MECHABOYS

JAMES KOCHALKA

TOP SHELF PRODUCTIONS
MARIETTA, GA

Mechaboys © 2018 James Kochalka.

Published by Top Shelf Productions, PO Box 1282, Marietta, GA 30061-1282, USA. Top Shelf Productions is an imprint of IDW Publishing, a division of Idea and Design Works, LLC. Offices: 2765 Truxtun Road, San Diego, CA 92106. Top Shelf Productions®, the Top Shelf logo, Idea and Design Works®, and the IDW logo are registered trademarks of Idea and Design Works, LLC. All Rights Reserved. With the exception of small excerpts of artwork used for review purposes, none of the contents of this publication may be reprinted without the permission of IDW Publishing. IDW Publishing does not read or accept unsolicited submissions of ideas, stories, or artwork.

Editor-in-Chief: Chris Staros.

Edited by Leigh Walton.

Back cover photo courtesy of Luke Awtry.

Visit our online catalog at www.topshelfcomix.com.

Printed in Korea.

ISBN 978-1-60309-423-8

FOR MYSELF,
WITH LOVE.

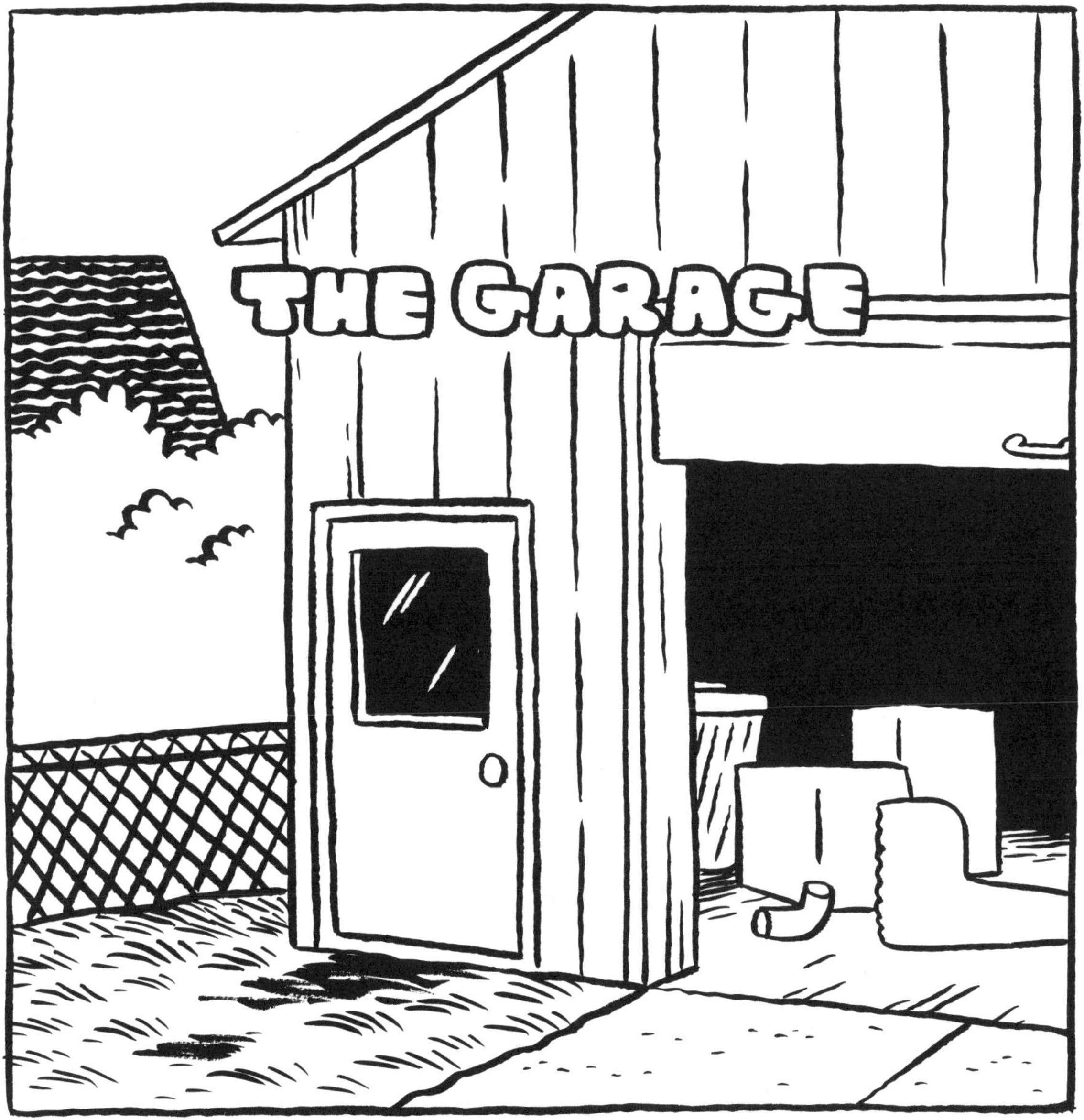
THE GARAGE

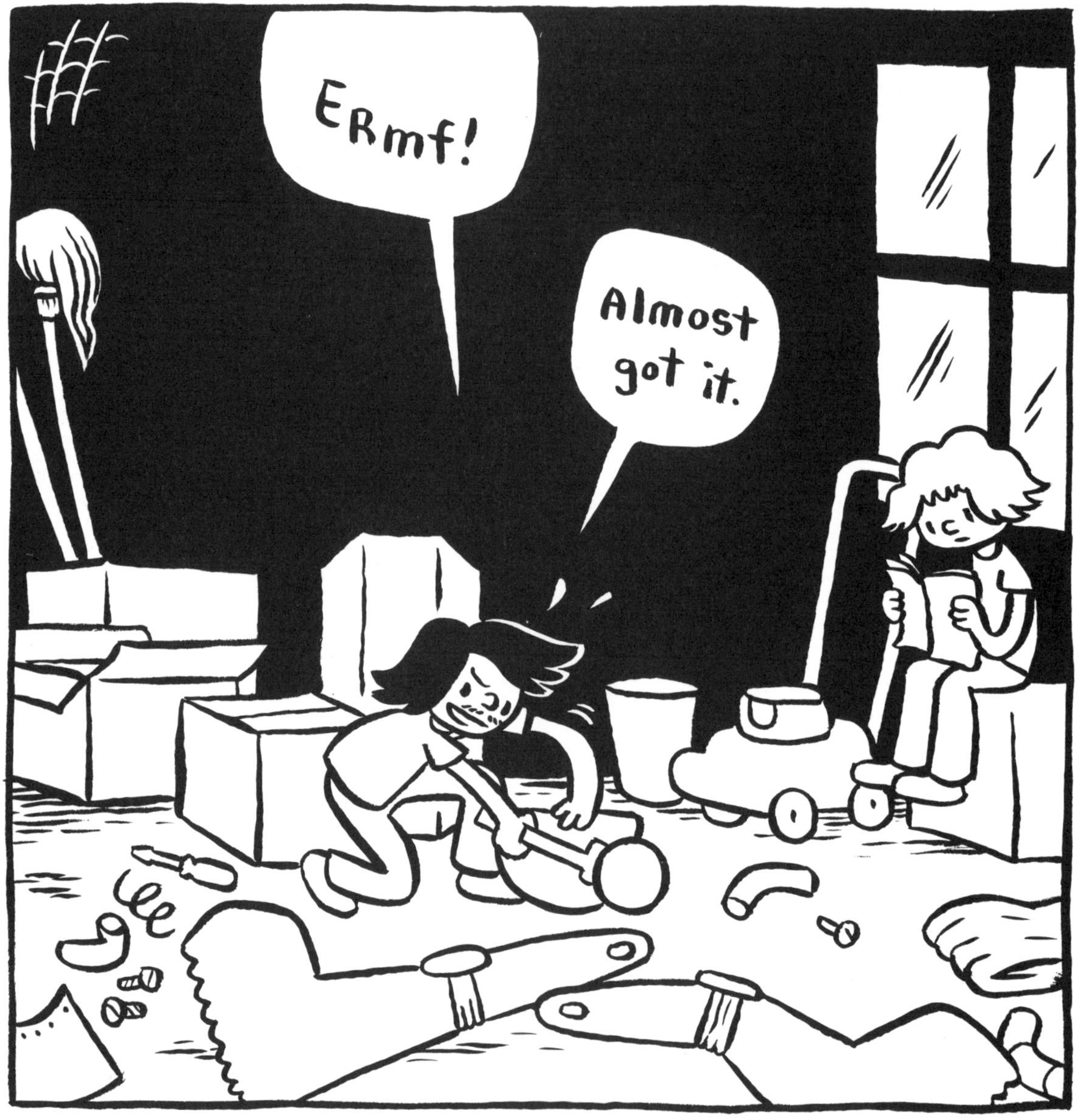
ERmf!
Almost got it.

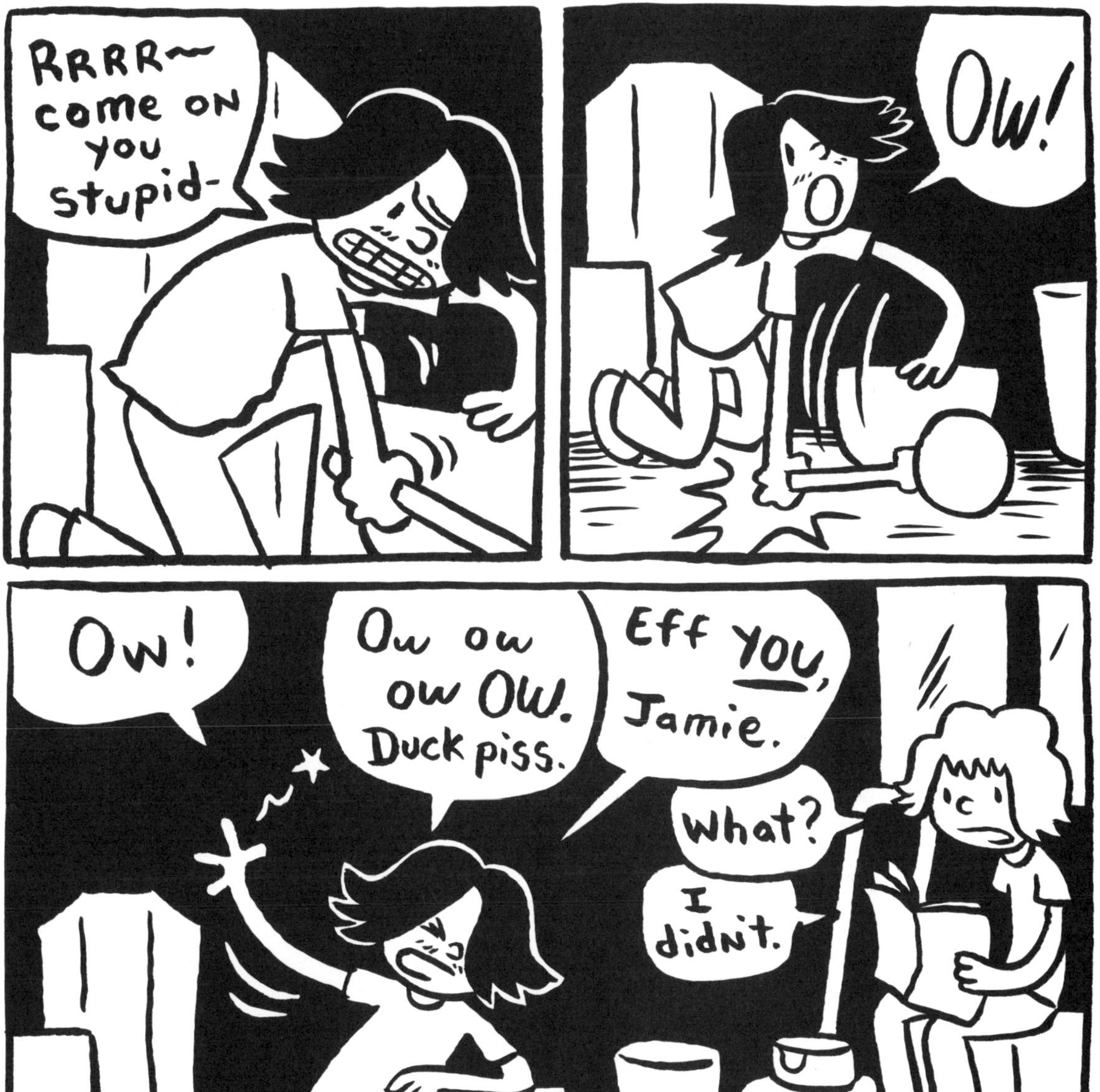
RRRR~ come on you stupid-
Ow!
Ow!
Ow ow ow OW. Duck piss.
Eff YOU, Jamie.
What?
I didn't.

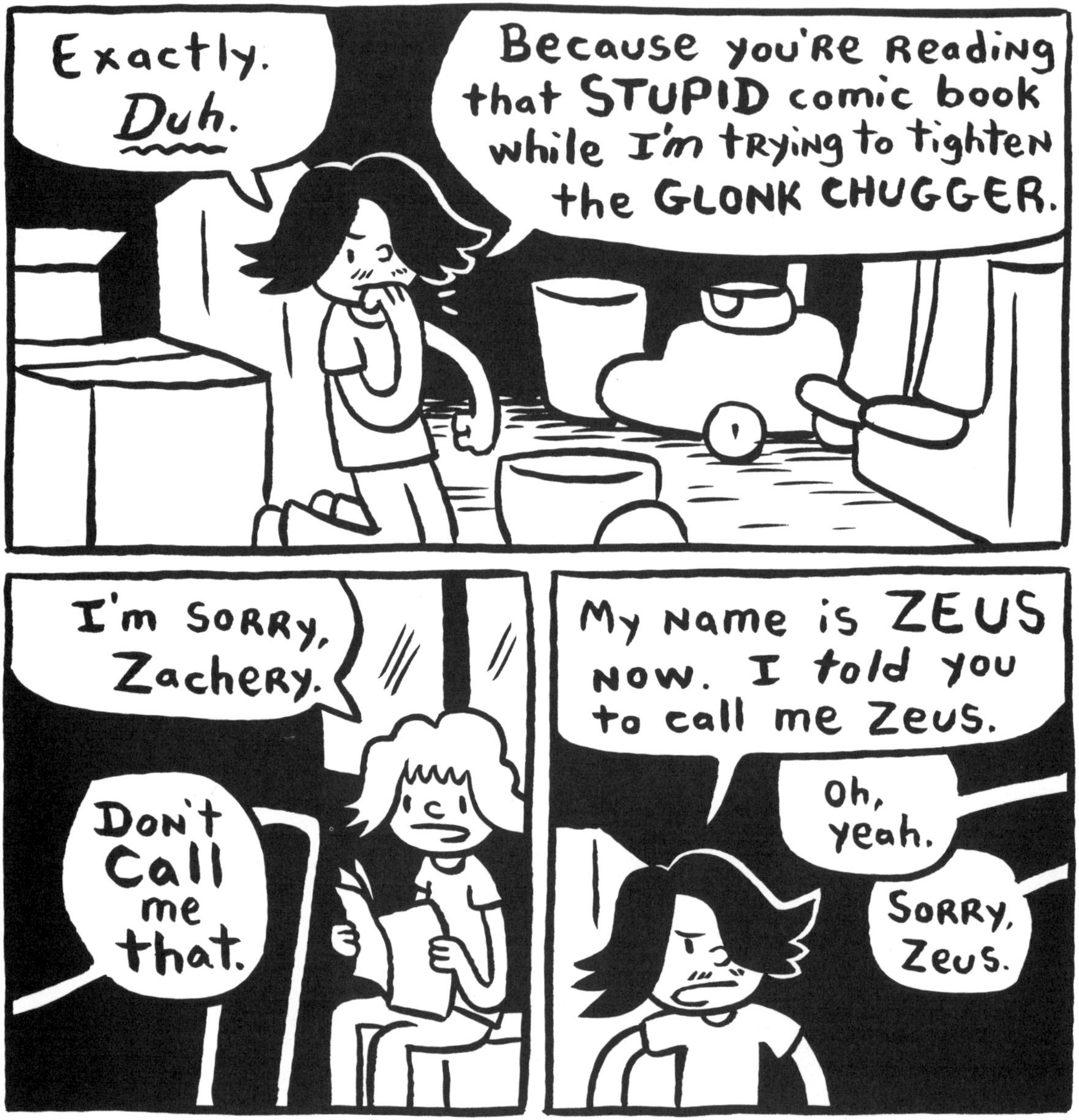
Exactly. Duh.
Because you're reading that STUPID comic book while I'm trying to tighten the GLONK CHUGGER.
I'm sorry, Zachery.
Don't call me that.
My name is ZEUS now. I told you to call me Zeus.
Oh, yeah.
Sorry, Zeus.

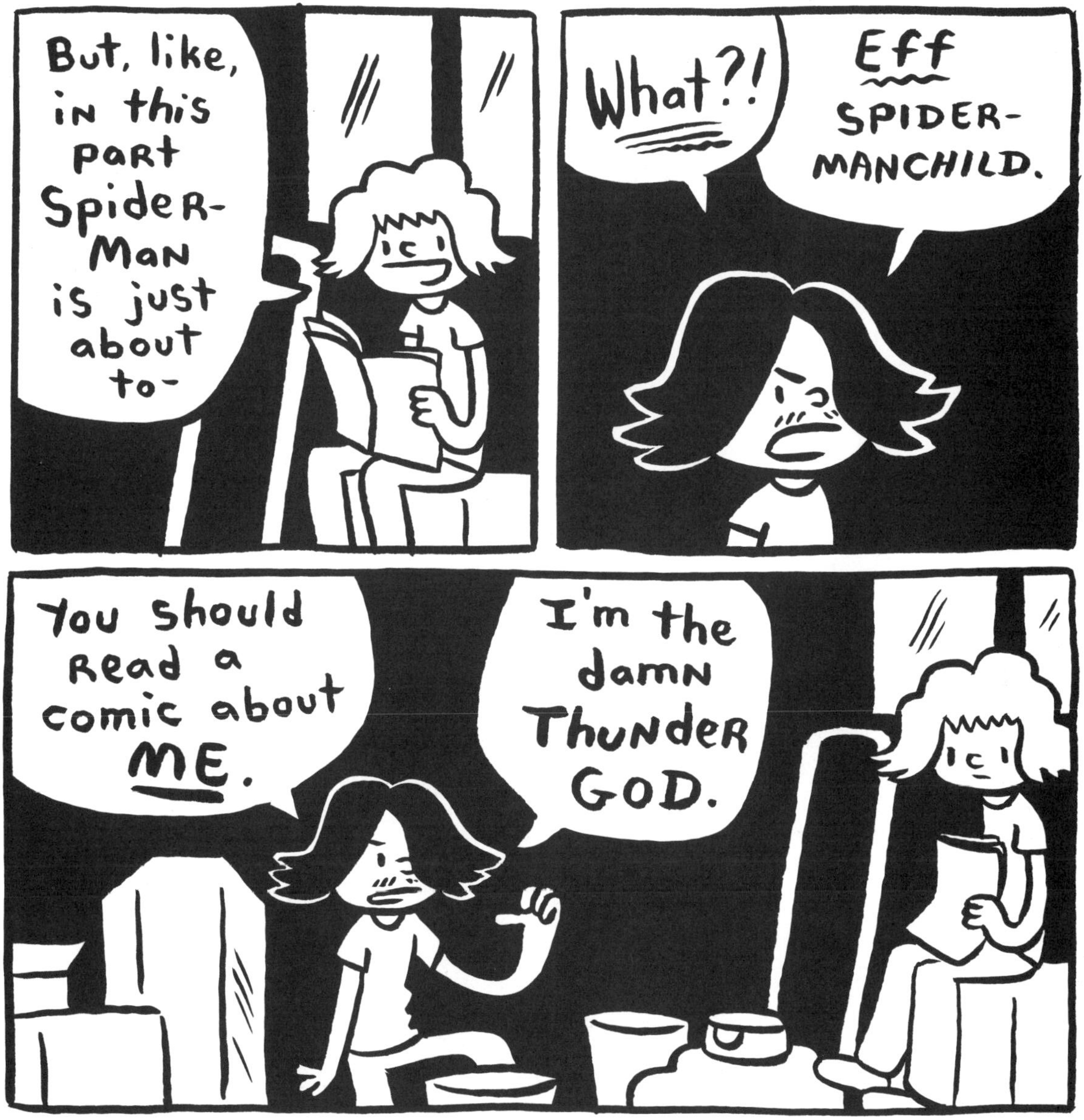
But, like, in this part Spider-Man is just about to-
What?!
Eff SPIDER-MANCHILD.
You should read a comic about ME.
I'm the damn Thunder GOD.

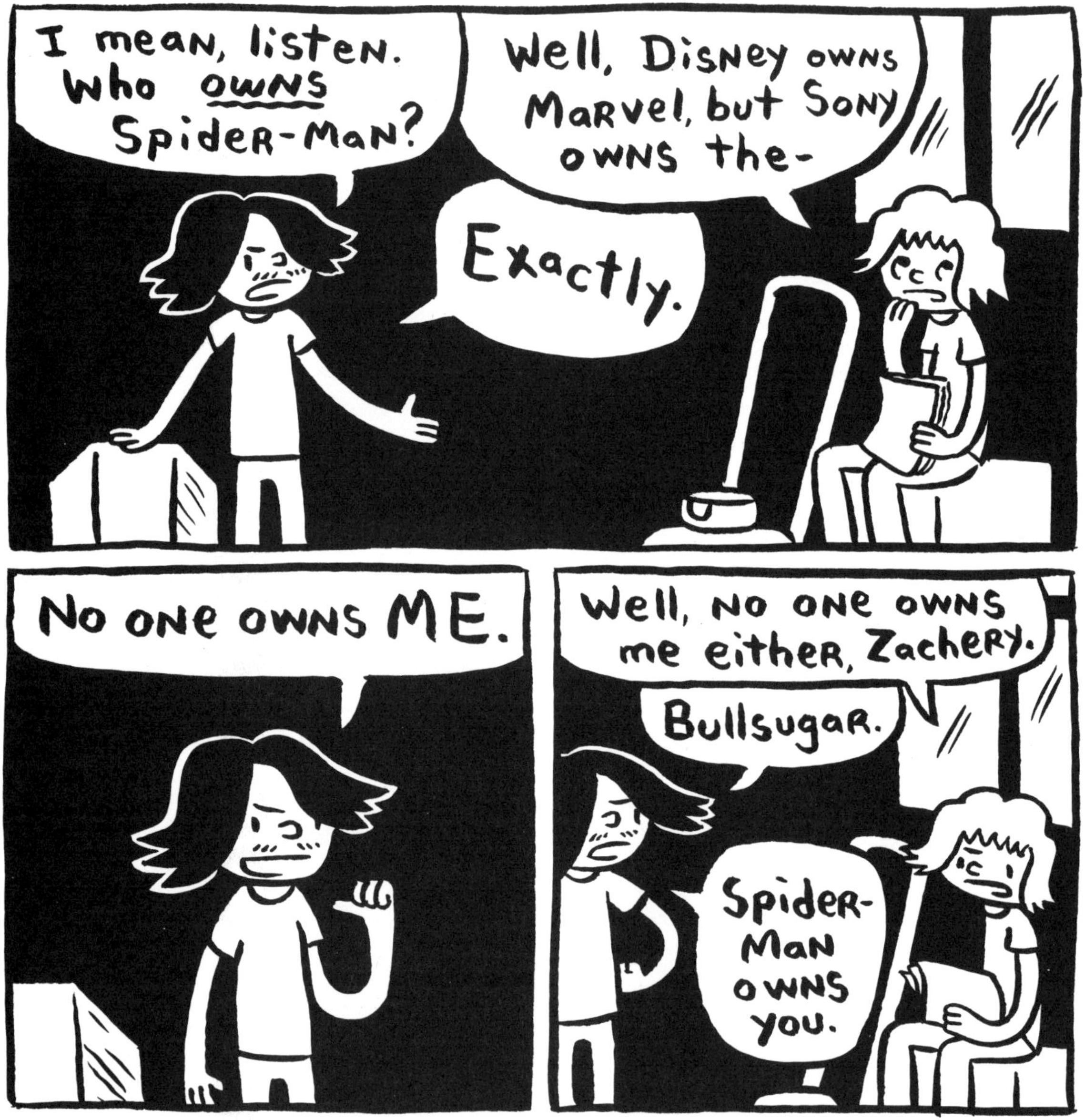
I mean, listen. Who OWNS Spider-Man?
Well, Disney owns Marvel, but Sony owns the-
Exactly.
No one owns ME.
Well, no one owns me either, Zachery.
Bullsugar.
Spider-Man owns you.

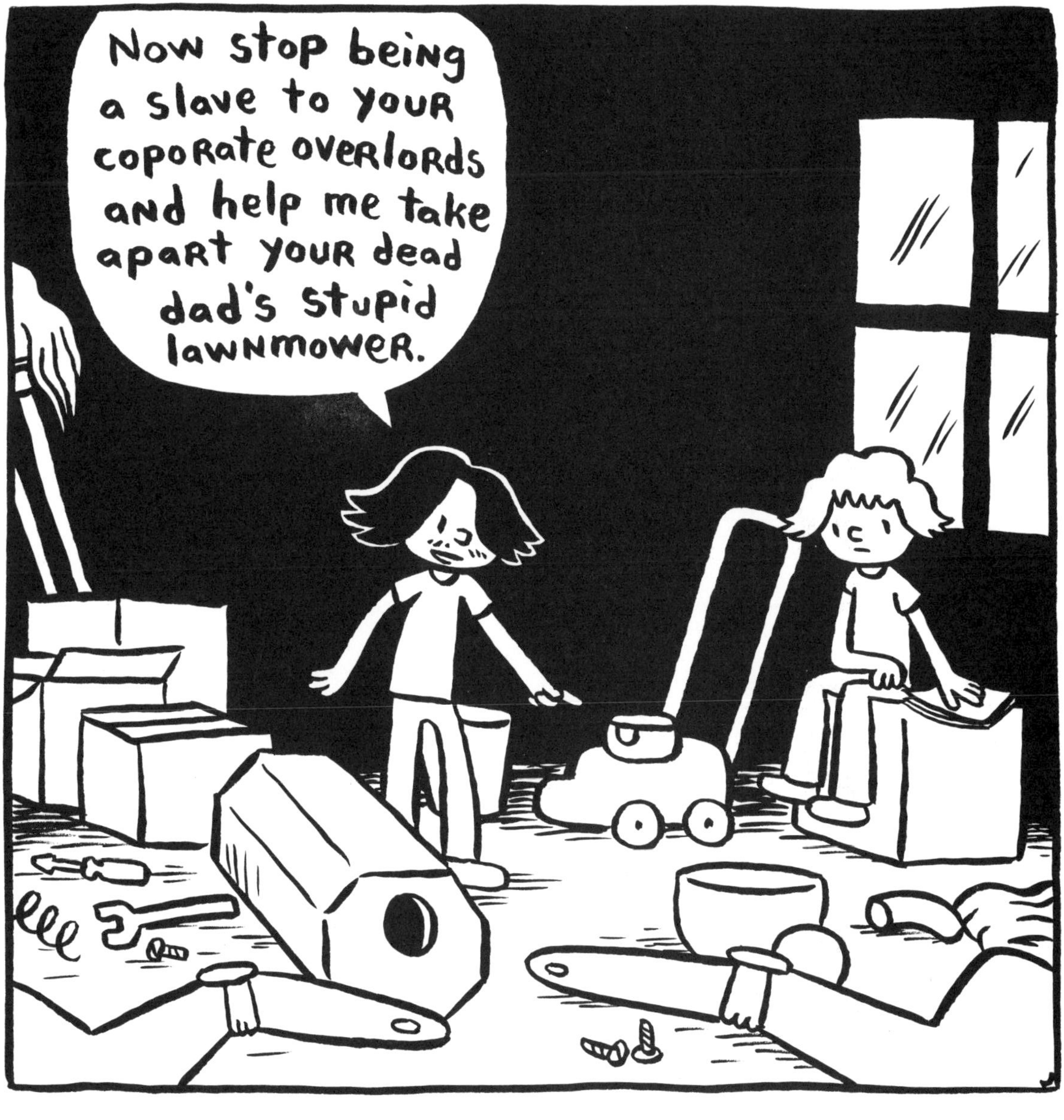
Now stop being a slave to your coporate overlords and help me take apart your dead dad's stupid lawnmower.

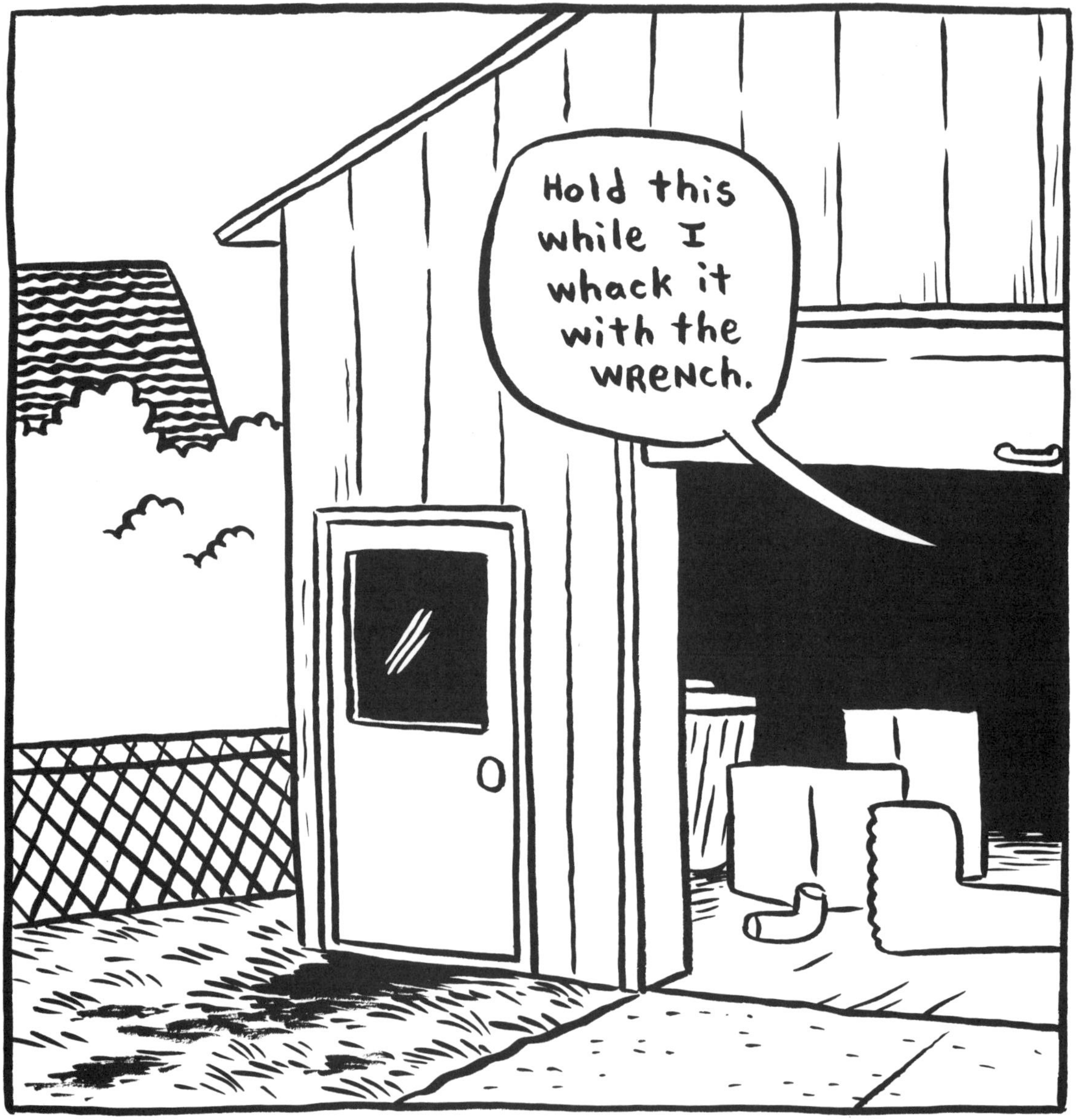
Hold this while I whack it with the WRENCH.

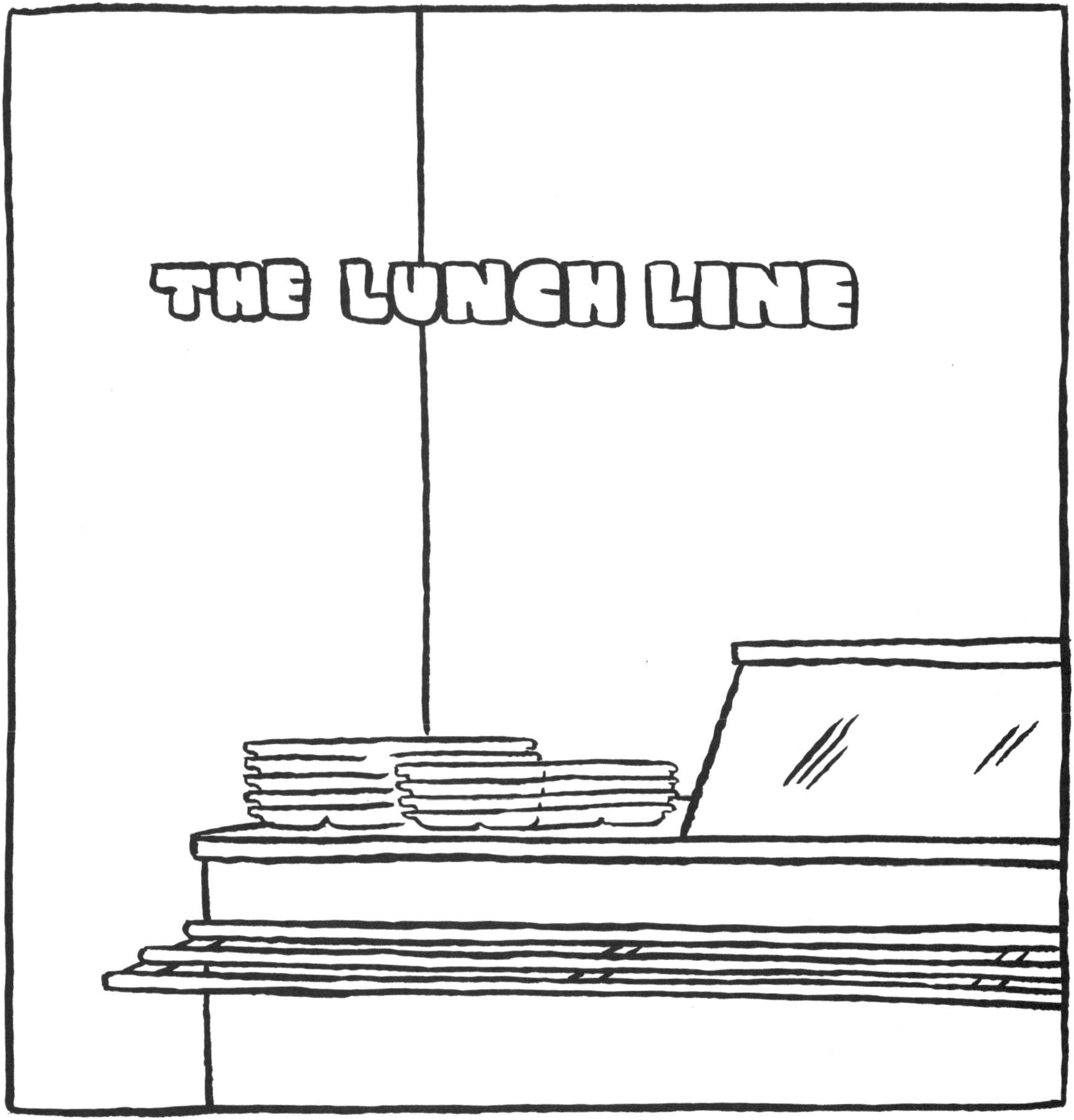
THE LUNCH LINE

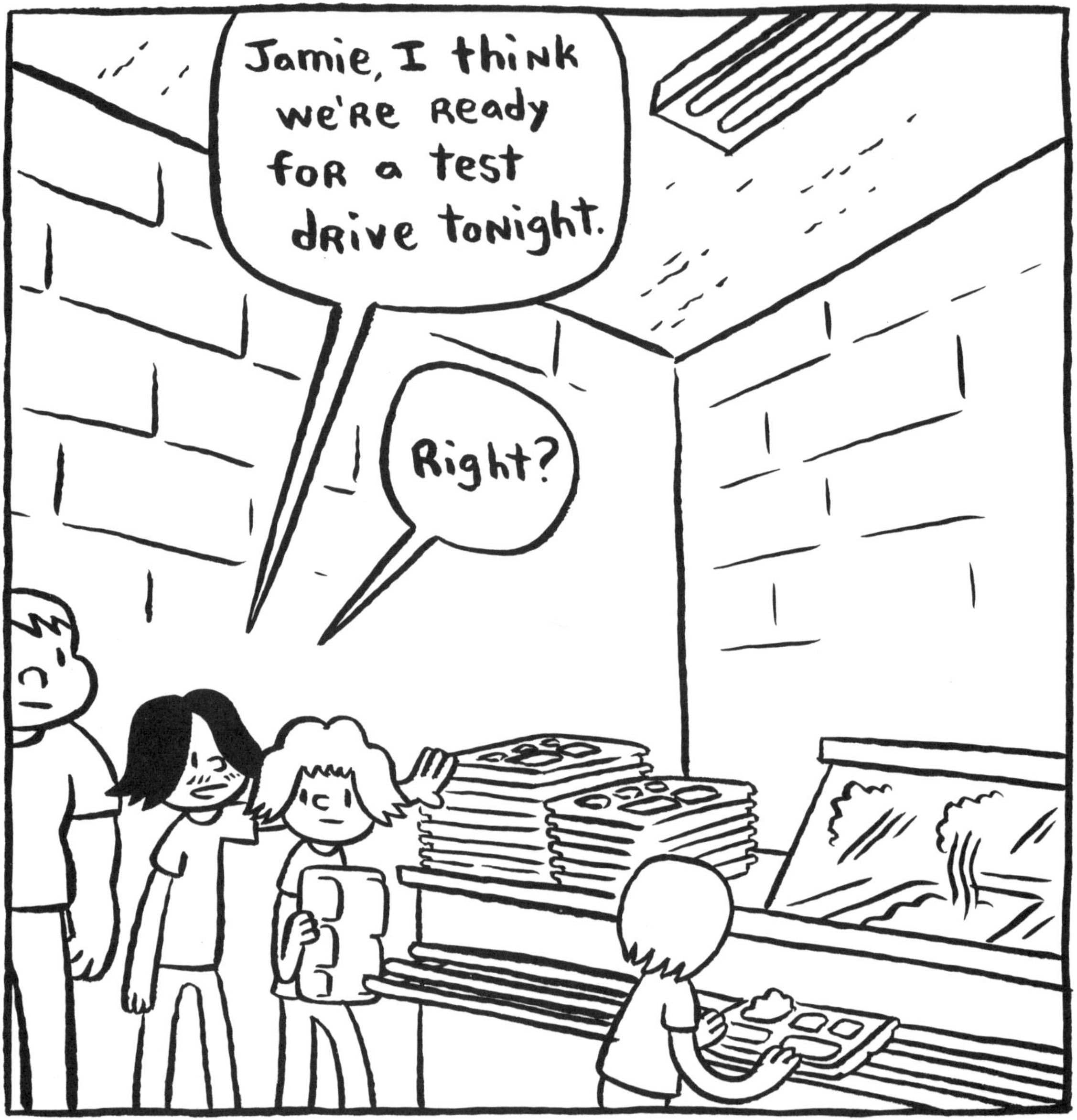
Jamie, I think we're ready for a test drive tonight.
Right?

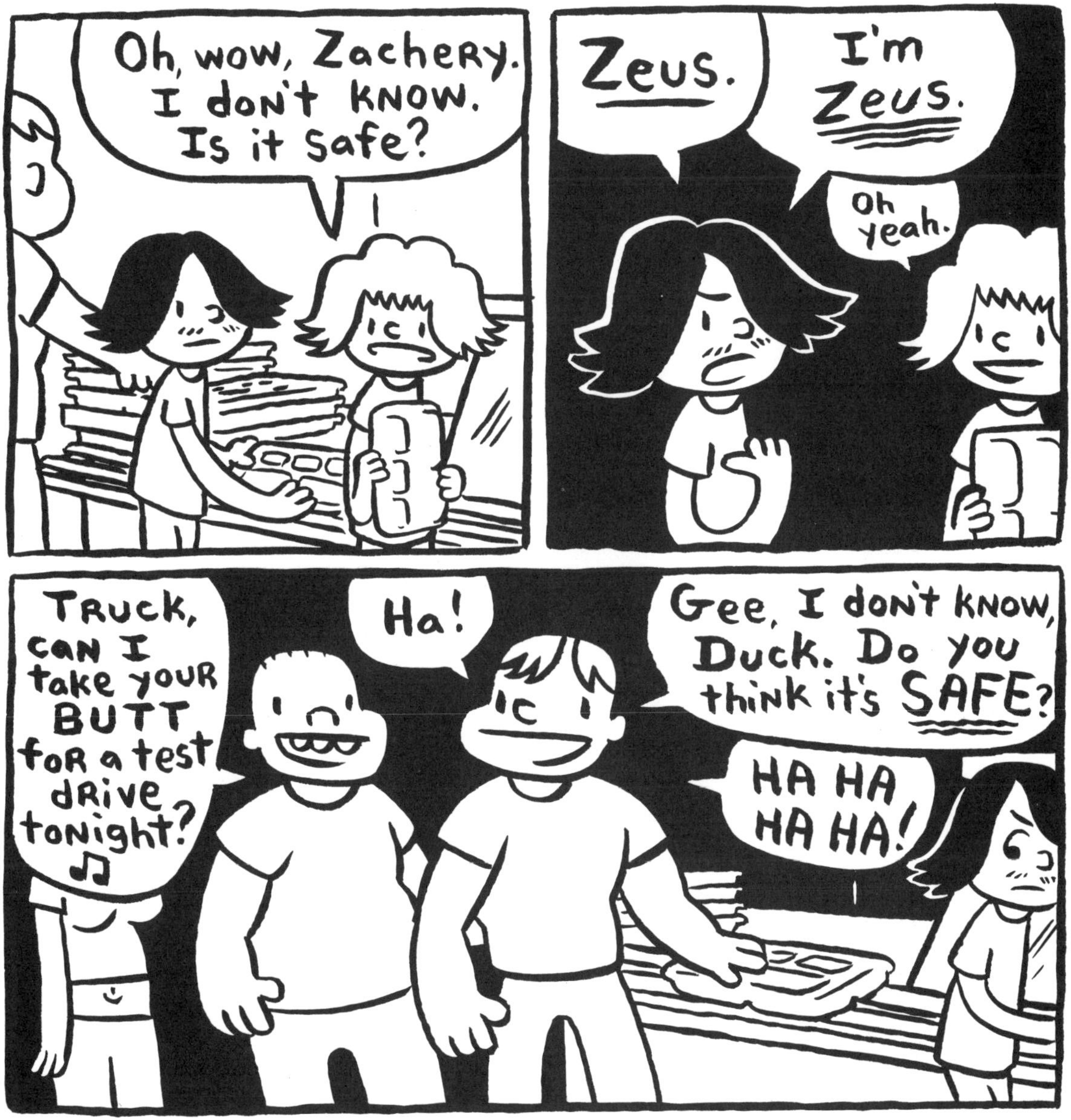
Oh, wow, Zachery. I don't know. Is it safe?
Zeus.
I'm Zeus.
Oh yeah.
Truck, can I take your BUTT for a test drive tonight? ♫
Ha!
Gee, I don't know, Duck. Do you think it's SAFE?
HA HA HA HA!

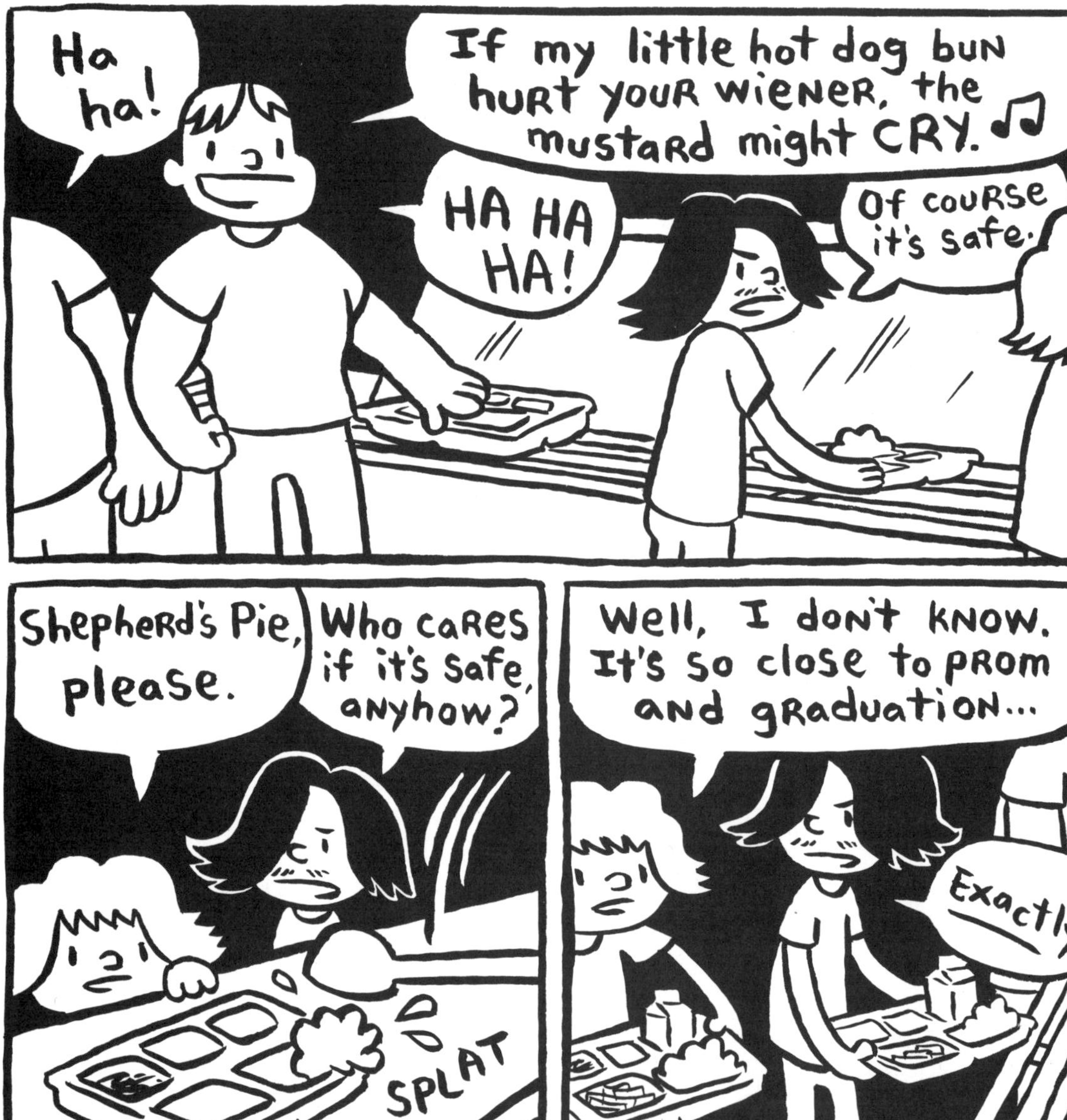
Ha ha!
If my little hot dog bun hurt your wiener, the mustard might CRY. ♫
HA HA HA!
Of course it's safe.
Shepherd's Pie, please.
Who cares if it's safe, anyhow?
SPLAT
Well, I don't know. It's so close to prom and graduation...
Exactly.

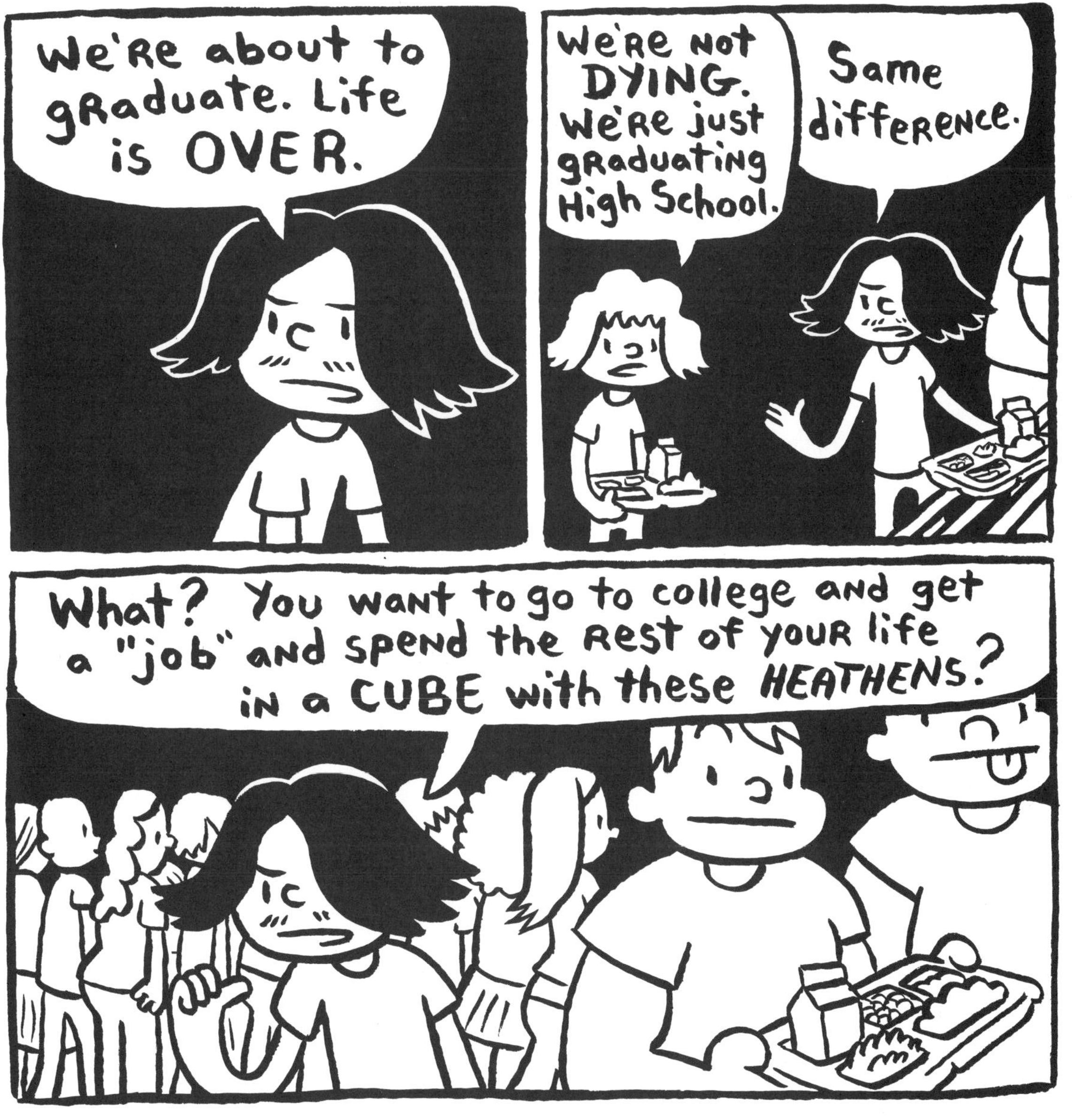
We're about to graduate. Life is OVER.
We're not DYING. We're just graduating High School.
Same difference.
What? You want to go to college and get a "job" and spend the rest of your life in a CUBE with these HEATHENS?

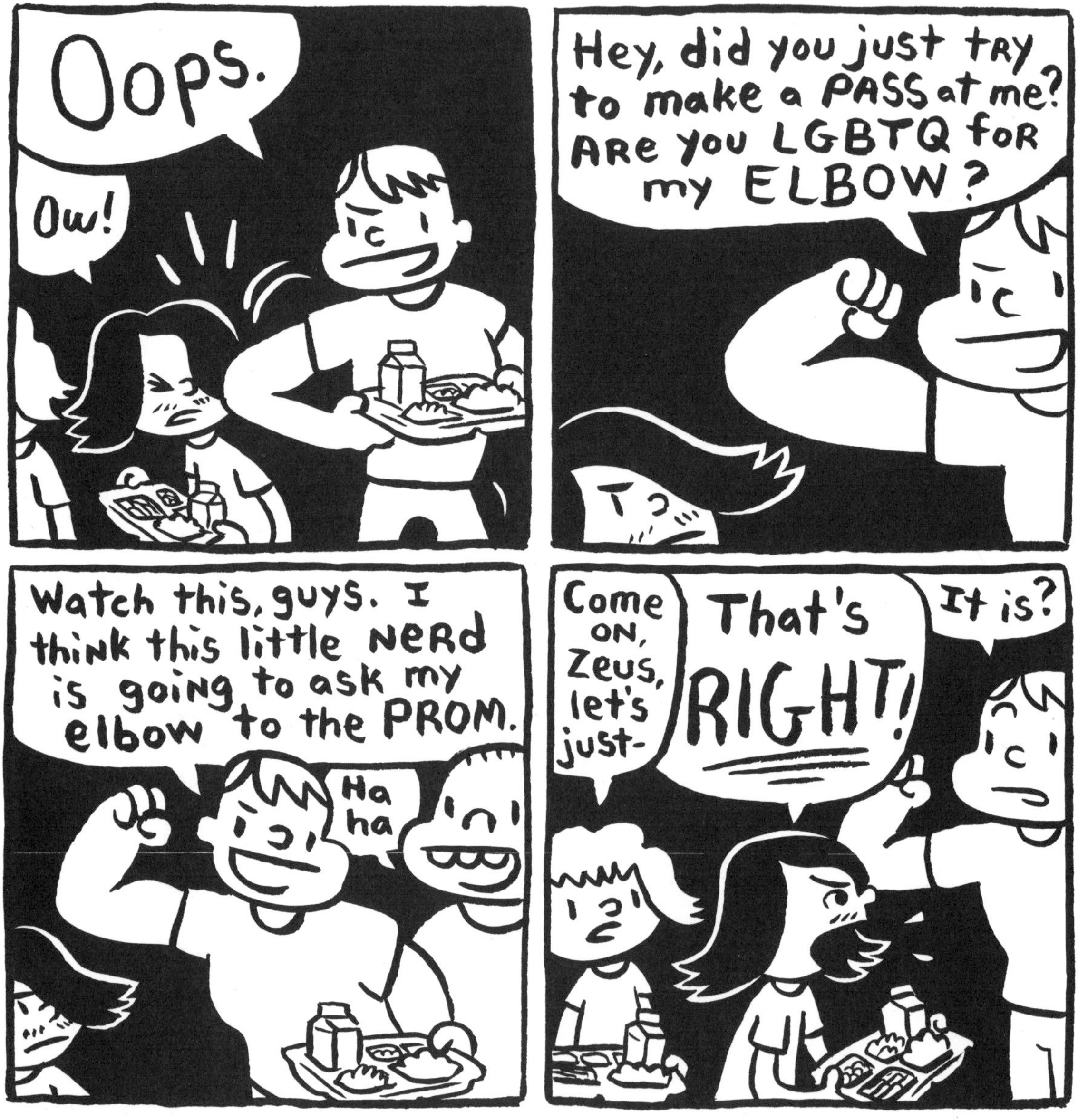
Oops.
Ow!
Hey, did you just TRY to make a PASS at me? ARE you LGBTQ for my ELBOW?
Watch this, guys. I think this little NERD is going to ask my elbow to the PROM.
Ha ha
Come ON, Zeus, let's just-
That's RIGHT!
It is?

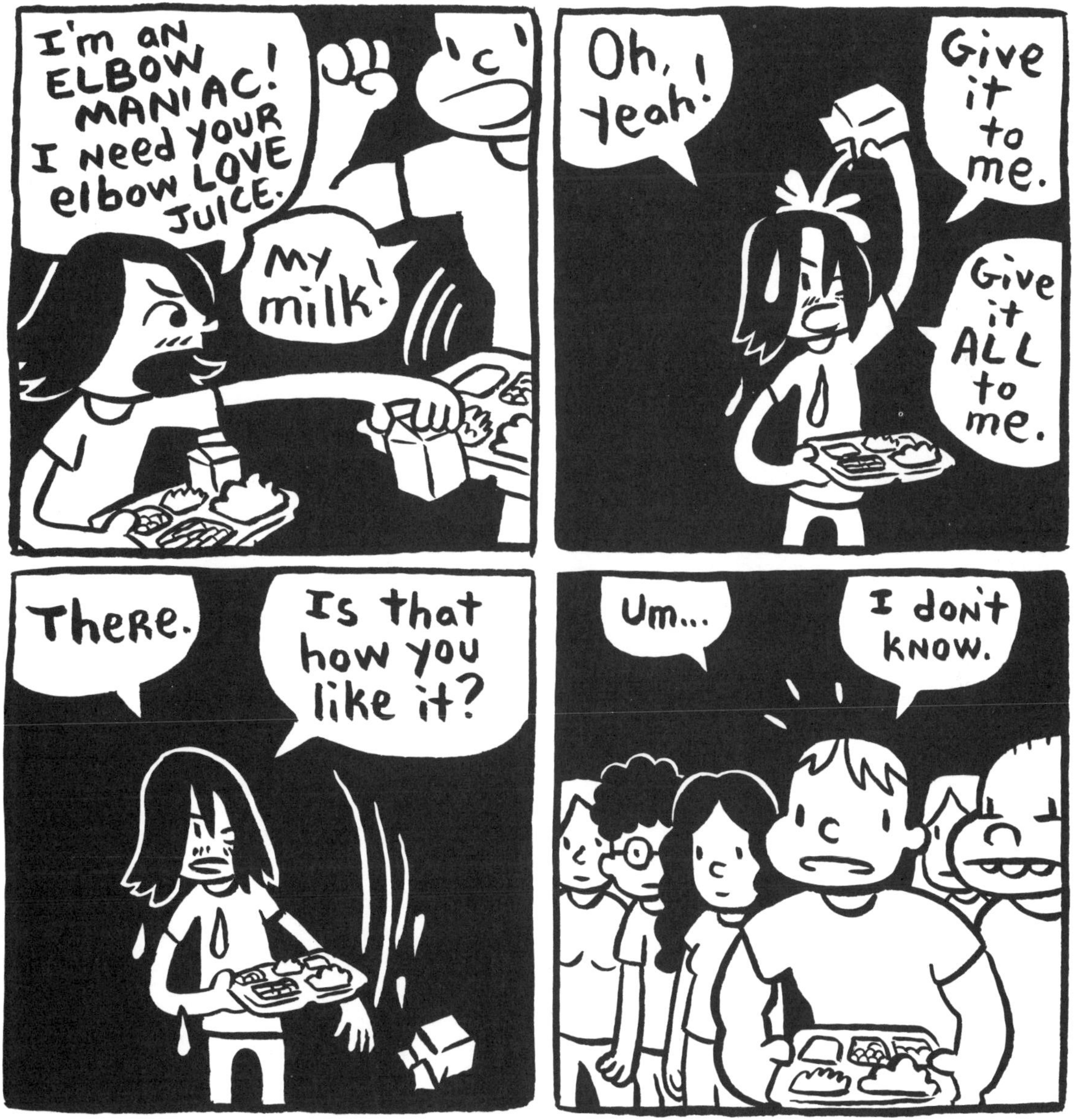
I'm an ELBOW MANIAC! I need YOUR elbow LOVE JUICE.
MY milk!
Oh, yeah!
Give it to me.
Give it ALL to me.
There.
Is that how you like it?
Um...
I don't know.

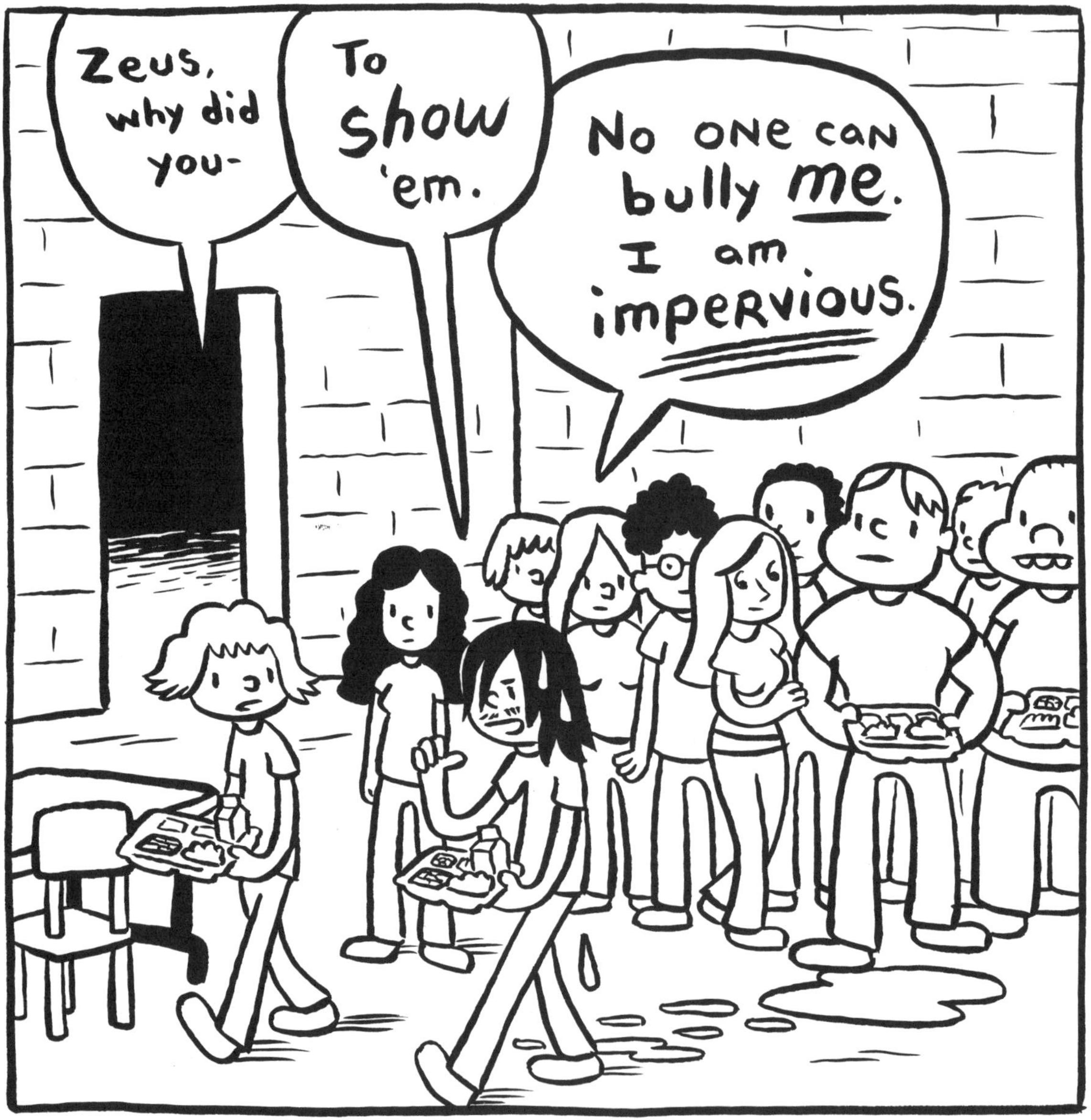
Zeus, why did you-
To show 'em.
No one can bully me. I am impervious.

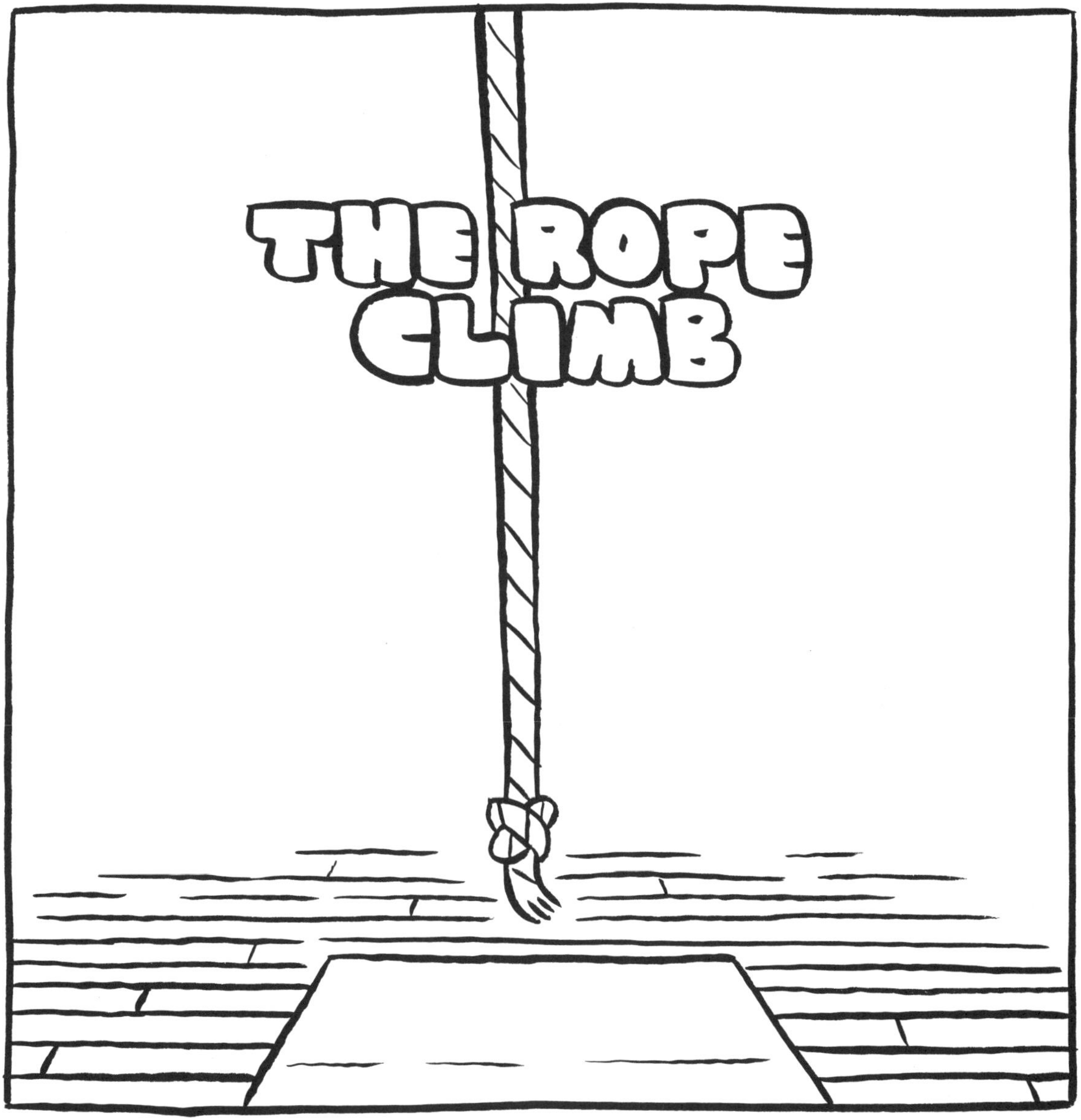
THE ROPE
CLIMB

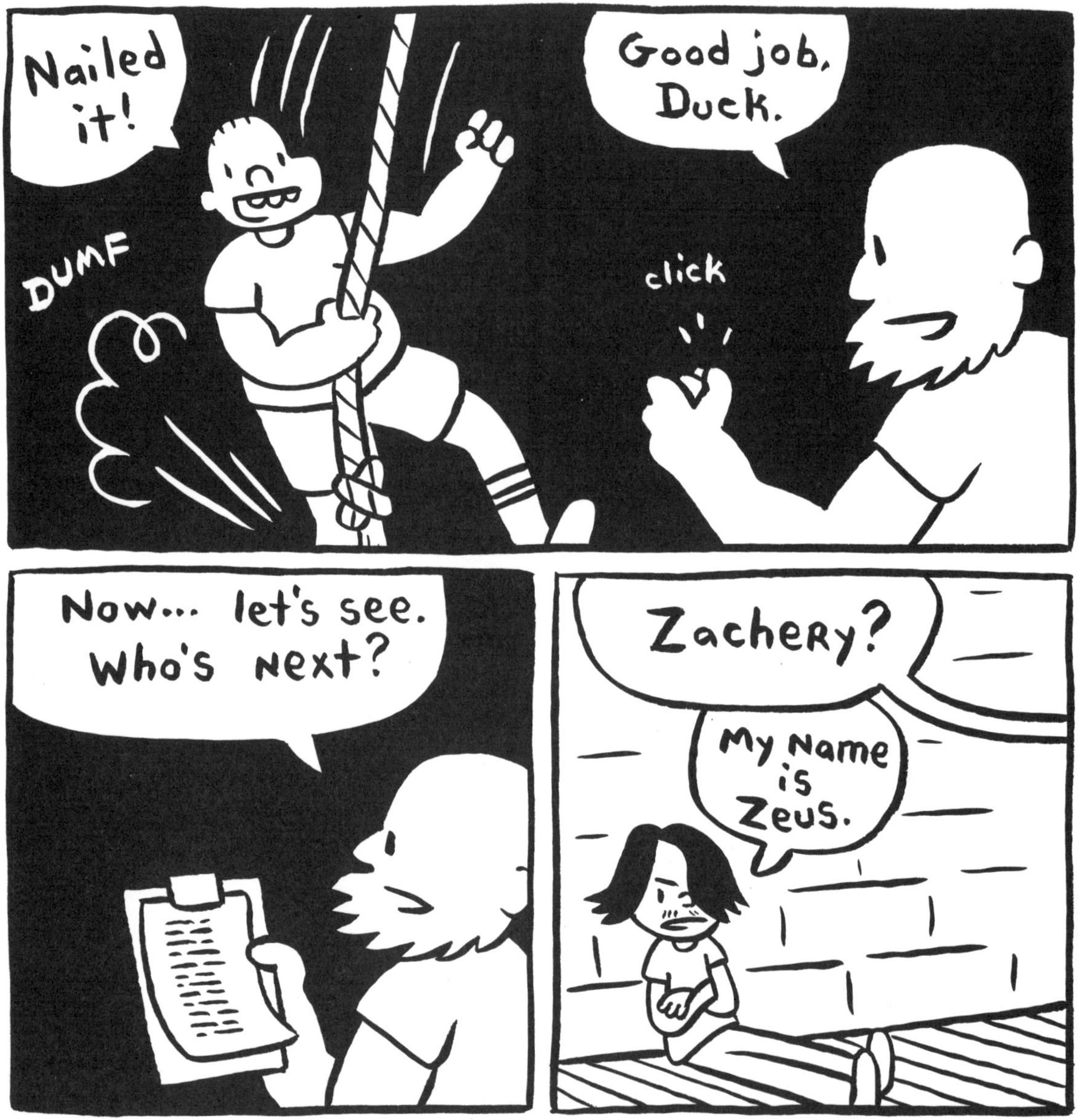
Nailed it!
DUMF
Good job, Duck.
click
Now... let's see. Who's next?
Zachery?
My name is Zeus.

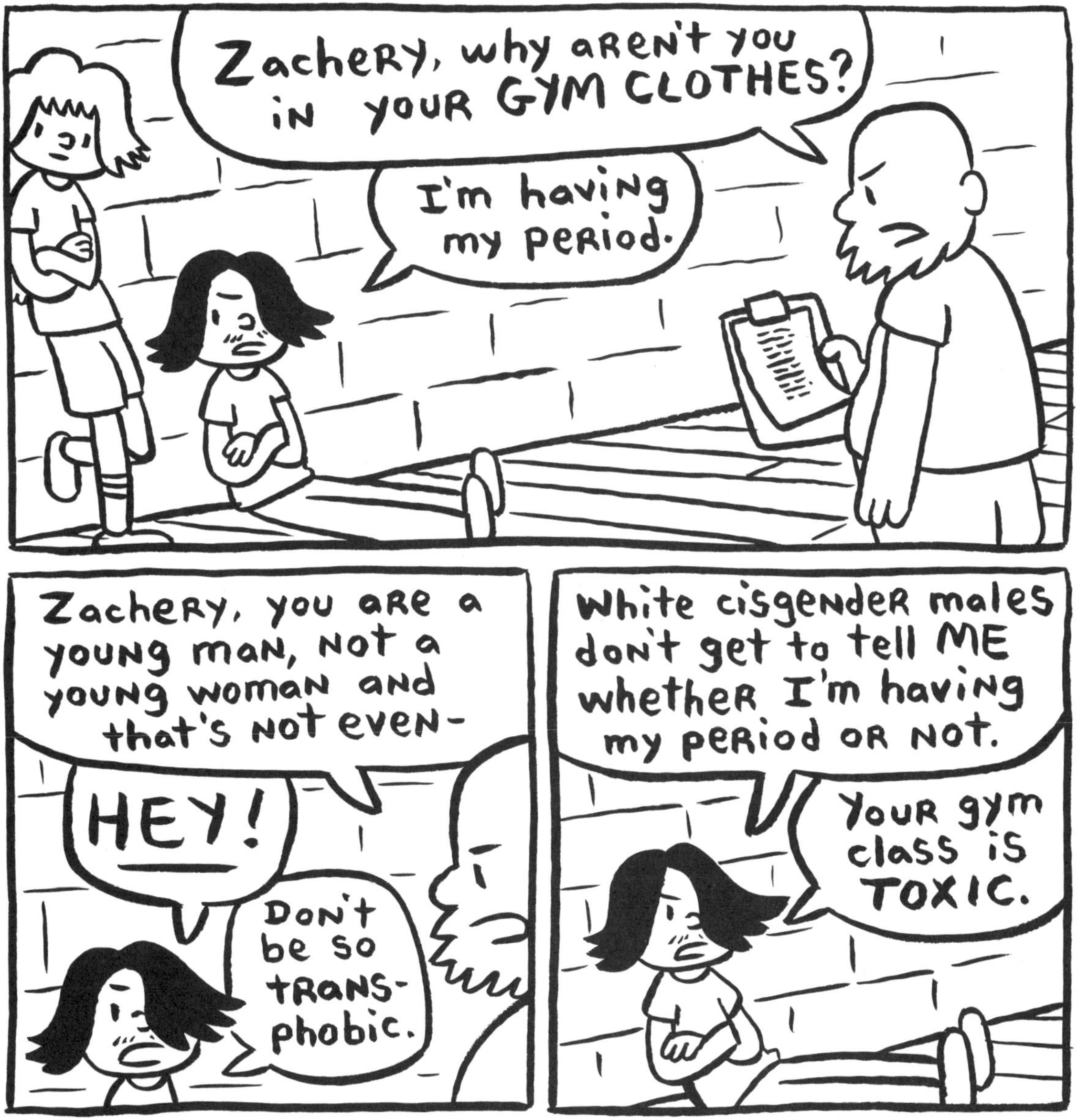
Zachery, why aren't you in your GYM CLOTHES?
I'm having my period.
Zachery, you are a young man, not a young woman and that's not even-
HEY!
Don't be so TRANS-phobic.
White cisgender males don't get to tell ME whether I'm having my period or not.
Your gym class is TOXIC.

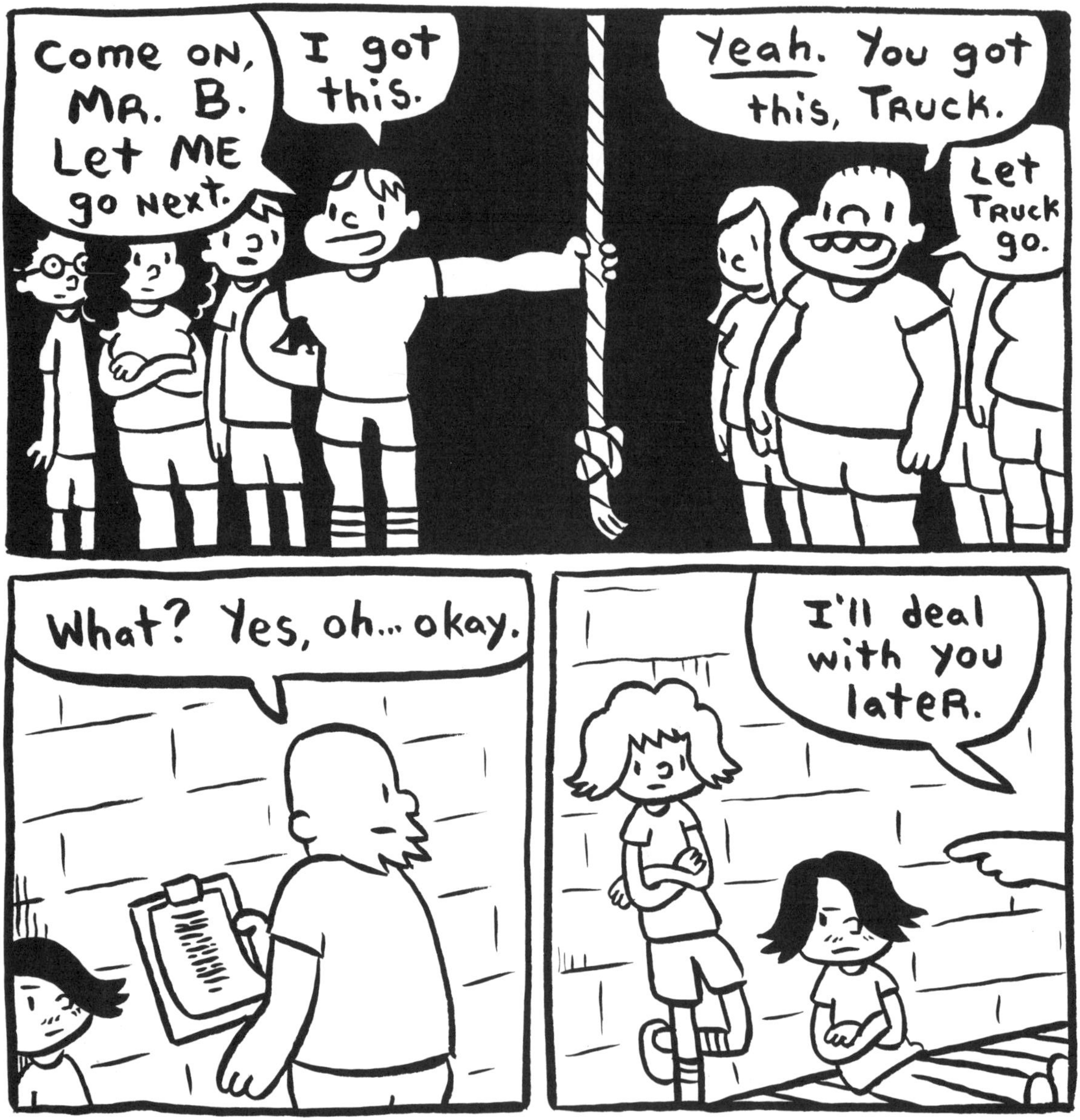
Come ON, MR. B. Let ME go Next.
I got this.
Yeah. You got this, TRUCK.
Let TRUCK go.
What? Yes, oh... okay.
I'll deal with you lateR.

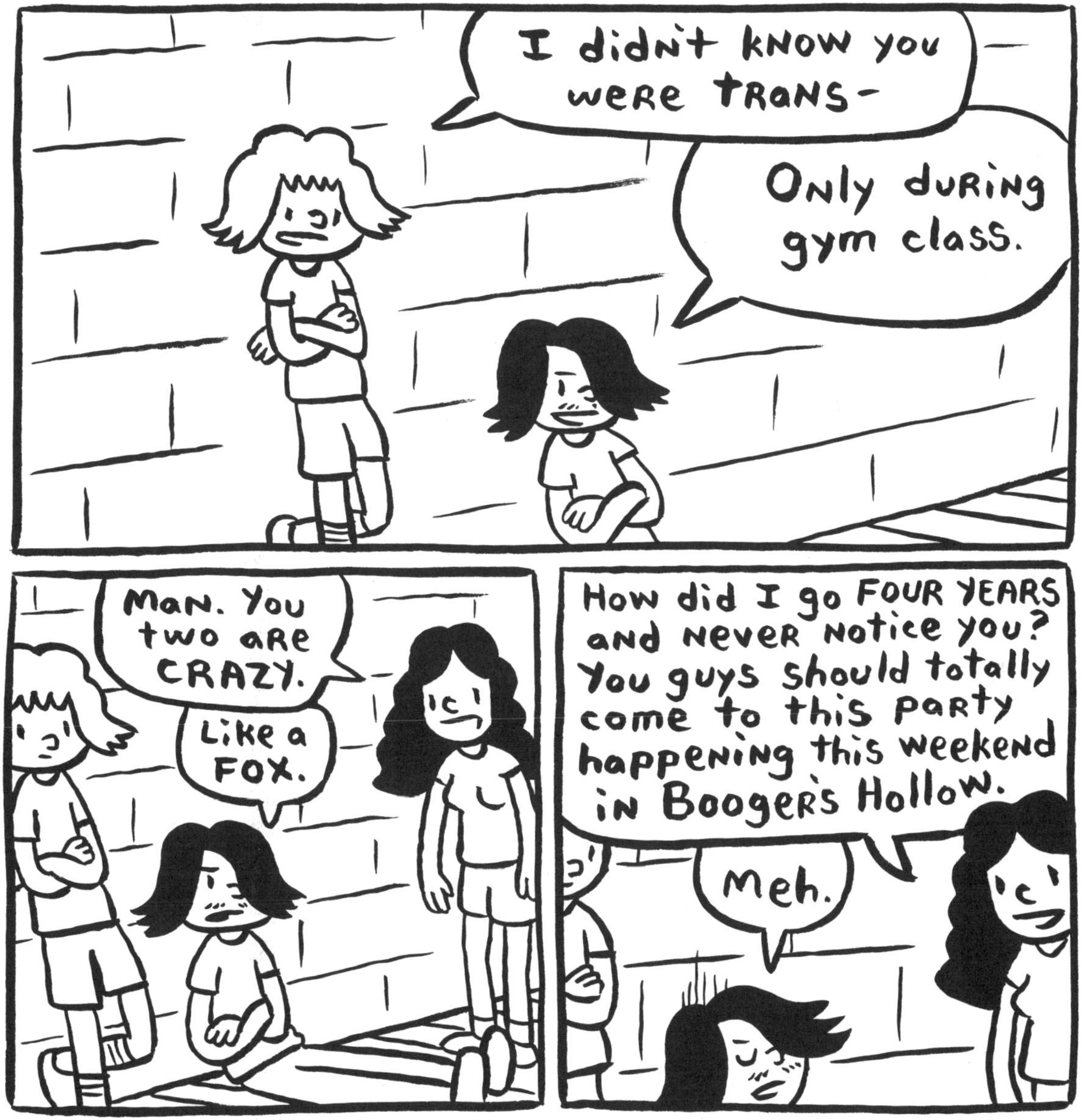
I didn't know you were trans-
Only during gym class.
Man. You two are CRAZY.
Like a FOX.
How did I go FOUR YEARS and never notice you? You guys should totally come to this party happening this weekend in Booger's Hollow.
Meh.

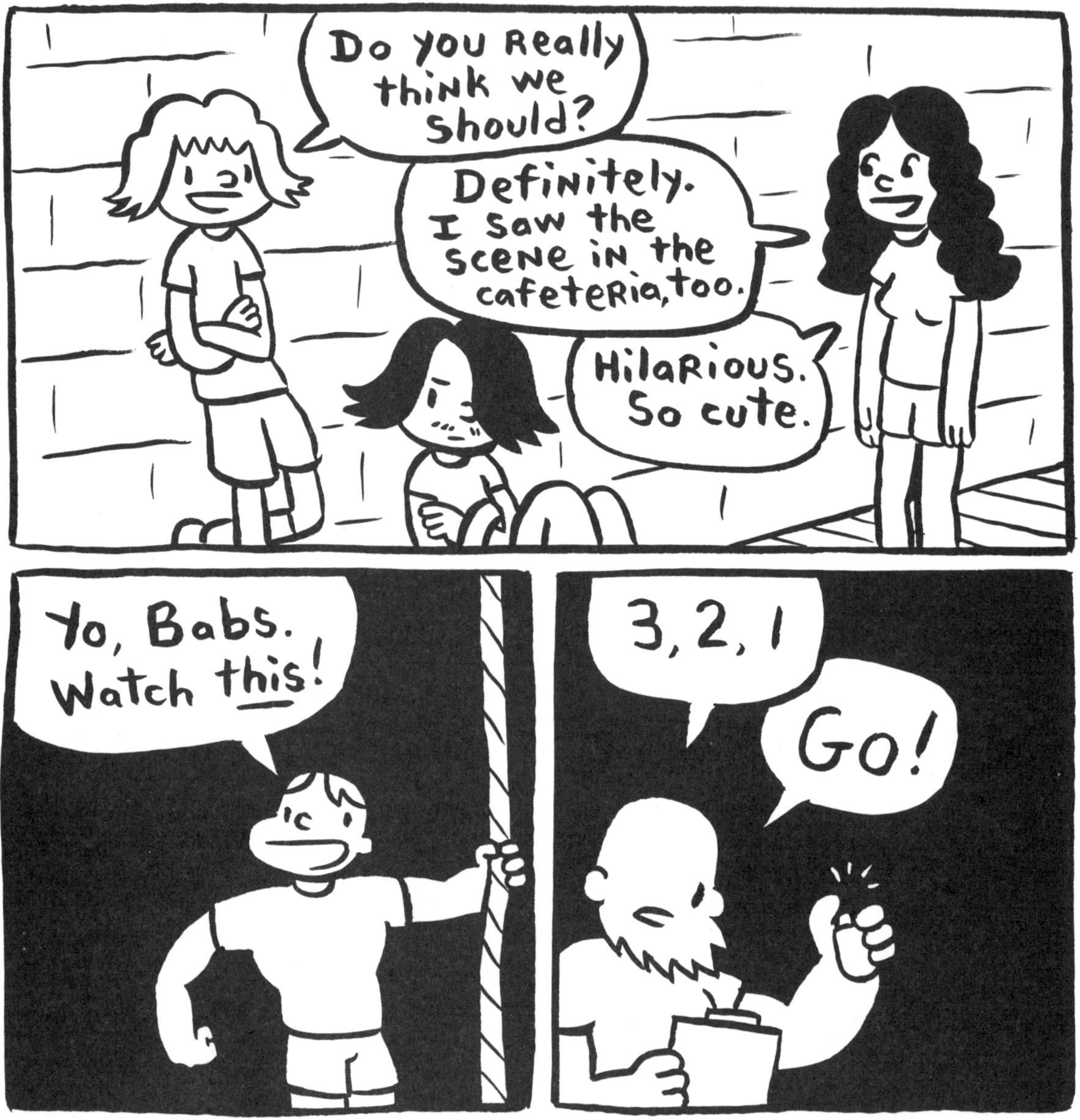
Do you Really think we should?
Definitely. I saw the scene in the cafeteria, too.
Hilarious. So cute.
Yo, Babs. Watch this!
3, 2, 1
Go!

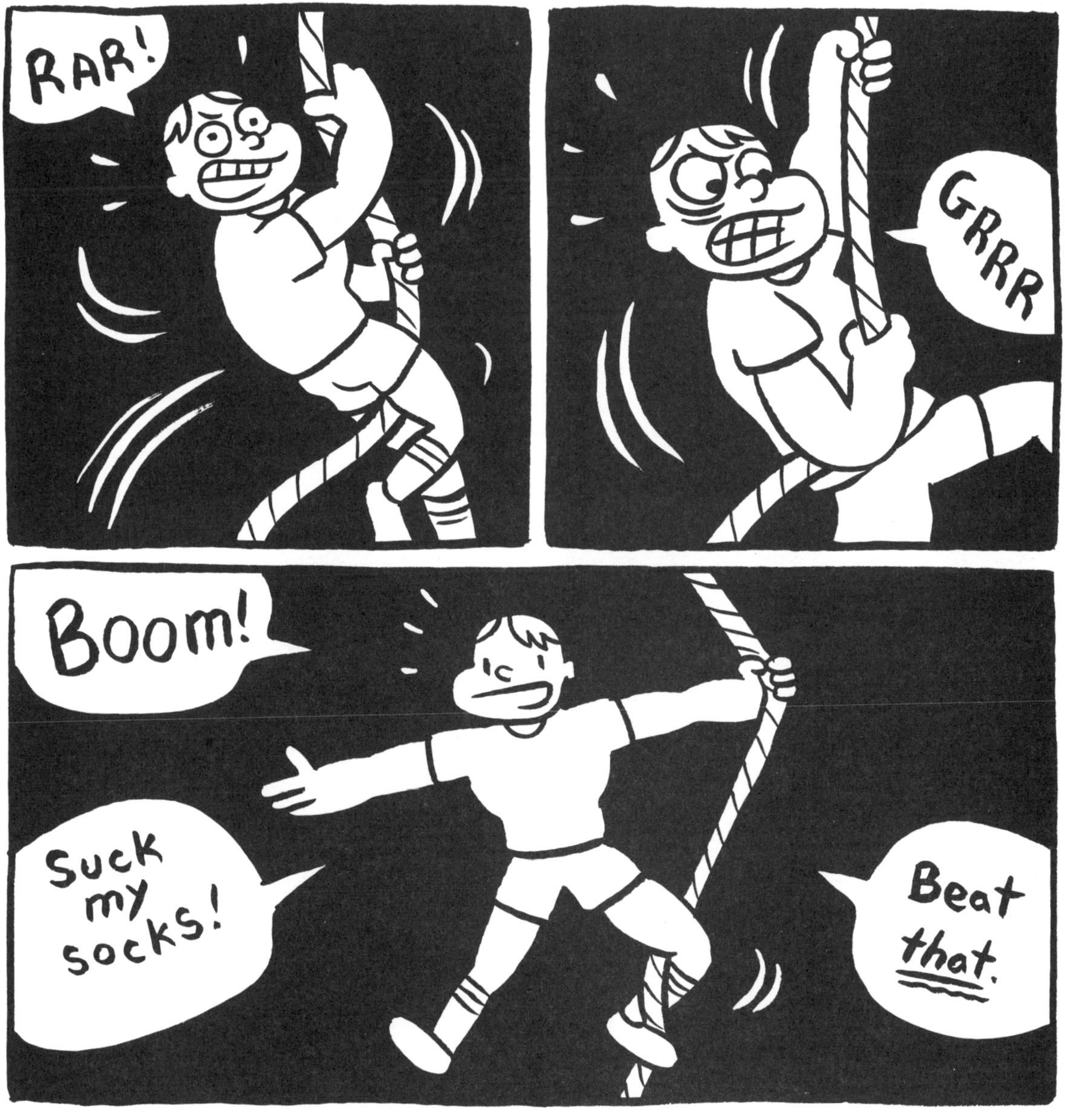
RAR!
GRRR
Boom!
Suck my socks!
Beat that.

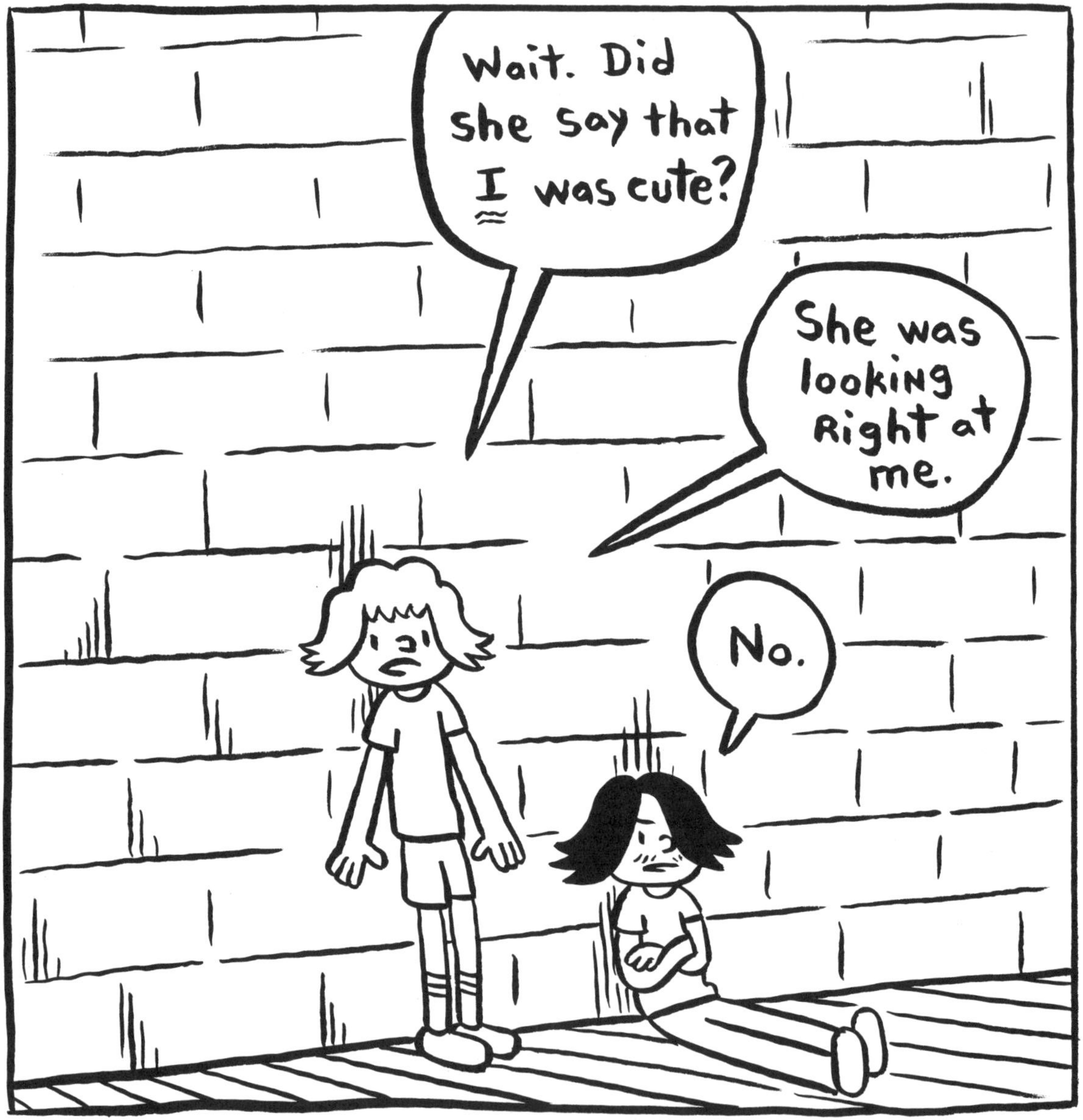
Wait. Did she say that I was cute?
She was looking right at me.
No.

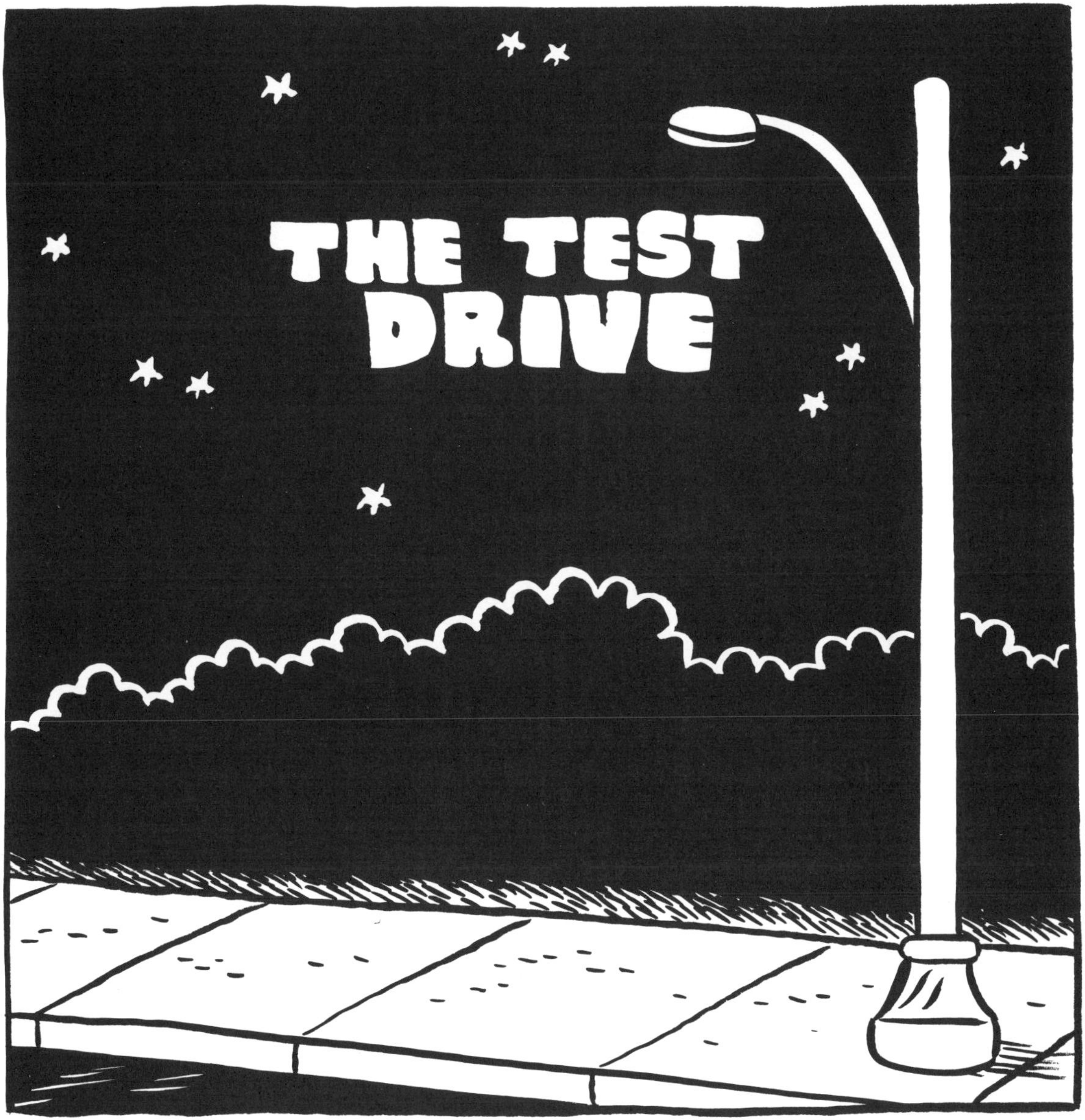
THE TEST
DRIVE

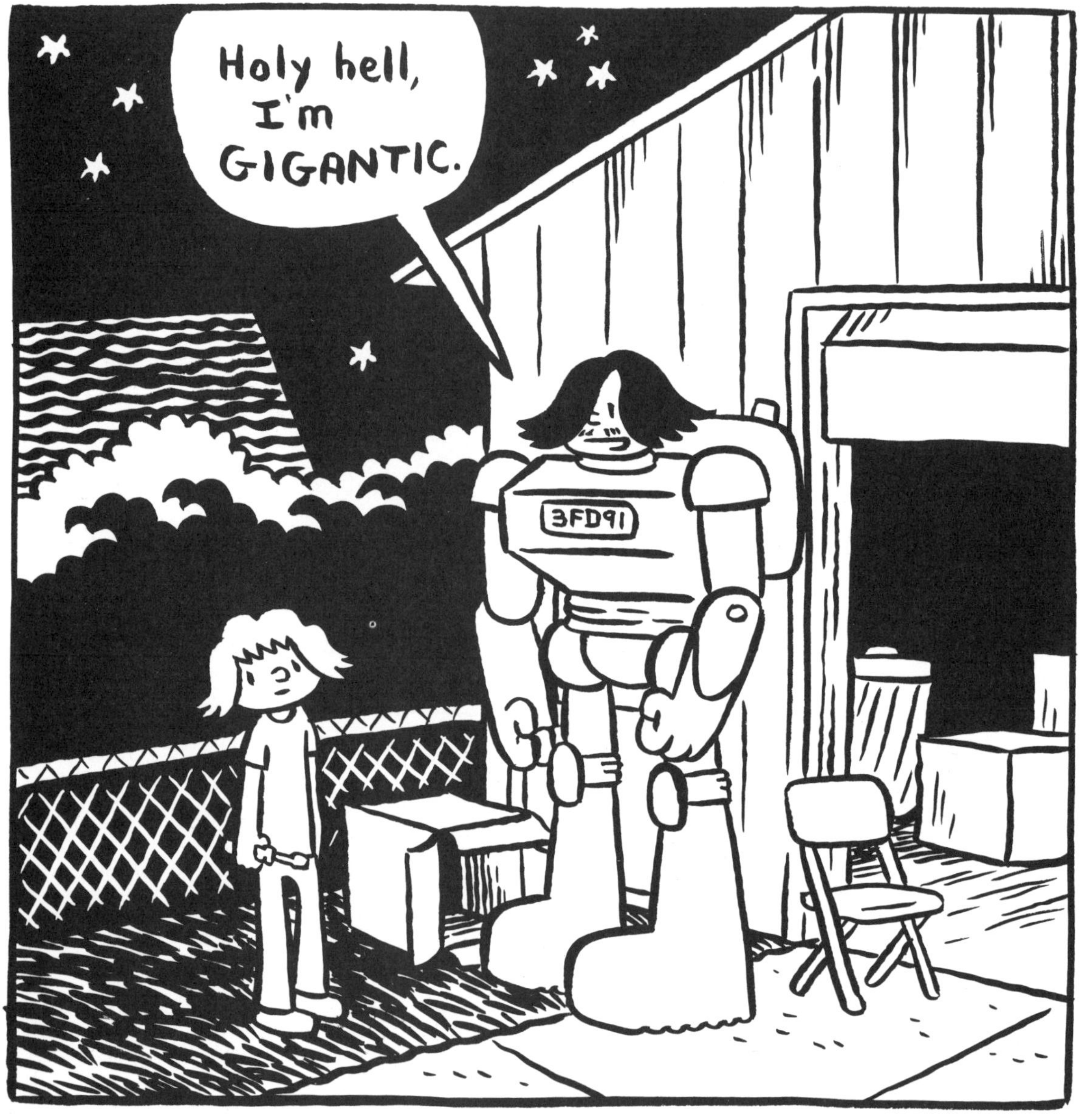
Holy hell, I'm GIGANTIC.
3FD91

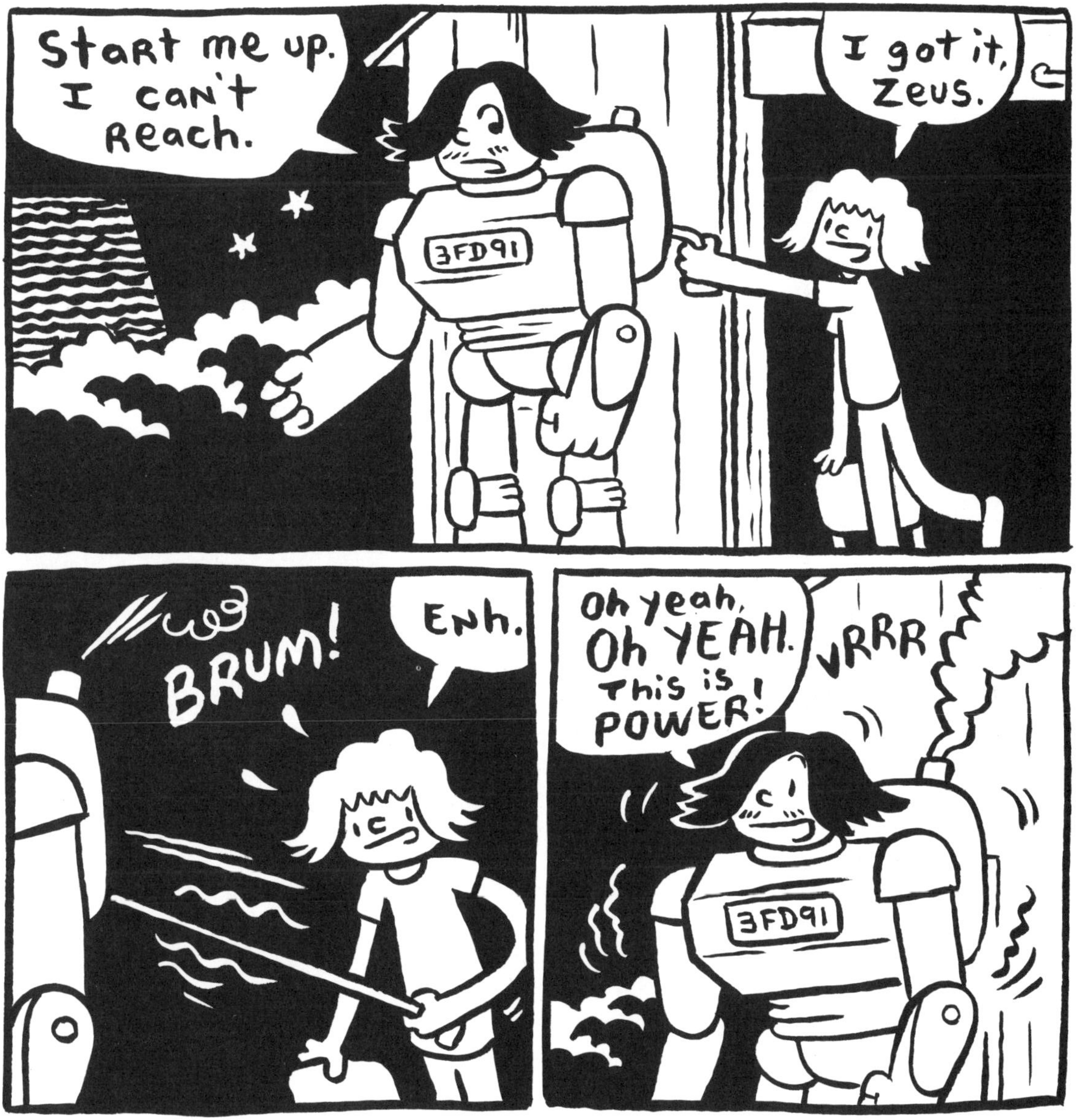
Start me up. I can't Reach.
I got it, Zeus.
3FD91
BRUM!
Enh.
Oh yeah, Oh YEAH. This is POWER!
VRRR
3FD91

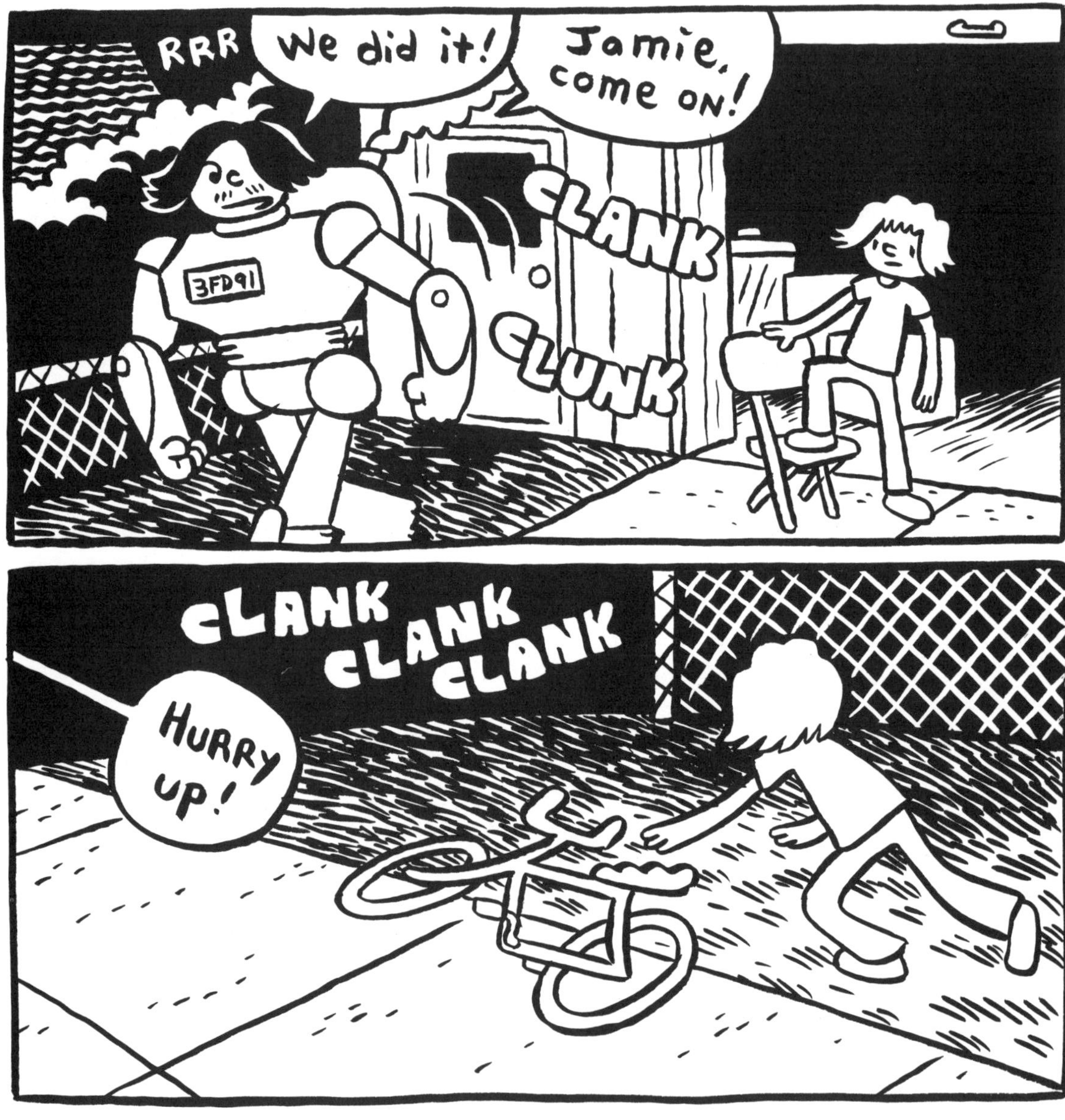
RRR
We did it!
Jamie, come on!
3FD91
CLANK
CLUNK
CLANK CLANK CLANK
HURRY UP!

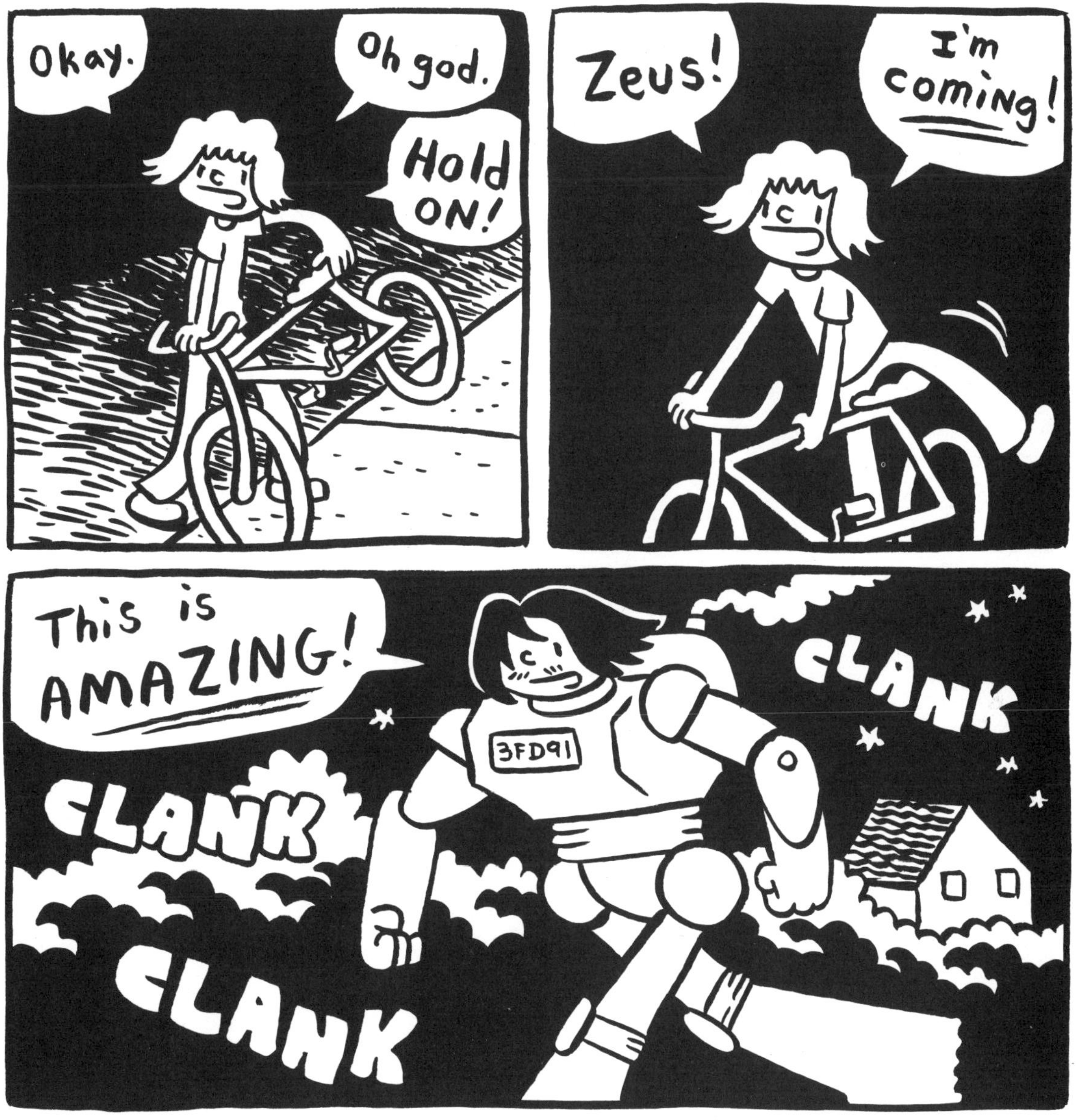
Okay.
Oh god.
Hold ON!
Zeus!
I'm coming!
This is AMAZING!
3FD91
CLANK
CLANK
CLANK

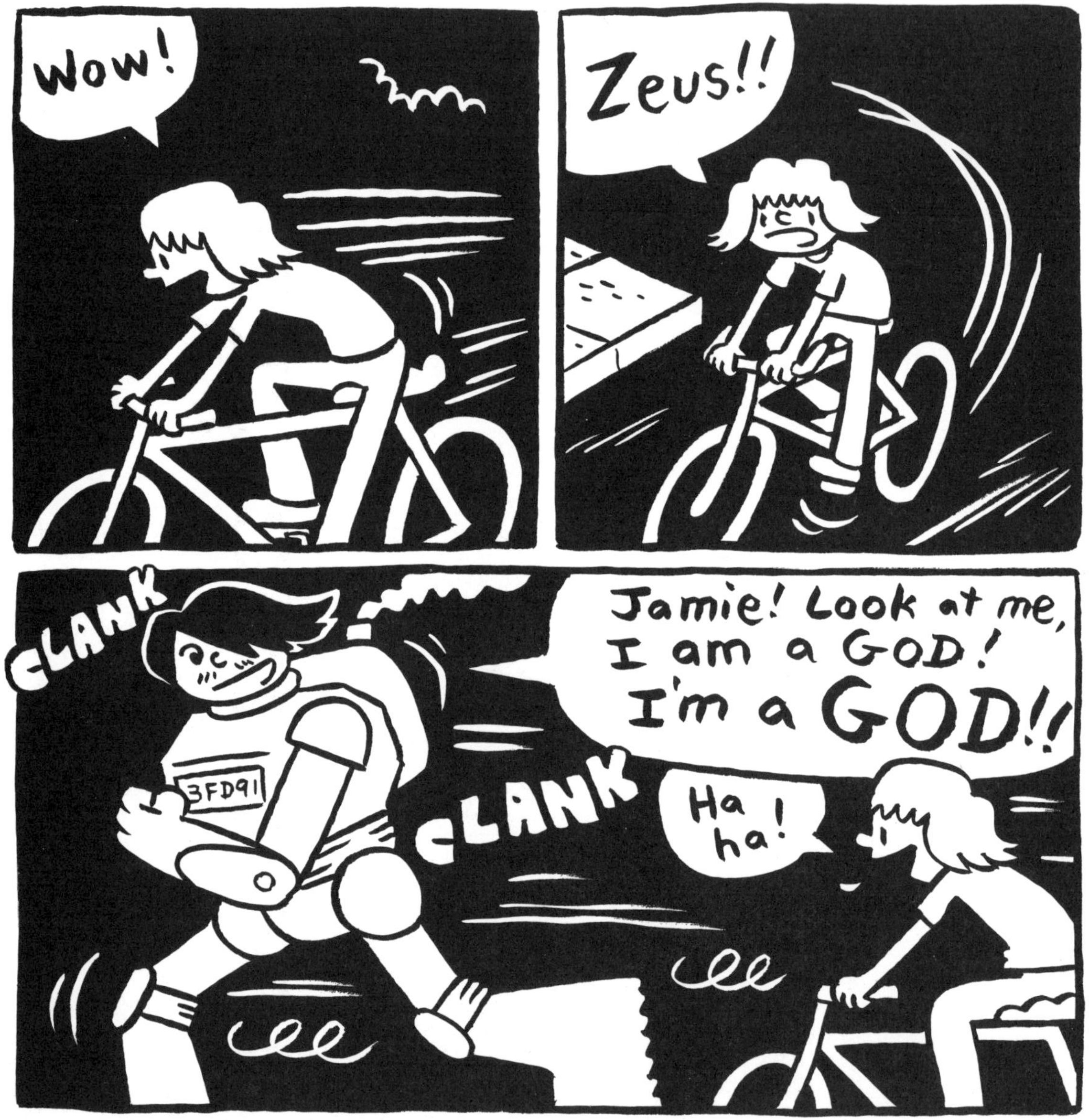
WOW!
Zeus!!
CLANK
Jamie! Look at me, I am a GOD! I'm a GOD!!
3FD91
CLANK
Ha ha!

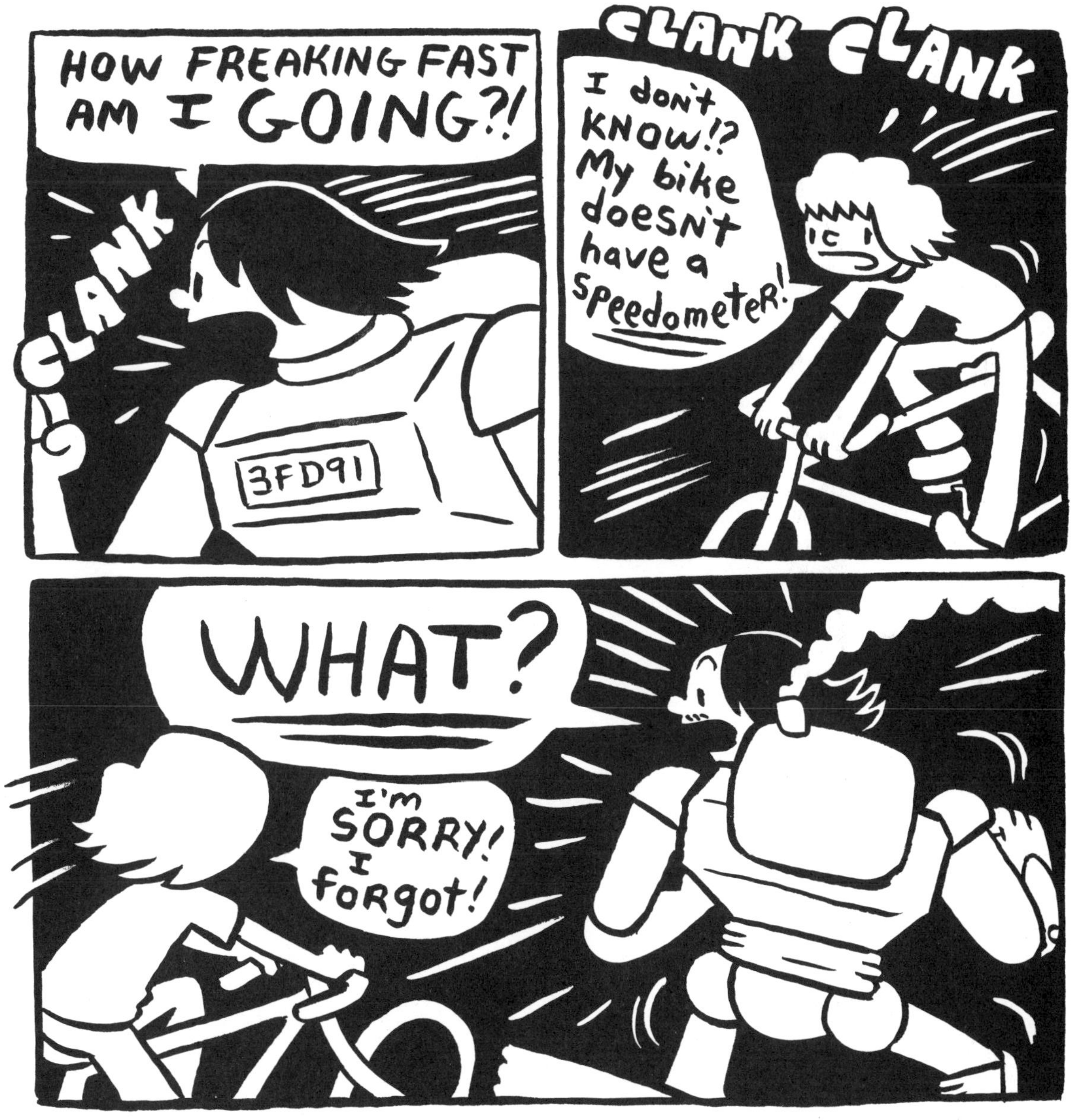

HOW FREAKING FAST AM I GOING?!
CLANK
3FD91
CLANK CLANK
I don't KNOW!? My bike doesn't have a speedometer!
WHAT?
I'm SORRY! I forgot!

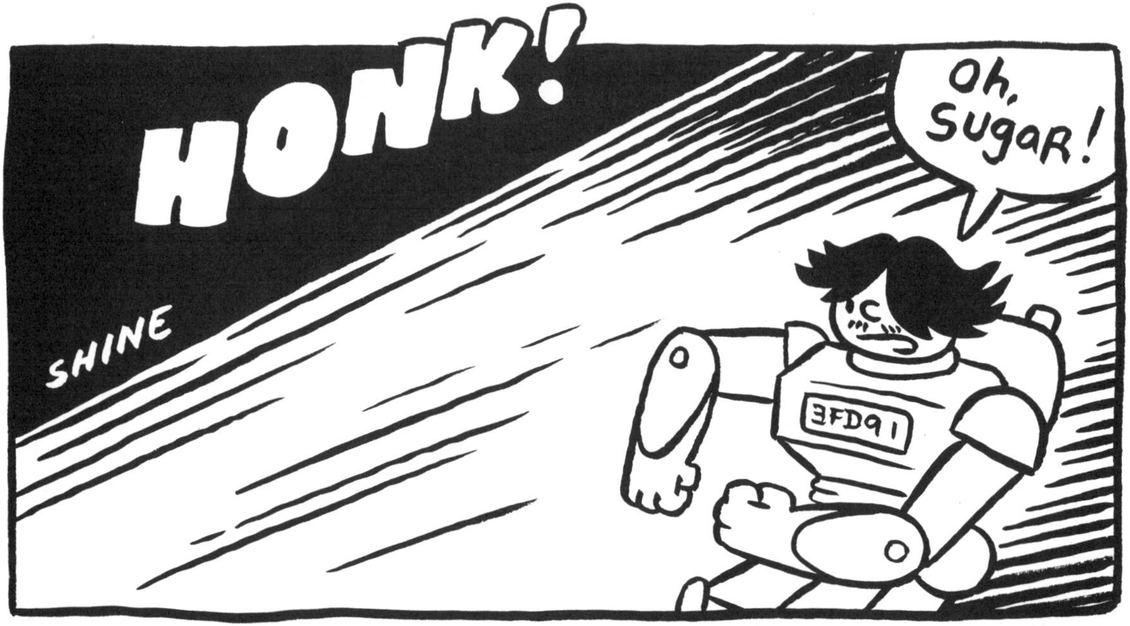
HONK!
Oh, Sugar!
SHINE
3FD91

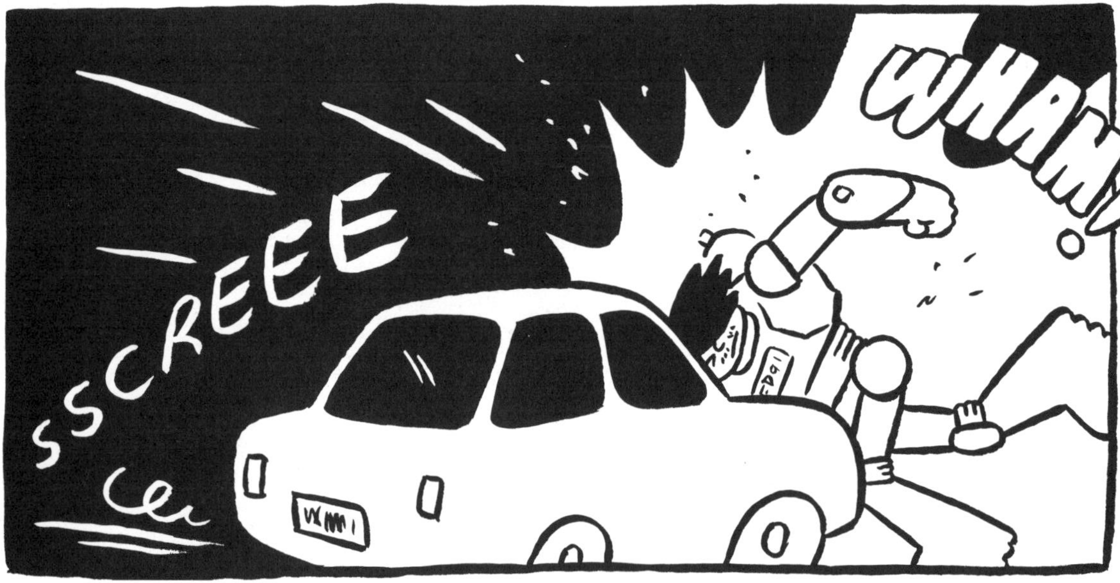
SSCREEEE
WHAM!

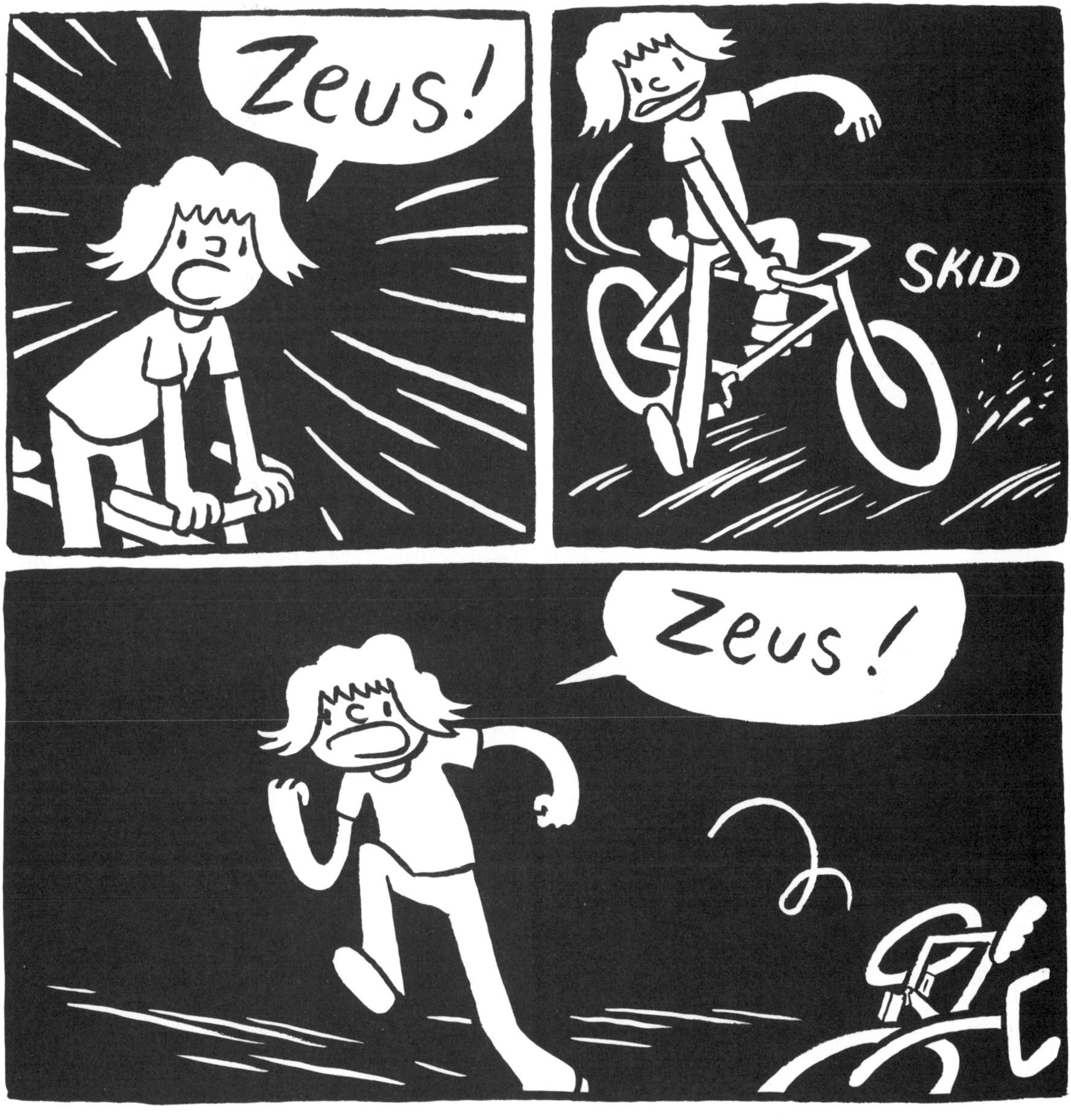
Zeus!
SKID
Zeus!

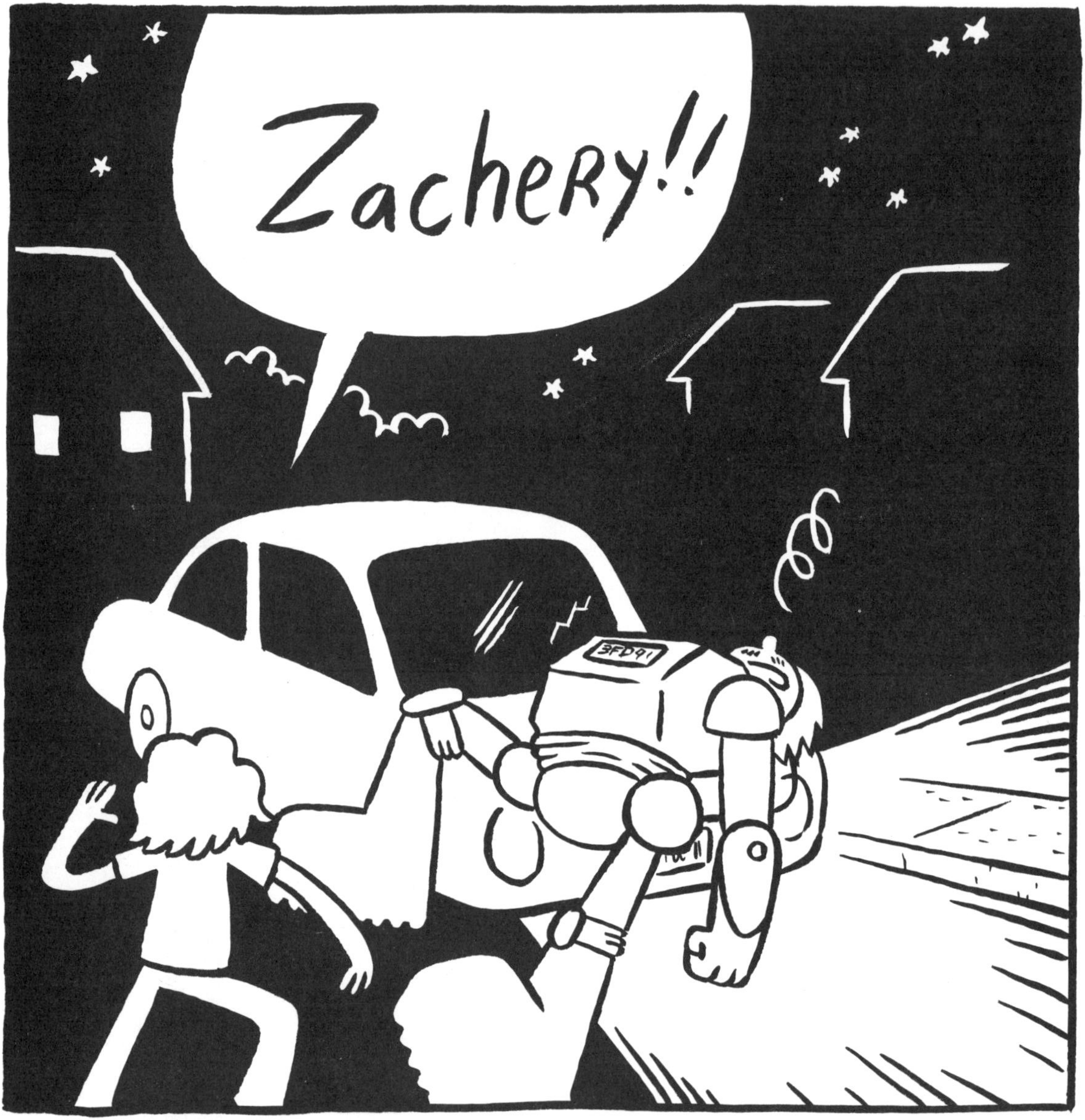
Zachery!!

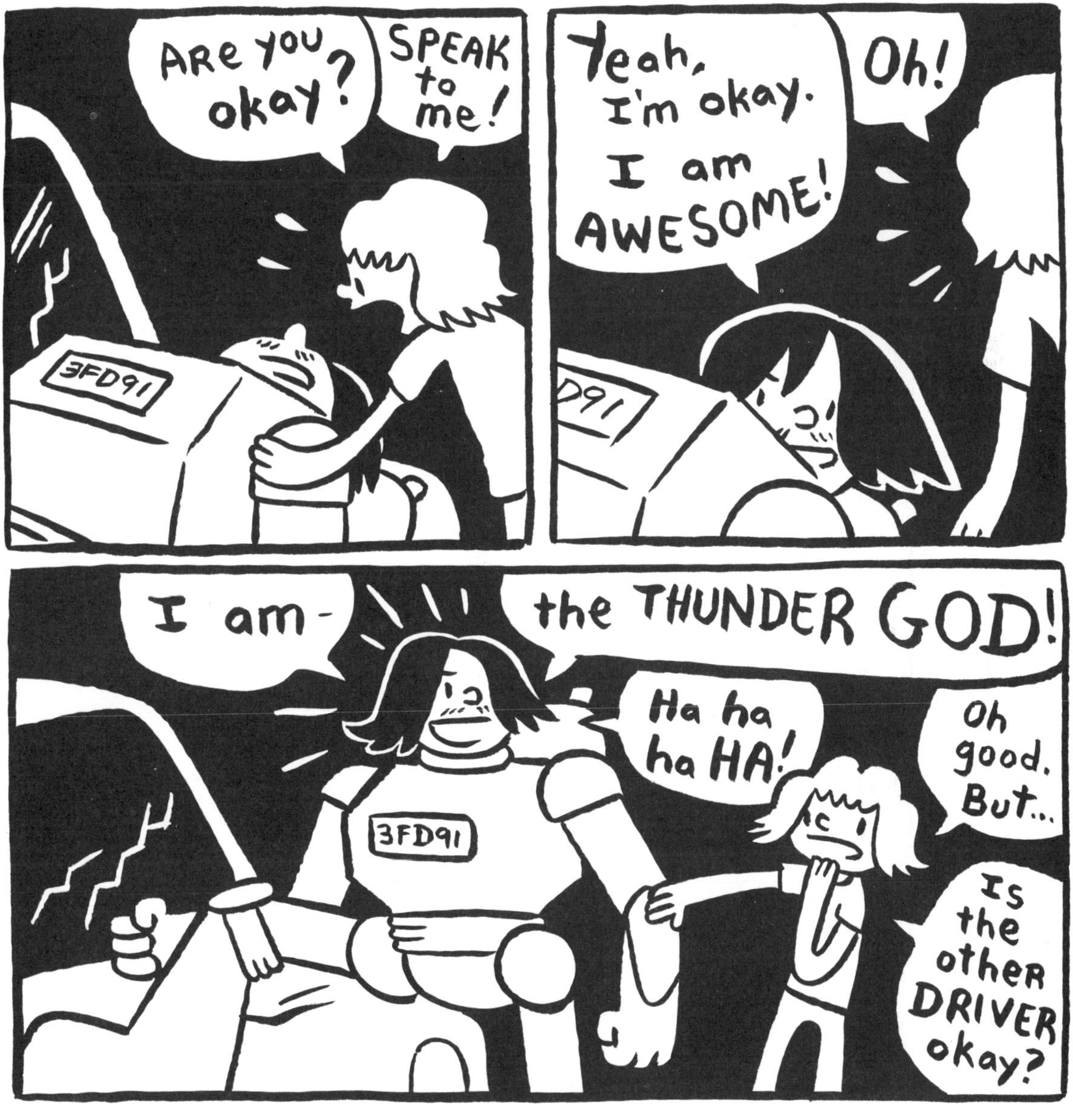
Are you okay?
SPEAK to me!
Yeah, I'm okay. I am AWESOME!
Oh!
3FD91
I am-
the THUNDER GOD!
Ha ha ha HA!
Oh good. But...
Is the other DRIVER okay?
3FD91

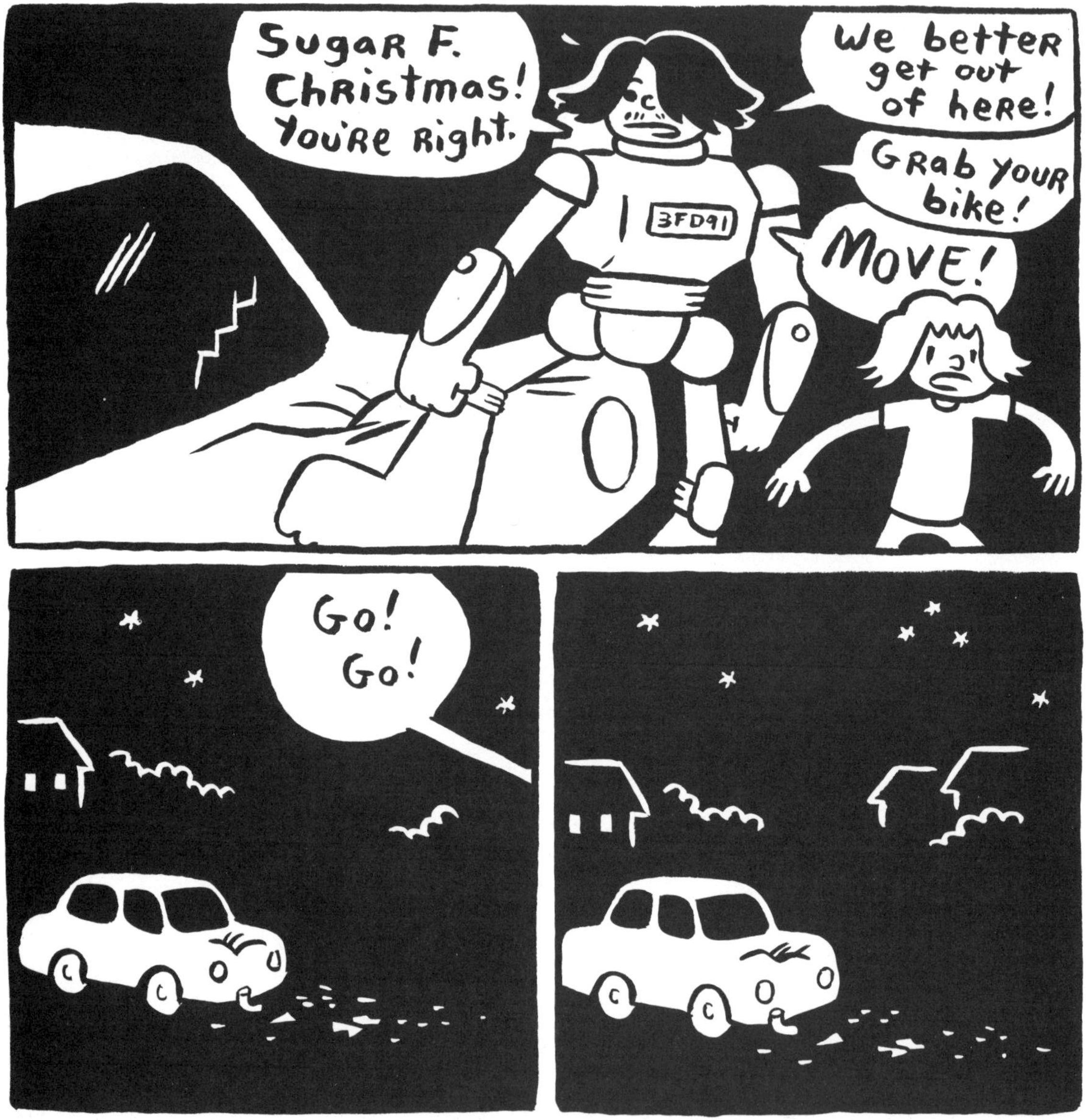
Sugar F. Christmas! You're Right.
We better get out of here!
Grab your bike!
MOVE!
3FD91
Go! Go!

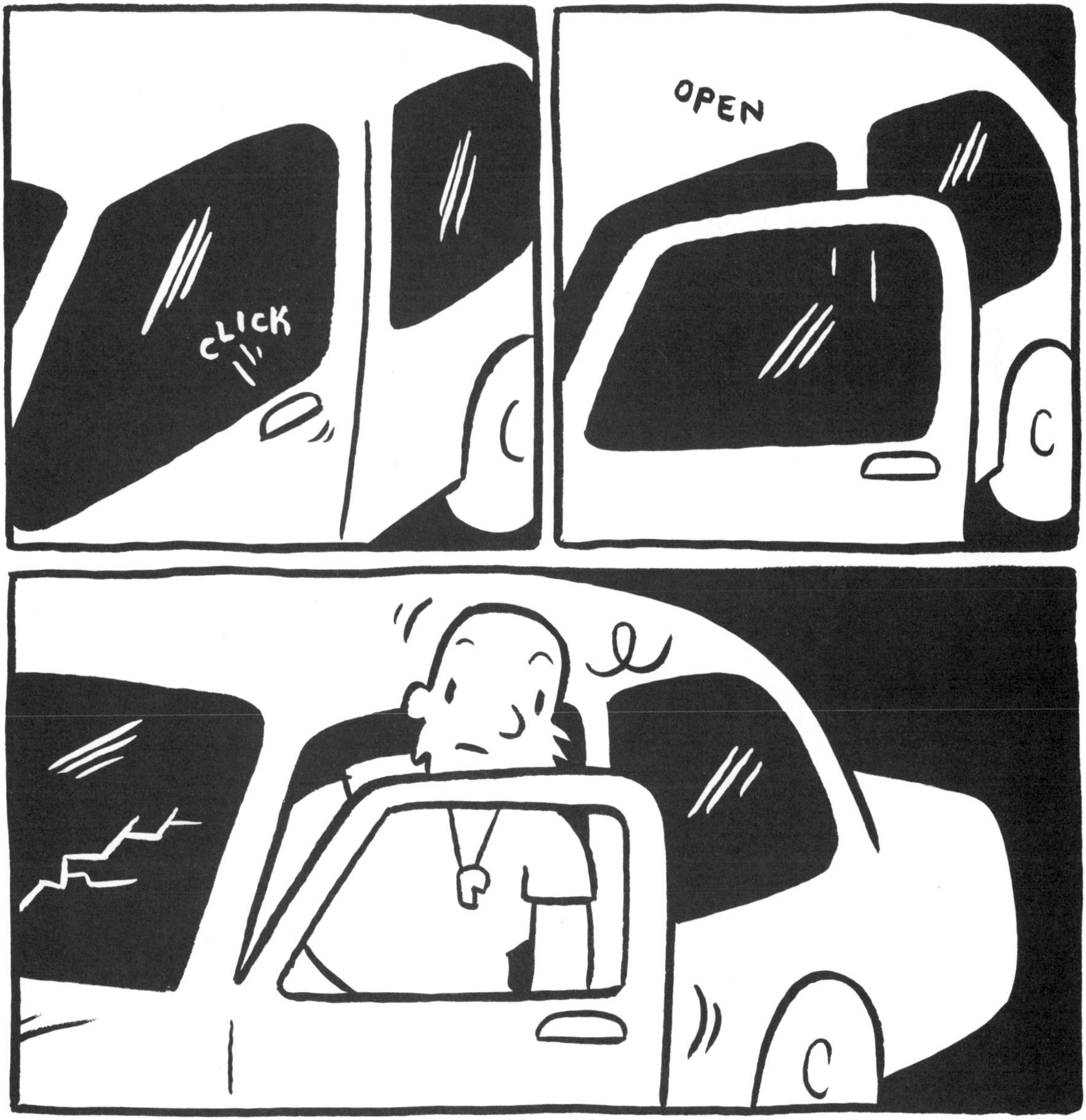
CLICK
OPEN

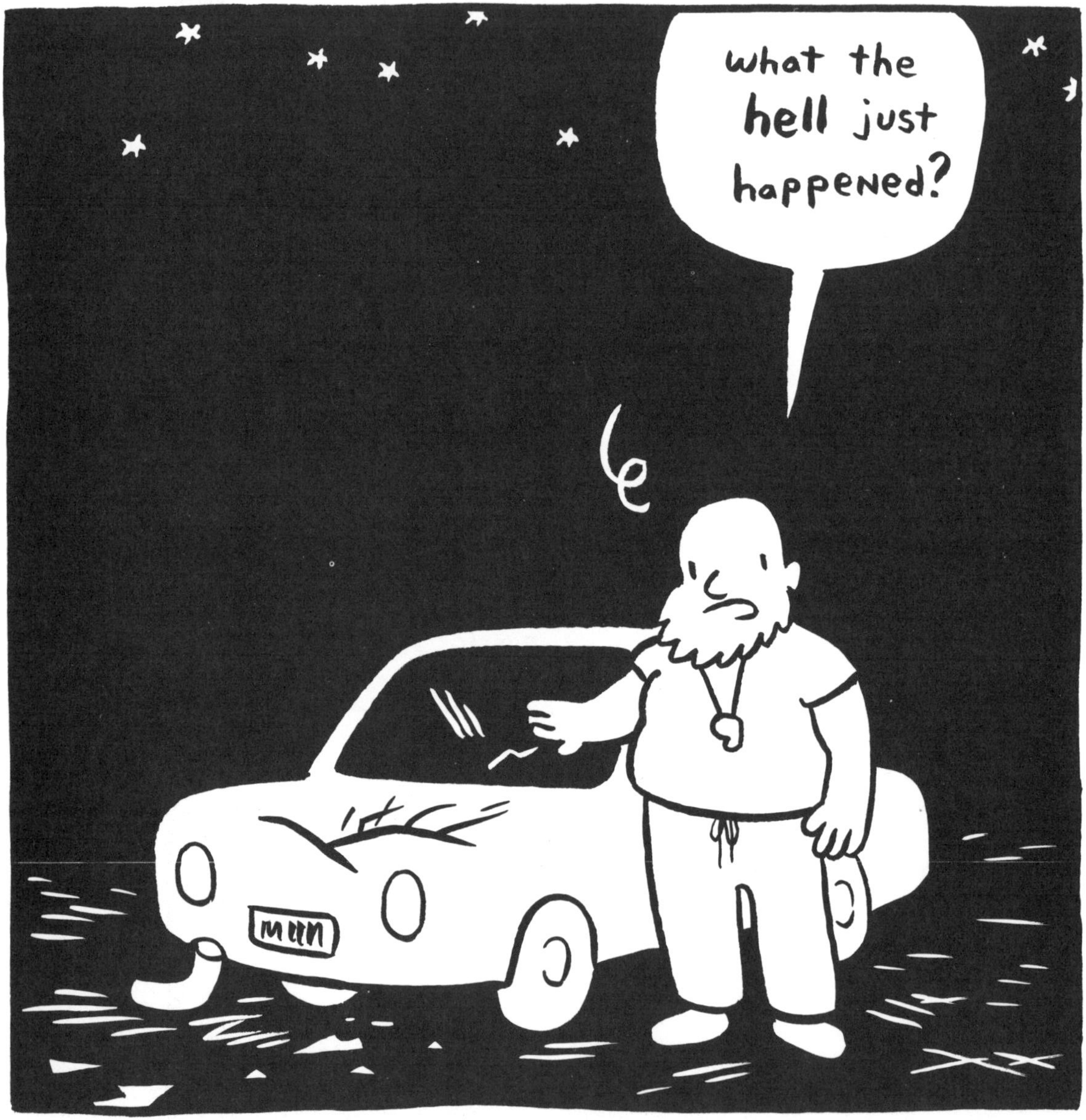
what the hell just happened?
MUN

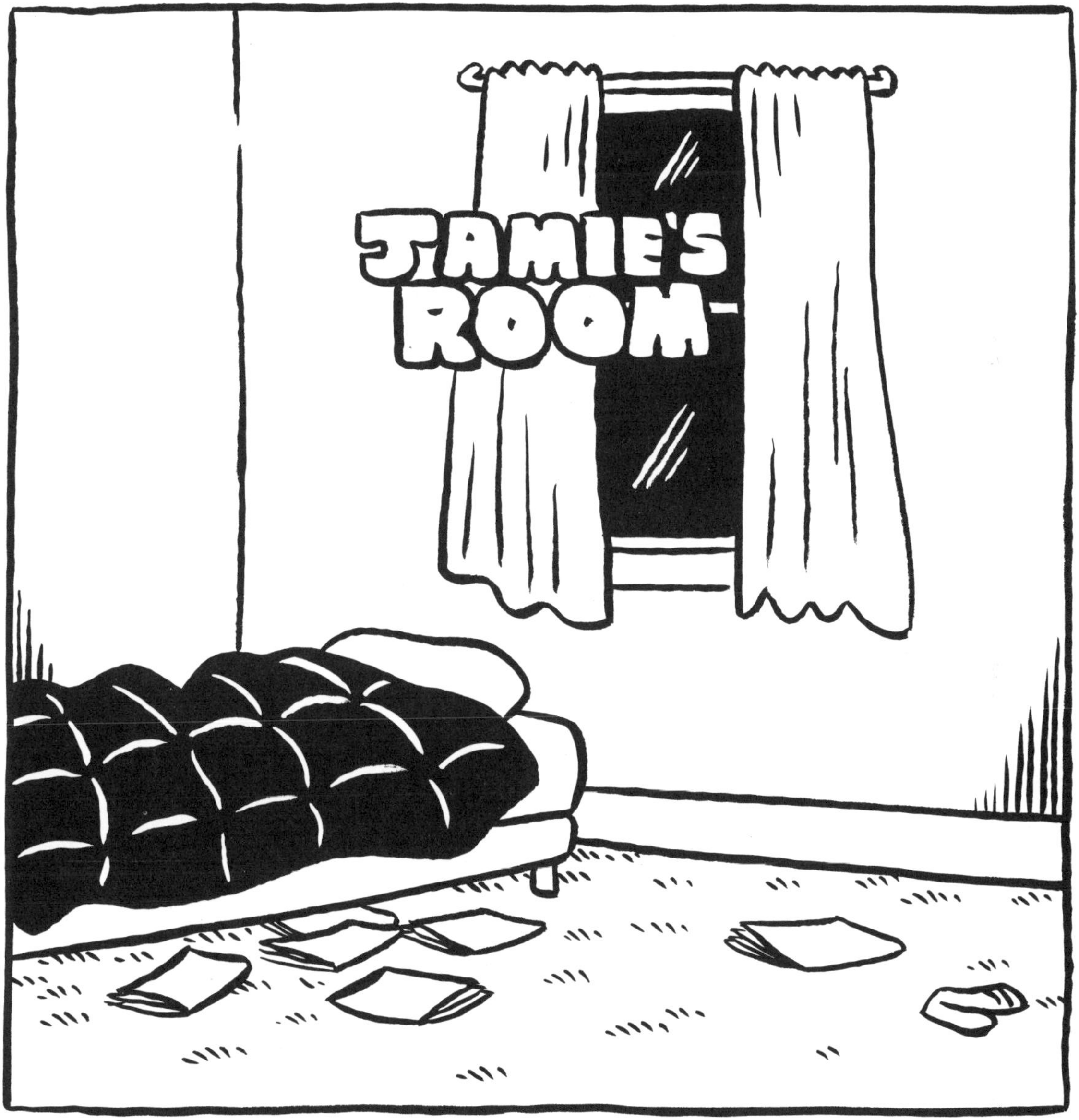
JAMIE'S
ROOM

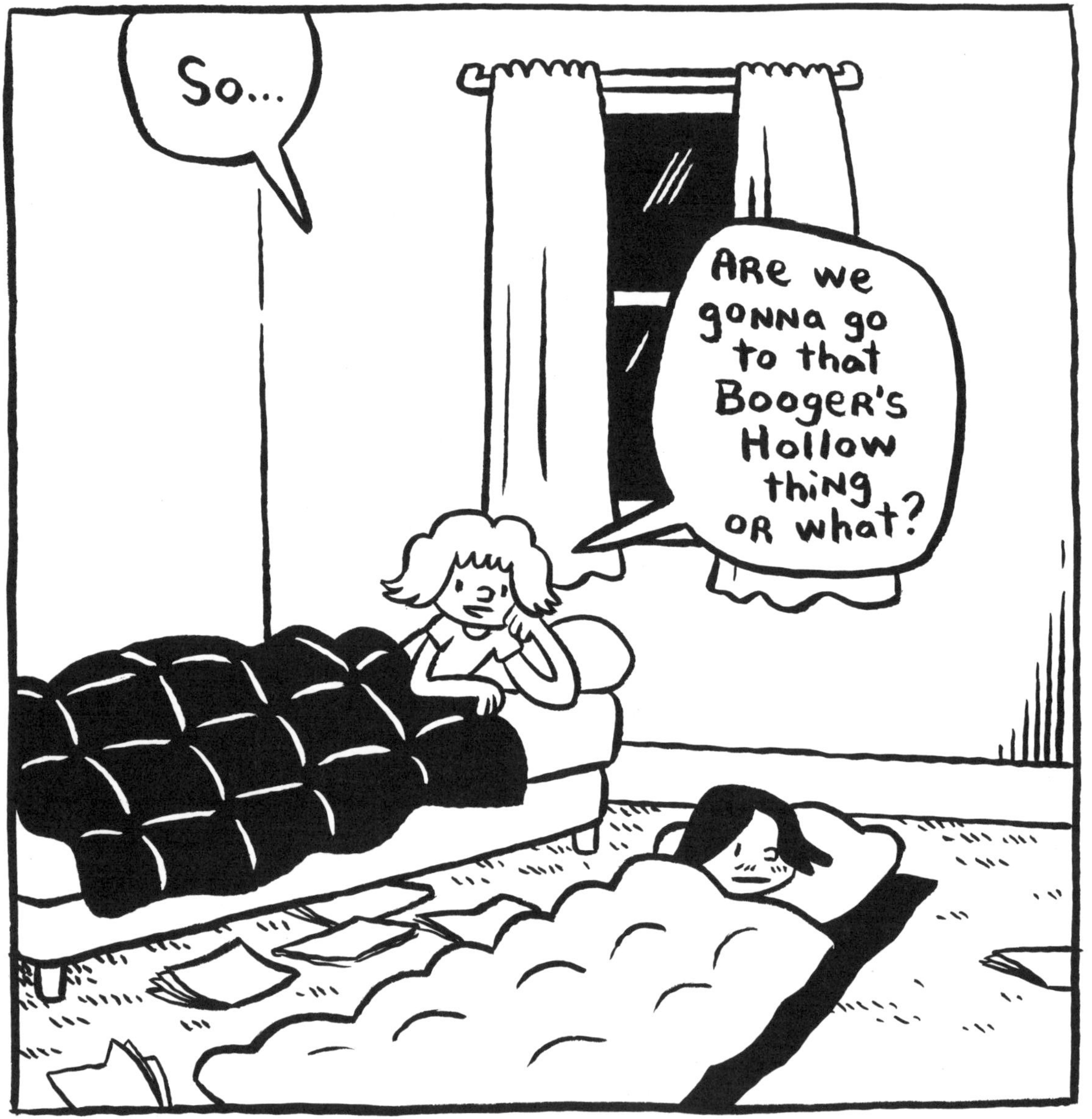
So...
Are we gonna go to that Booger's Hollow thing or what?

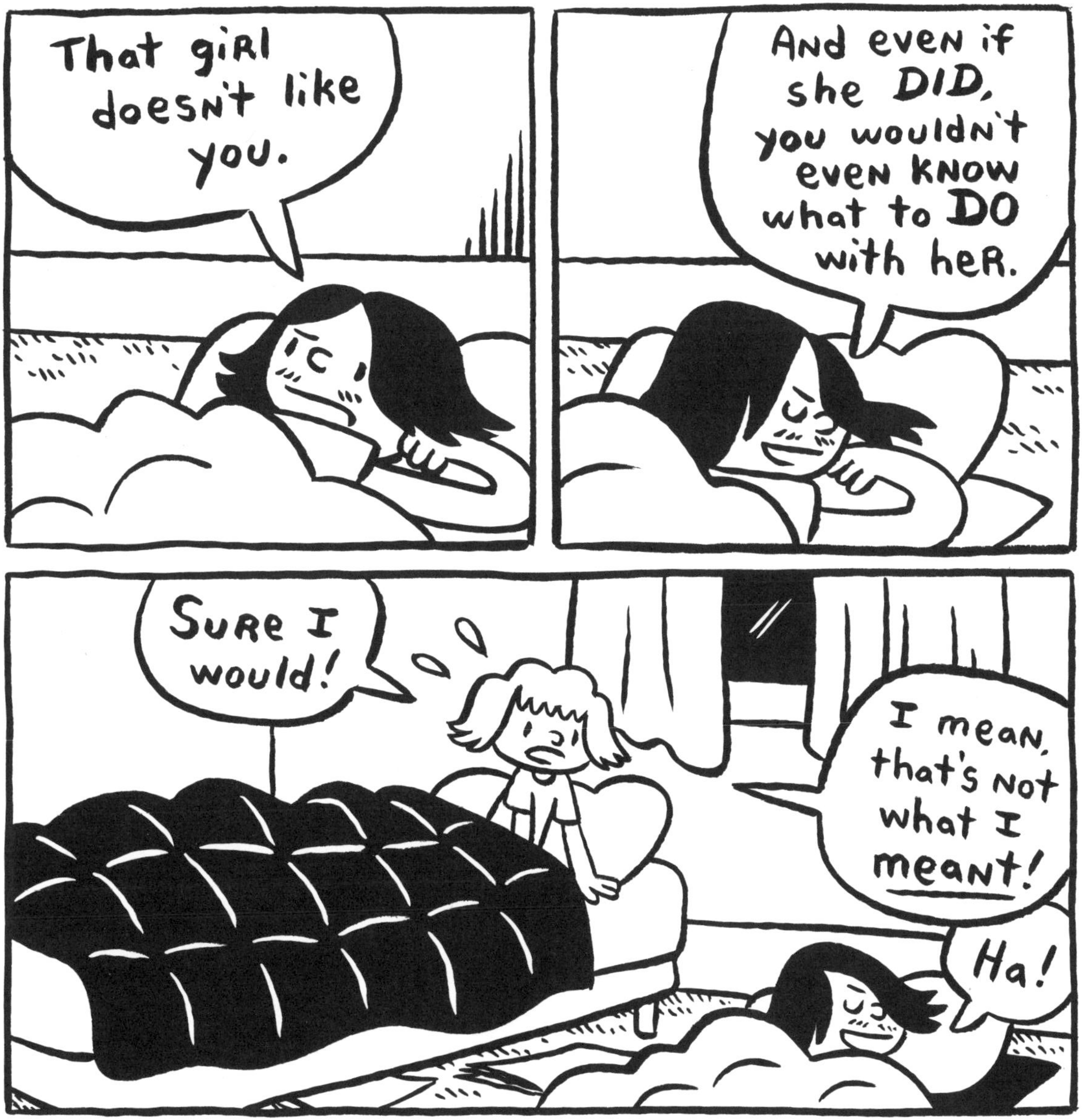
That girl doesn't like you.
And even if she DID, you wouldn't even KNOW what to DO with her.
Sure I would!
I mean, that's not what I meant!
Ha!

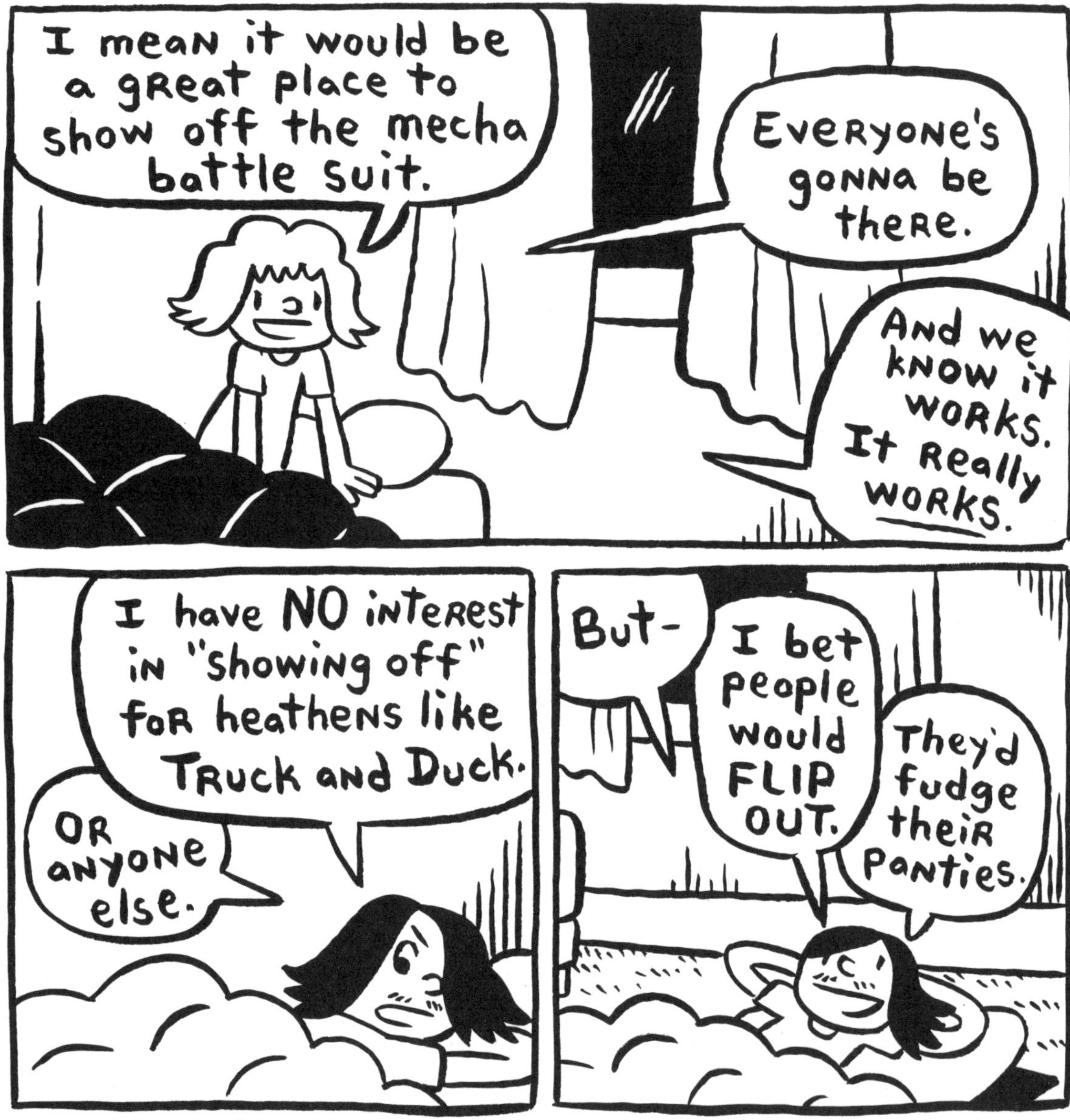
I mean it would be a great place to show off the mecha battle suit.
Everyone's gonna be there.
And we know it works. It really WORKS.
I have NO interest in "showing off" for heathens like Truck and Duck.
OR anyone else.
But-
I bet people would FLIP OUT.
They'd fudge their panties.

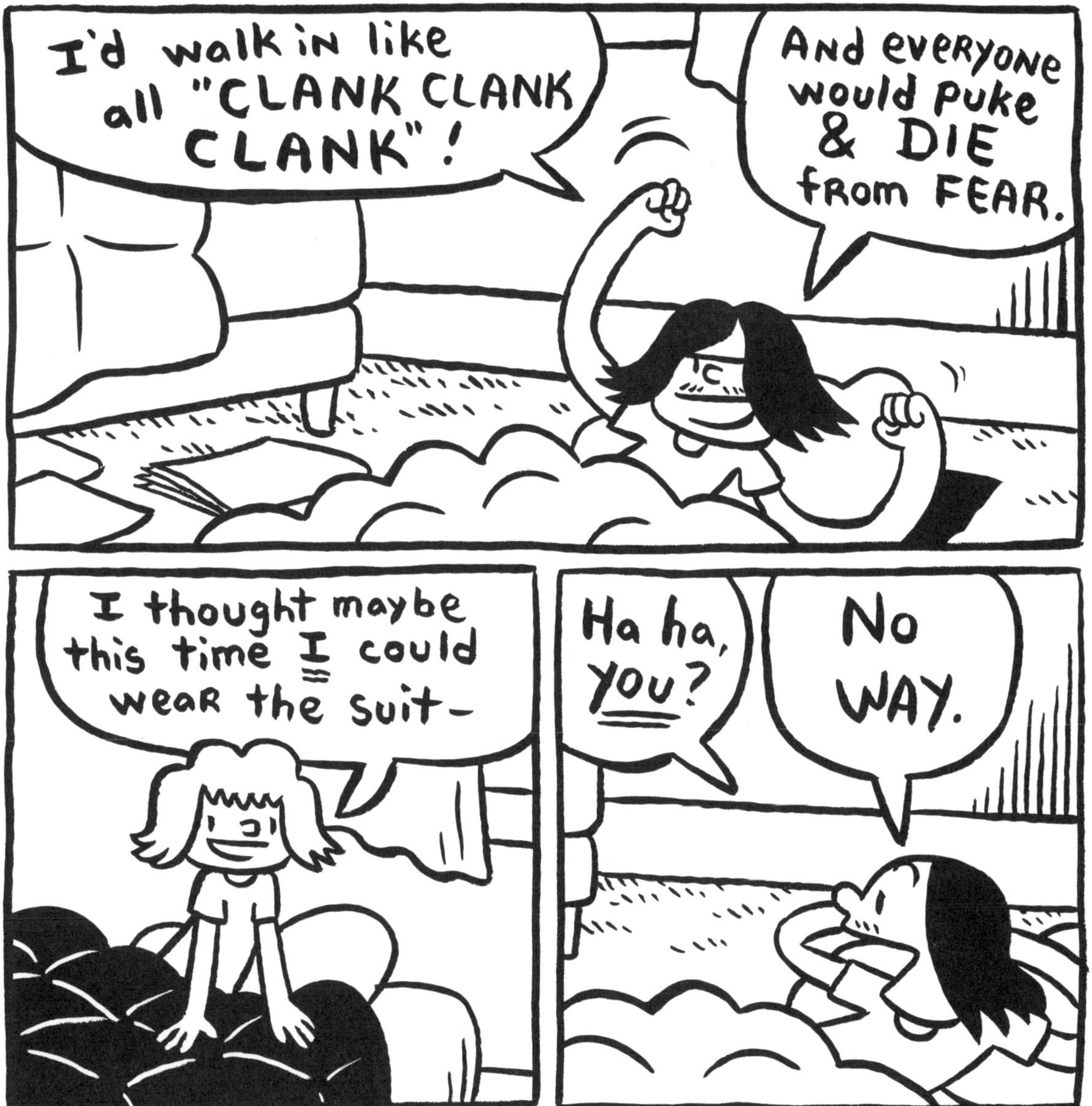
I'd walk in like all "CLANK CLANK CLANK"!
And everyone would puke & DIE from FEAR.
I thought maybe this time I could wear the suit-
Ha ha, YOU?
No WAY.

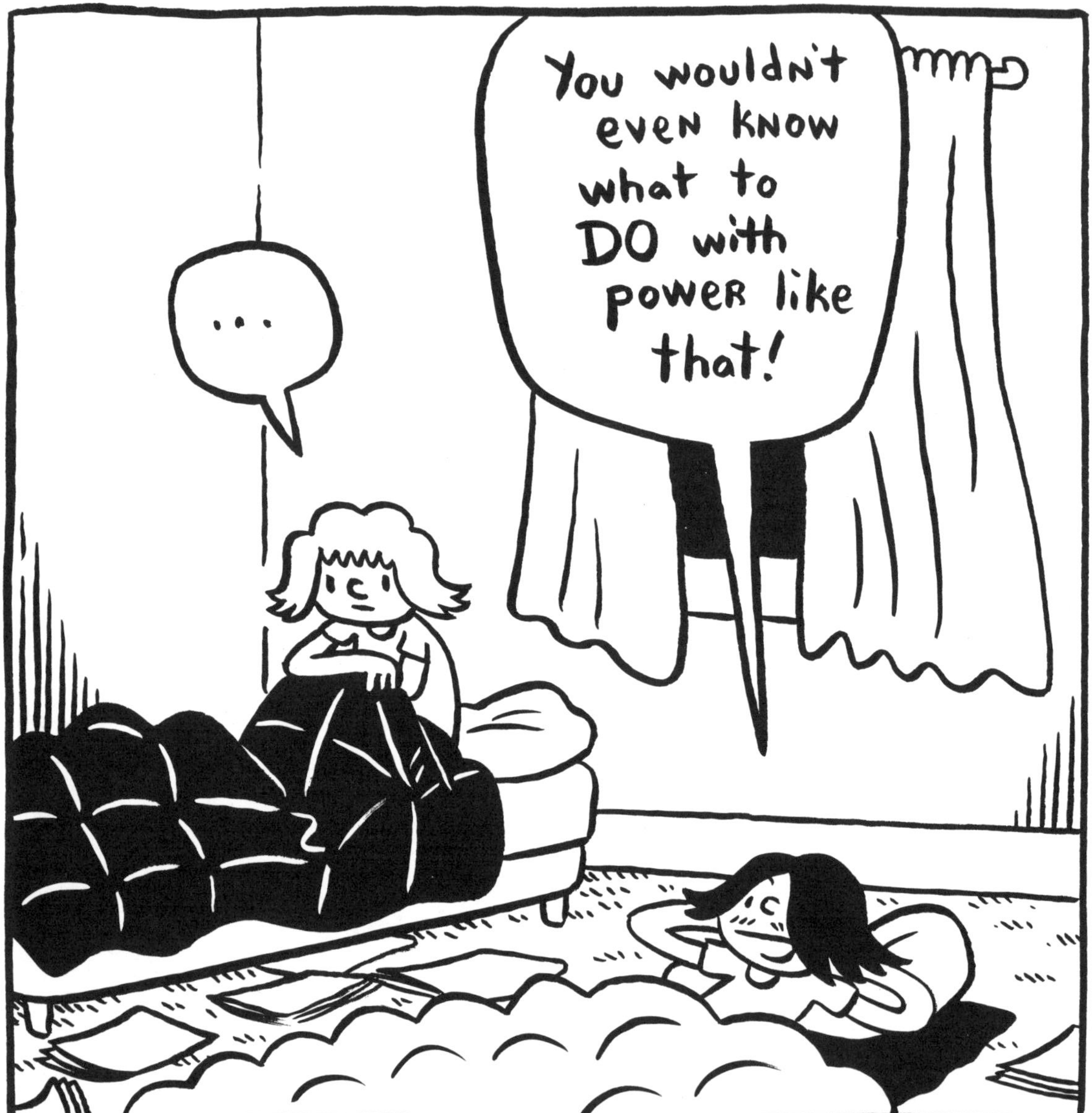
...
You wouldn't even know what to DO with power like that!

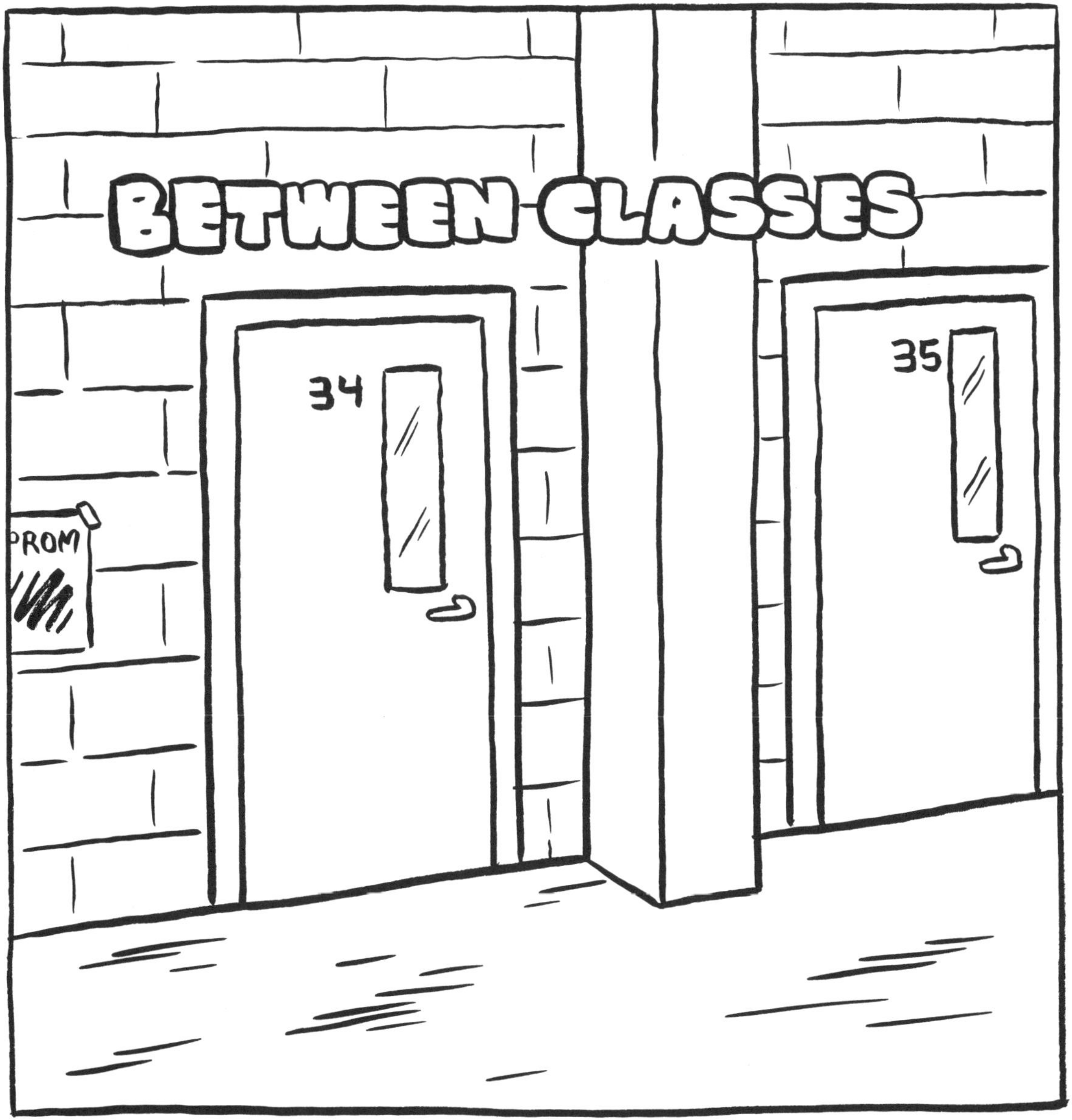
BETWEEN CLASSES
34
35
PROM

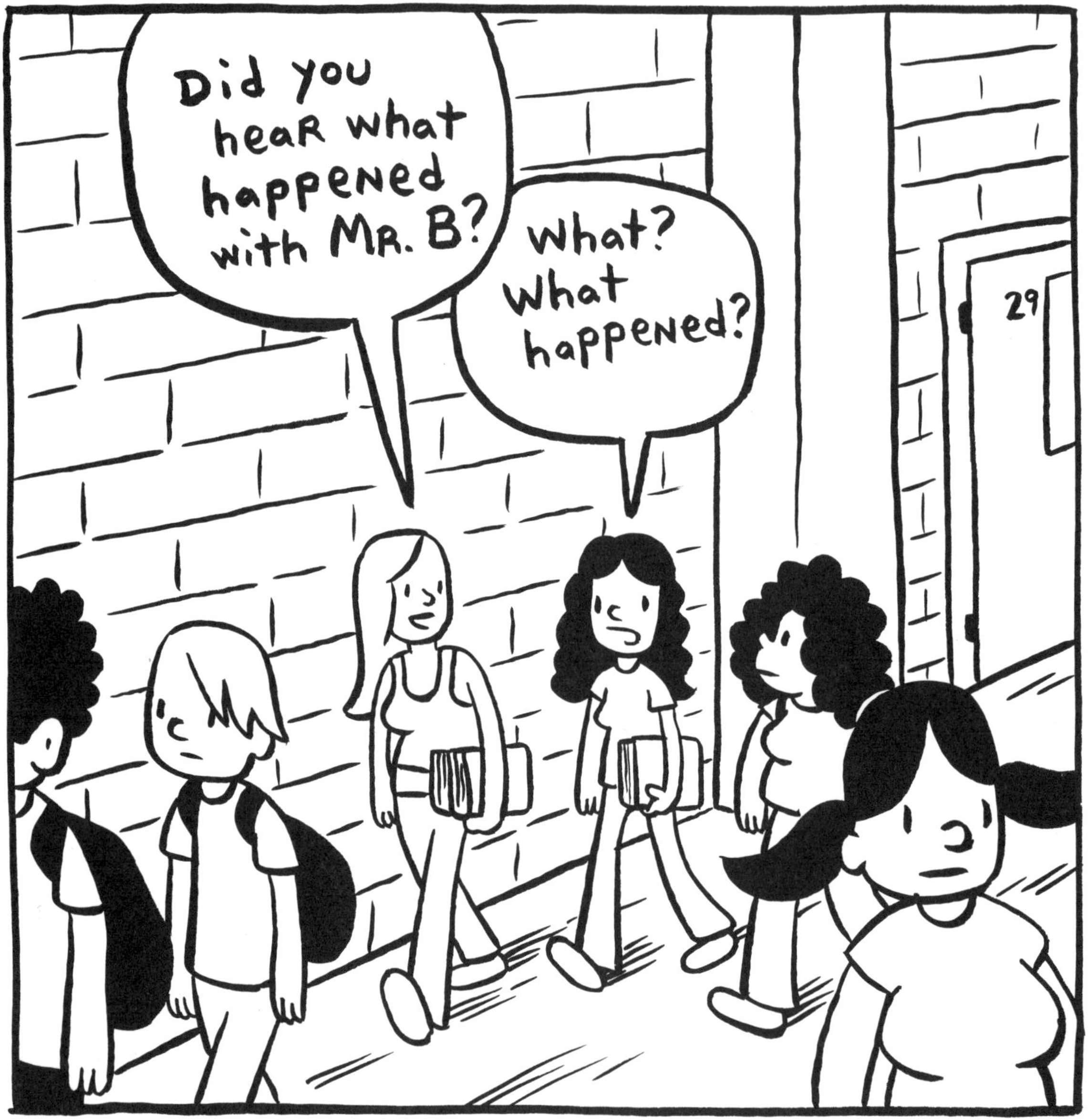
Did you hear what happened with MR. B?
What? What happened?
29

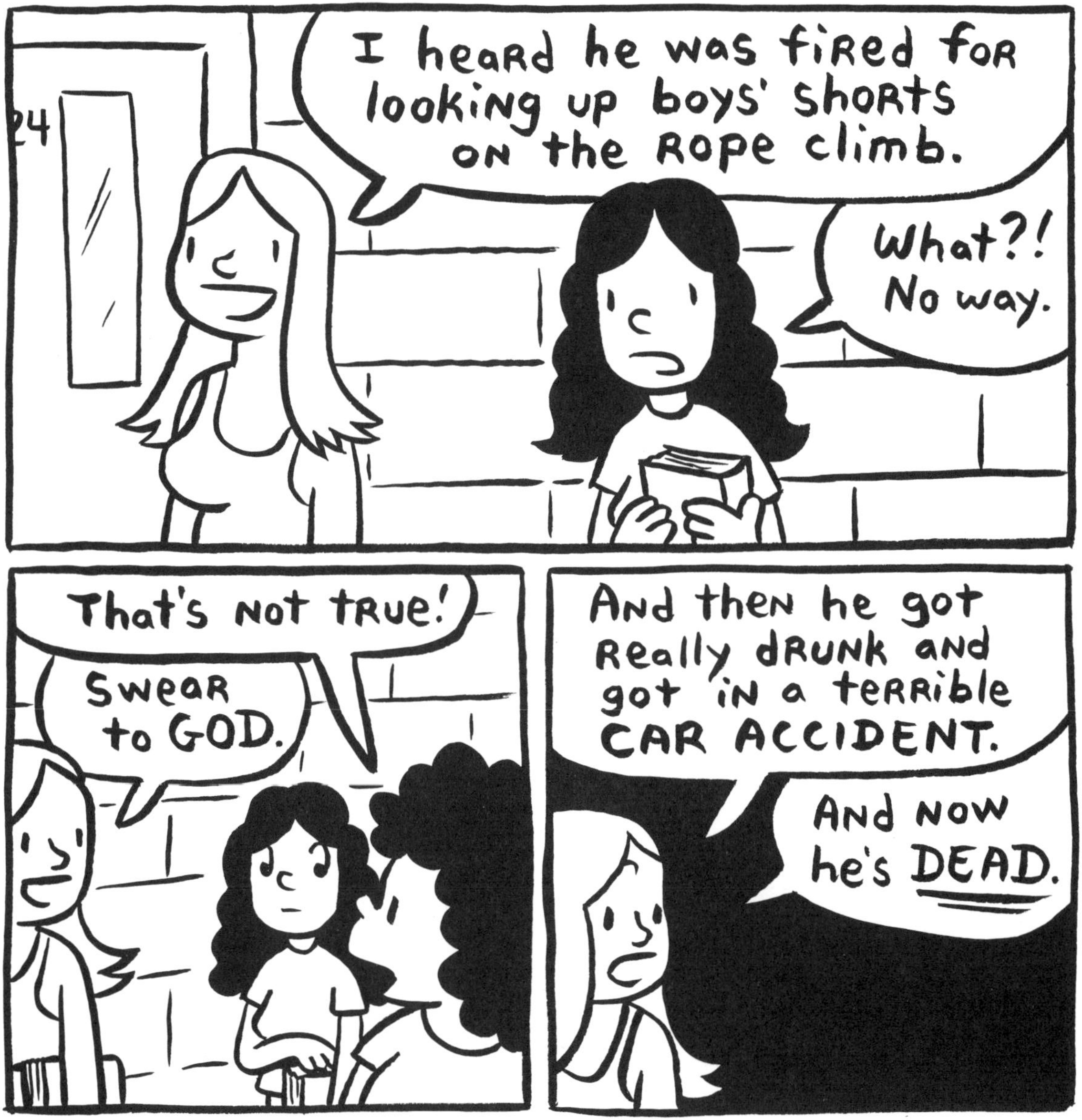
24
I heard he was fired for looking up boys' shorts on the rope climb.
What?! No way.
That's not true!
Swear to GOD.
And then he got really drunk and got in a terrible CAR ACCIDENT.
And now he's DEAD.

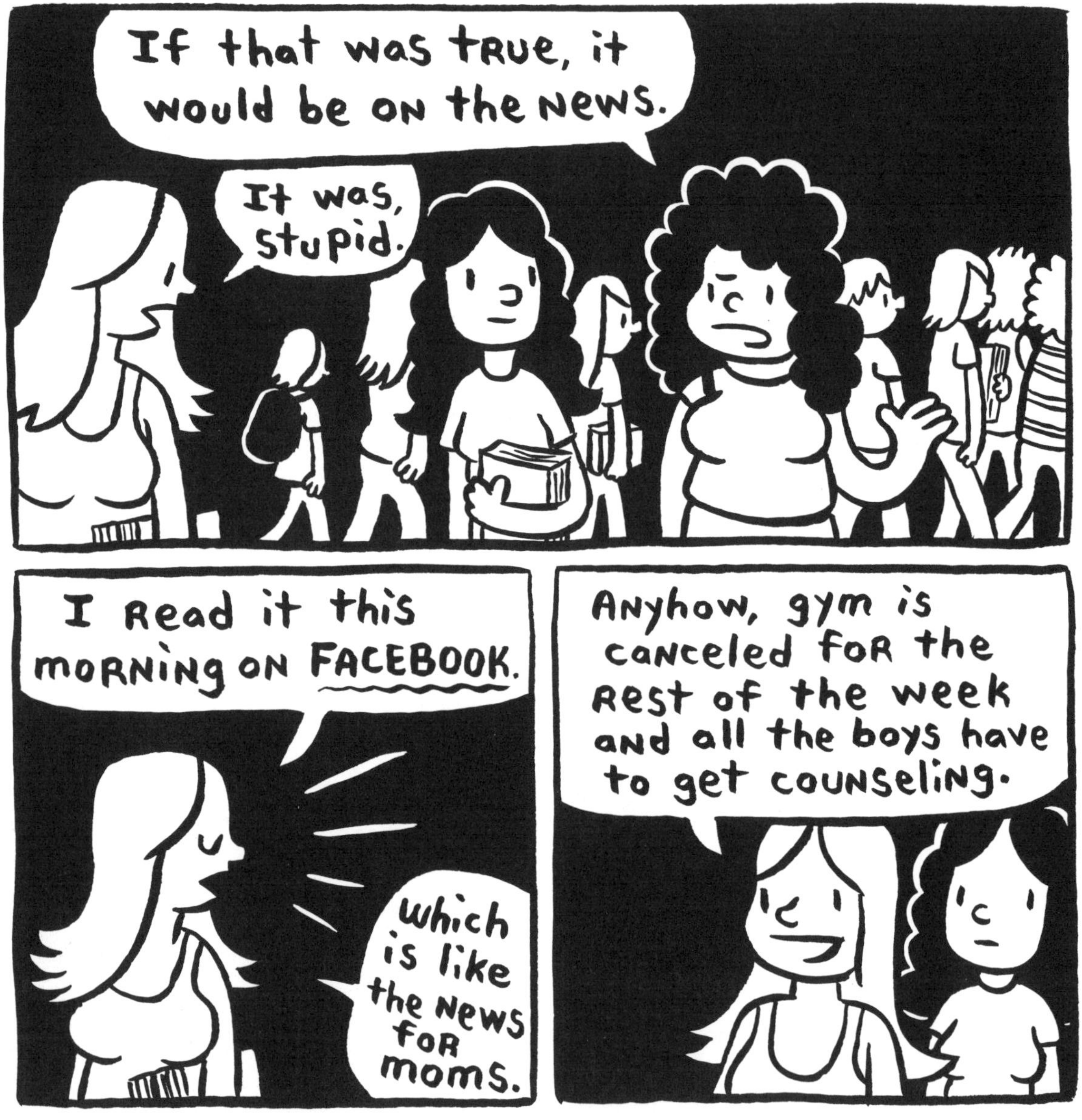
If that was true, it would be on the news.
It was, stupid.
I read it this morning on FACEBOOK.
which is like the news for moms.
Anyhow, gym is canceled for the rest of the week and all the boys have to get counseling.

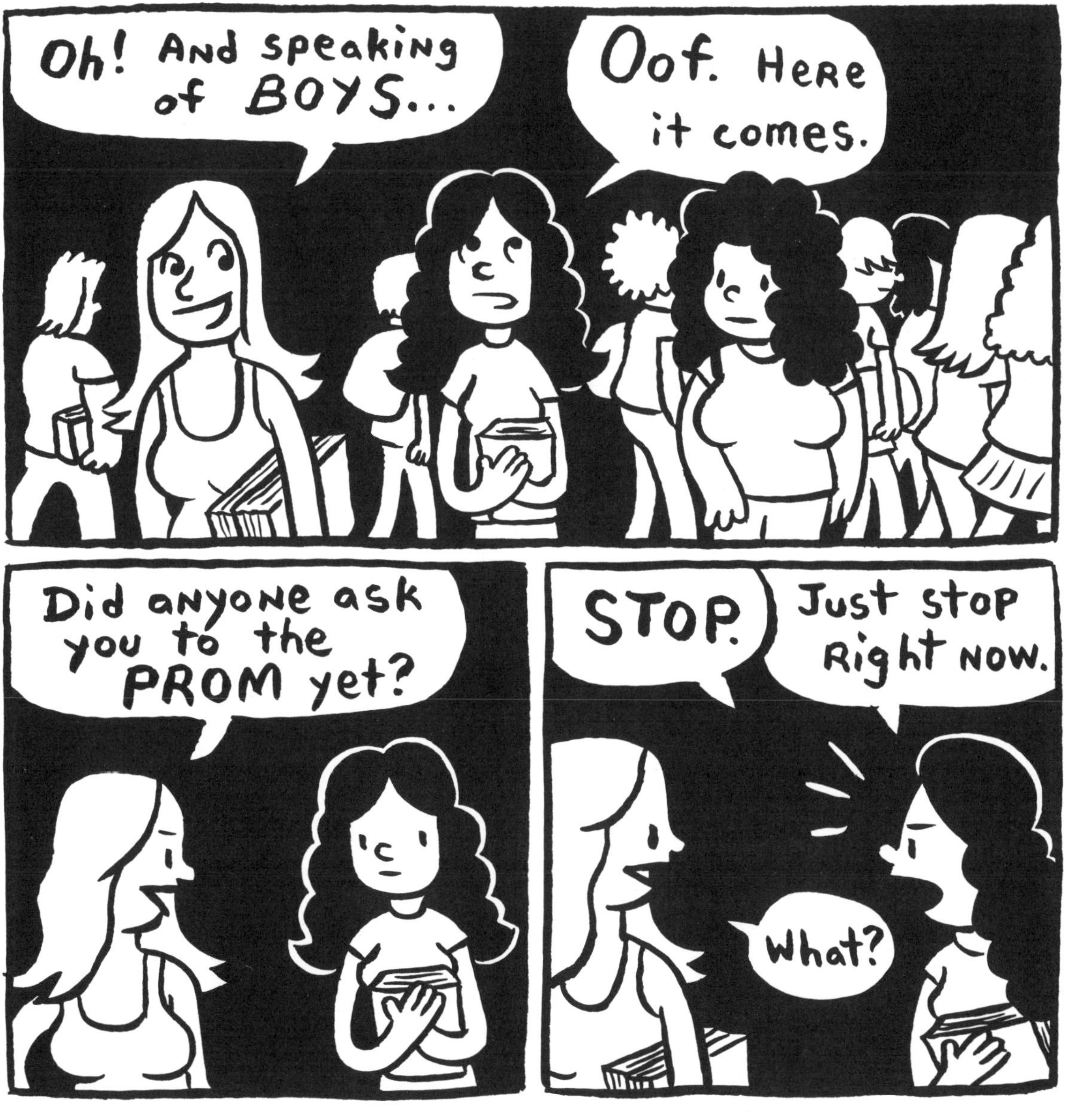
Oh! And speaking of BOYS...
Oof. Here it comes.
Did anyone ask you to the PROM yet?
STOP.
Just stop Right now.
What?

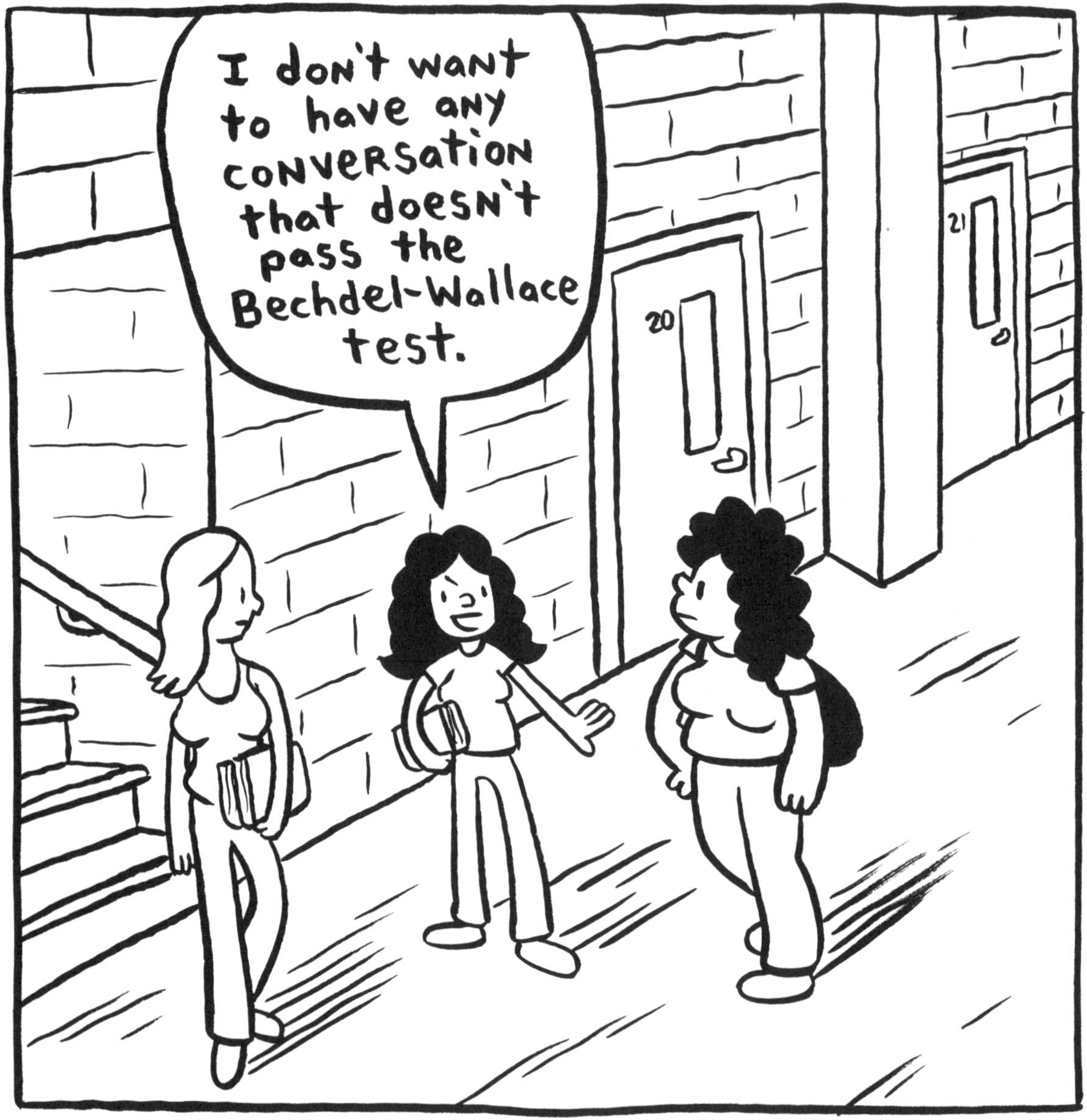
I don't want to have any conversation that doesn't pass the Bechdel-Wallace test.
20
21

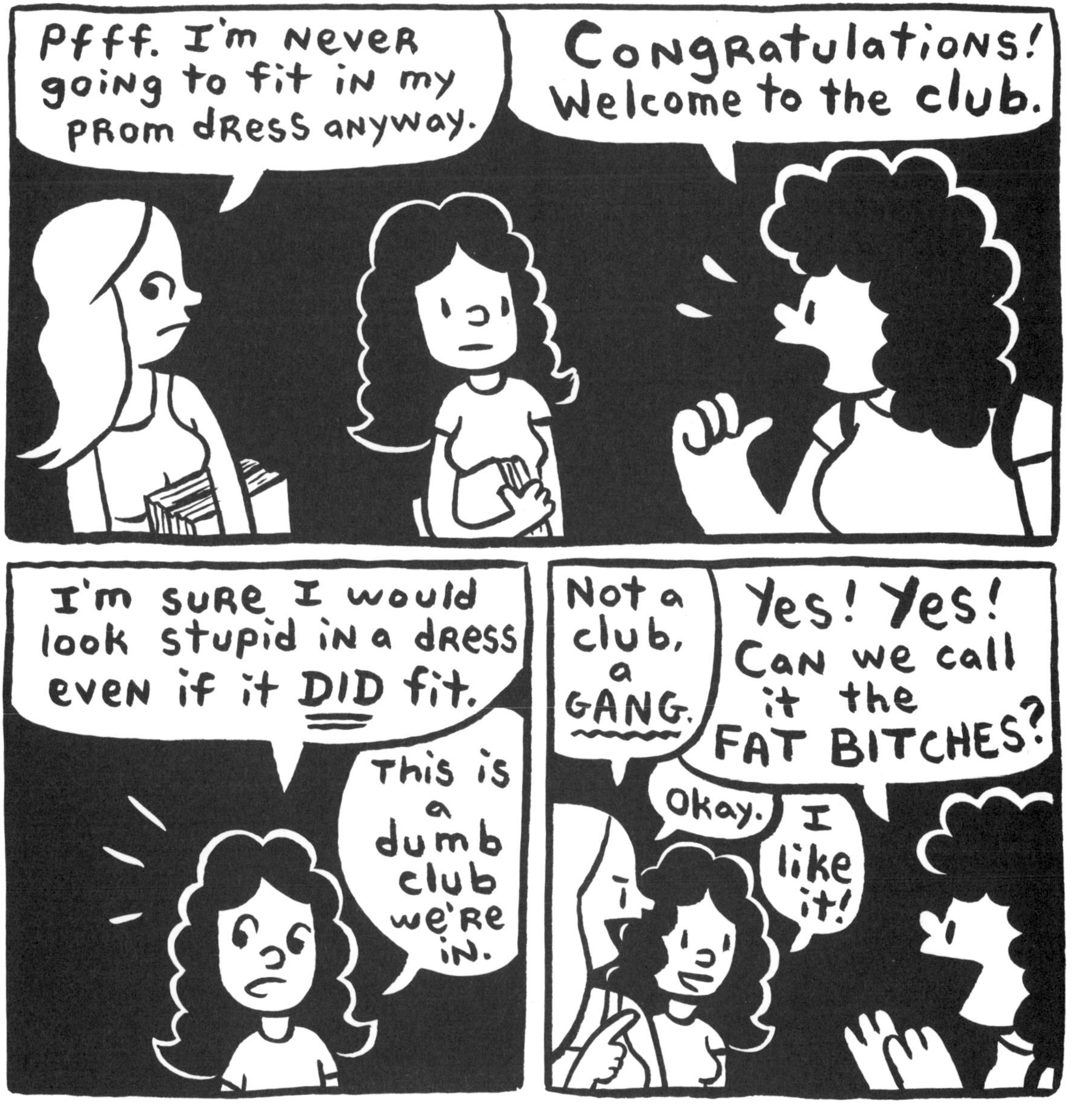

Pfff. I'm never going to fit in my prom dress anyway.
Congratulations! Welcome to the club.
I'm sure I would look stupid in a dress even if it DID fit.
This is a dumb club we're in.
Not a club, a GANG.
Yes! Yes! Can we call it the FAT BITCHES?
Okay.
I like it!

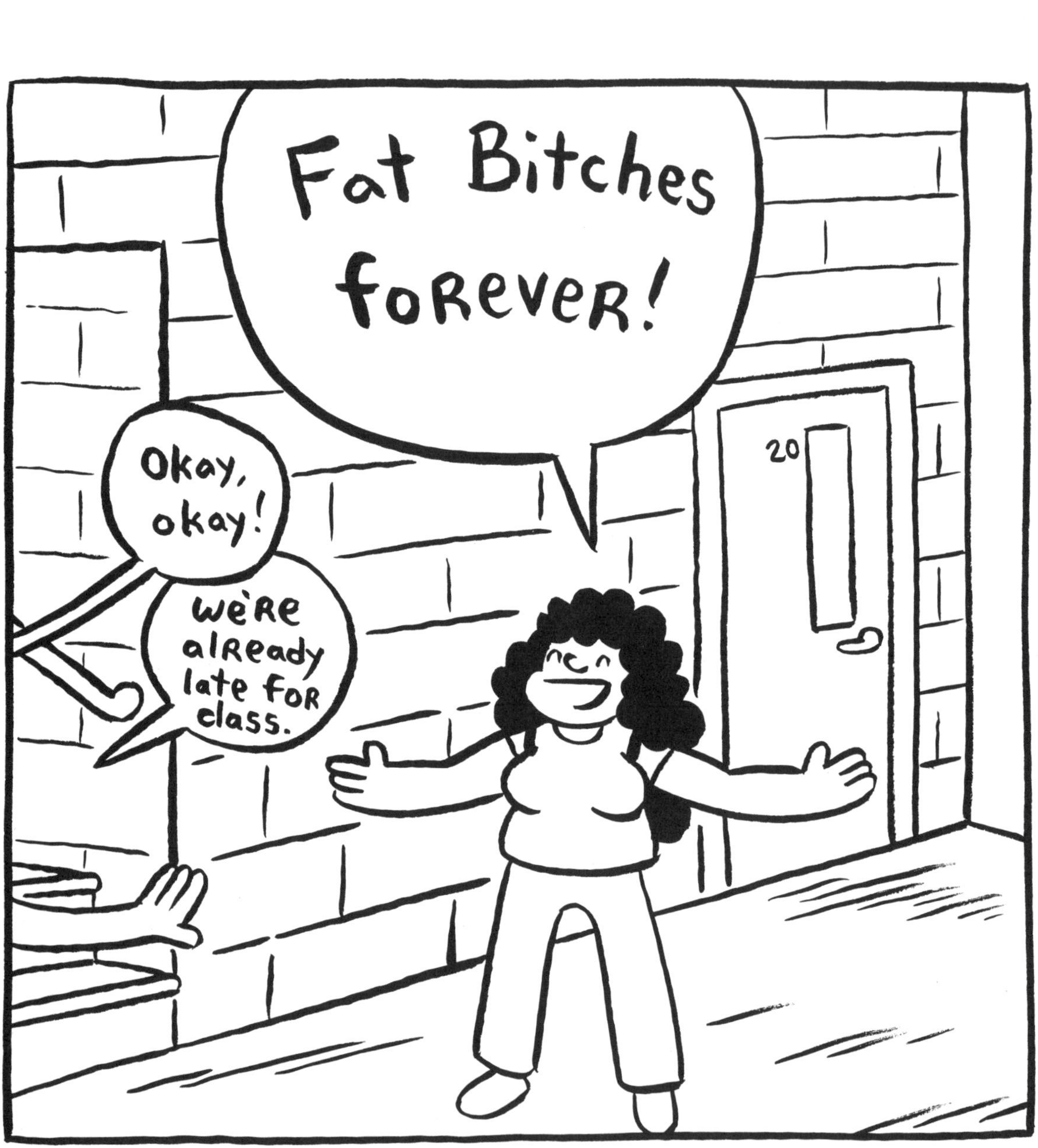
Fat Bitches forever!
Okay, okay!
we're already late for class.
20

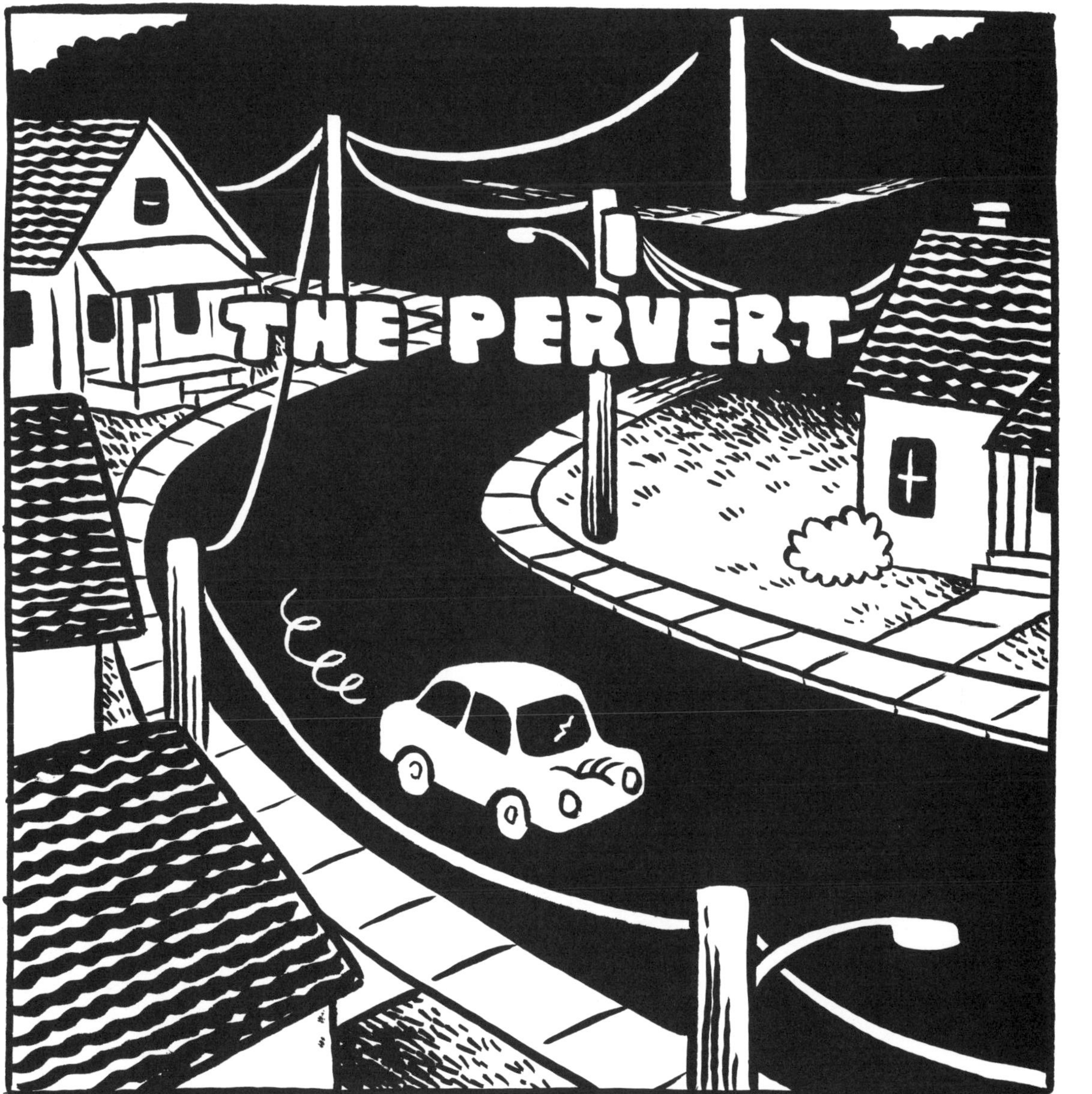
THE PERVERT

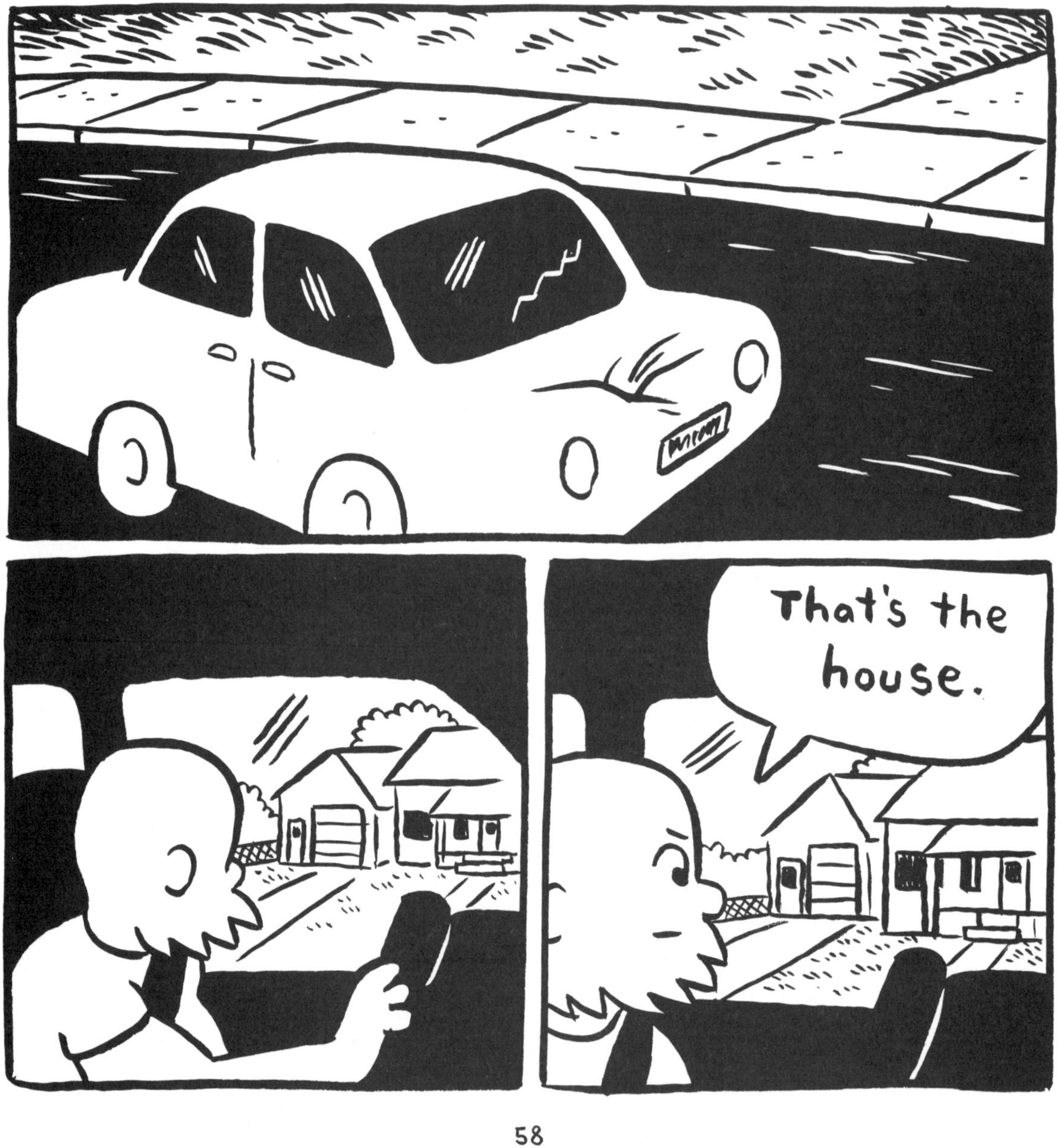
That's the house.

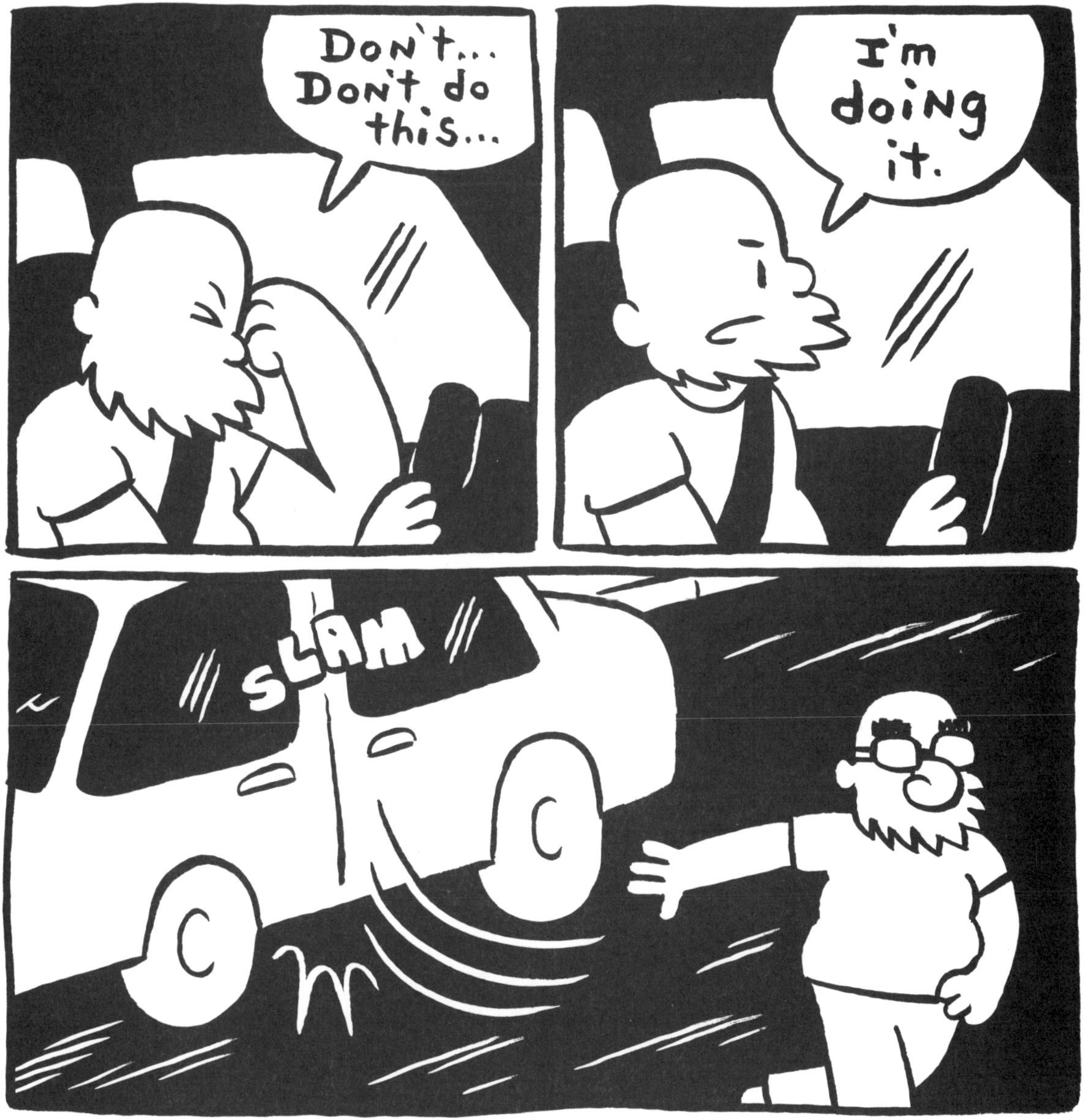
Don't... Don't do this...
I'm doing it.
SLAM

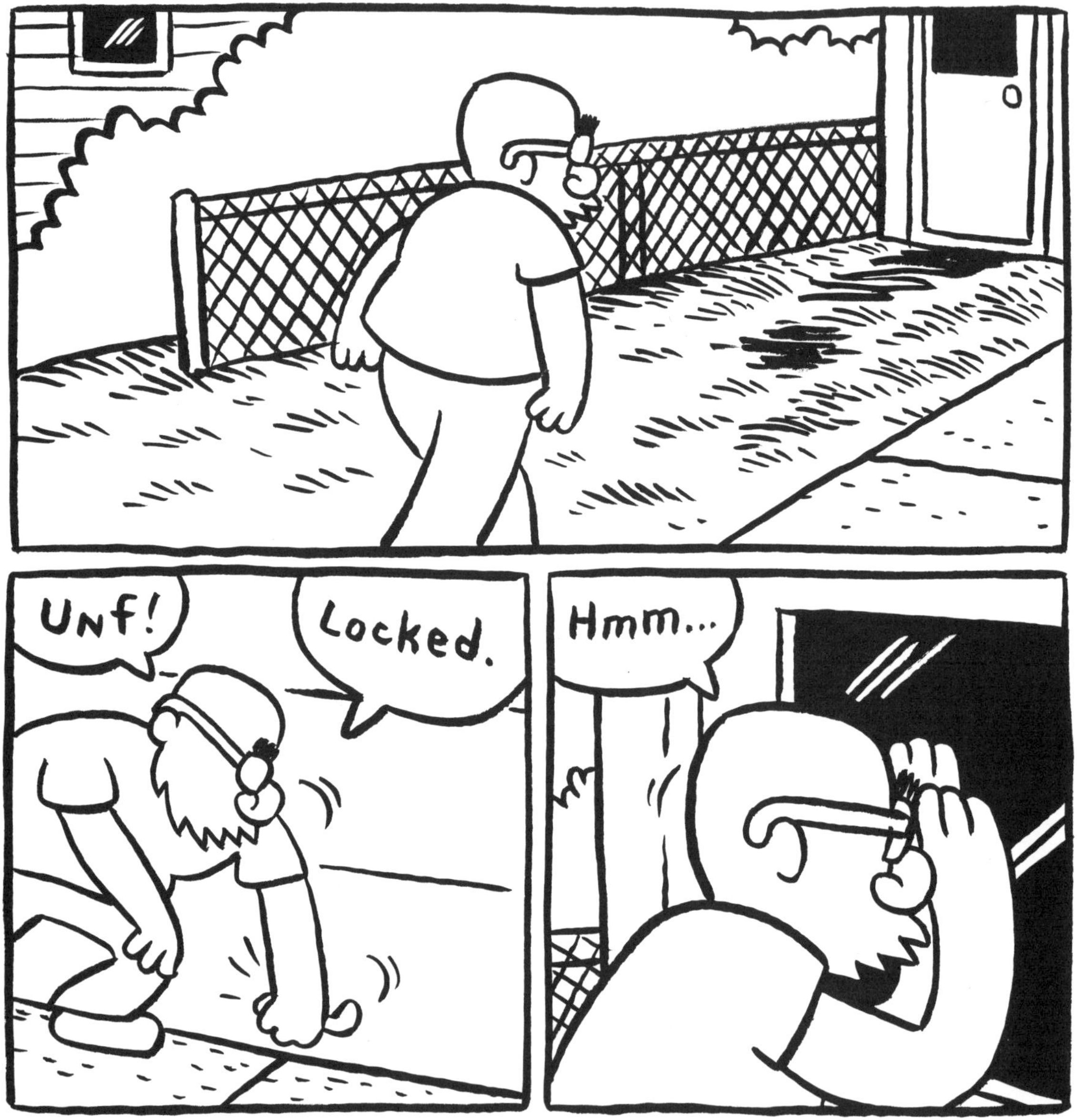
Unf!
Locked.
Hmm...

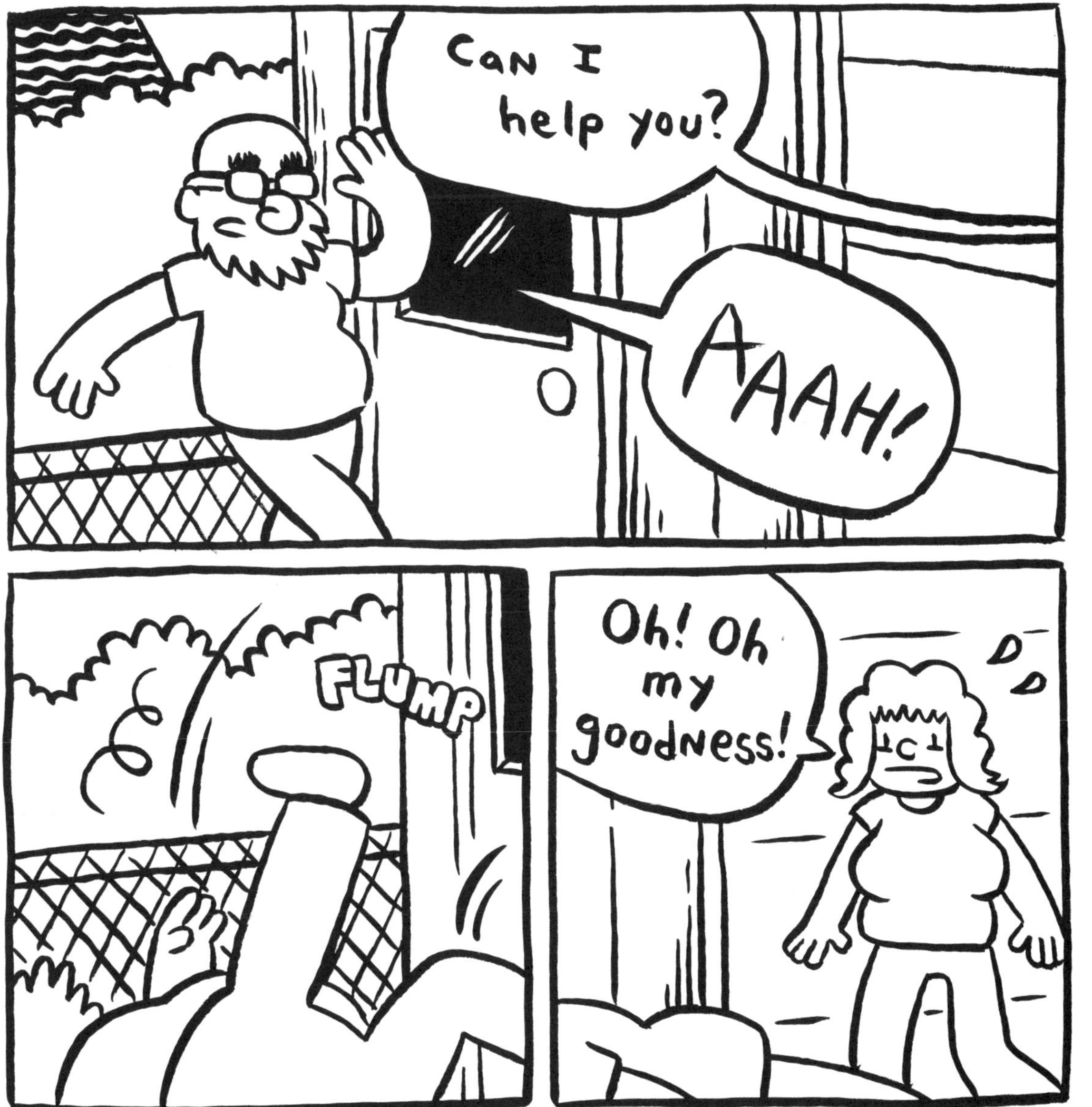

Can I help you?
AAAH!
FLUMP
Oh! Oh my goodness!

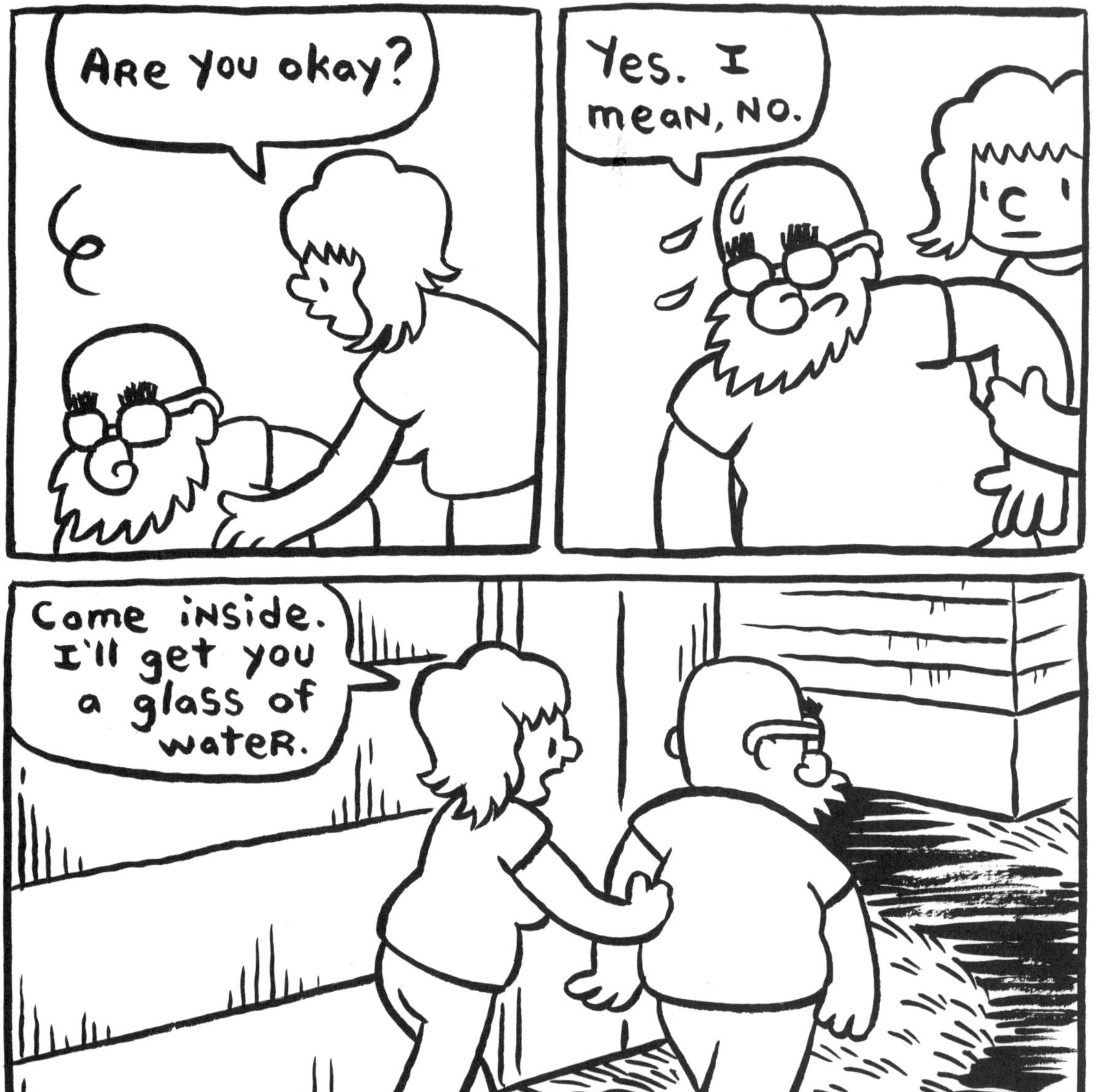
Are you okay?
Yes. I mean, no.
Come inside. I'll get you a glass of water.

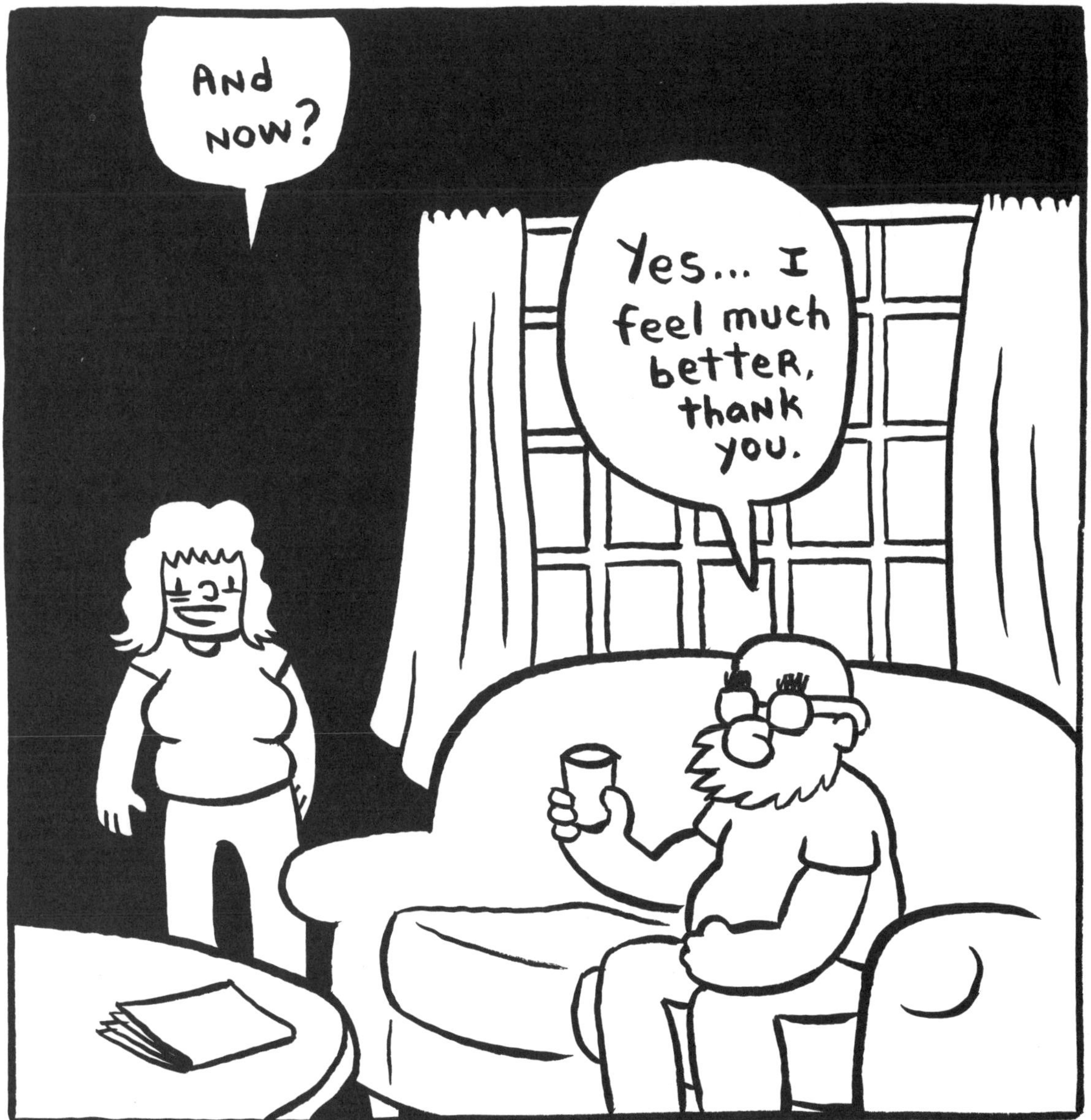
And now?
Yes... I feel much better, thank you.

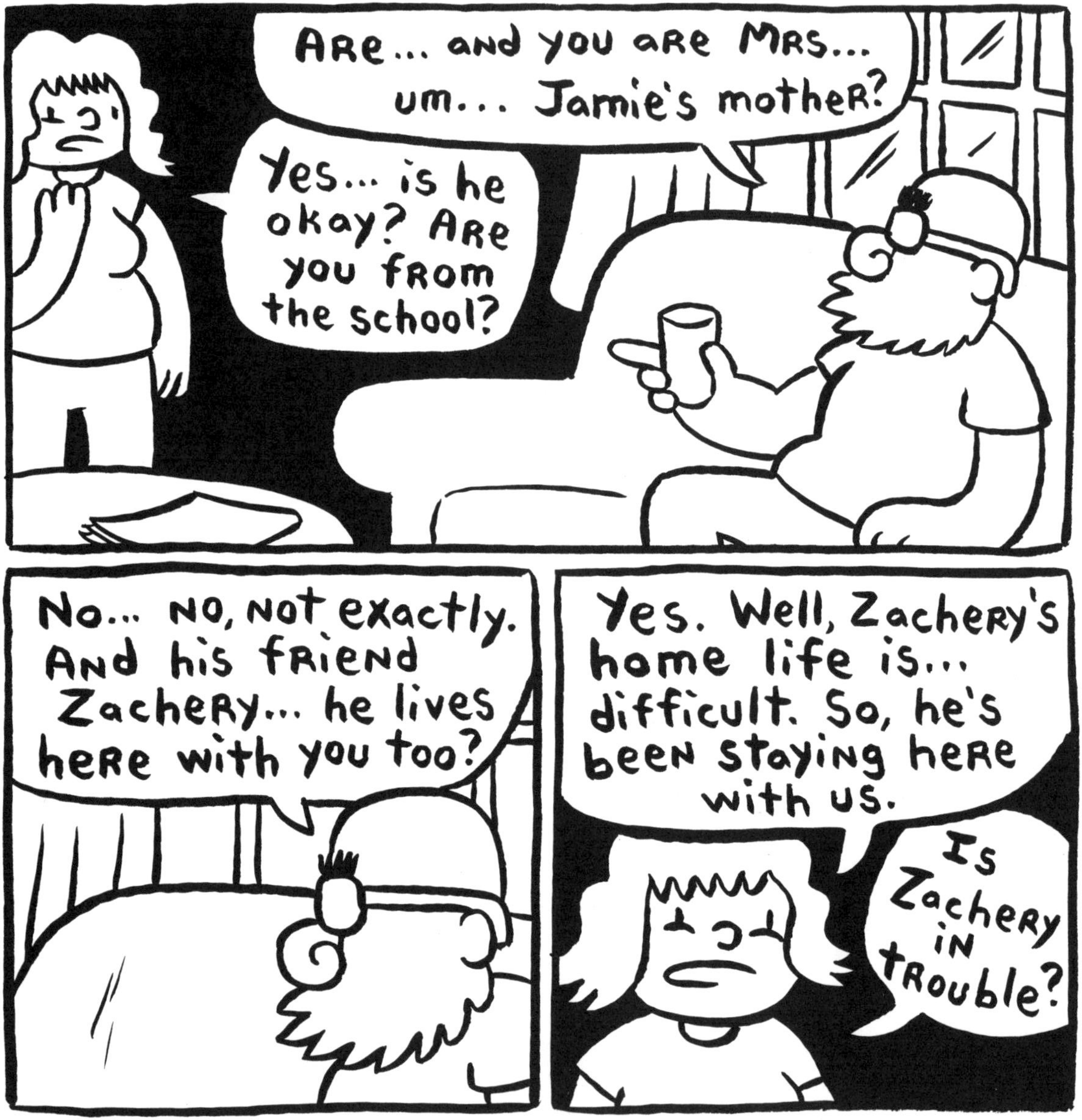
ARE... and you are MRS... um... Jamie's mother?
Yes... is he okay? ARE you FROM the school?
No... NO, not exactly. AND his FRIEND Zachery... he lives here with you too?
Yes. Well, Zachery's home life is... difficult. So, he's been staying here with us.
Is Zachery in trouble?

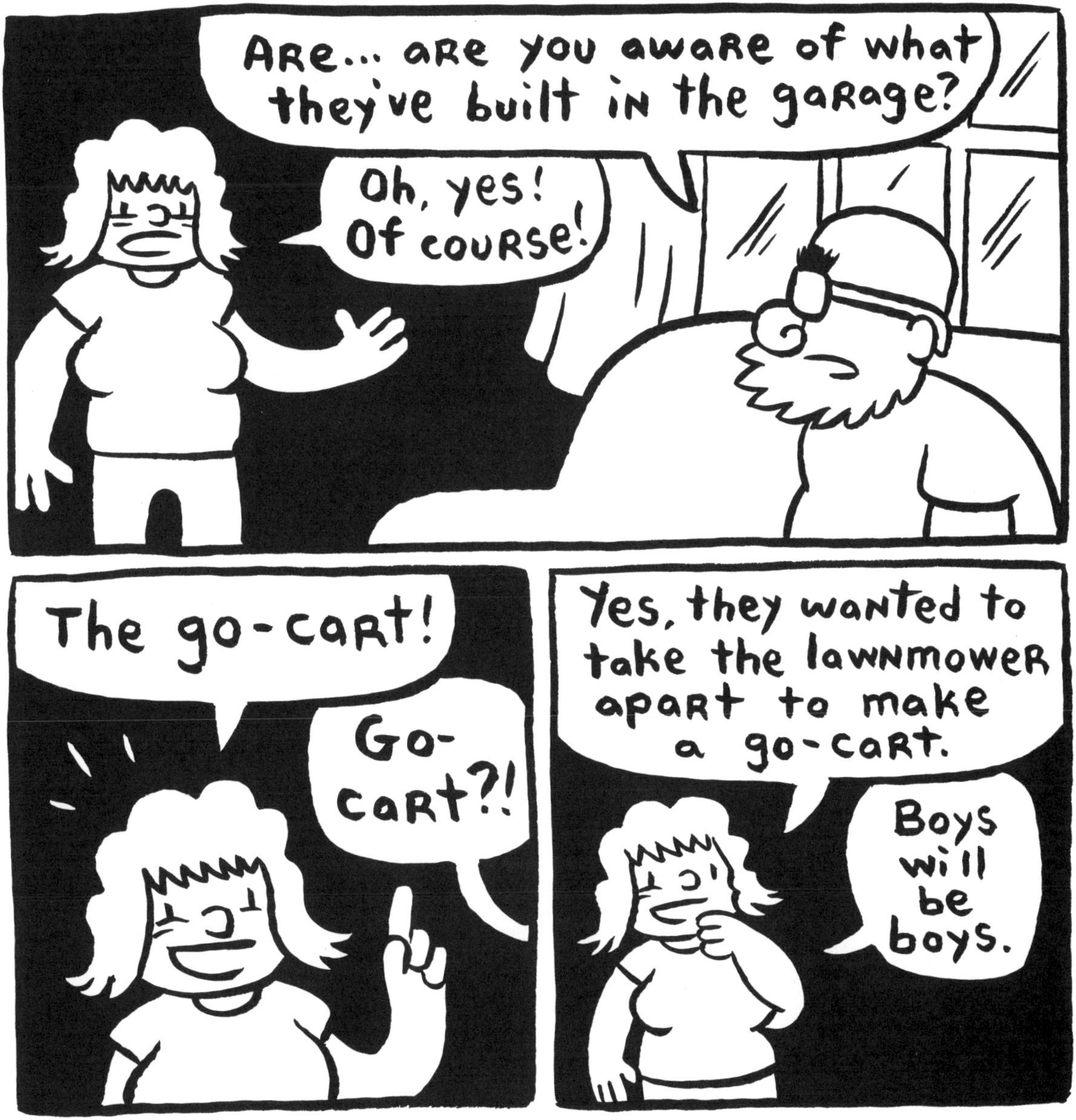
Are... are you aware of what they've built in the garage?
Oh, yes! Of course!
The go-cart!
Go-cart?!
Yes, they wanted to take the lawnmower apart to make a go-cart.
Boys will be boys.

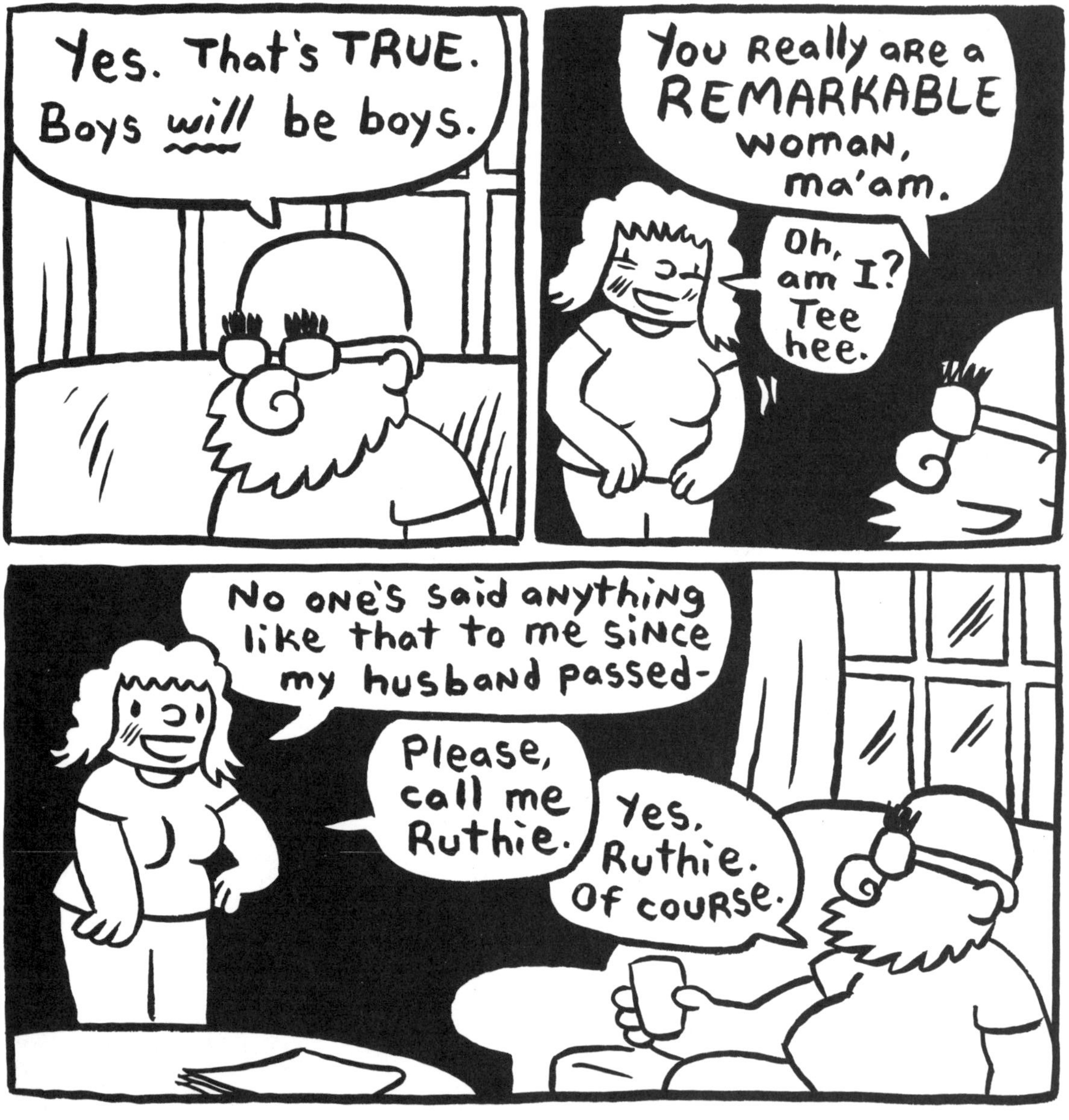
Yes. That's TRUE. Boys will be boys.
You really are a REMARKABLE woman, ma'am.
Oh, am I? Tee hee.
No one's said anything like that to me since my husband passed-
Please, call me Ruthie.
Yes, Ruthie. Of course.

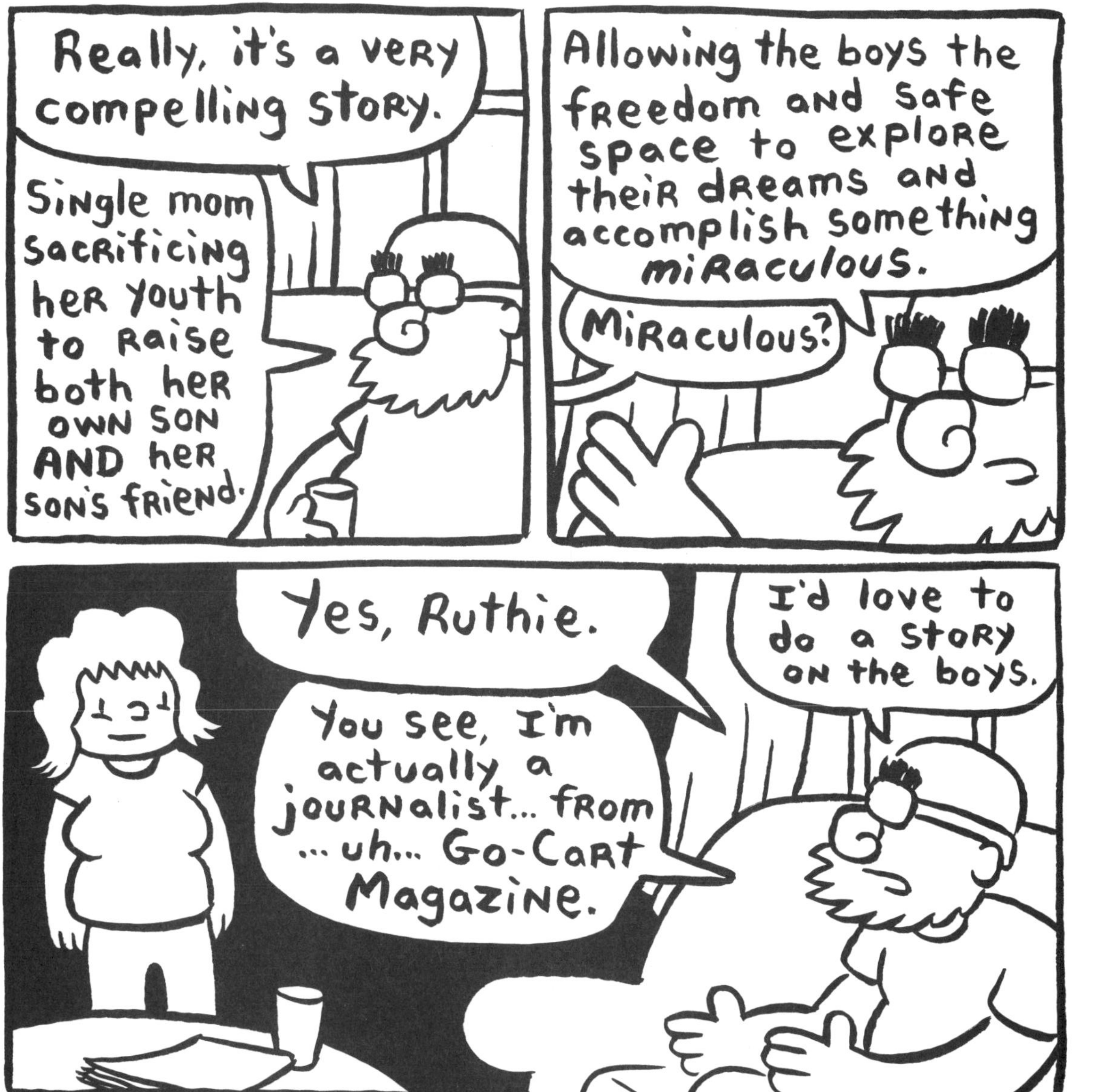
Really, it's a very compelling story.
Single mom sacrificing her youth to raise both her own son AND her son's friend.
Allowing the boys the freedom and safe space to explore their dreams and accomplish something *miraculous*.
Miraculous?
Yes, Ruthie.
You see, I'm actually a journalist... from ...uh... Go-Cart Magazine.
I'd love to do a story on the boys.

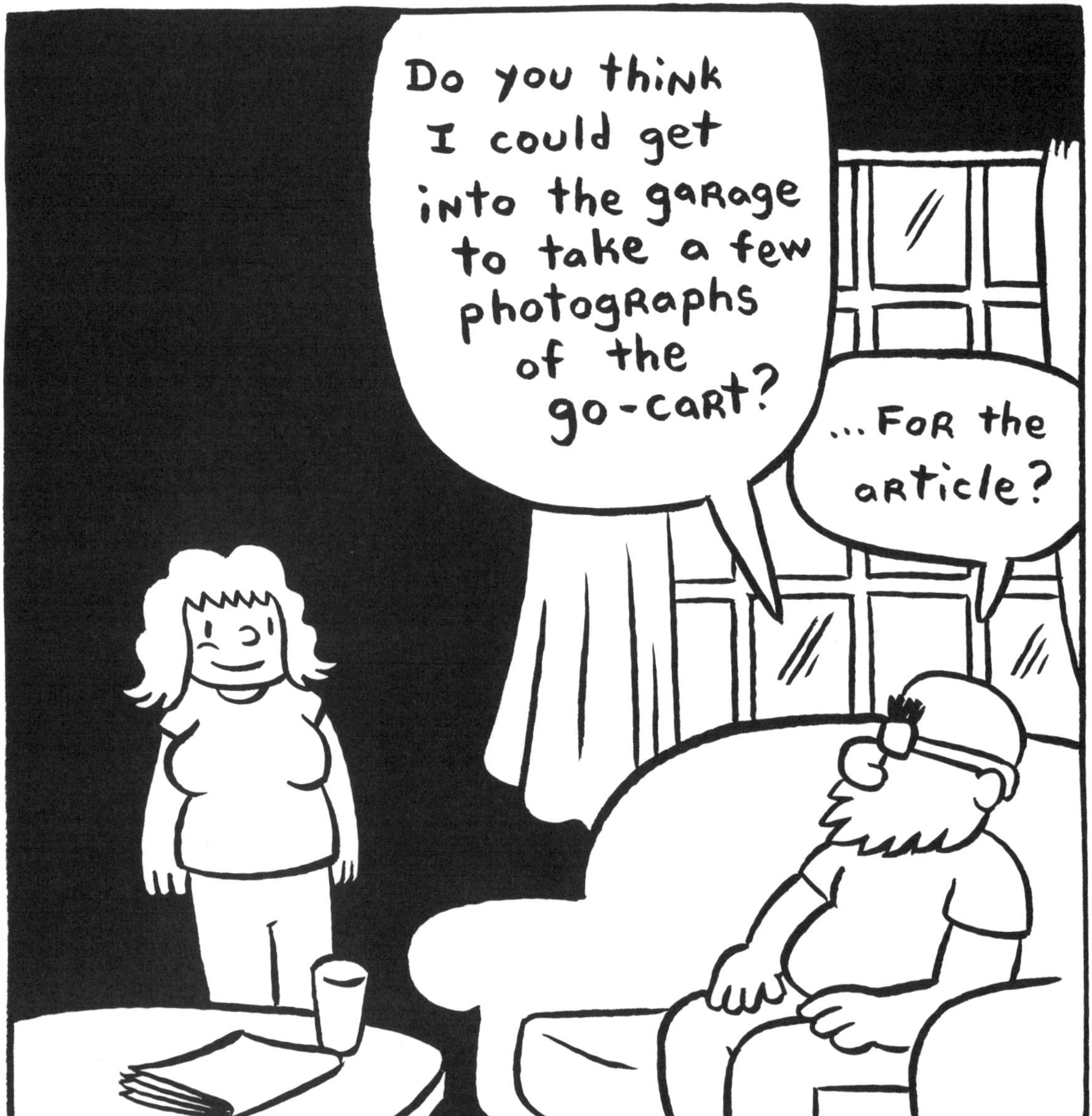
Do you think I could get into the garage to take a few photographs of the go-cart?
...For the article?

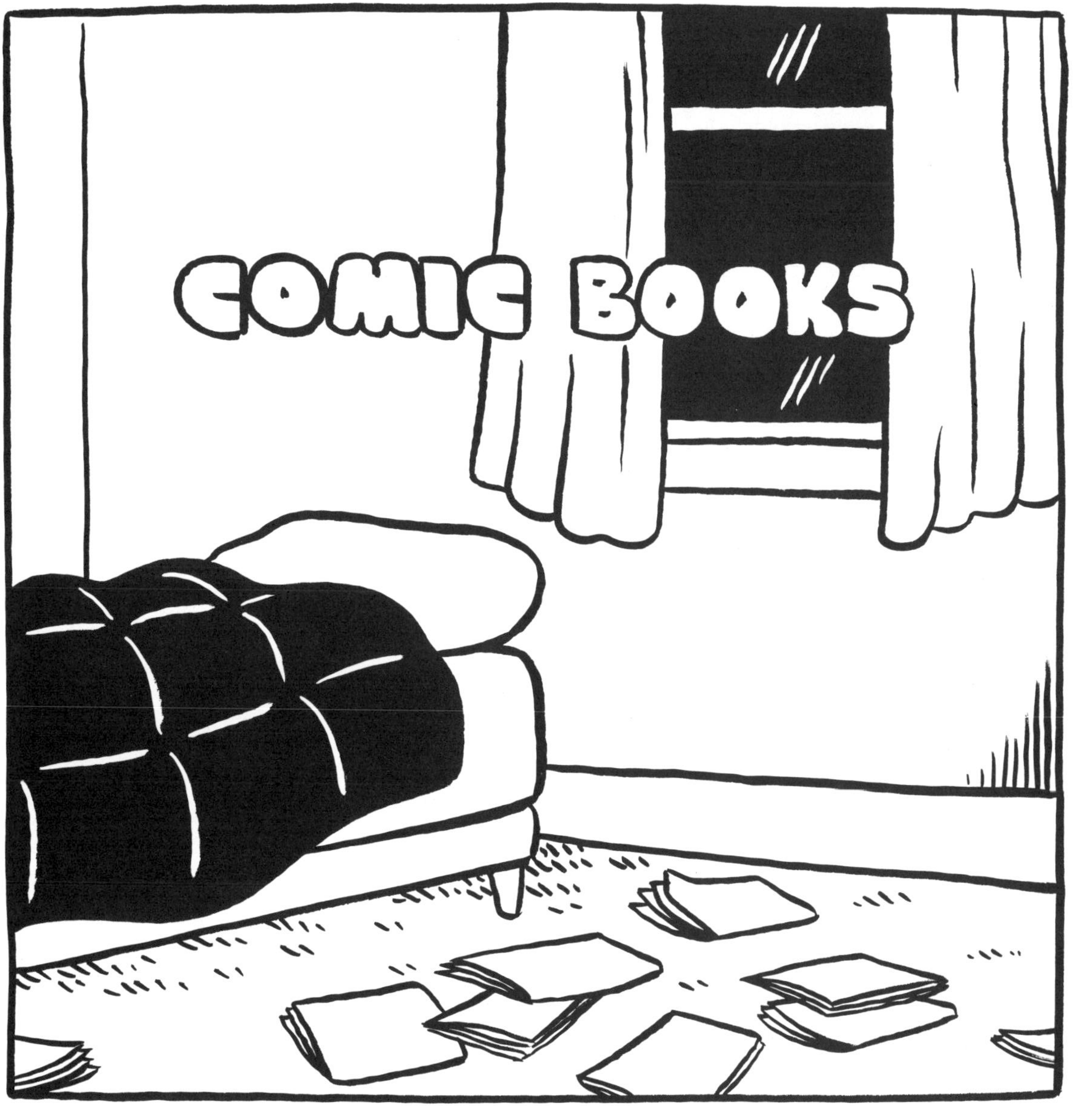
COMIC BOOKS

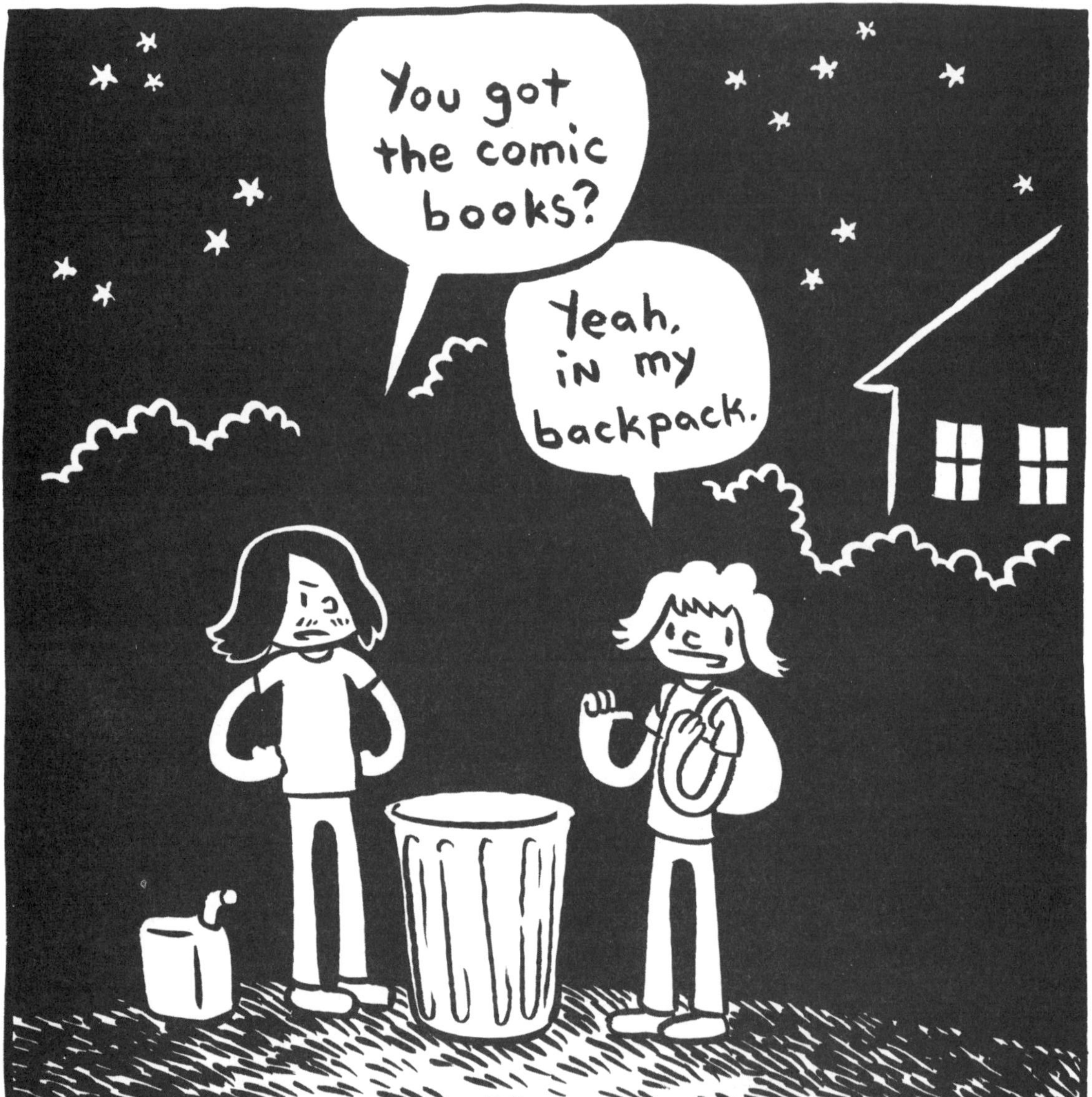
You got the comic books?
Yeah, in my backpack.

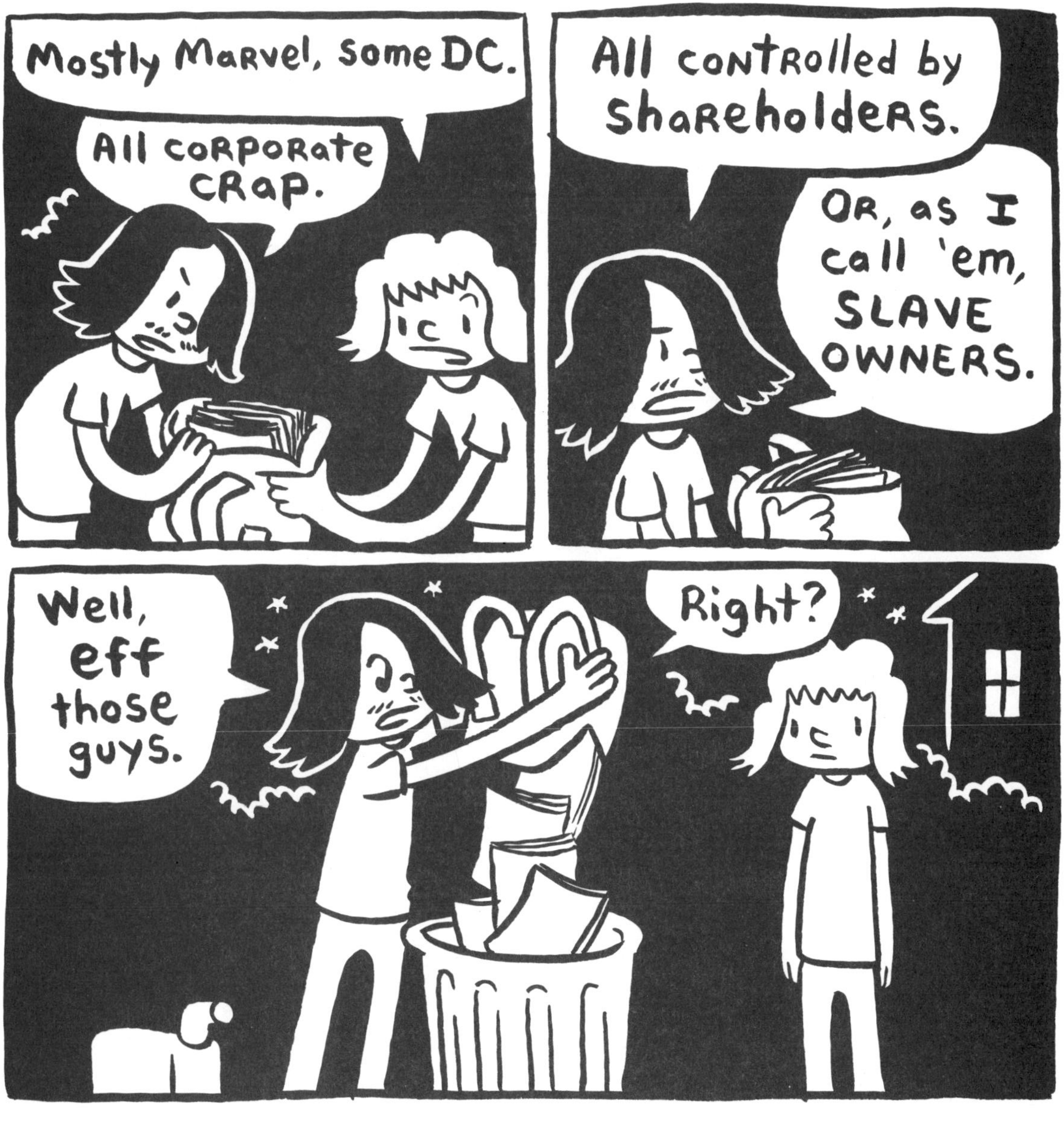
Mostly Marvel, some DC.
All corporate crap.
All controlled by shareholders.
Or, as I call 'em, SLAVE OWNERS.
Well, eff those guys.
Right?

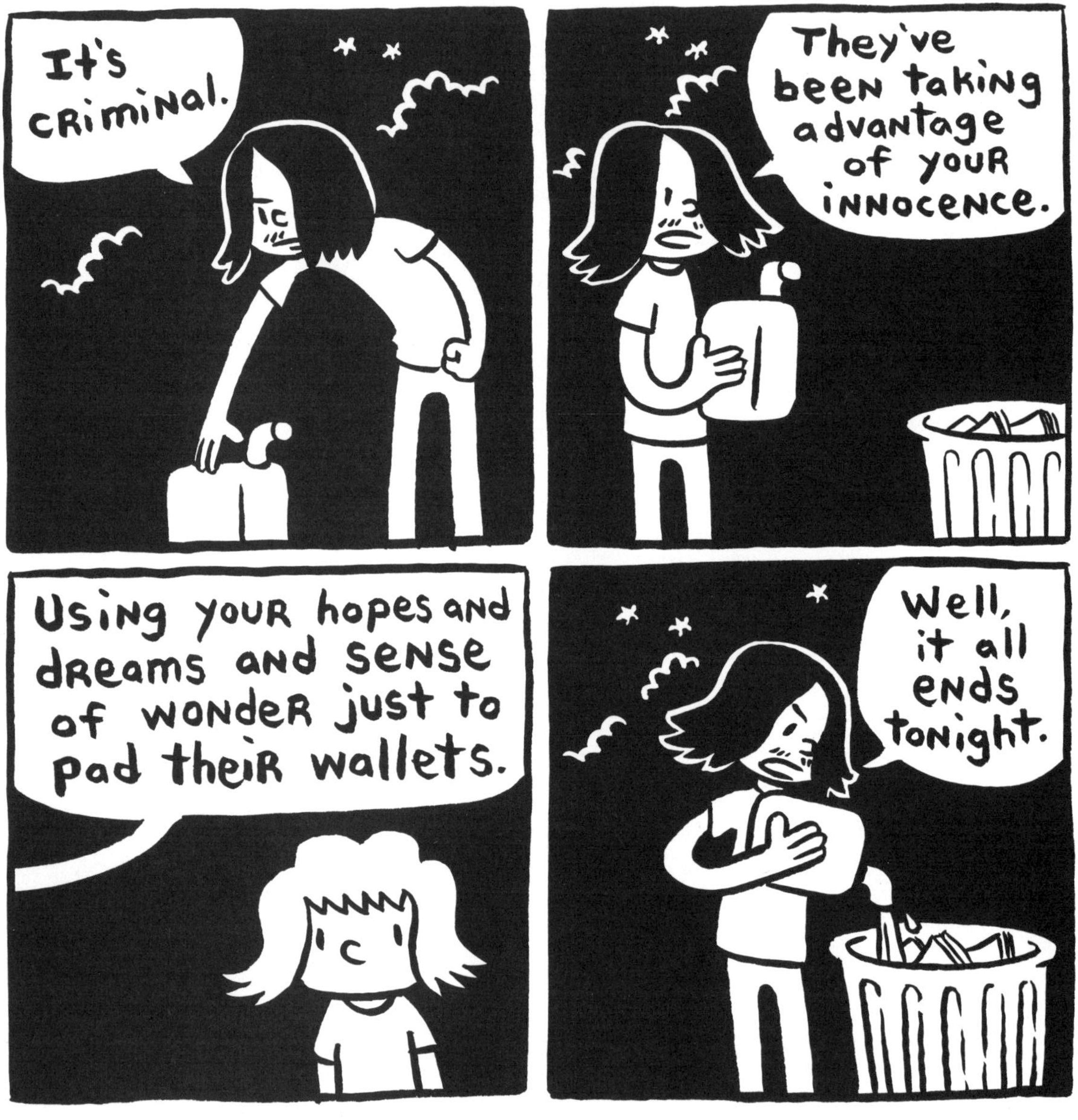
It's criminal.
They've been taking advantage of your innocence.
Using your hopes and dreams and sense of wonder just to pad their wallets.
Well, it all ends tonight.

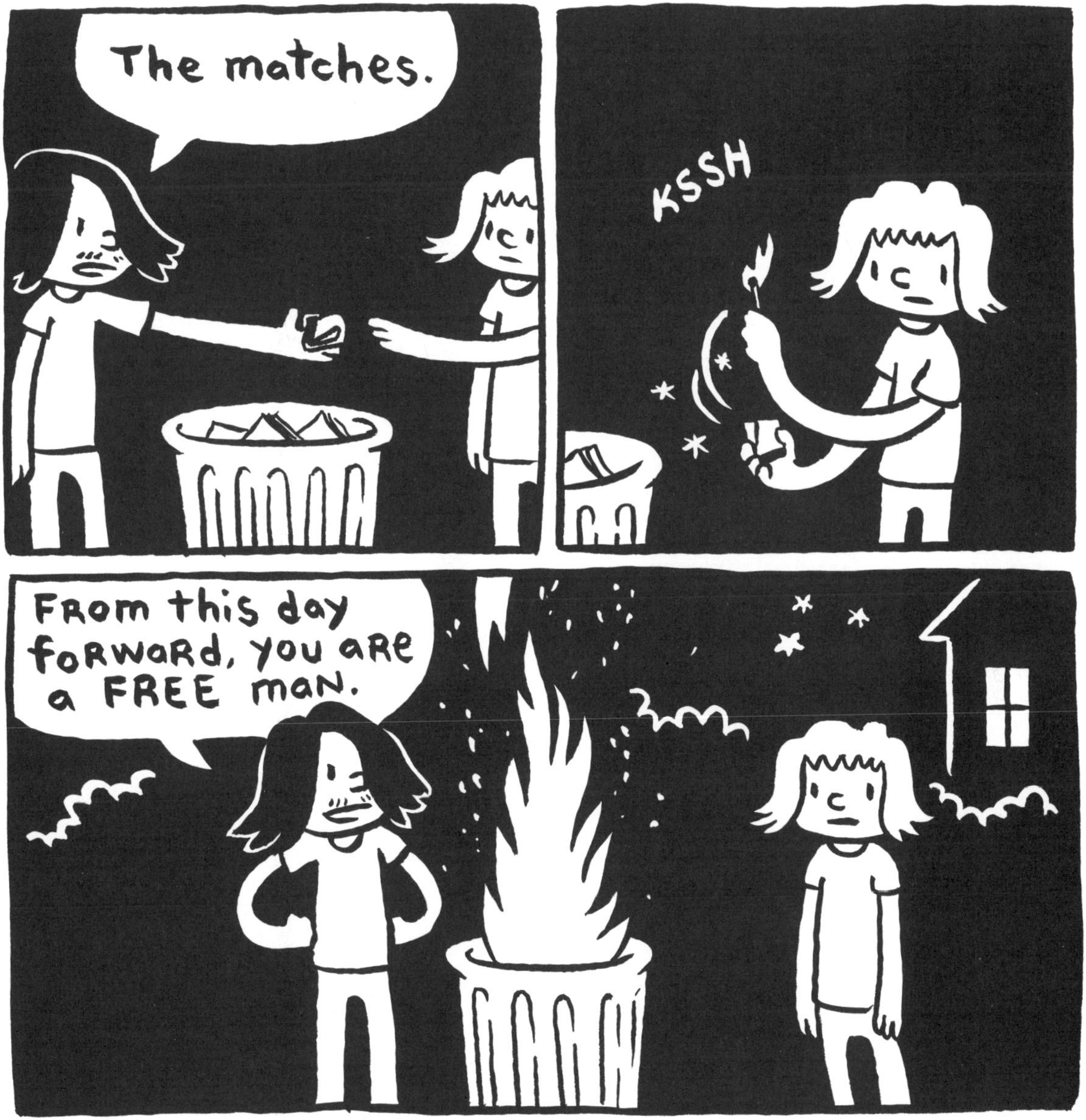
The matches.
KSSH
FROM this day forward, you are a FREE man.

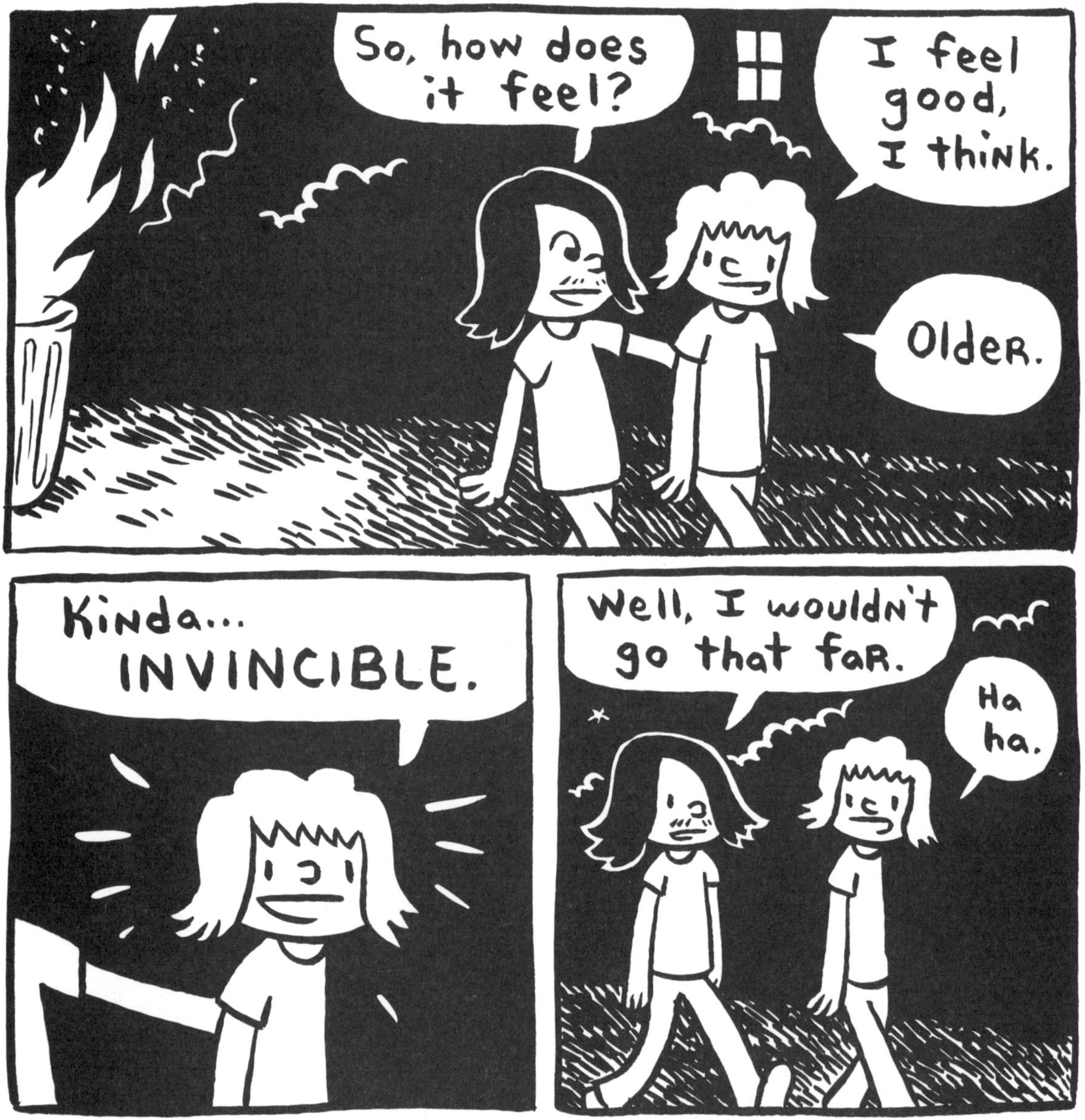
So, how does it feel?
I feel good, I think.
Older.
Kinda... INVINCIBLE.
Well, I wouldn't go that far.
Ha ha.

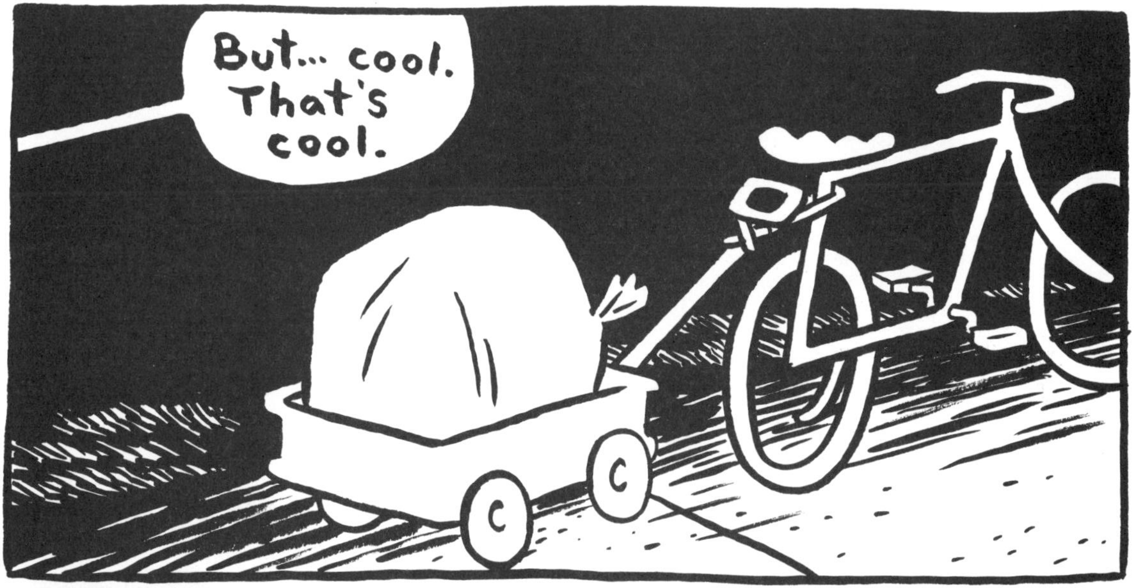
But... cool. That's cool.

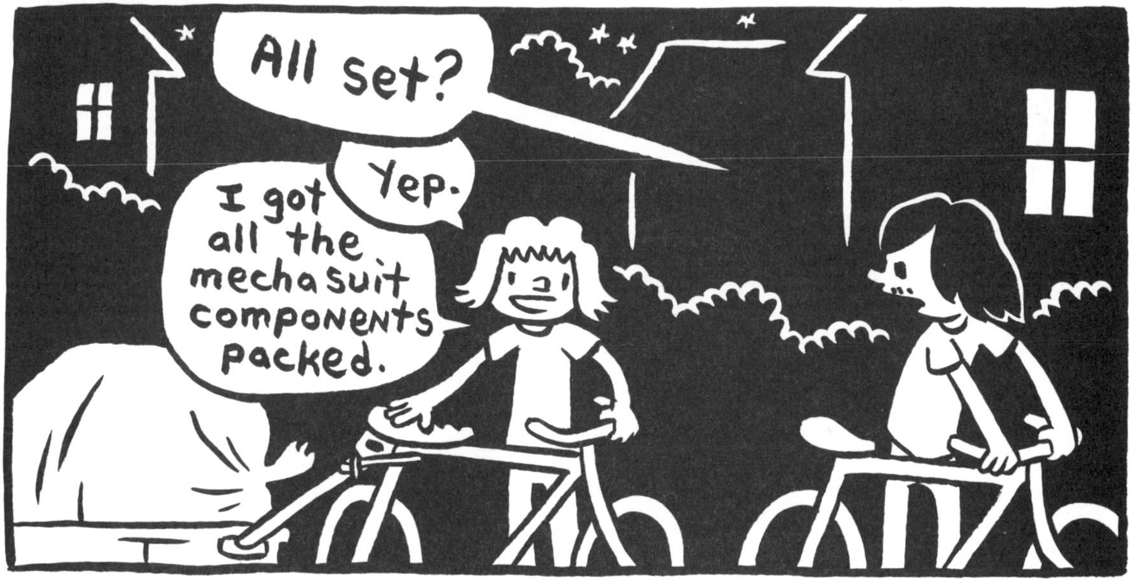
All set?
Yep.
I got all the mechasuit components packed.

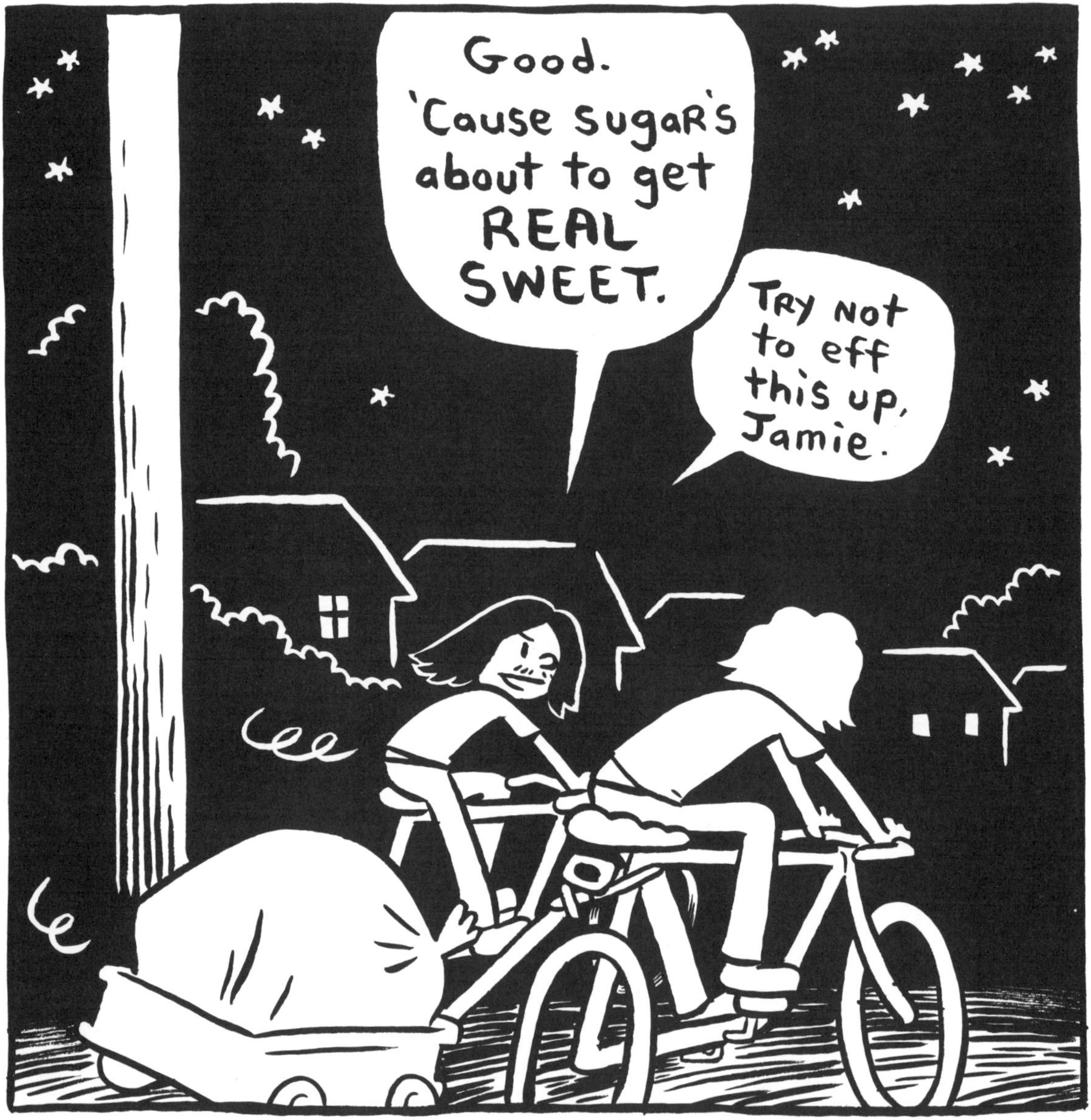
Good. 'Cause sugar's about to get REAL SWEET.
Try not to eff this up, Jamie.

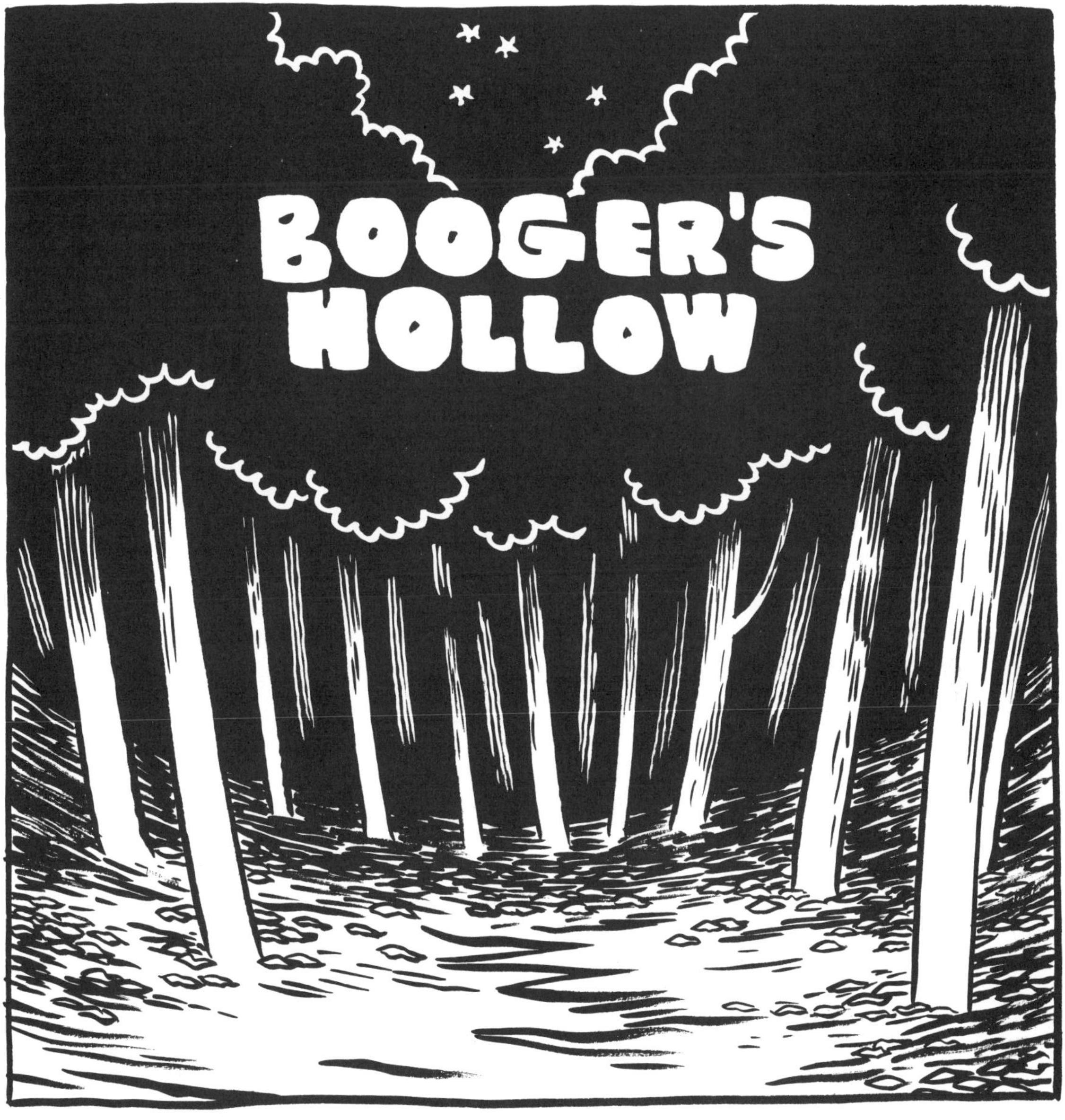
BOOGER'S
HOLLOW

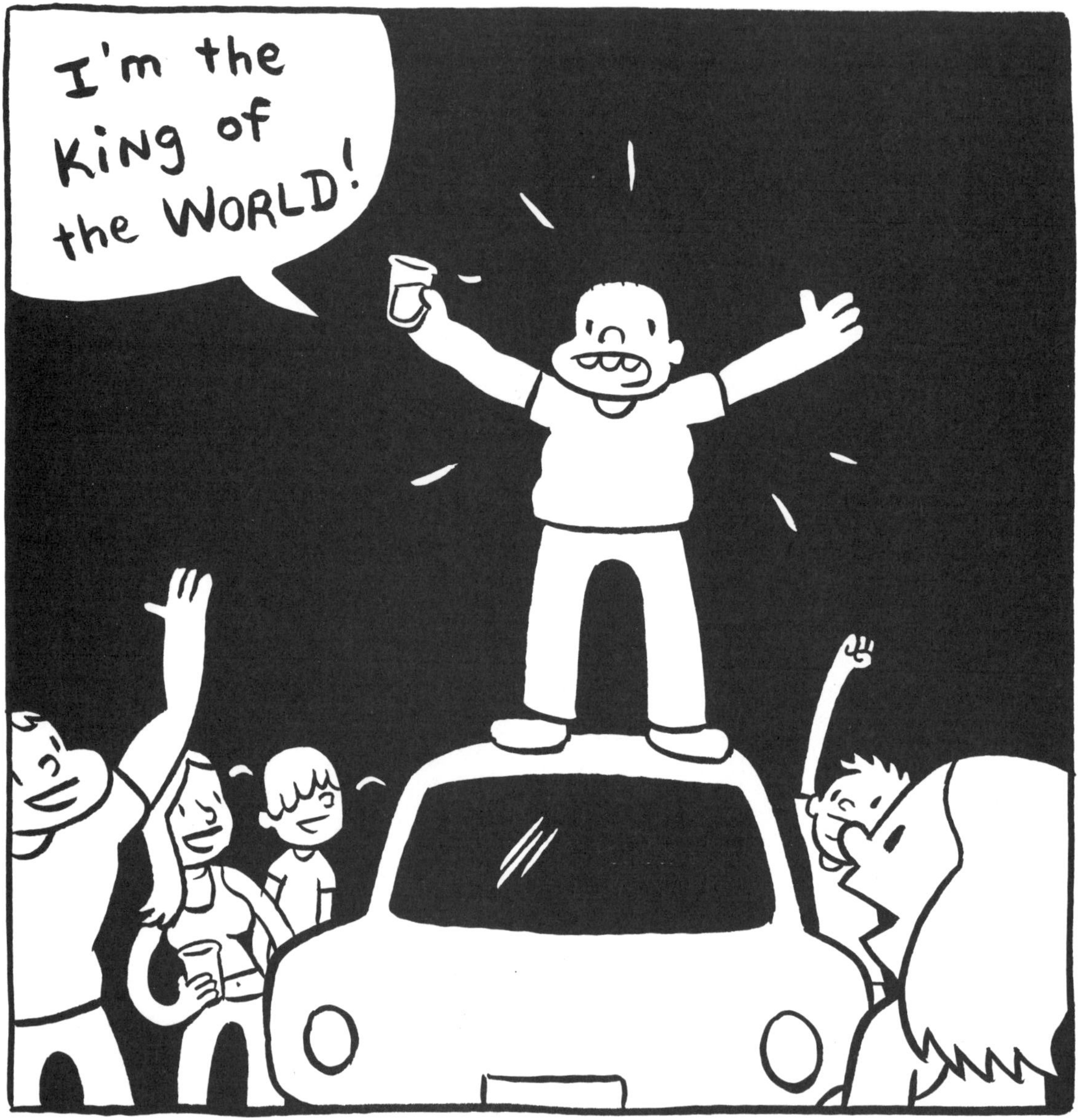
I'm the King of the WORLD!

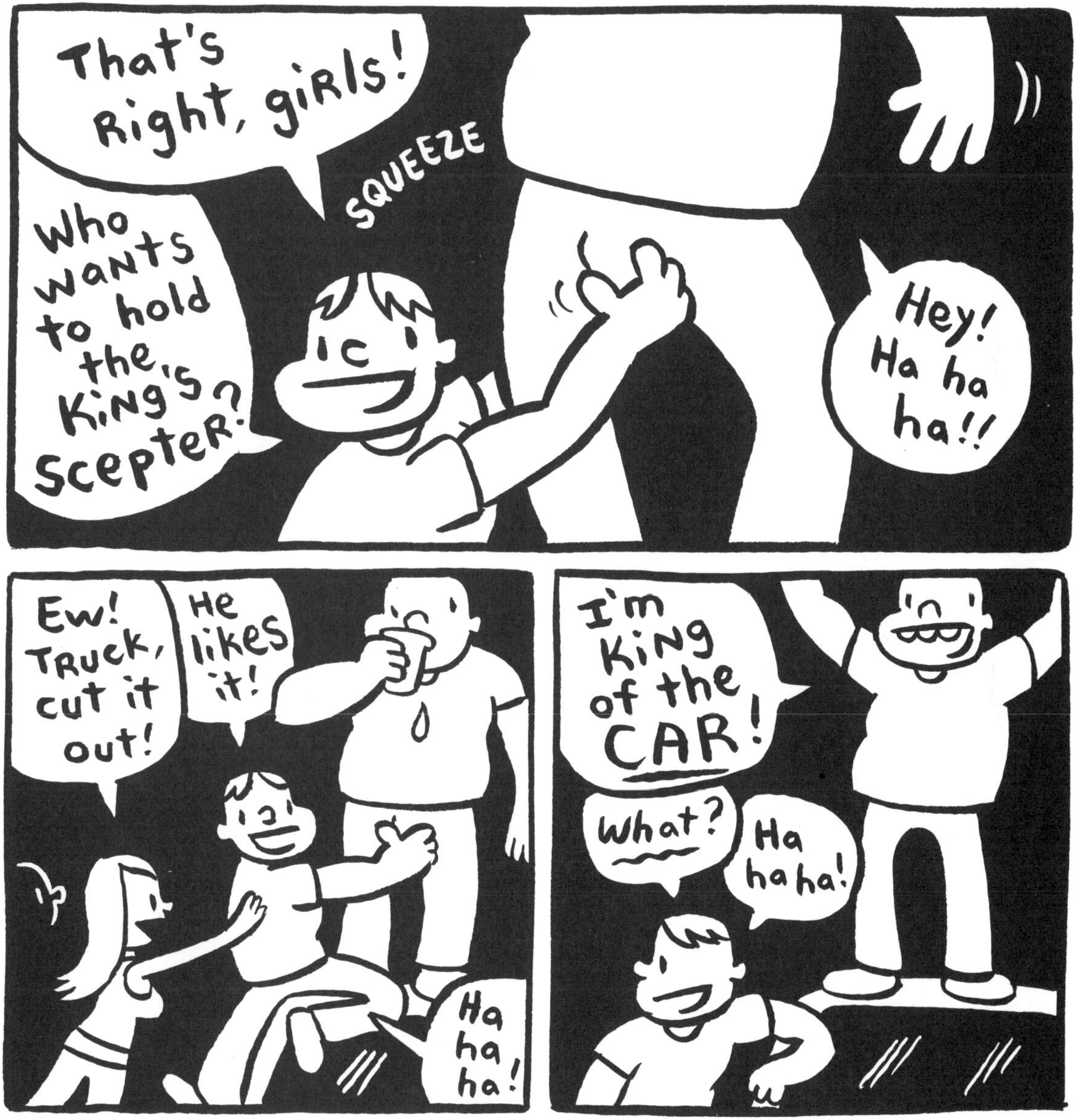
That's Right, girls!
SQUEEZE
Who wants to hold the King's Scepter?
Hey! Ha ha ha!!
Ew! Truck, cut it out!
He likes it!
Ha ha ha!
I'm King of the CAR!
What?
Ha ha ha!

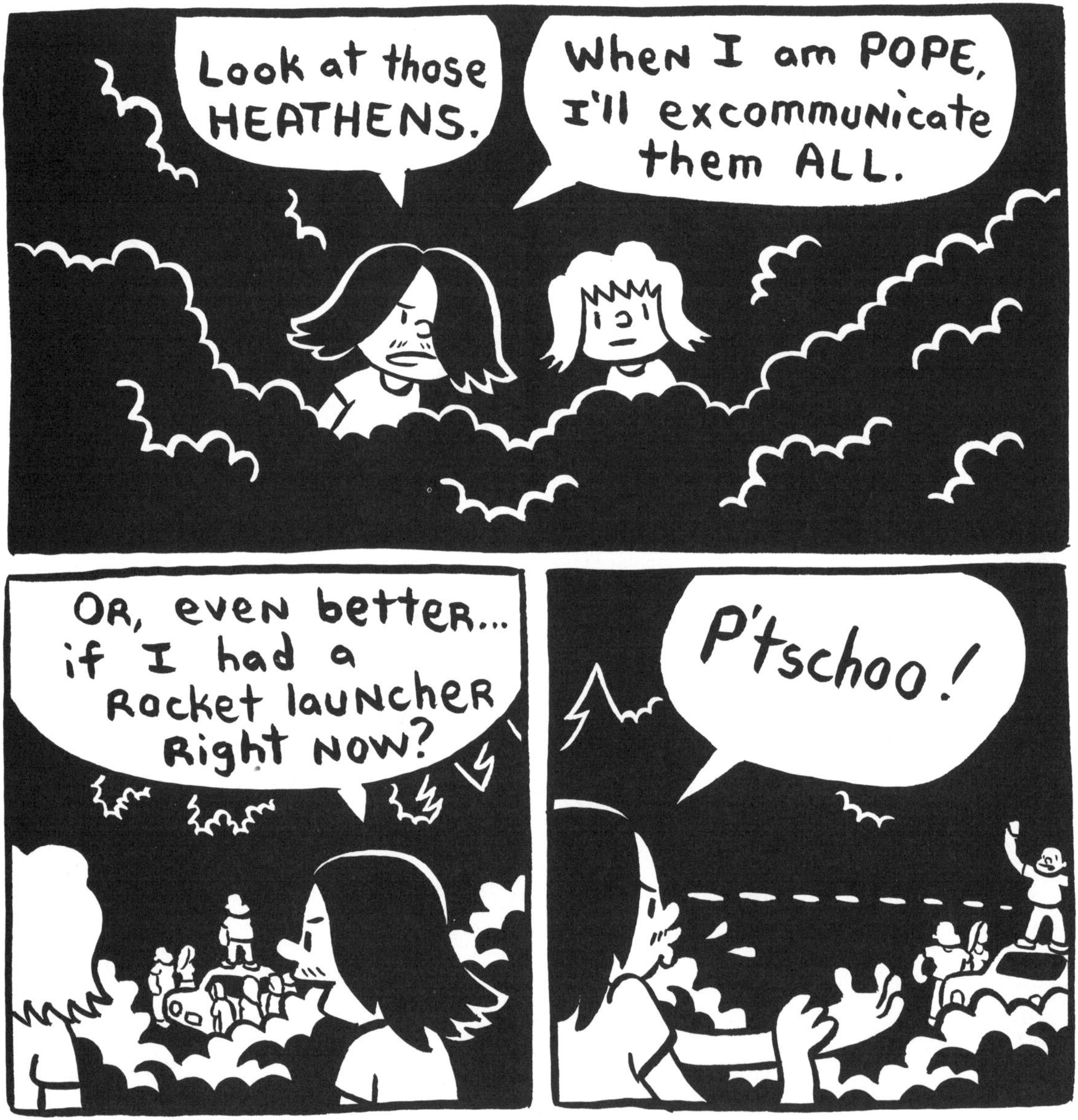
Look at those HEATHENS.
When I am POPE, I'll excommunicate them ALL.
OR, even better... if I had a Rocket launcher Right NOW?
P'tschoo!

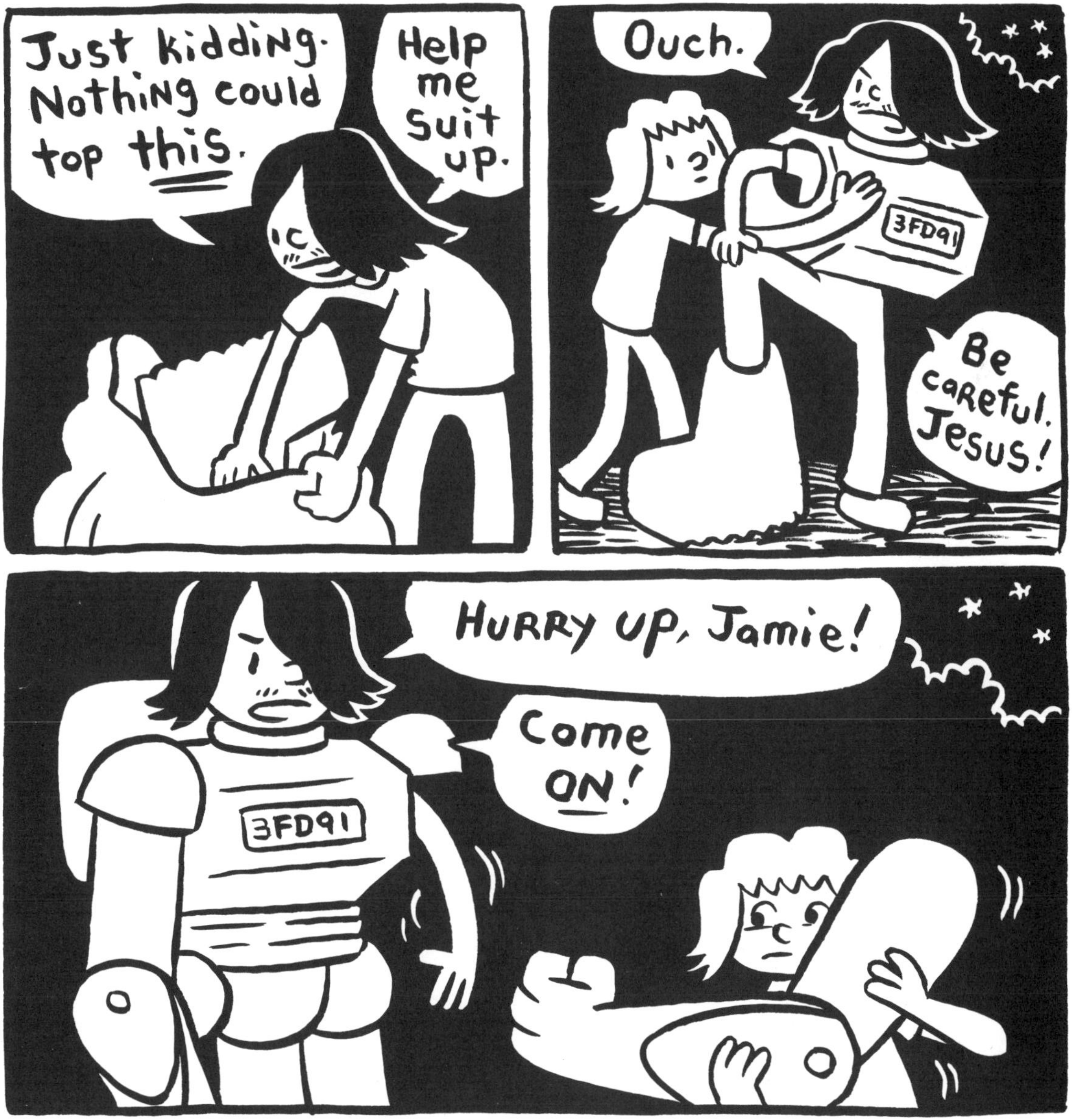
Just kidding. Nothing could top this.
Help me suit up.
Ouch.
3FD91
Be careful. Jesus!
HURRY UP, Jamie!
Come ON!
3FD91

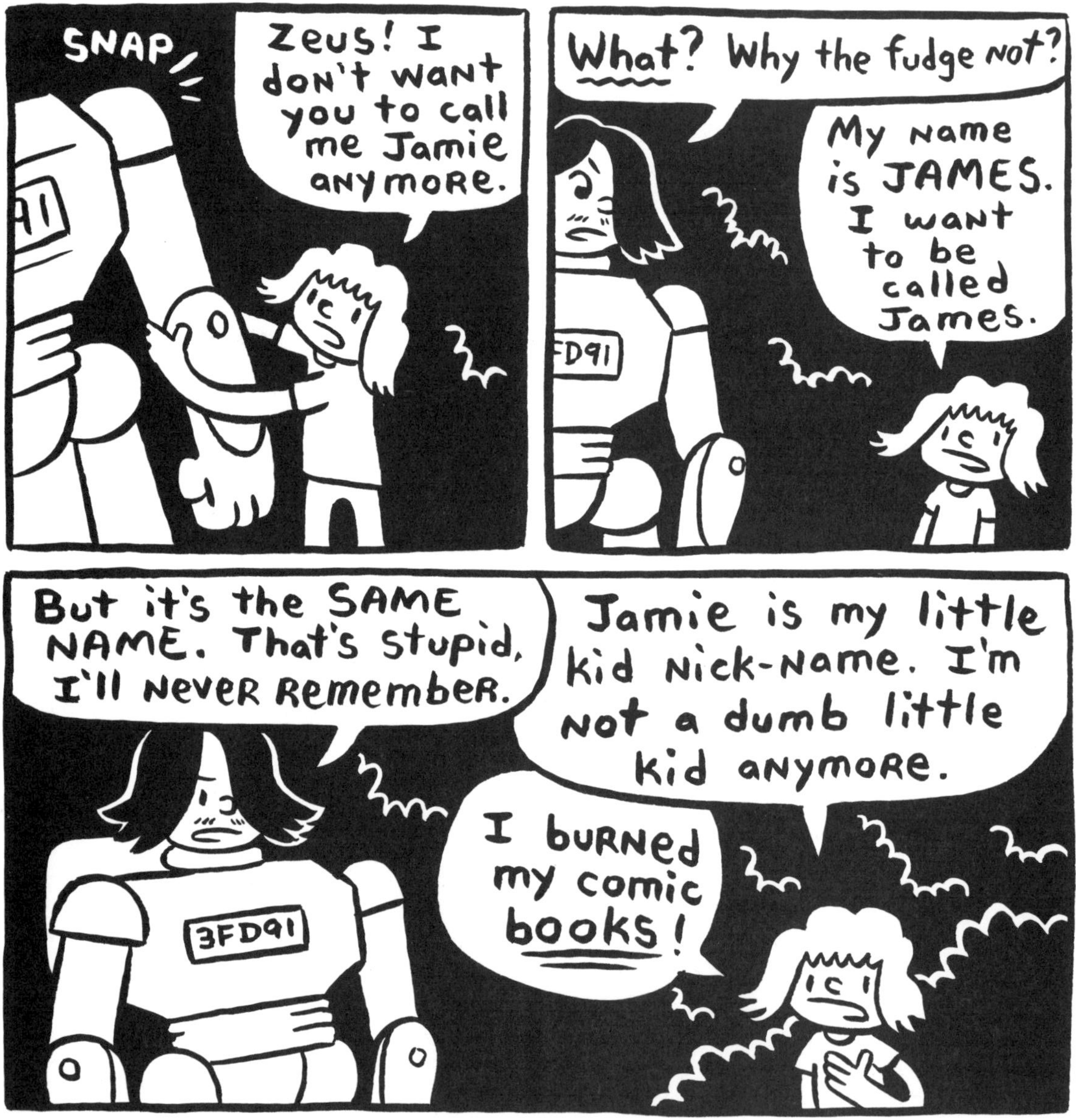
SNAP
Zeus! I don't want you to call me Jamie anymore.
What? Why the fudge not?
My name is JAMES. I want to be called James.
3FD91
But it's the SAME NAME. That's stupid, I'll never remember.
Jamie is my little kid nick-name. I'm not a dumb little kid anymore.
I burned my comic books!

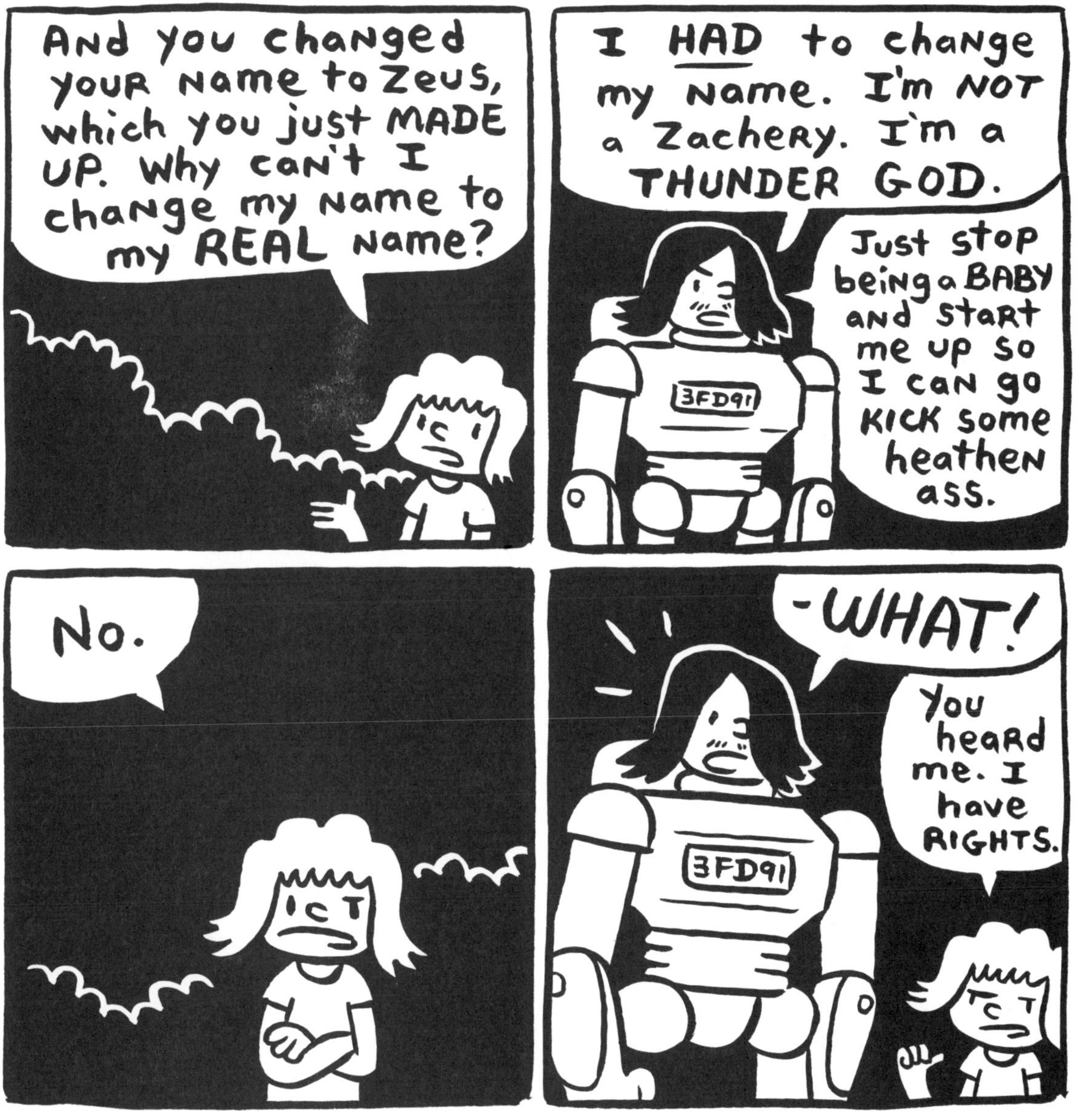
And you changed your name to Zeus, which you just MADE UP. Why can't I change my name to my REAL name?
I HAD to change my name. I'm NOT a Zachery. I'm a THUNDER GOD.
3FD91
Just stop being a BABY and start me up so I can go KICK some heathen ass.
No.
-WHAT!
3FD91
You heard me. I have RIGHTS.

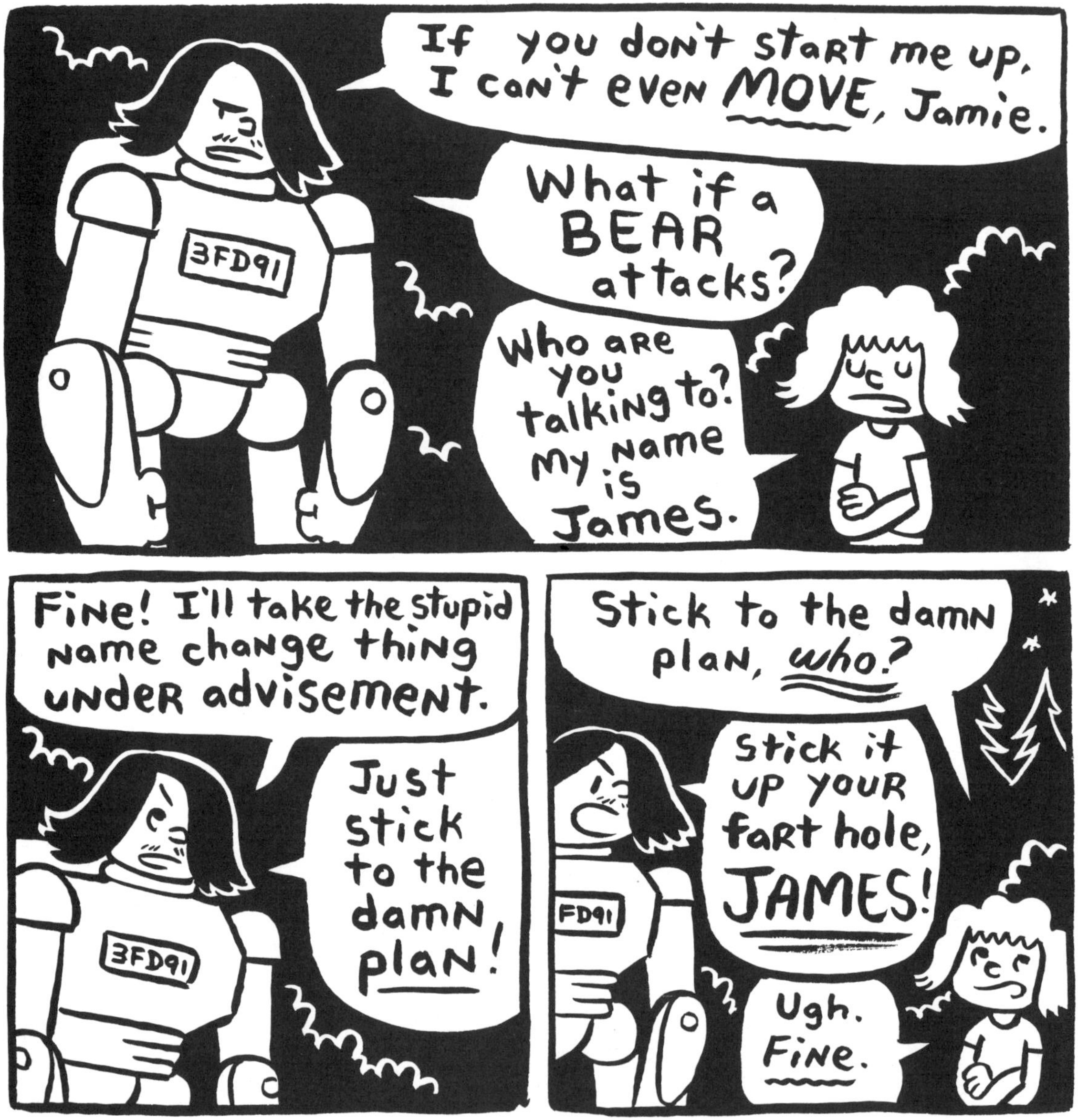
If you don't start me up, I can't even MOVE, Jamie.
What if a BEAR attacks?
Who are you talking to? My name is James.
3FD91
Fine! I'll take the stupid name change thing under advisement.
Just stick to the damn plan!
3FD91
Stick to the damn plan, who?
Stick it up your fart hole, JAMES!
FD91
Ugh. Fine.

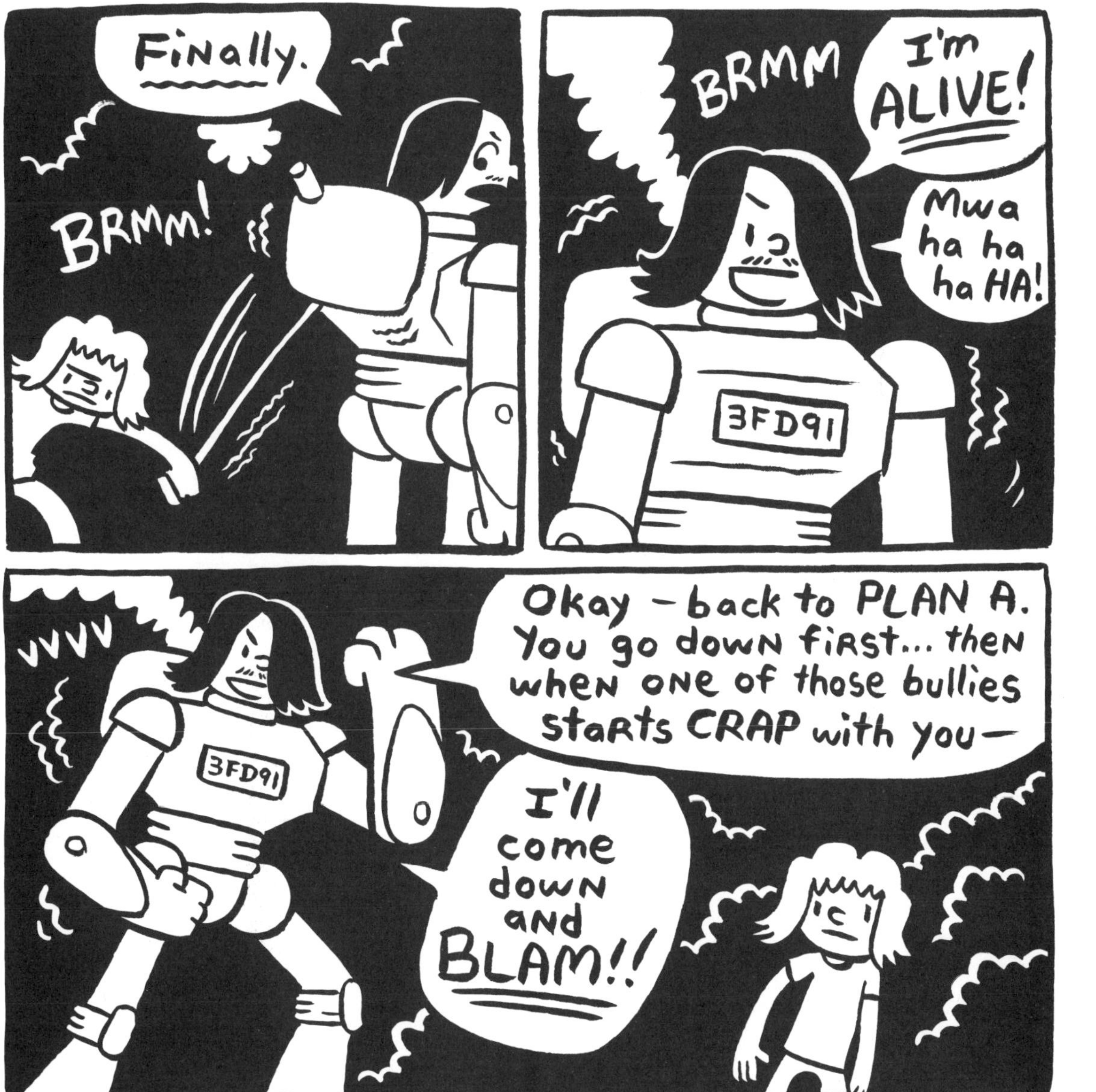
Finally.
BRMM!
BRMM
I'm ALIVE!
Mwa ha ha ha HA!
3FD91
Okay - back to PLAN A. You go down first... then when one of those bullies starts CRAP with you—
3FD91
I'll come down and BLAM!!

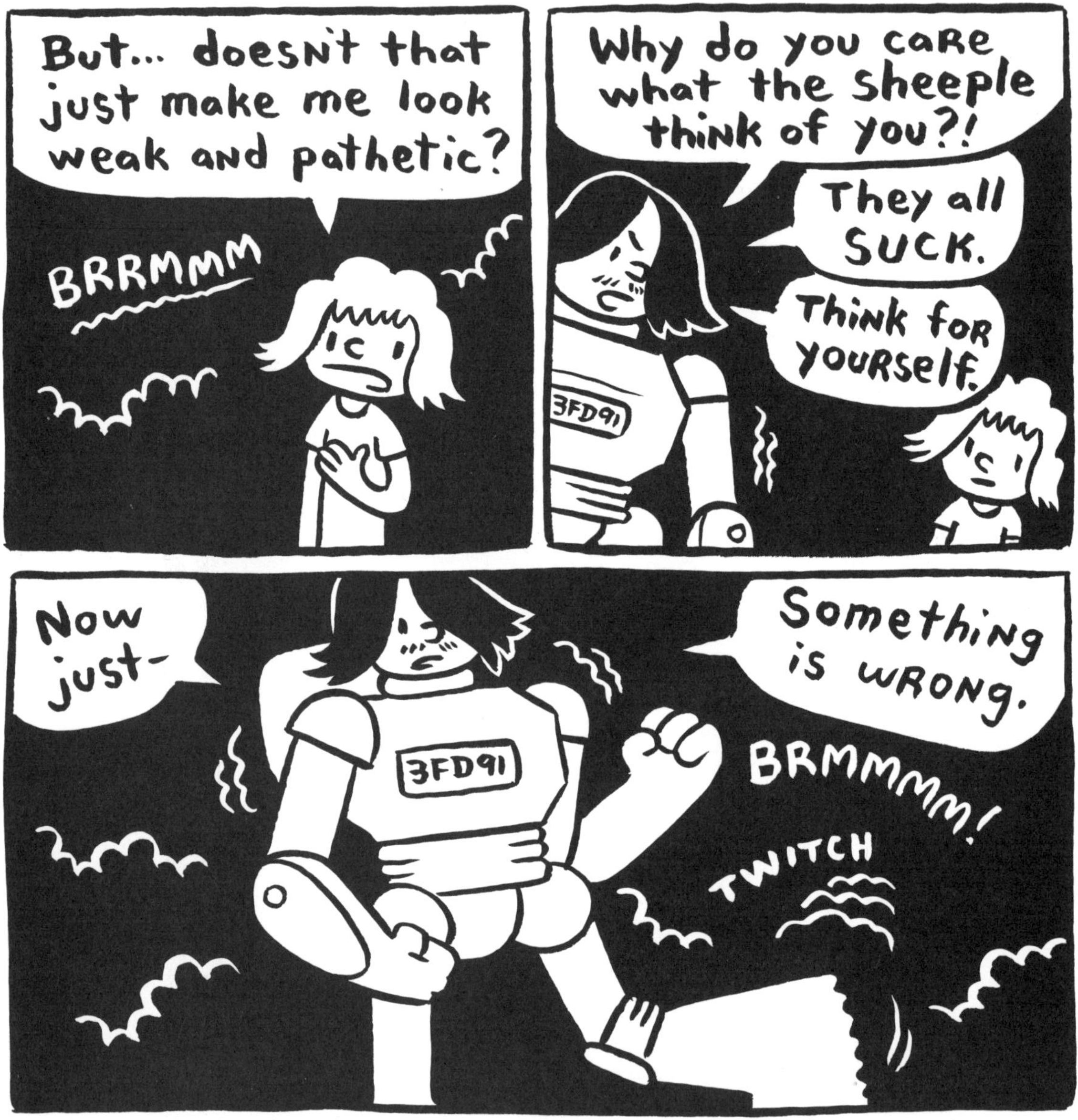
But... doesn't that just make me look weak and pathetic?
BRRMMM
Why do you care what the sheeple think of you?!
They all SUCK.
Think for yourself.
3FD91
Now just-
Something is wrong.
3FD91
BRMMMM!
TWITCH

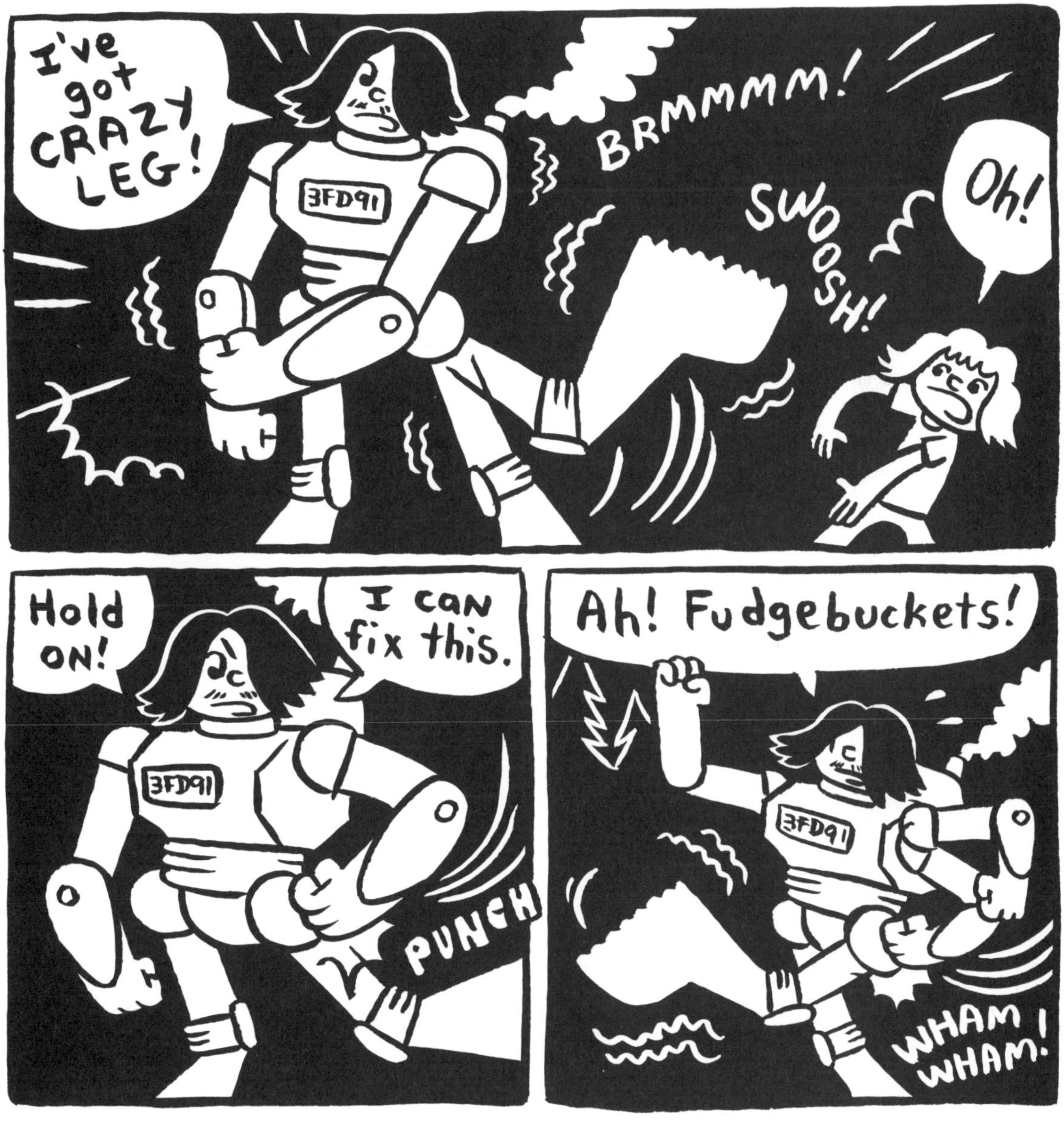
I've got CRAZY LEG!
BRMMMM!
SWOOOSH!
Oh!
Hold ON!
I can fix this.
PUNCH
Ah! Fudgebuckets!
WHAM WHAM!

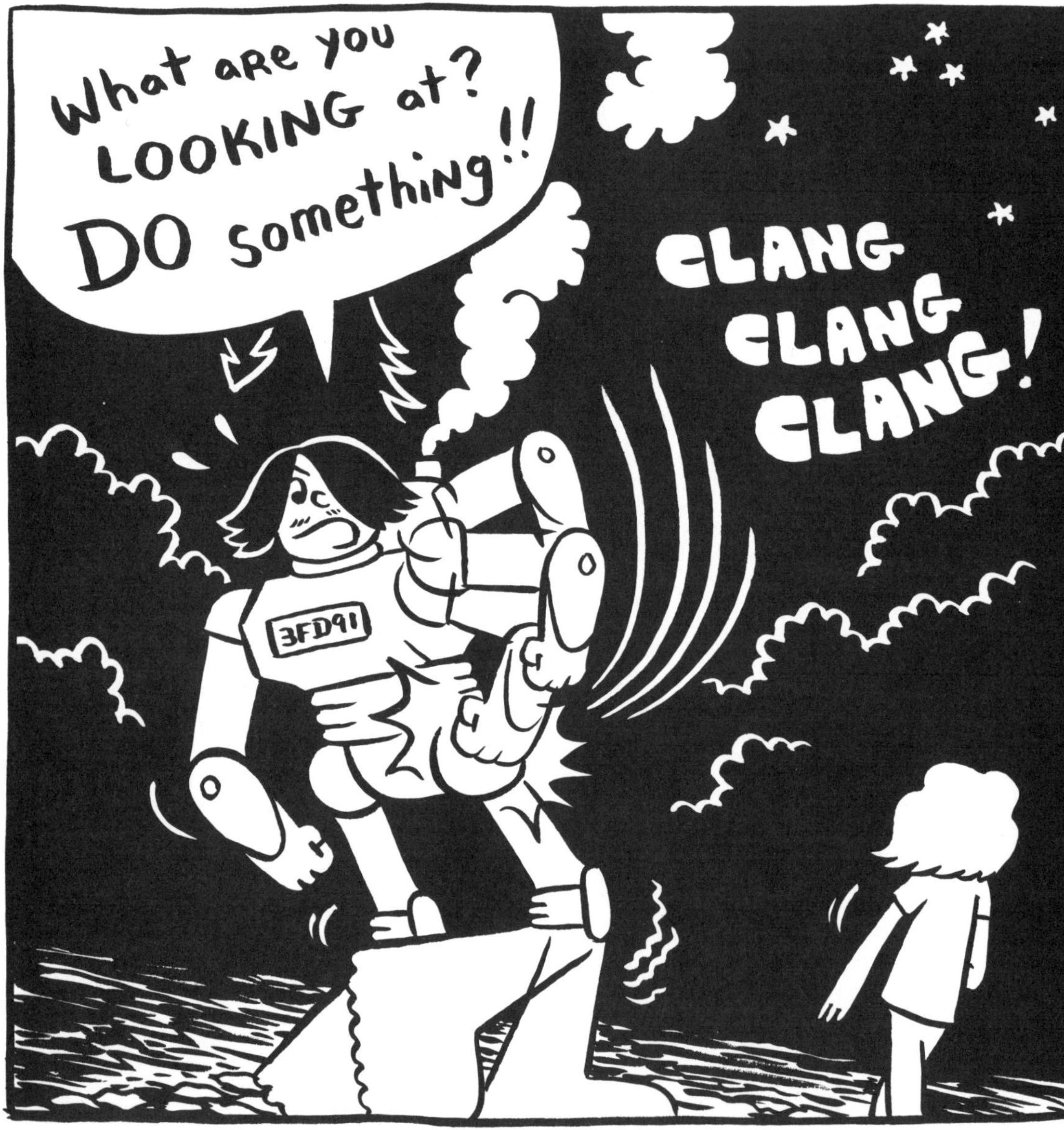
What are you LOOKING at? DO something!!
CLANG CLANG CLANG!
3FD91

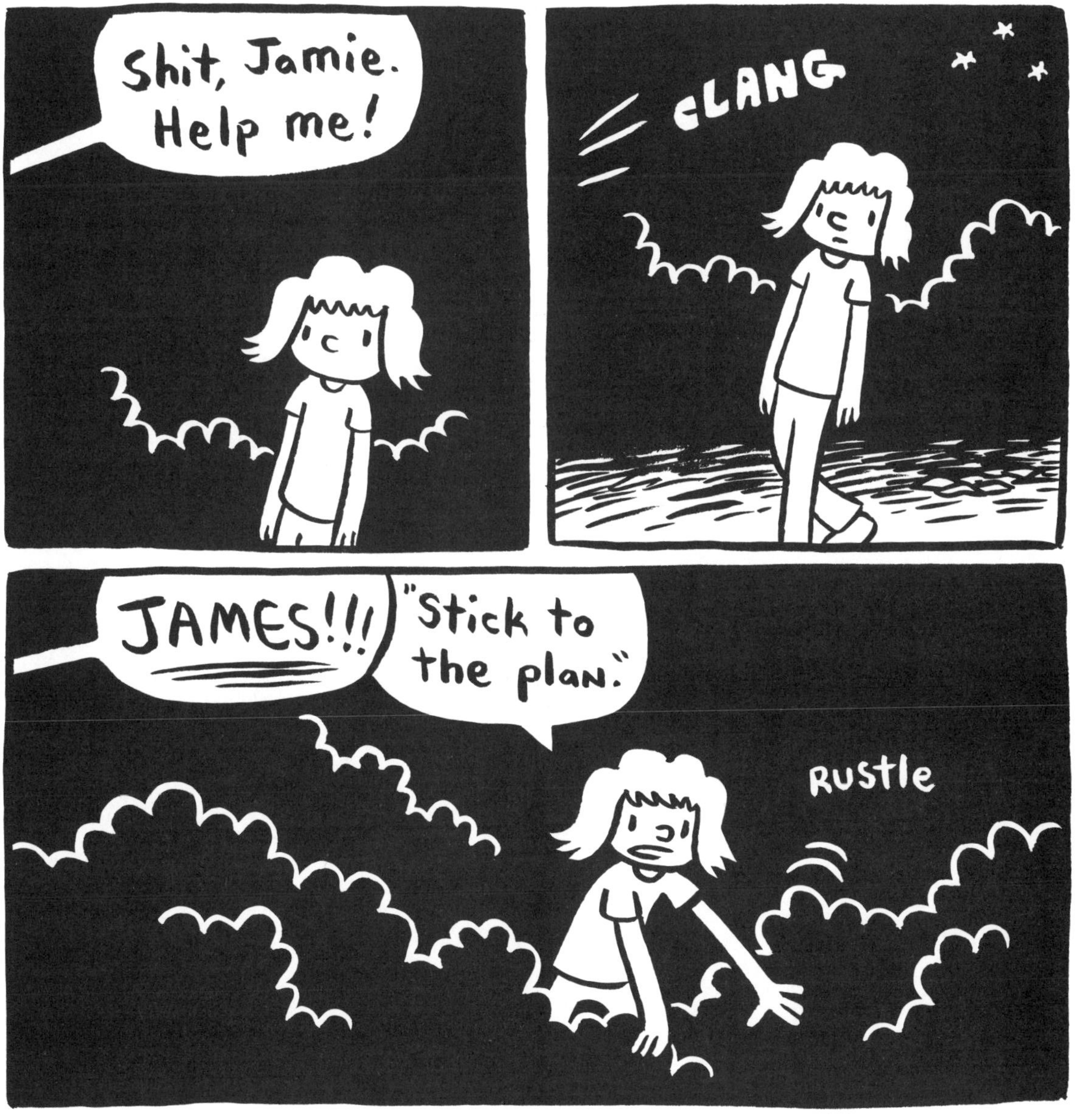
Shit, Jamie. Help me!
CLANG
JAMES!!!
"Stick to the plan."
RUSTLE

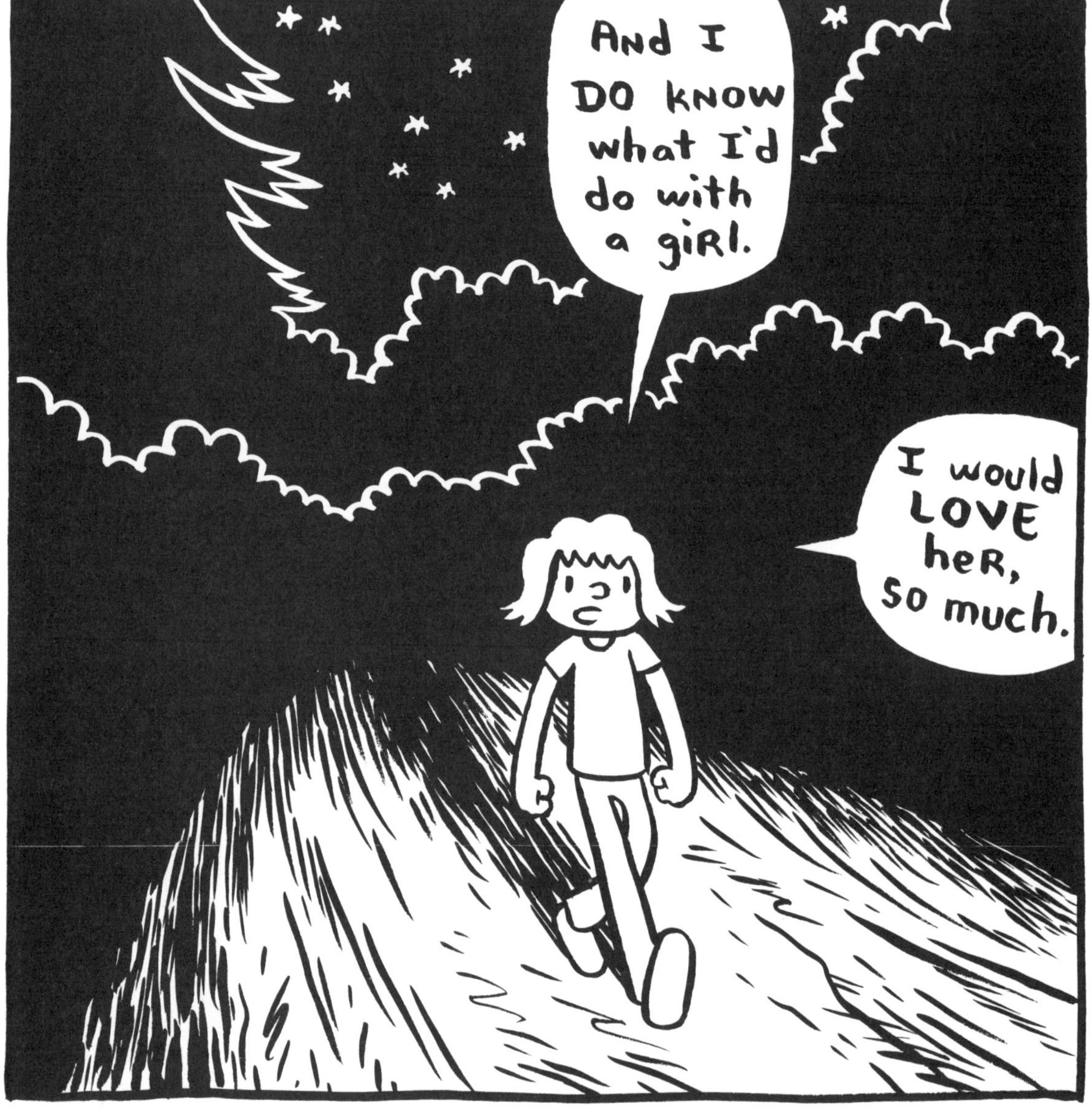
And I DO KNOW what I'd do with a girl.
I would LOVE her, so much.

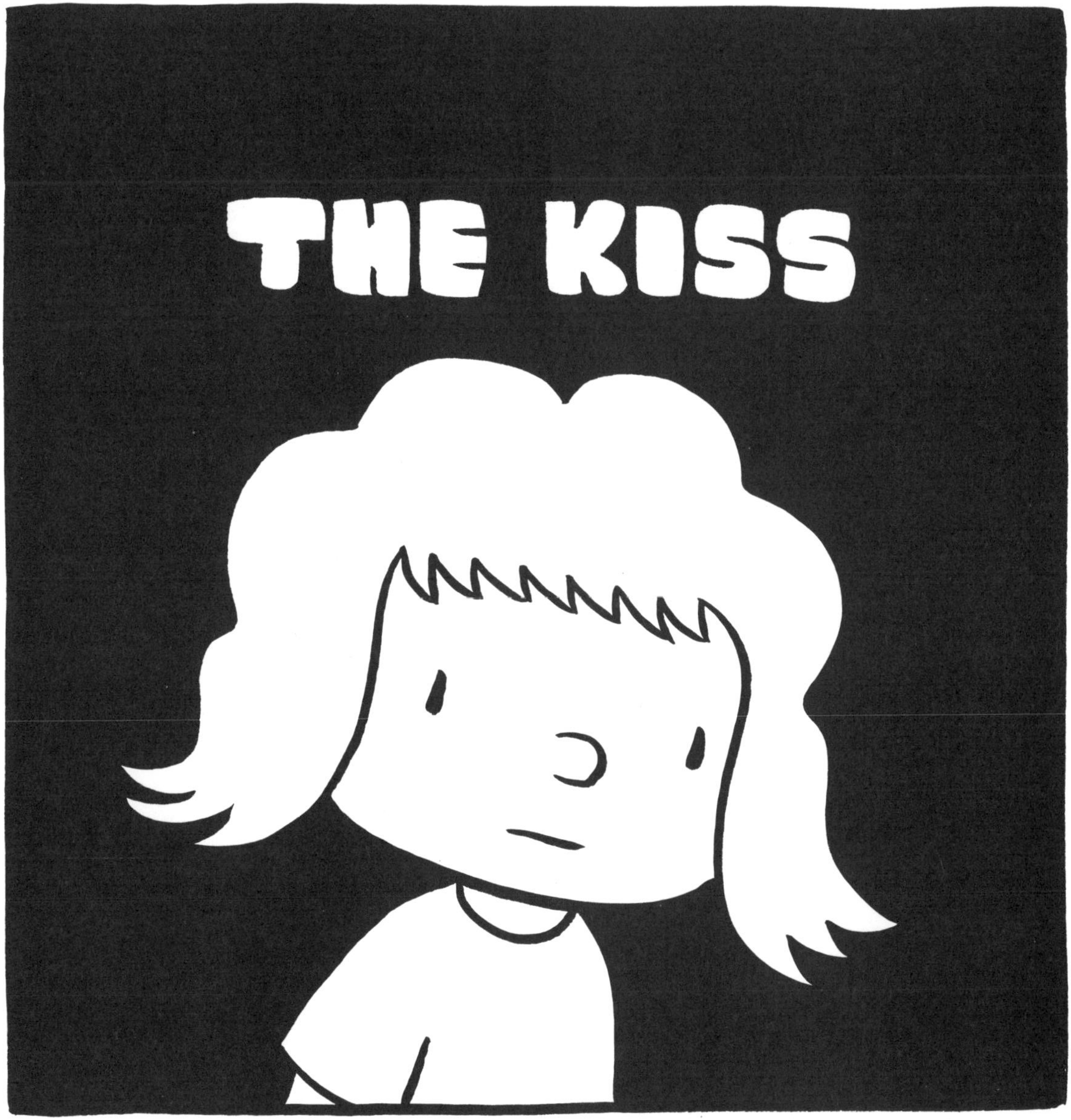
THE KISS

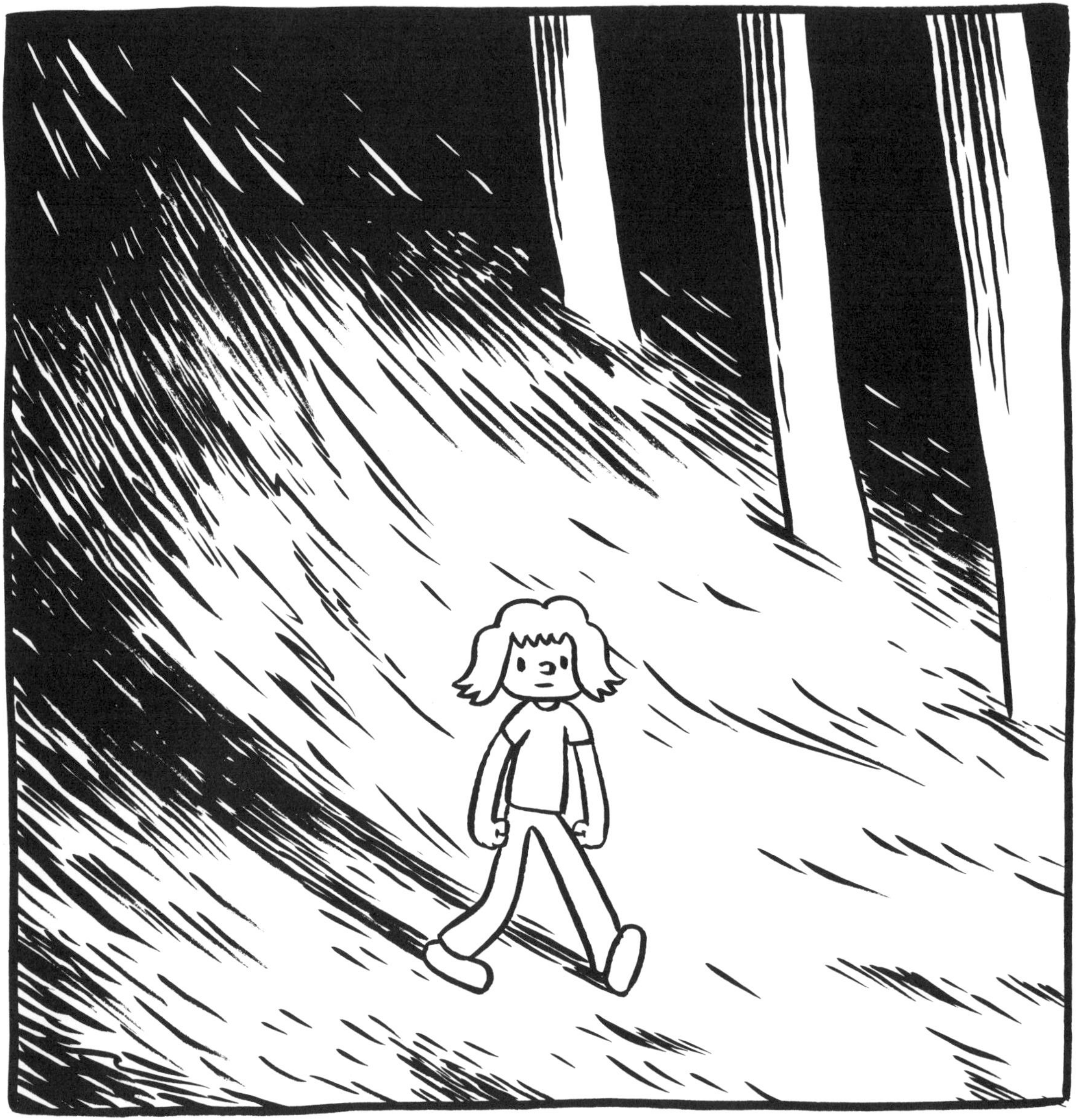

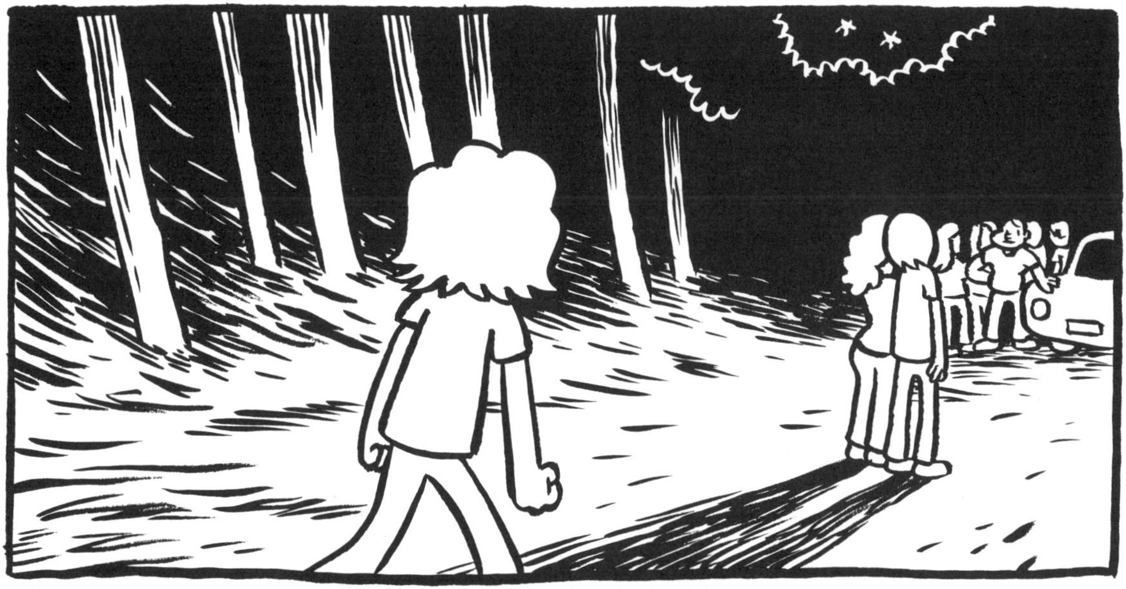

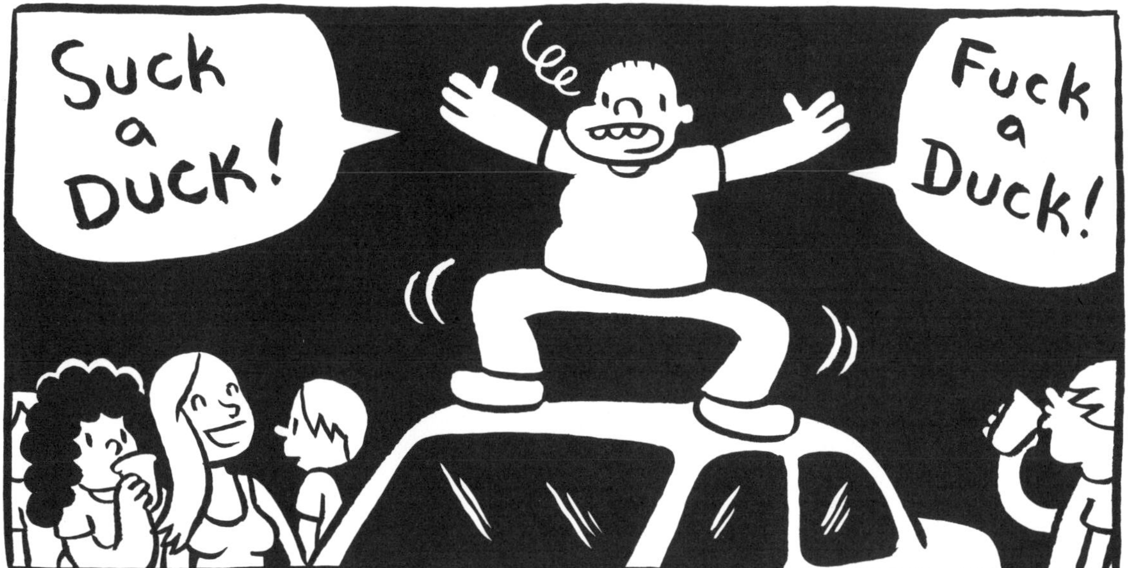
Suck a Duck!
Fuck a Duck!

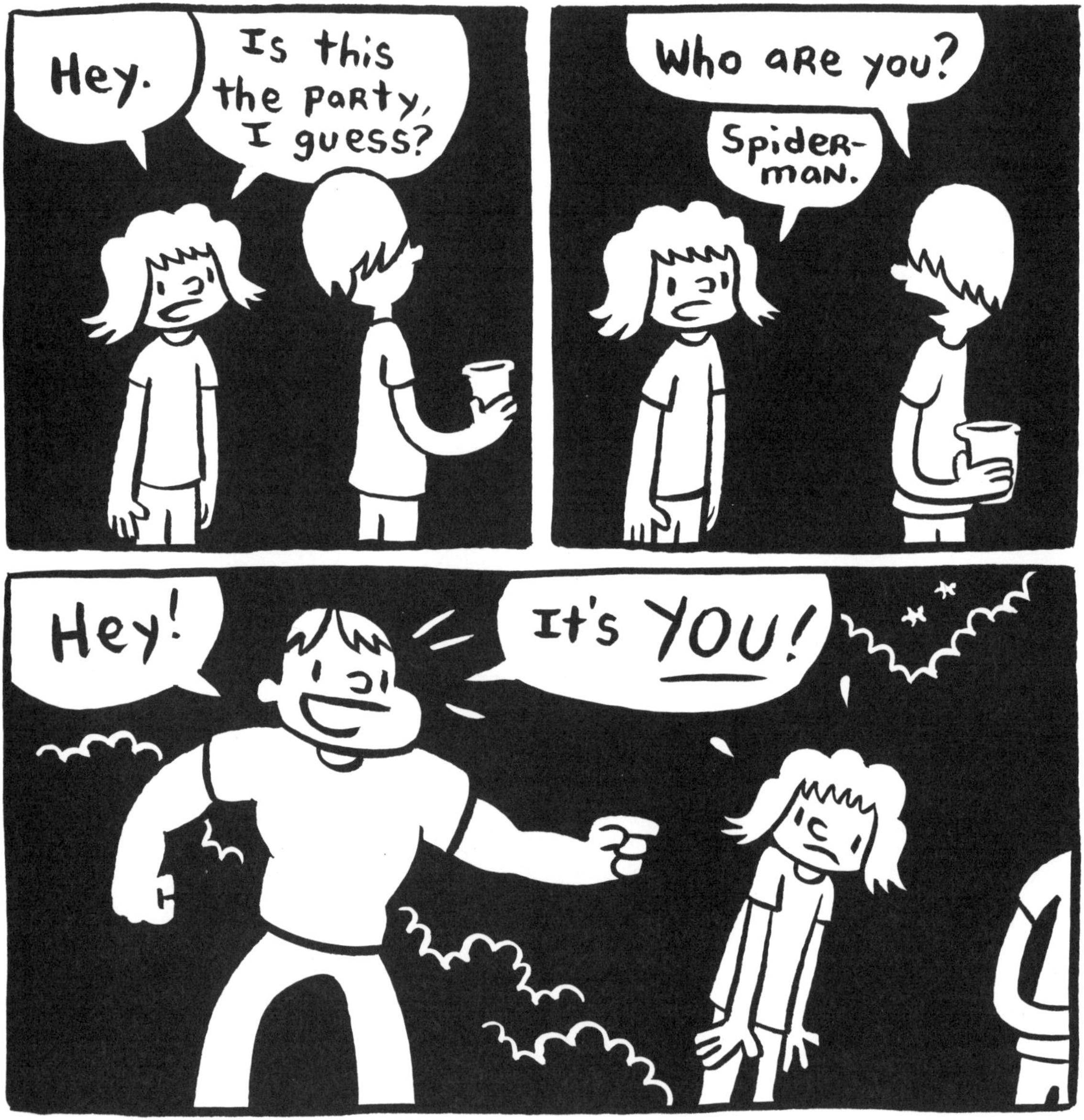
Hey.
Is this the party, I guess?
Who are you?
Spider-man.
Hey!
It's YOU!

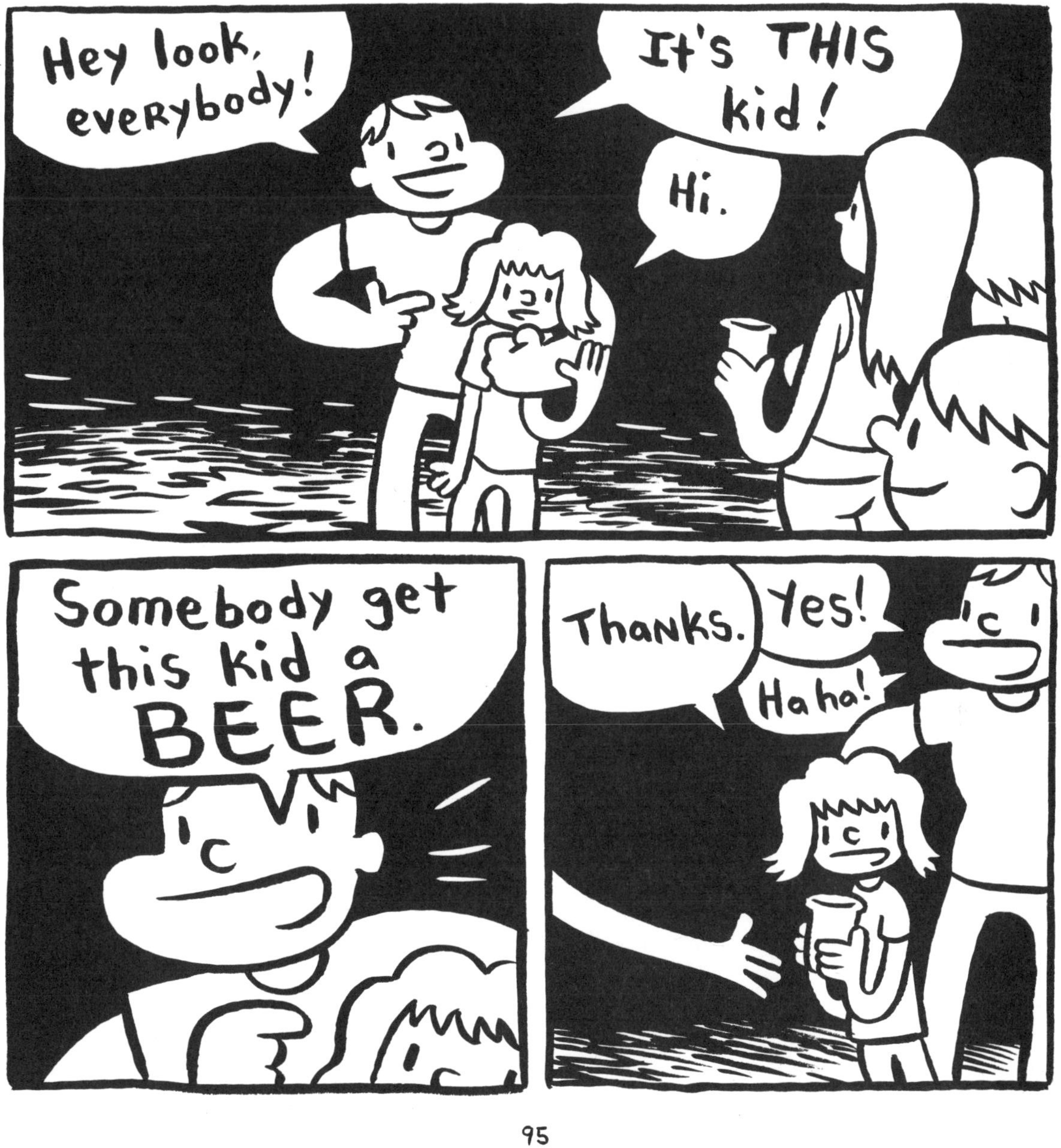
Hey look, everybody!
It's THIS kid!
Hi.
Somebody get this kid a BEER.
Thanks.
Yes!
Ha ha!

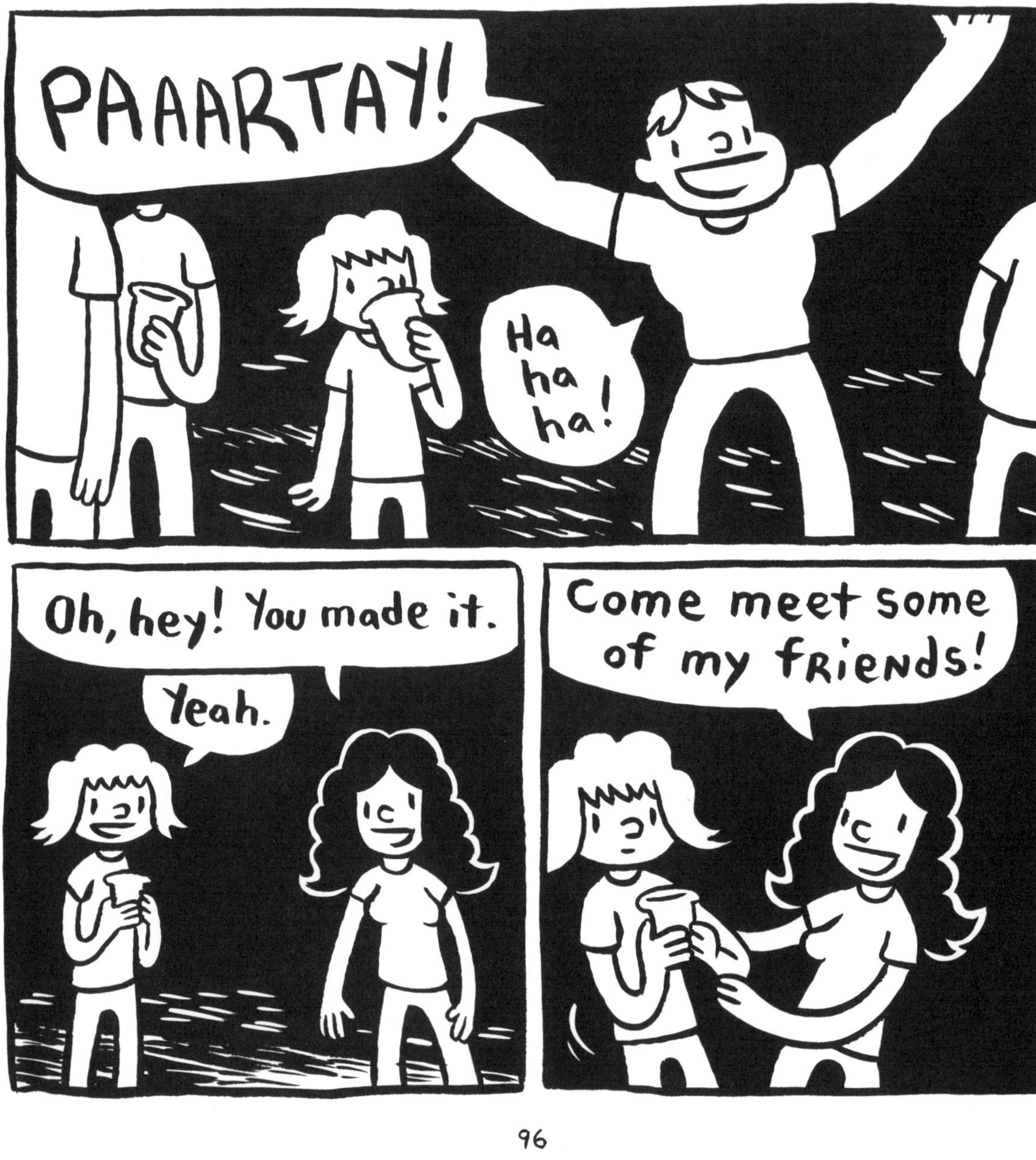
PAAARTAY!
Ha ha ha!
Oh, hey! You made it.
Yeah.
Come meet some of my friends!

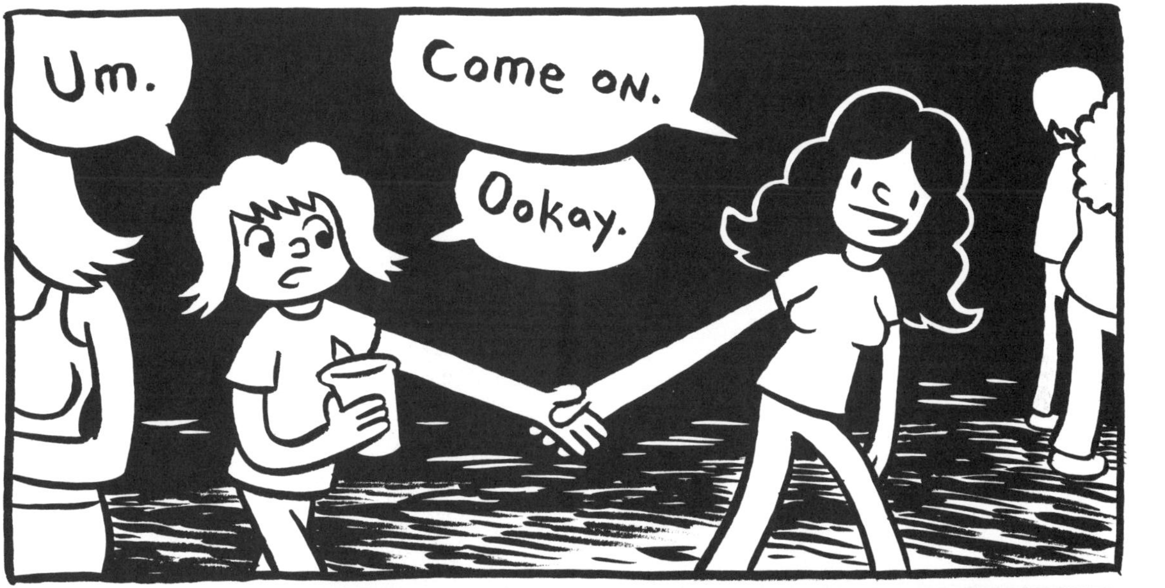
Um.
Come on.
Ookay.

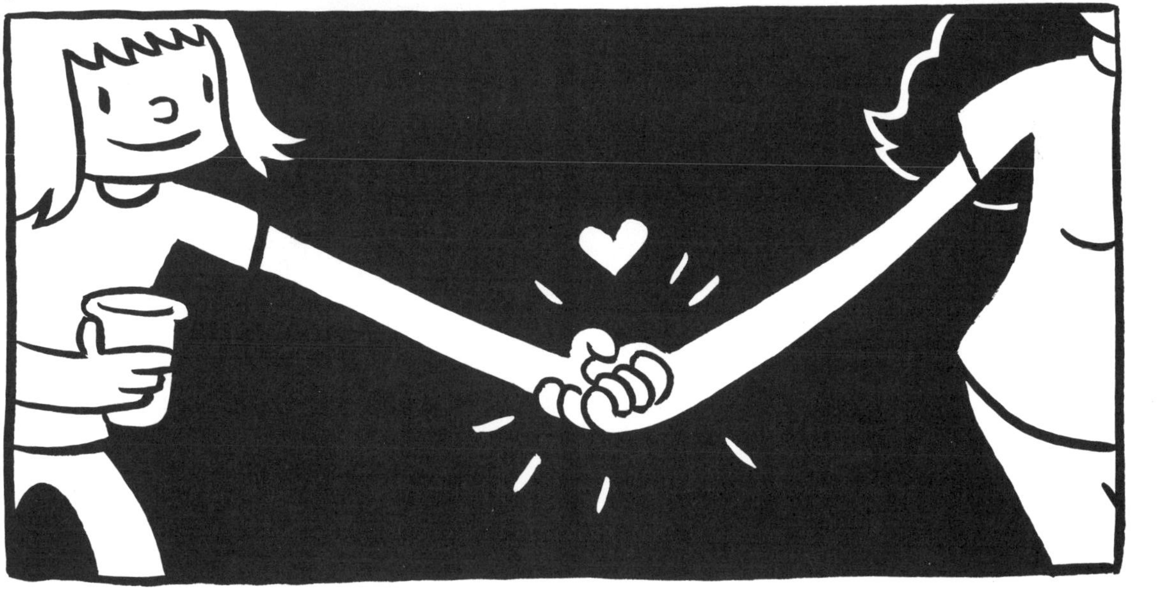

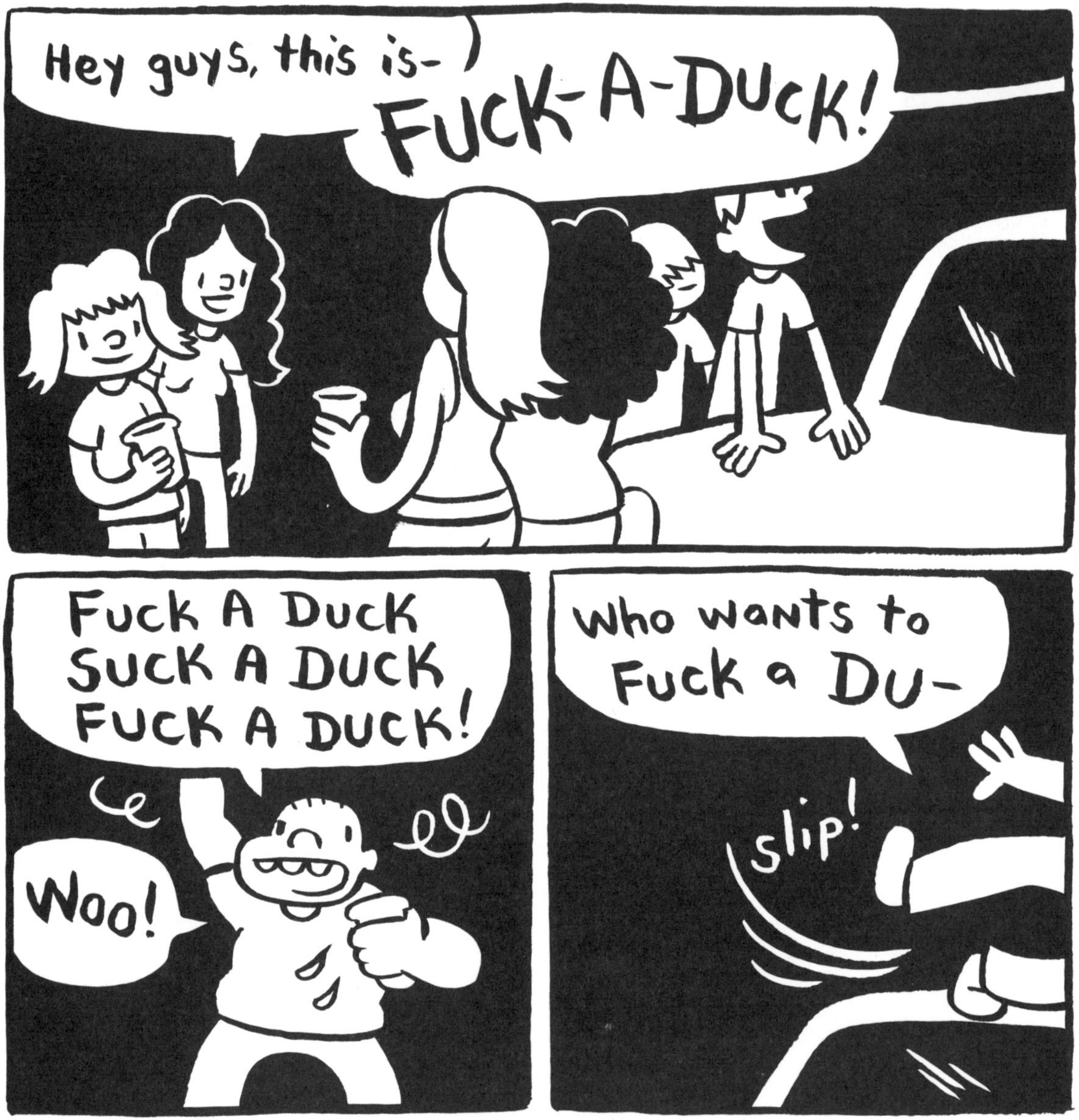
Hey guys, this is-
FUCK-A-DUCK!
Fuck A Duck
SUCK A DUCK
FUCK A DUCK!
Woo!
Who wants to
Fuck a DU-
slip!

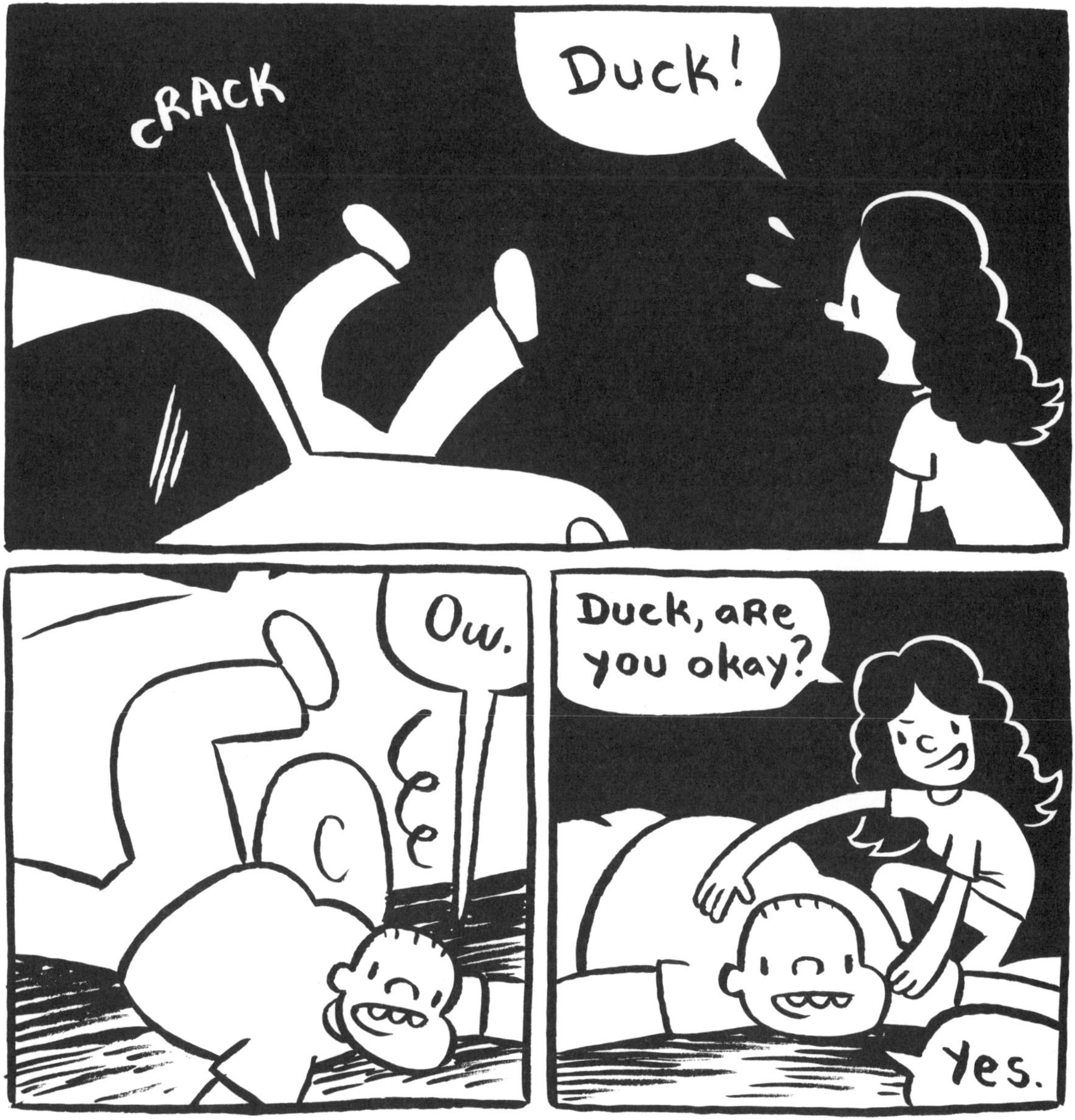
CRACK
Duck!
Ow.
Duck, aRe you okay?
Yes.

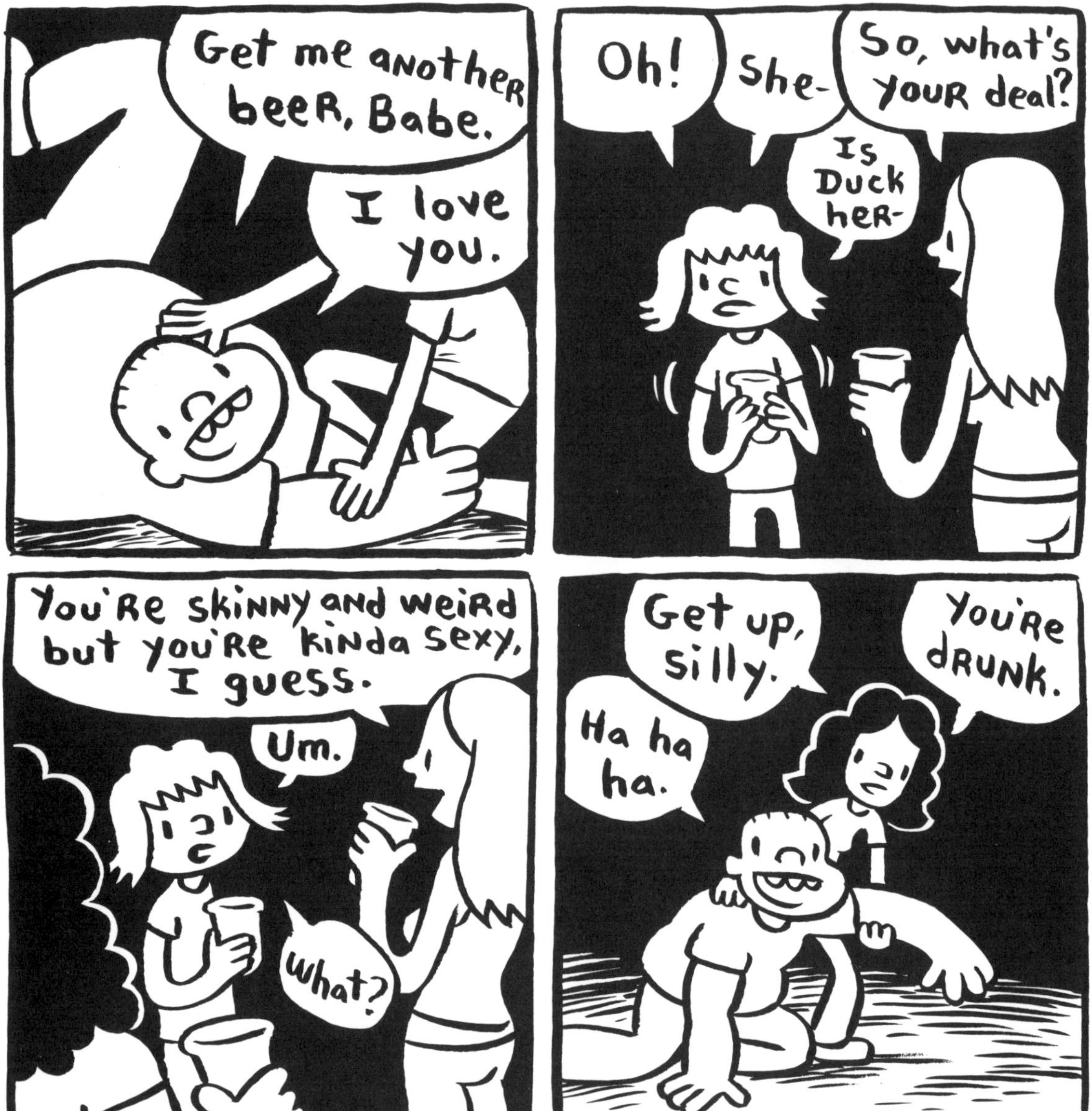

Get me another beer, Babe.
I love you.
Oh!
She-
So, what's your deal?
Is Duck her-
You're skinny and weird but you're kinda sexy, I guess.
Um.
What?
Get up, silly.
You're drunk.
Ha ha ha.

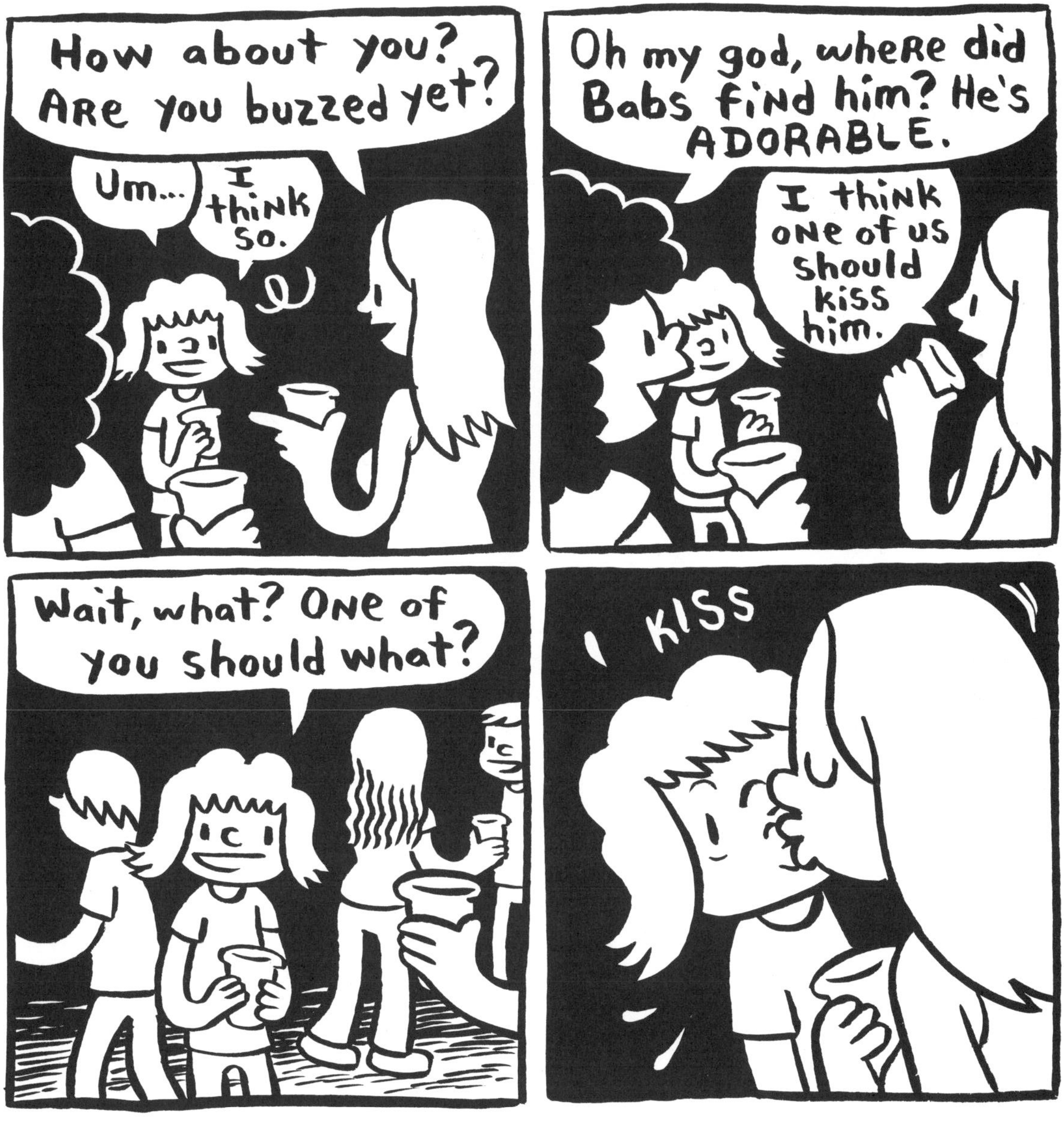
How about you? Are you buzzed yet?
Um...
I think so.
Oh my god, where did Babs find him? He's ADORABLE.
I think one of us should kiss him.
Wait, what? One of you should what?
KISS

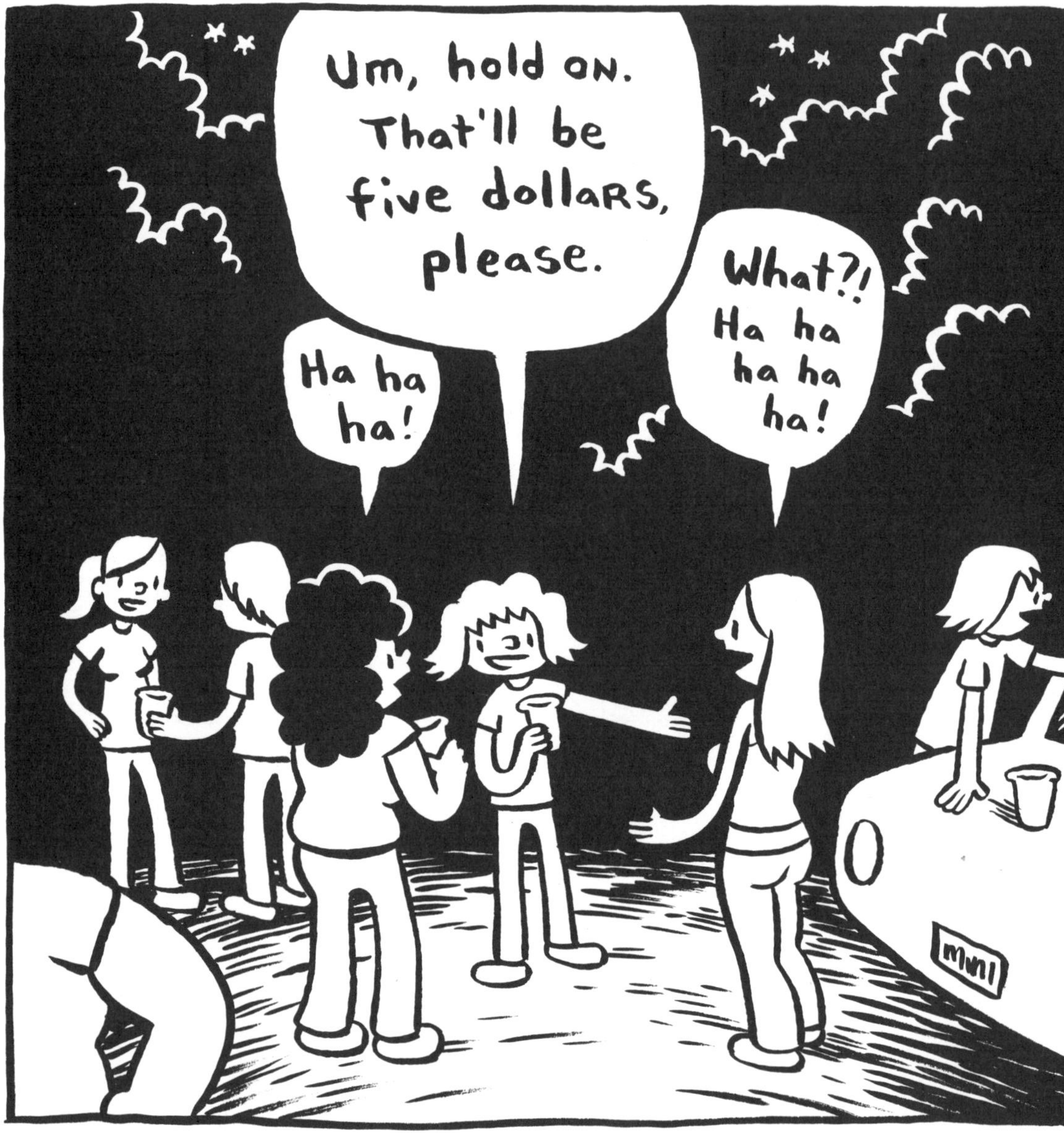
Um, hold on. That'll be five dollars, please.
Ha ha ha!
What?! Ha ha ha ha ha!
mini

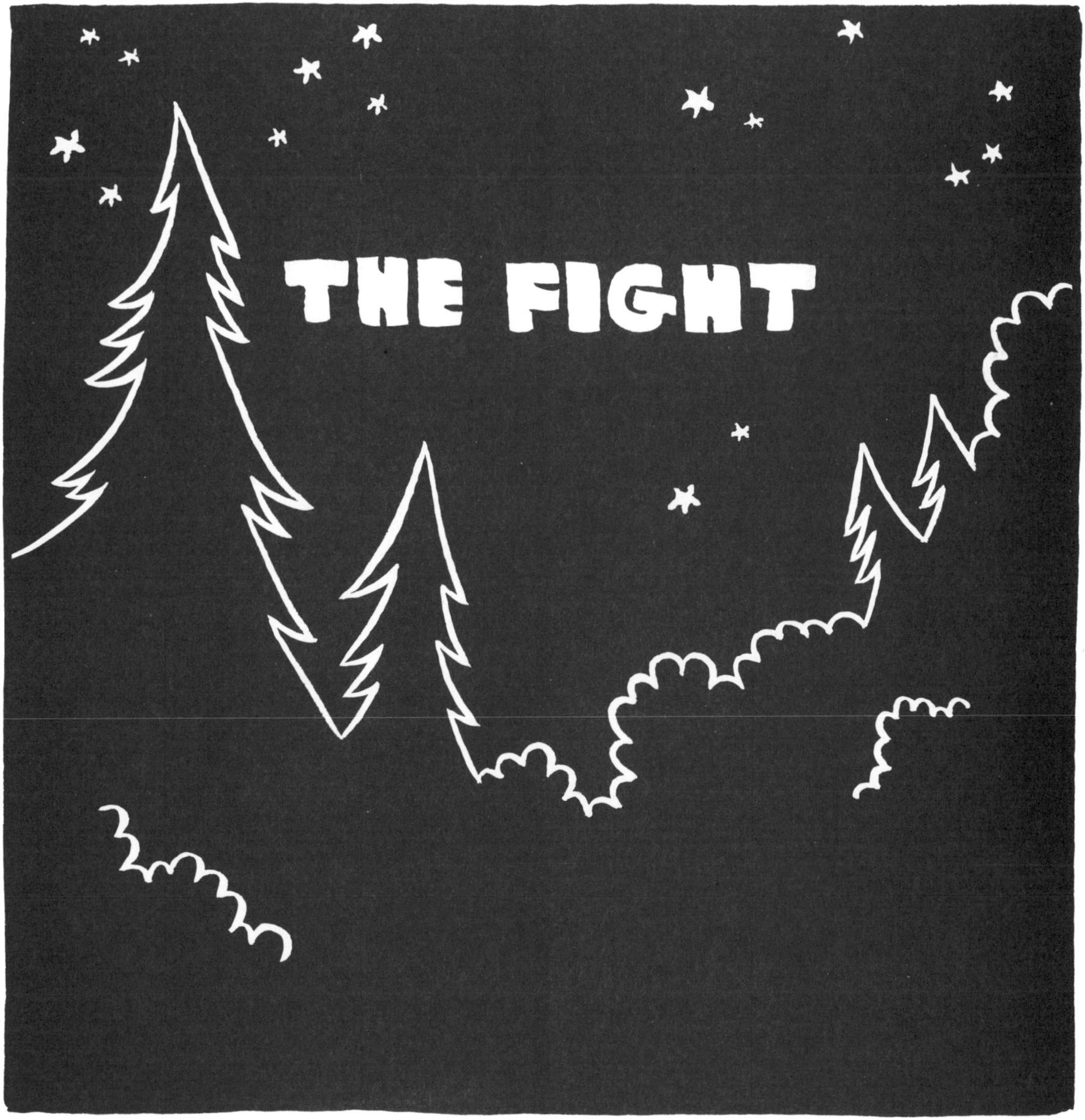
THE FIGHT

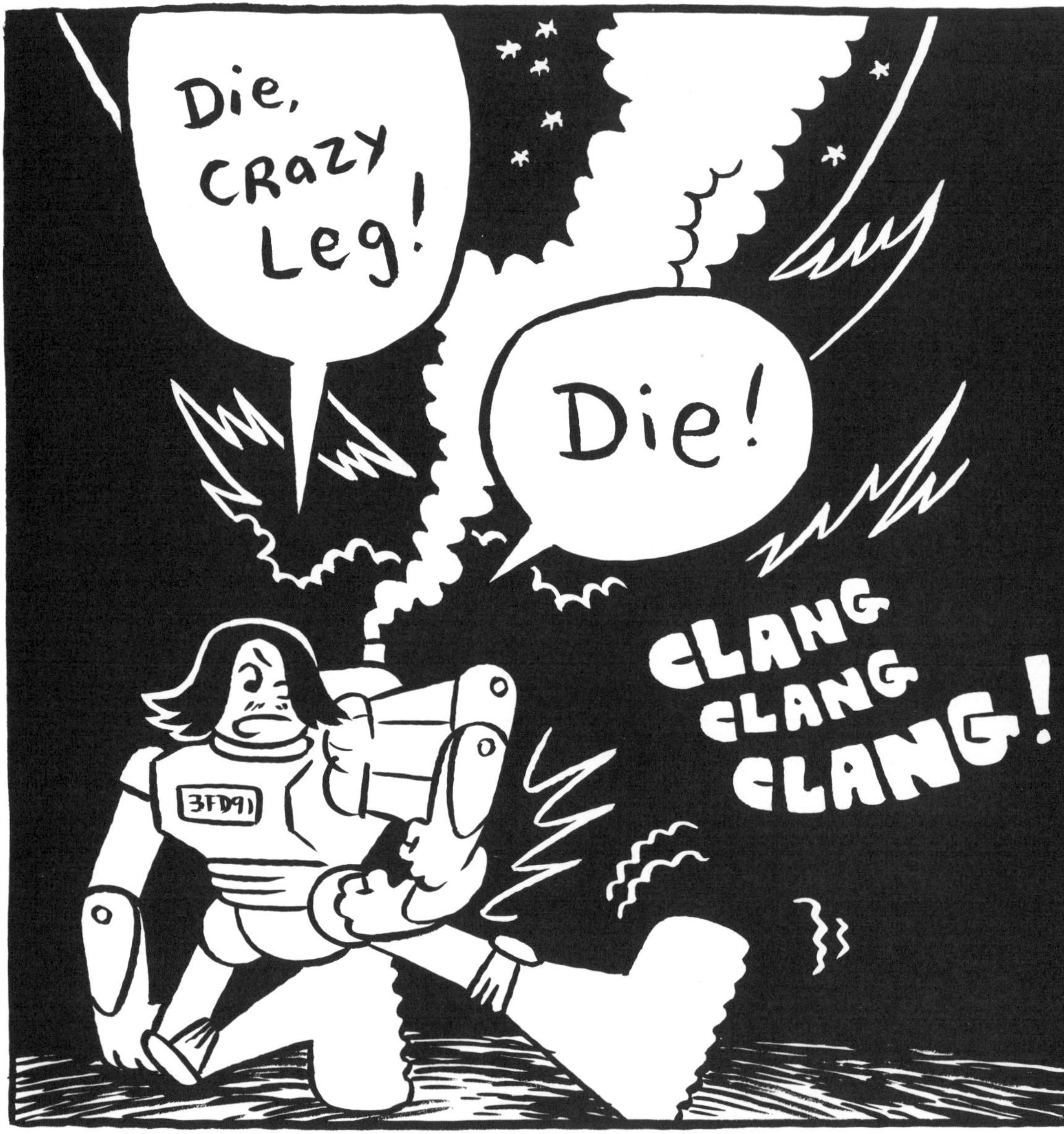
Die, crazy Leg!
Die!
CLANG CLANG CLANG!
3FD91

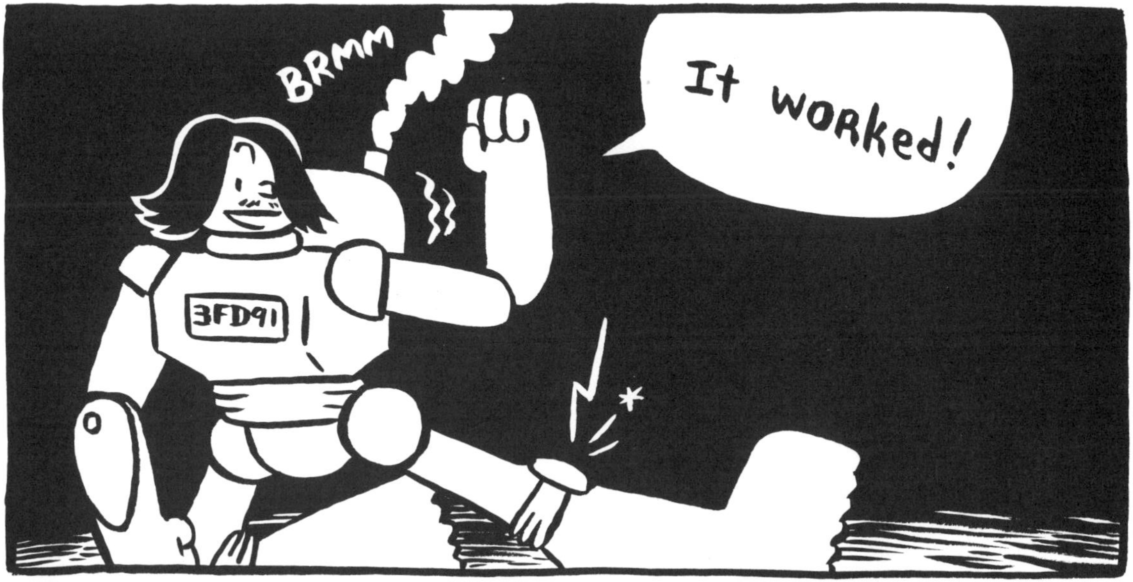
BRMM
It worked!
3FD91

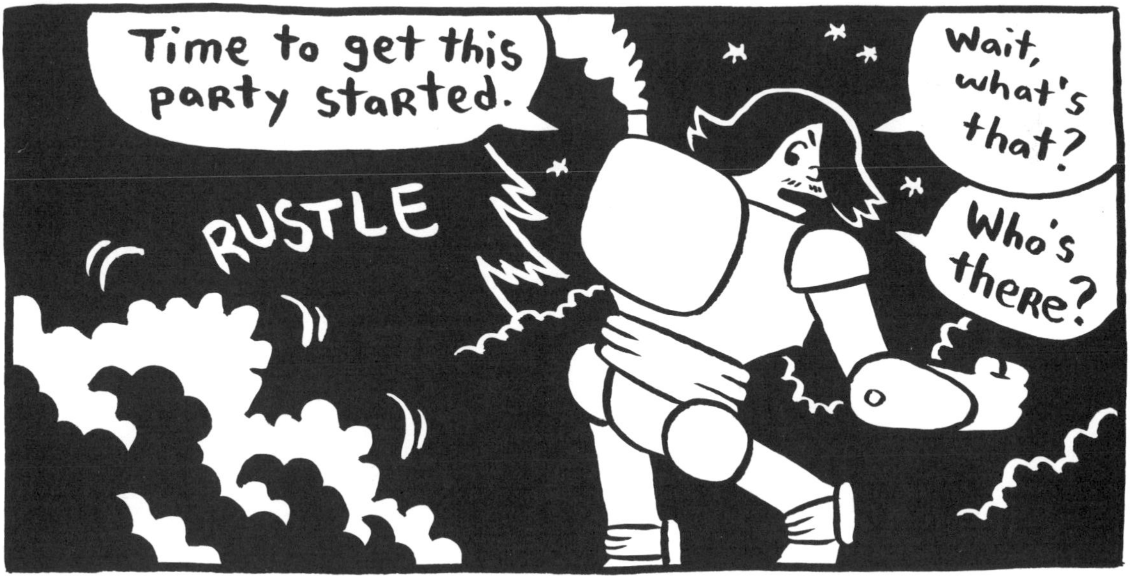
Time to get this party started.
Wait, what's that?
Who's there?
RUSTLE

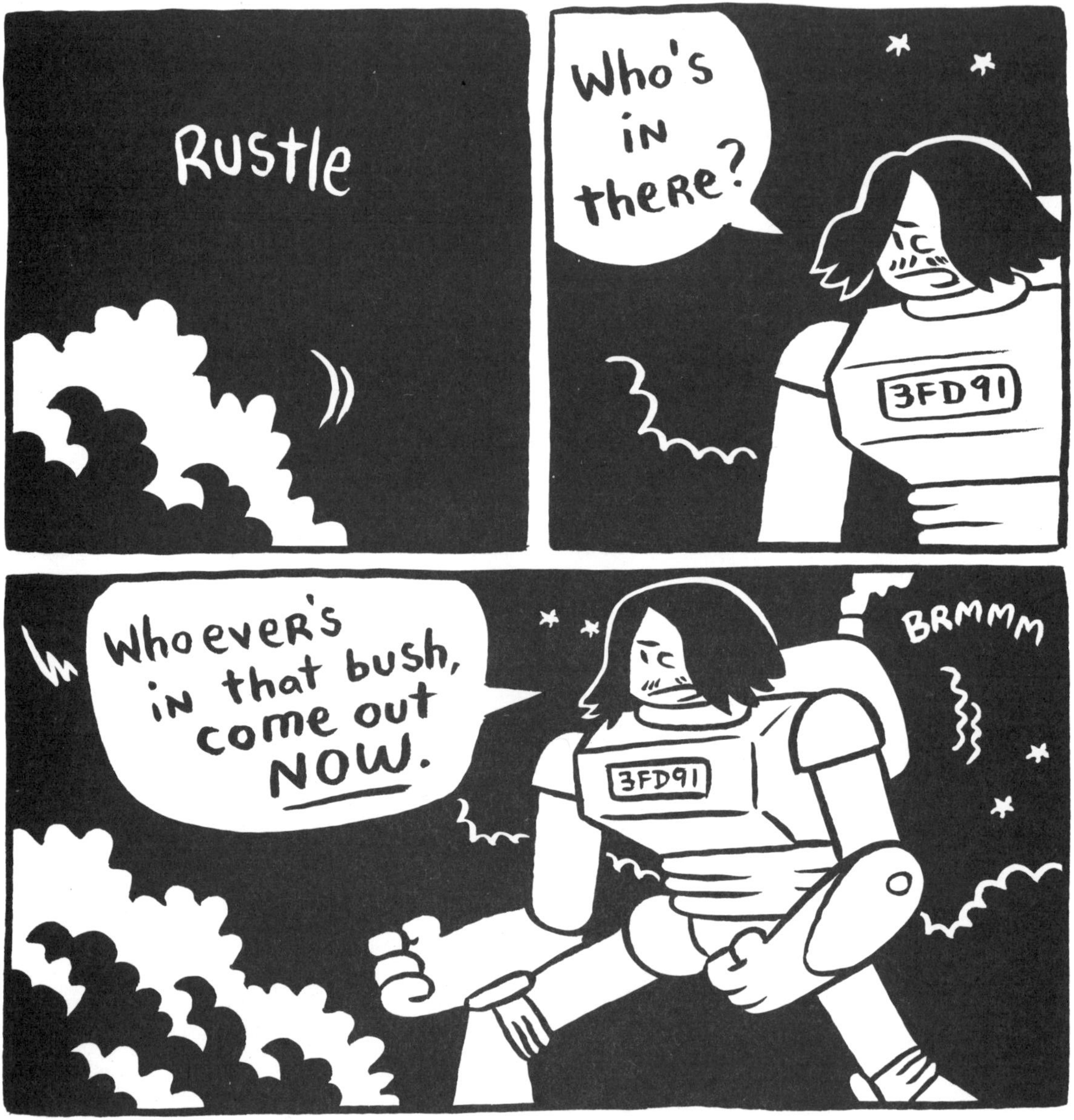
RUSTLE
Who's in there?
Whoever's in that bush, come out NOW.
BRMMM
3FD91

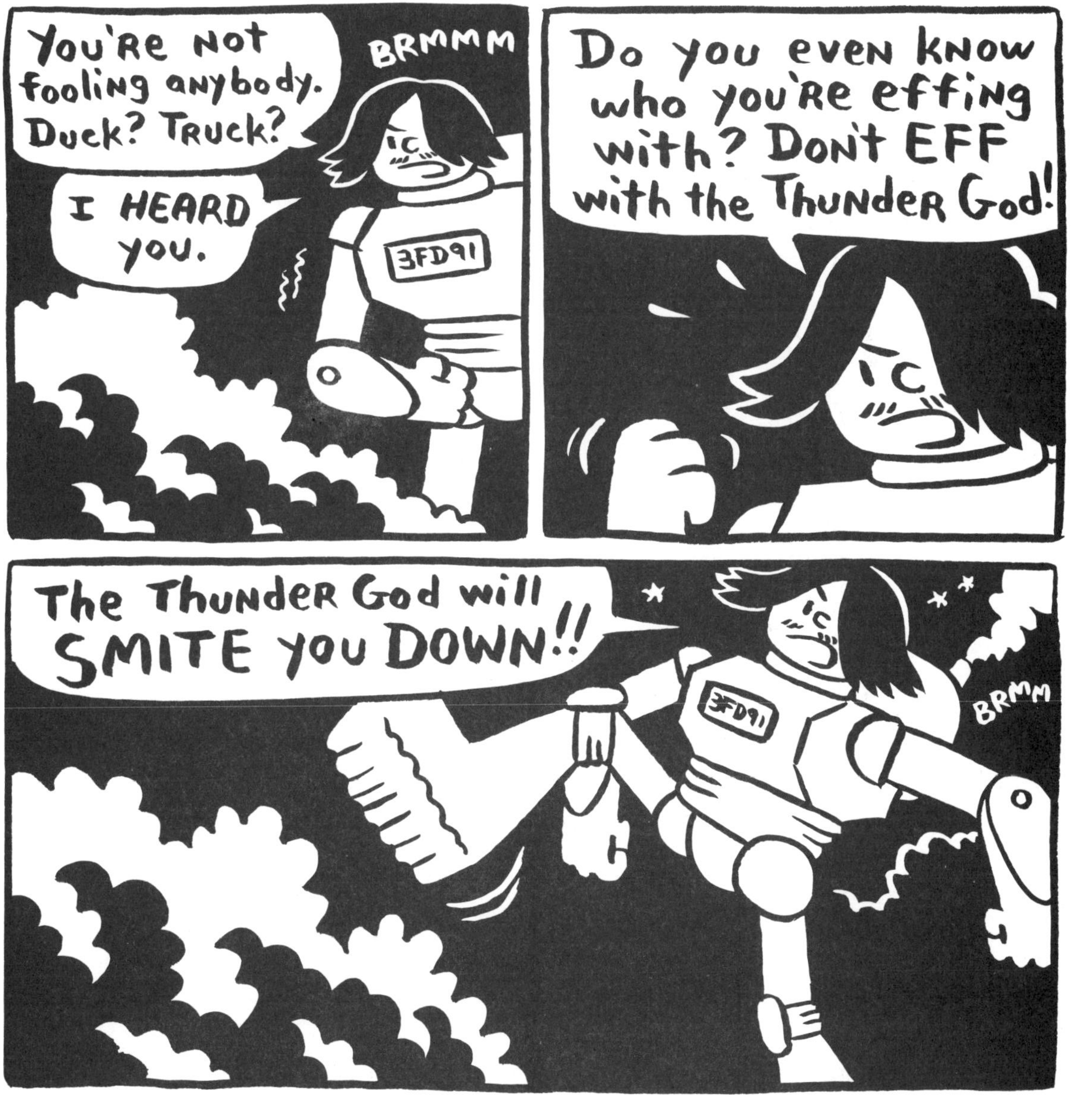
You're not fooling anybody. Duck? Truck?
BRMMM
I HEARD you.
3FD91
Do you even know who you're effing with? Don't EFF with the Thunder God!
The Thunder God will SMITE you DOWN!!
3FD91
BRMM

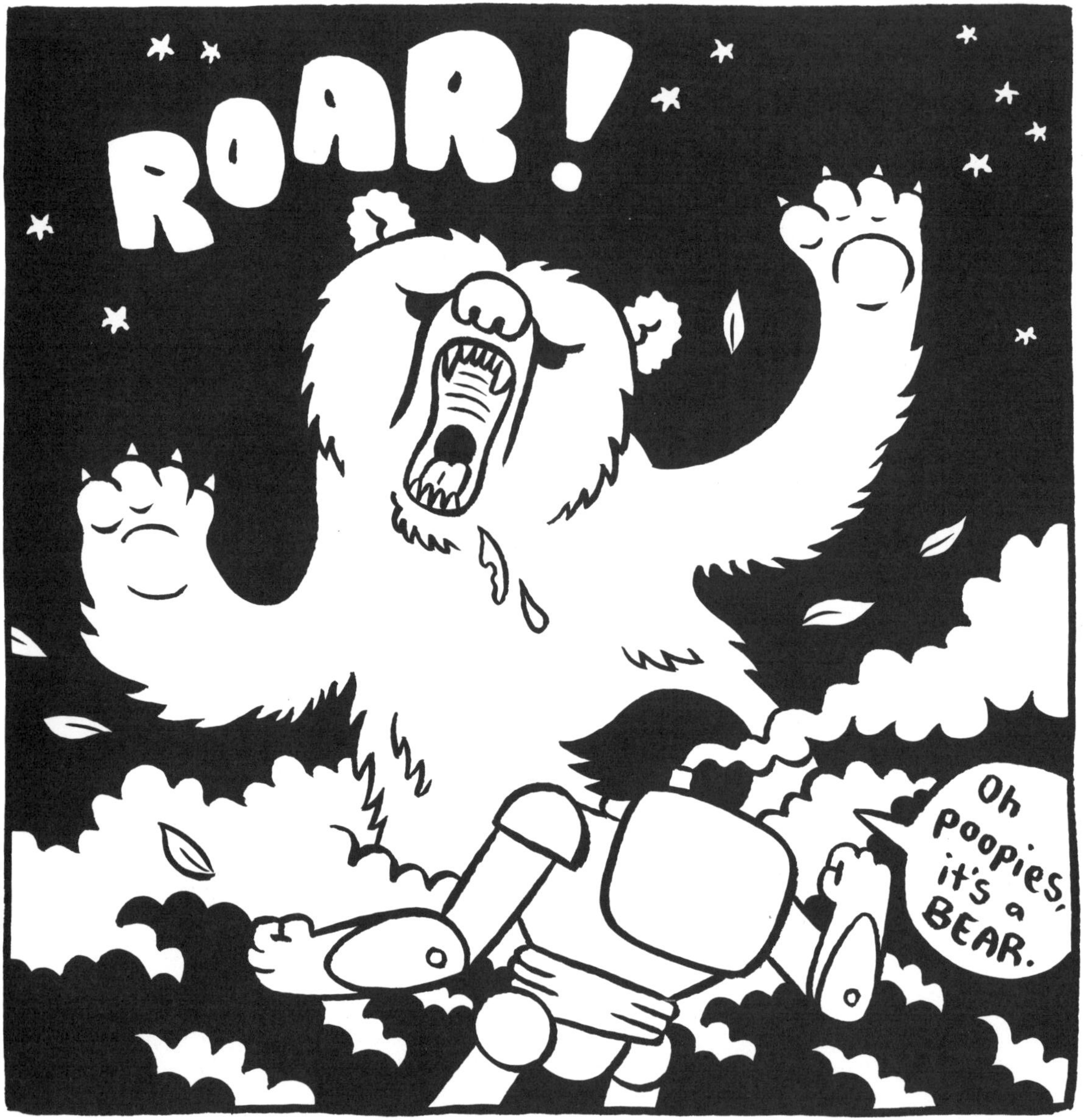
ROAR!
Oh poopies, it's a BEAR.

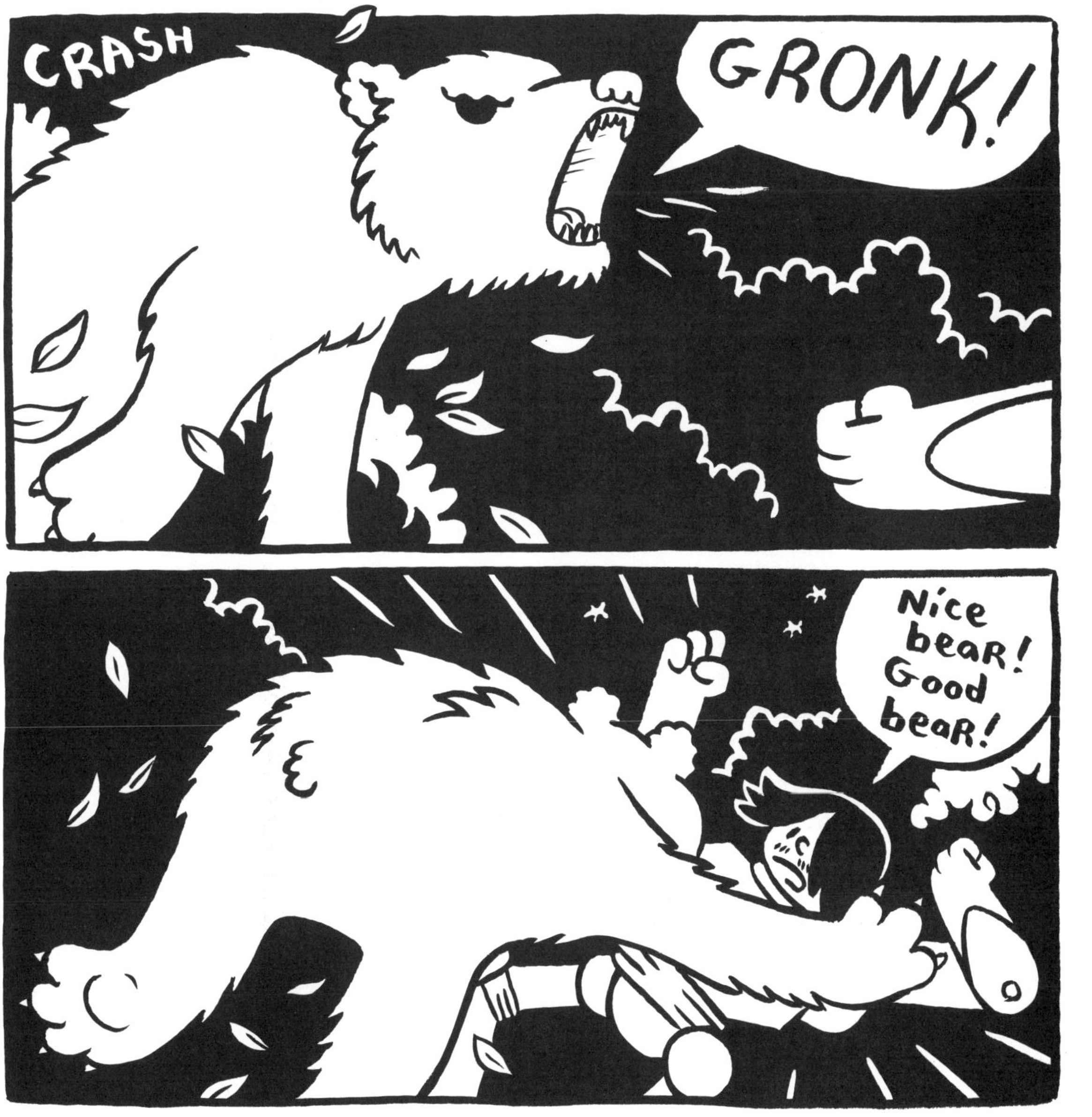
CRASH
GRONK!
Nice bear! Good bear!

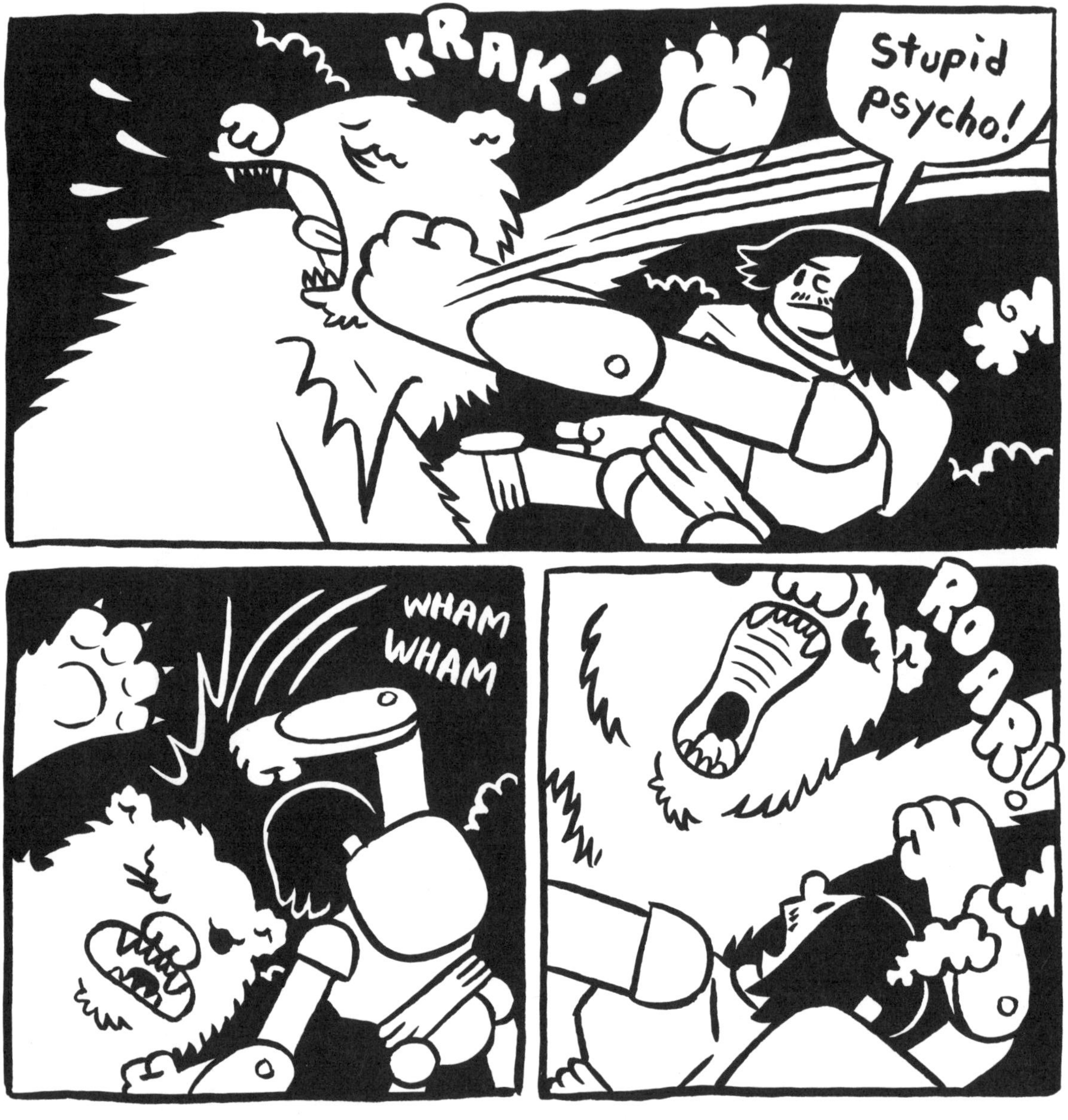
KRAK!
Stupid psycho!
WHAM
WHAM
ROAR!

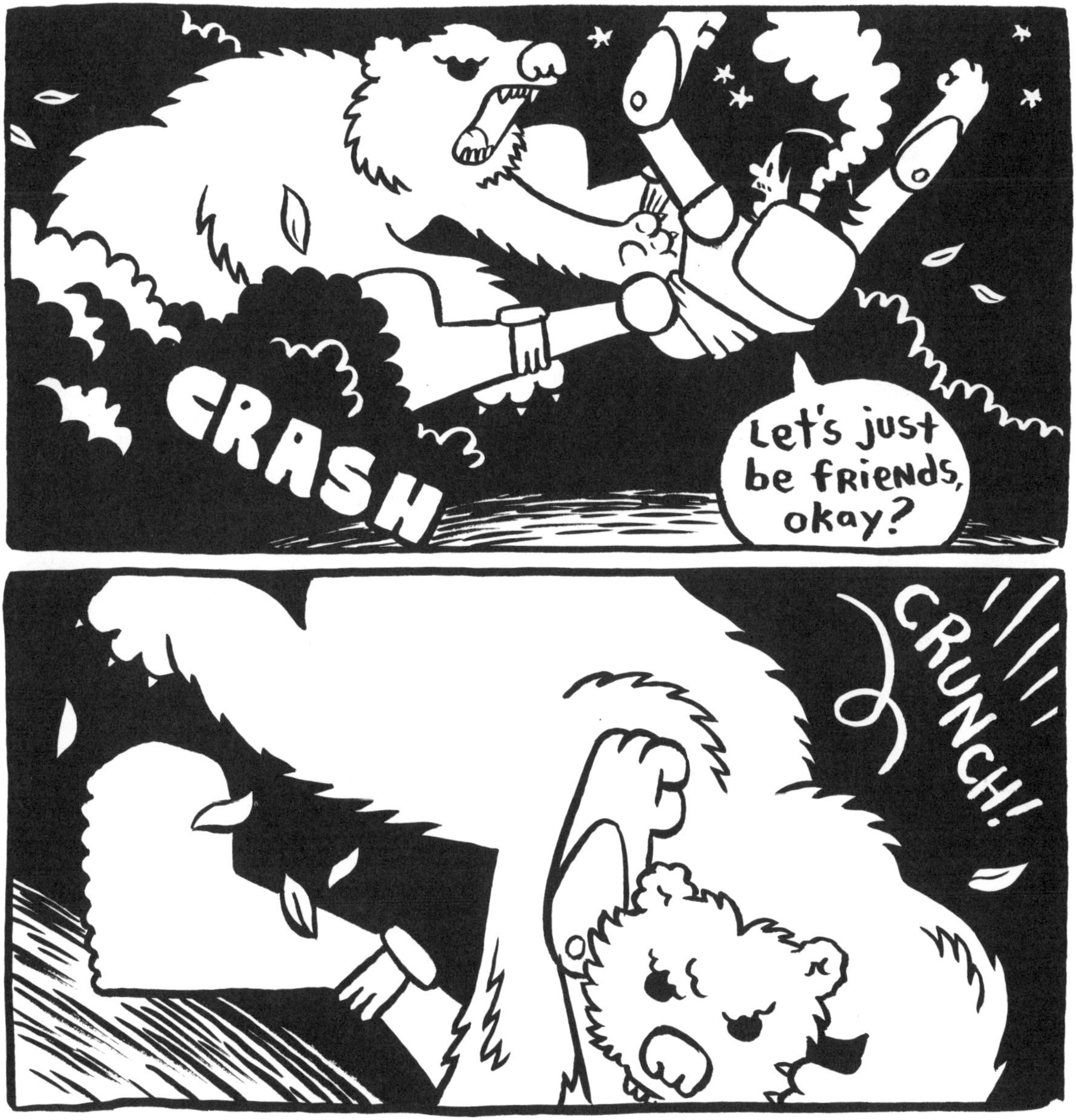
CRASH
Let's just be friends, okay?
CRUNCH!

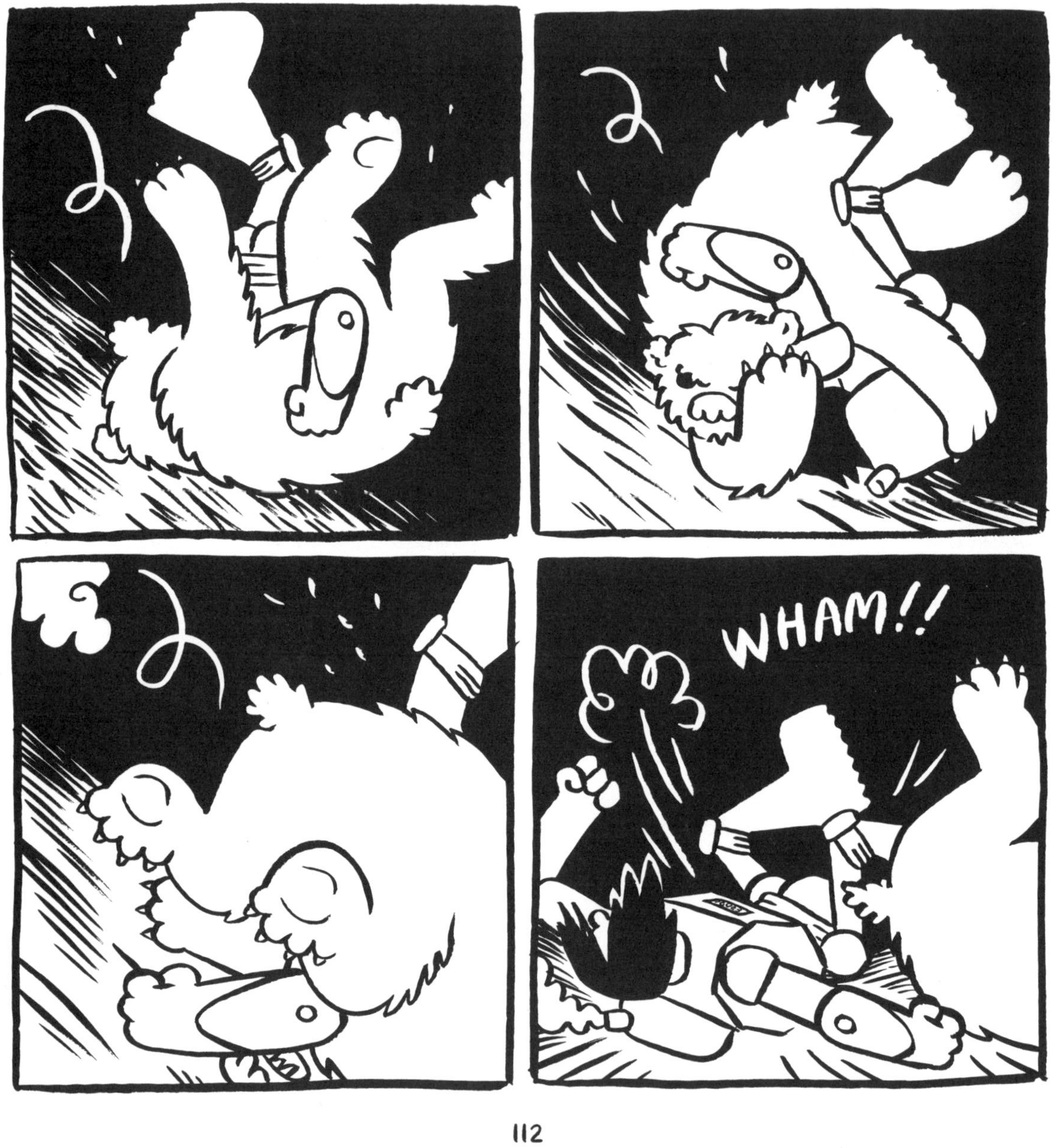
WHAM!!

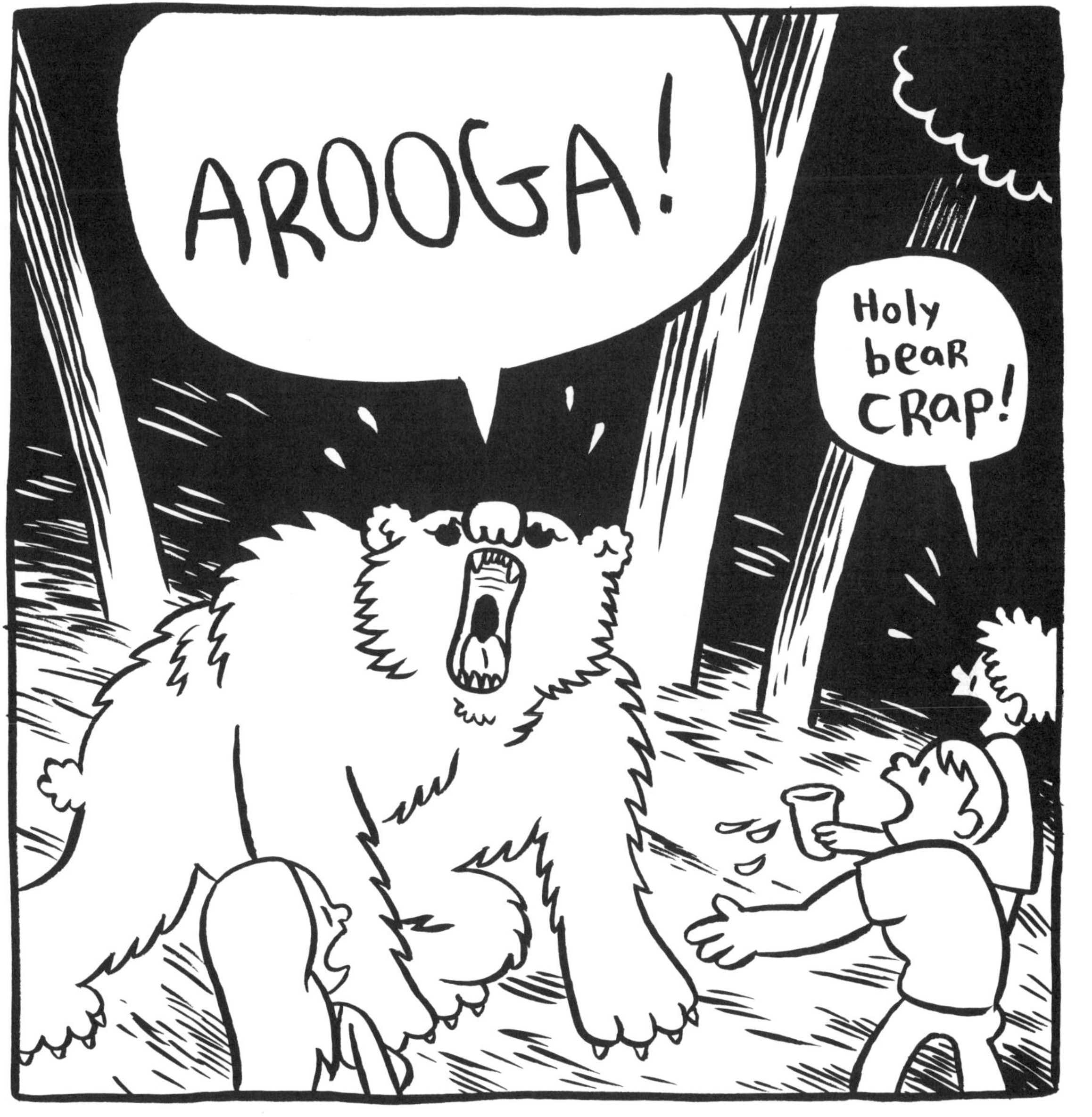
AROOGA!
Holy bear CRAP!

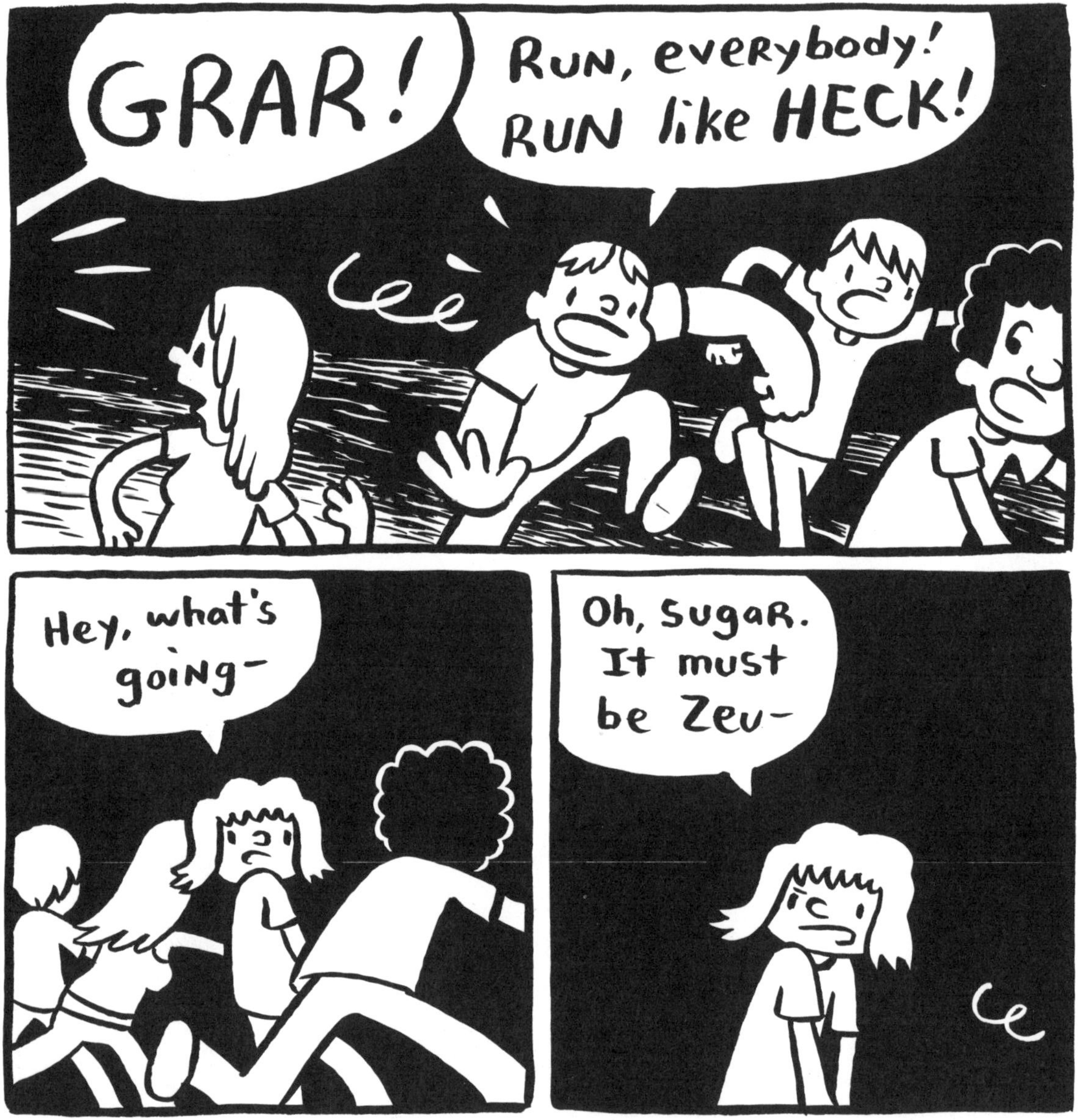
GRAR!
RUN, everybody! RUN like HECK!
Hey, what's going-
Oh, sugar. It must be Zeu-

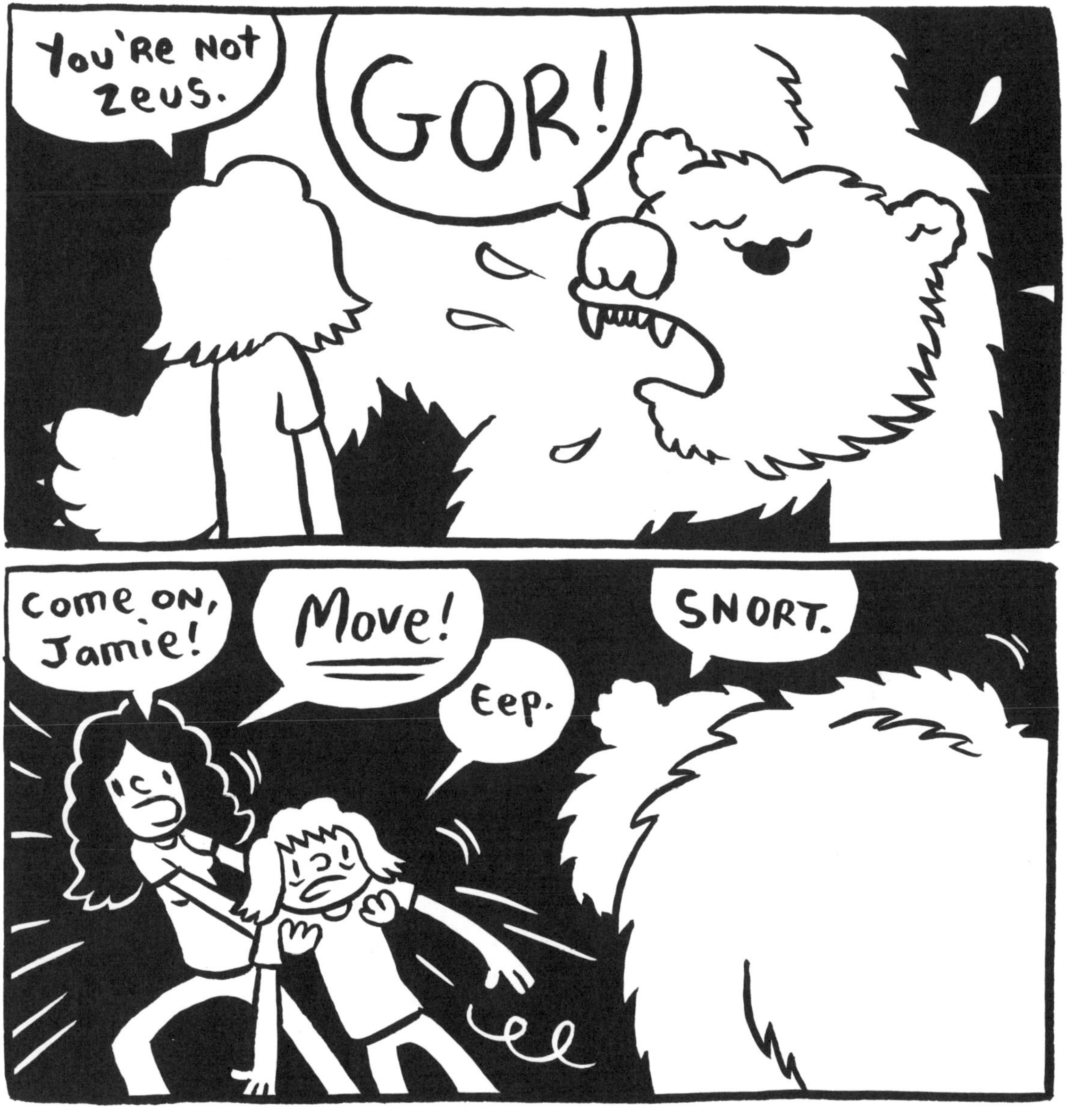
You're not Zeus.
GOR!
Come on, Jamie!
Move!
Eep.
SNORT.

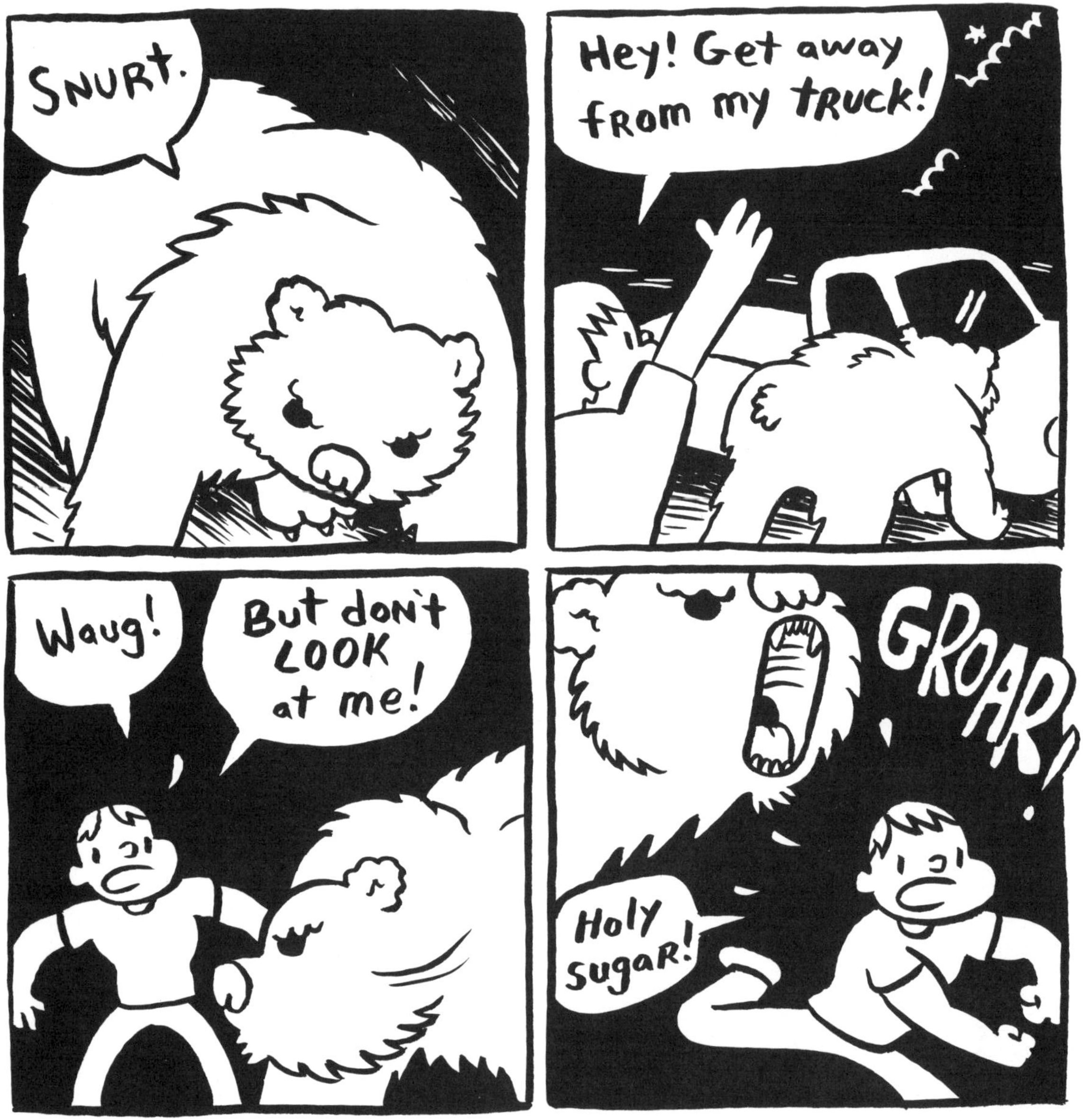
SNURT.
Hey! Get away from my TRUCK!
Waug!
But don't LOOK at me!
GROAR!
Holy sugaR!

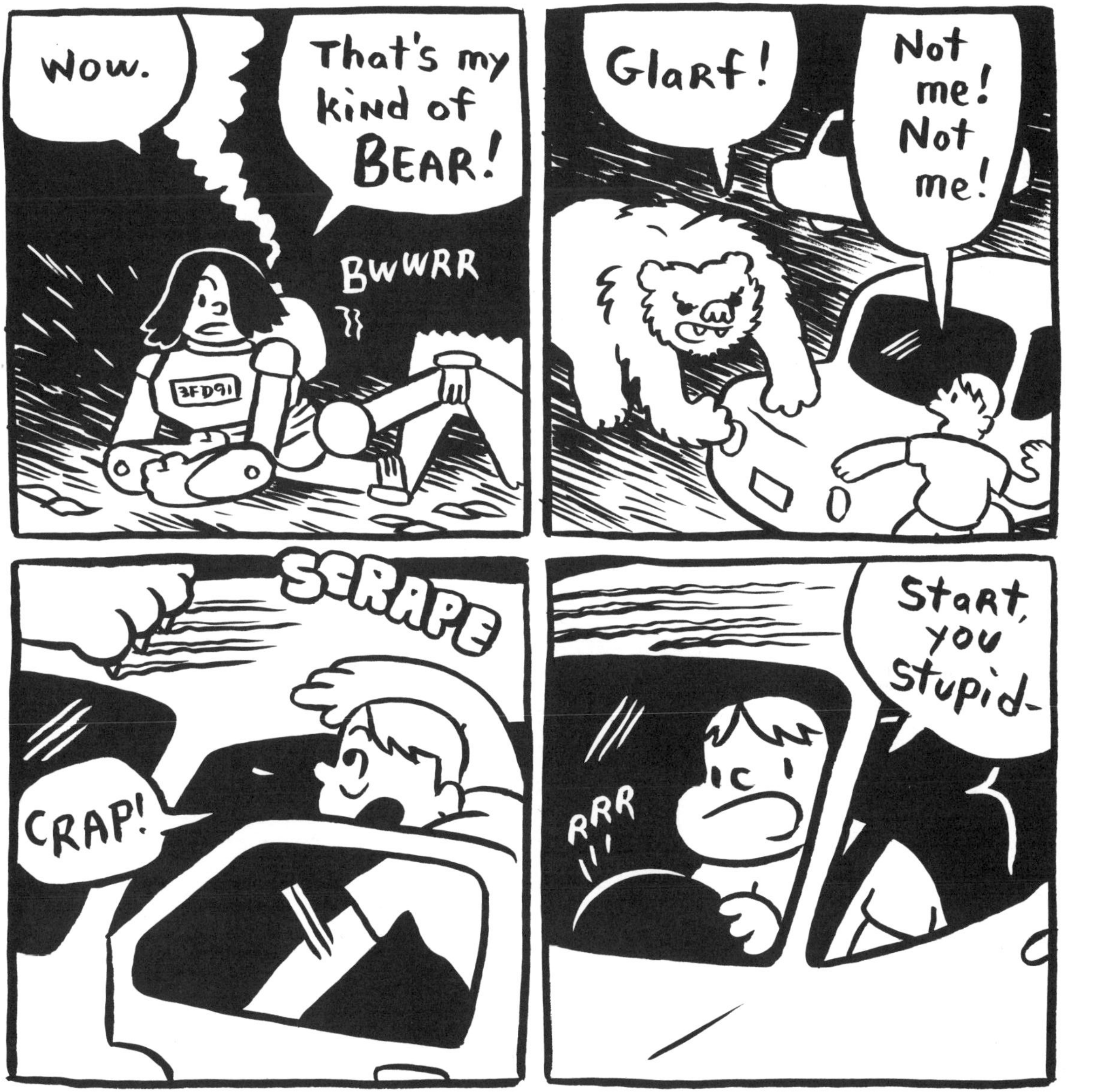
Wow.
That's my kind of BEAR!
BWWRR
3FD91
Glarf!
Not me! Not me!
SCRAPE
CRAP!
Start, you stupid-
RRR

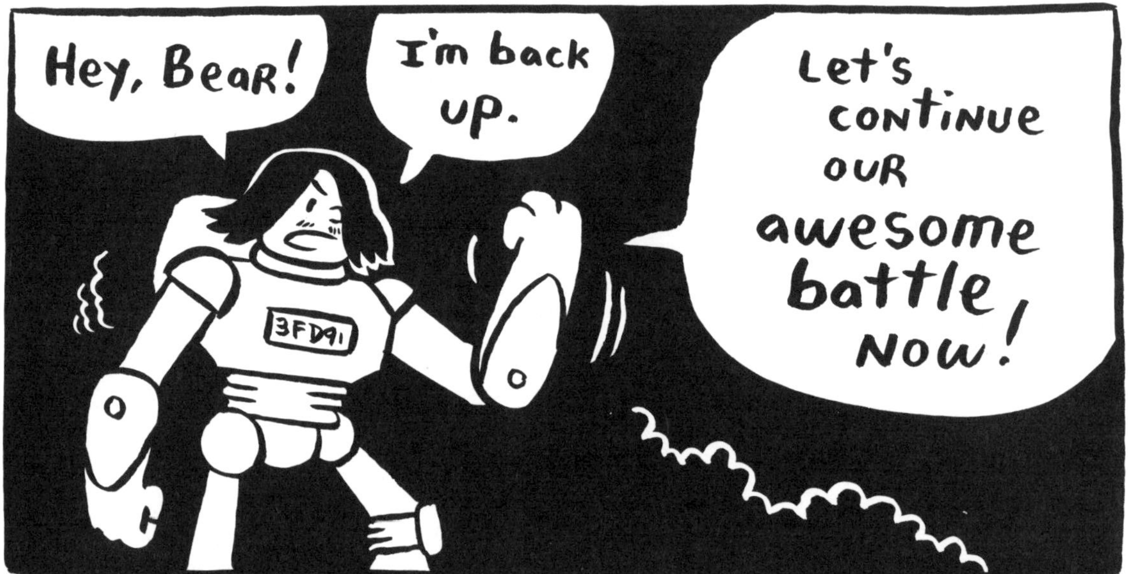
Hey, Bear!
I'm back up.
Let's continue our awesome battle now!
3FD91

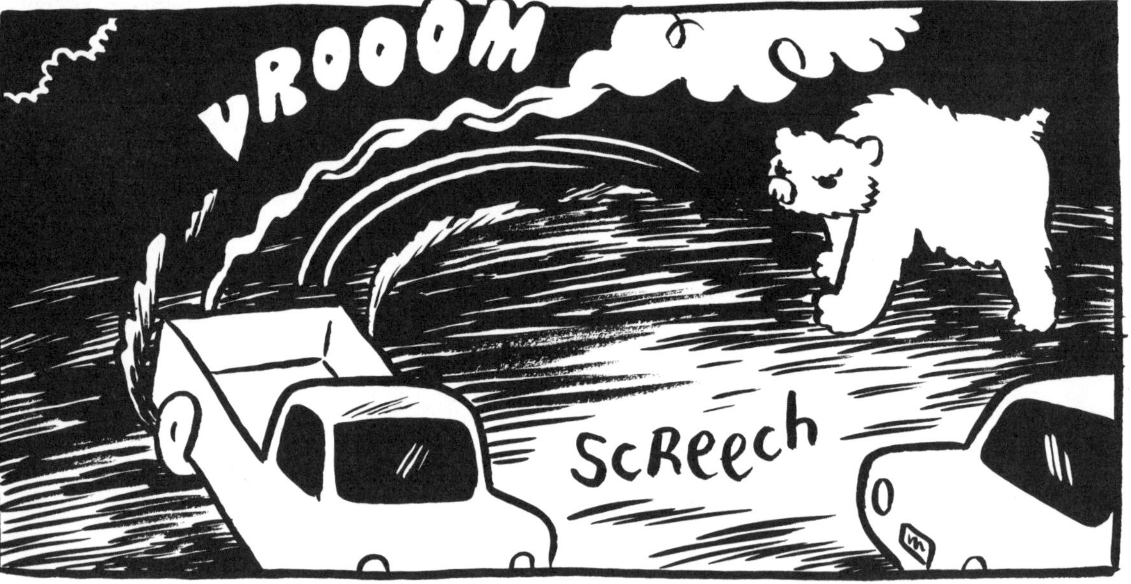
VROOOM
SCReech

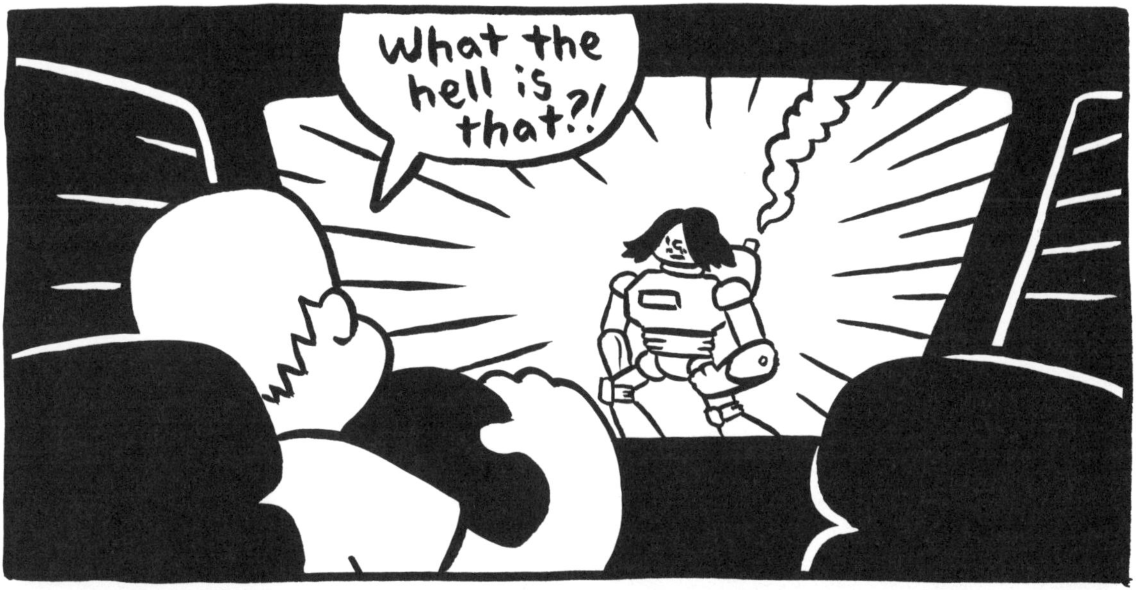
What the hell is that?!

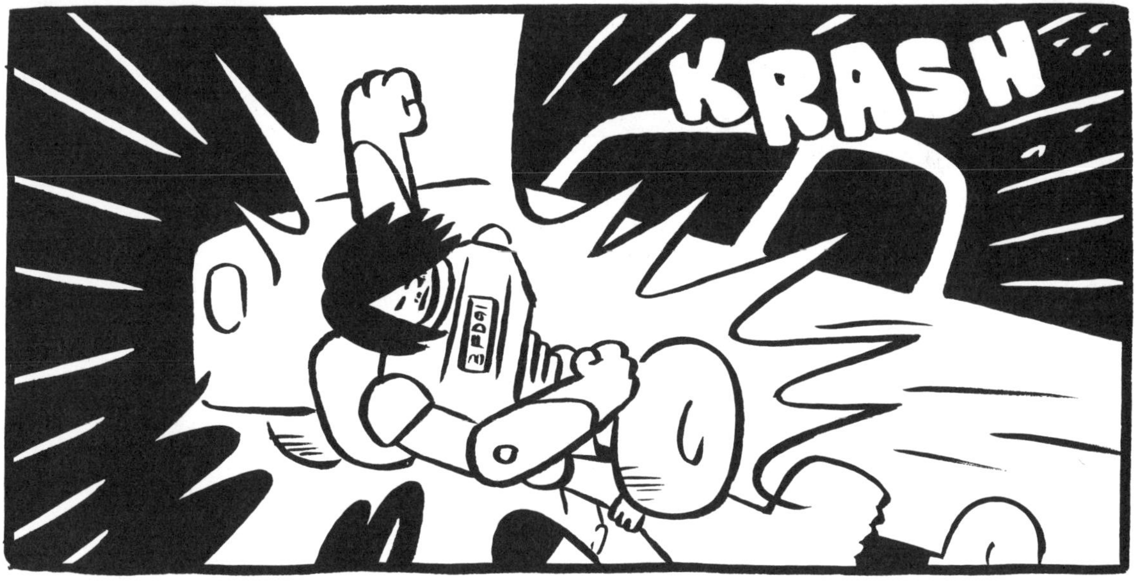
KRASH

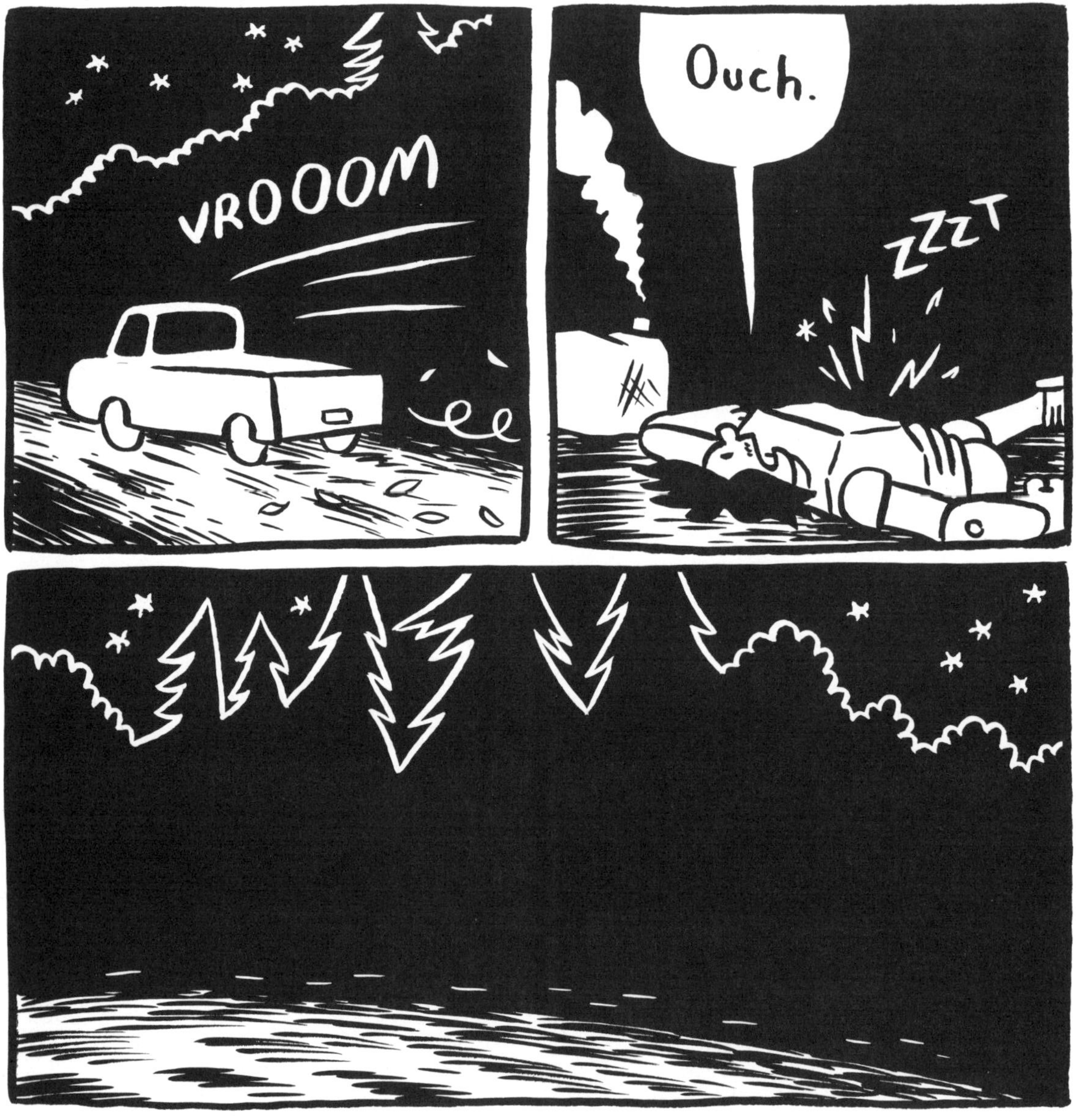
VROOOM
Ouch.
ZZZT

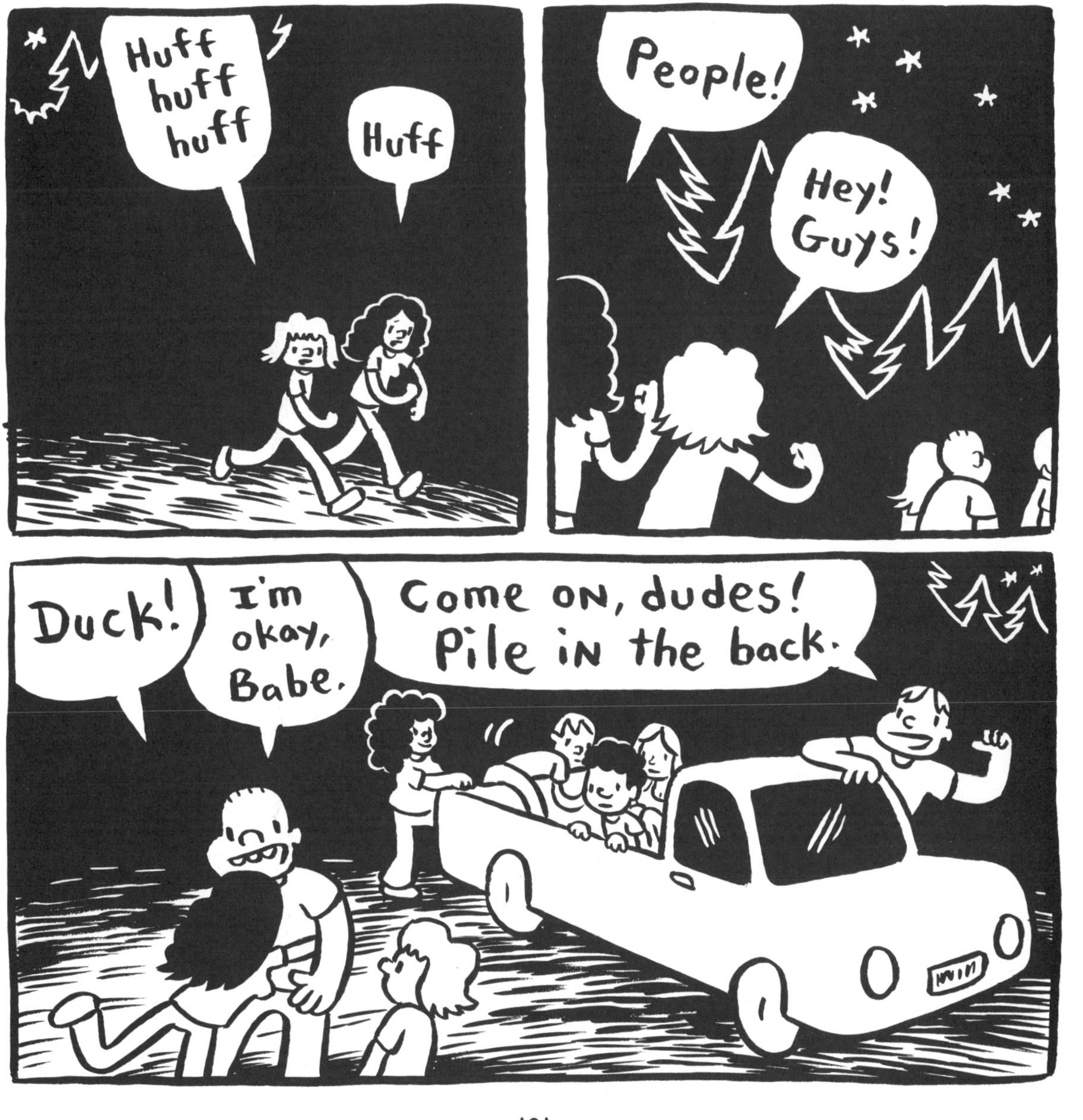
Huff huff huff huff
Huff
People!
Hey! Guys!
Duck!
I'm okay, Babe.
Come on, dudes! Pile in the back.

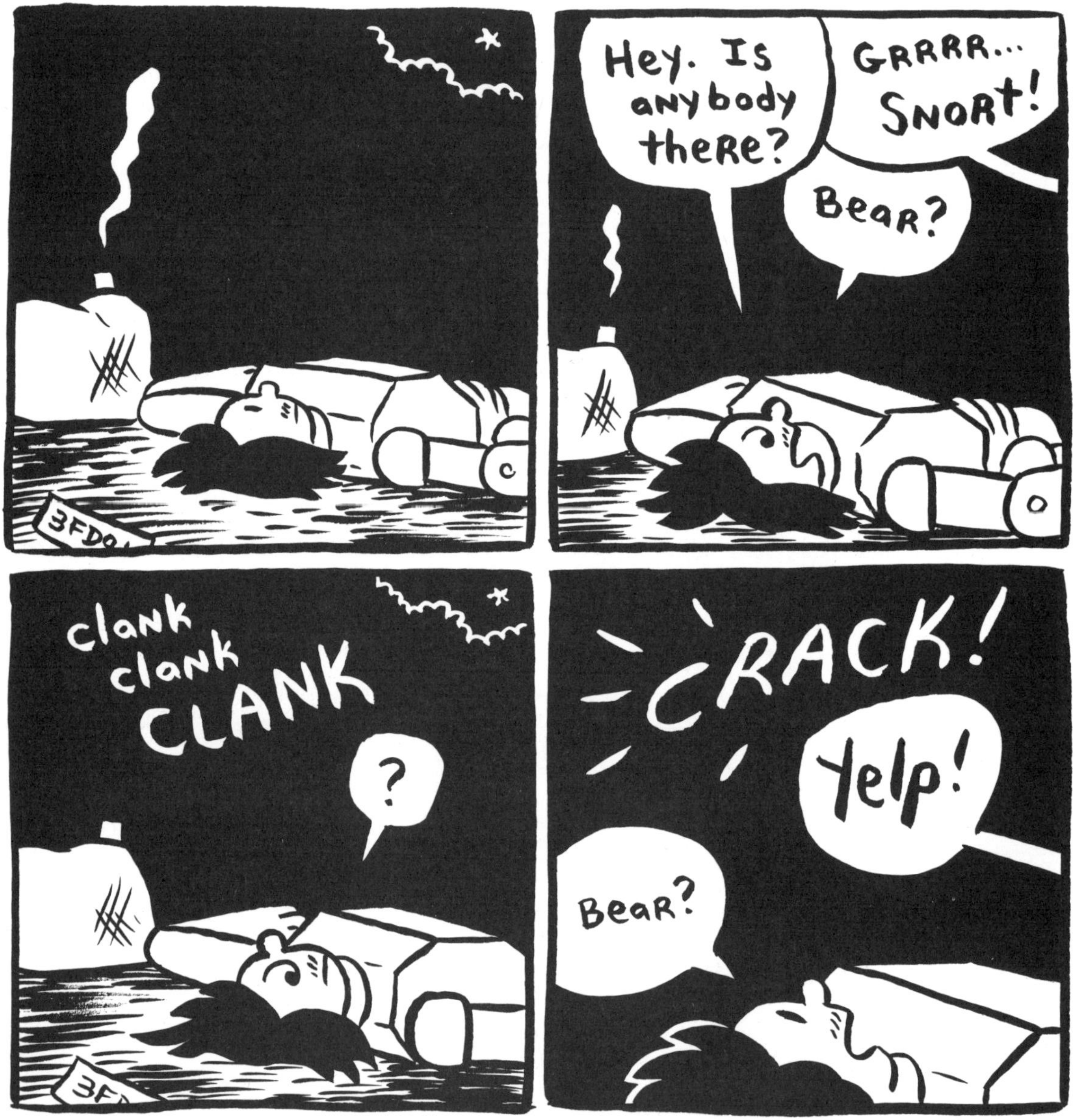
Hey. Is anybody there?
GRRRR... SNORT!
Bear?
clank clank CLANK
?
CRACK!
Yelp!
Bear?

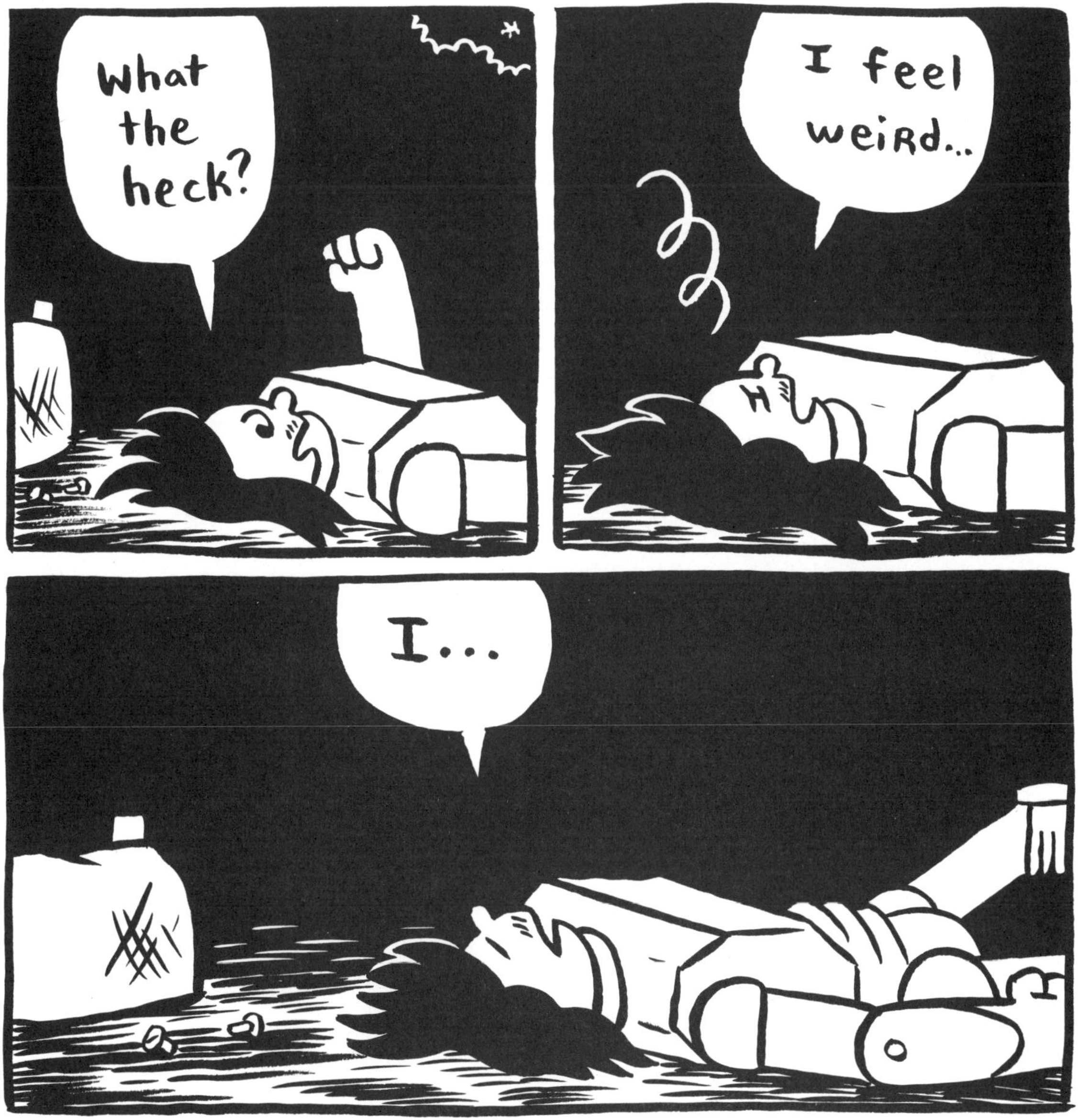
What the heck?
I feel weird...
I...

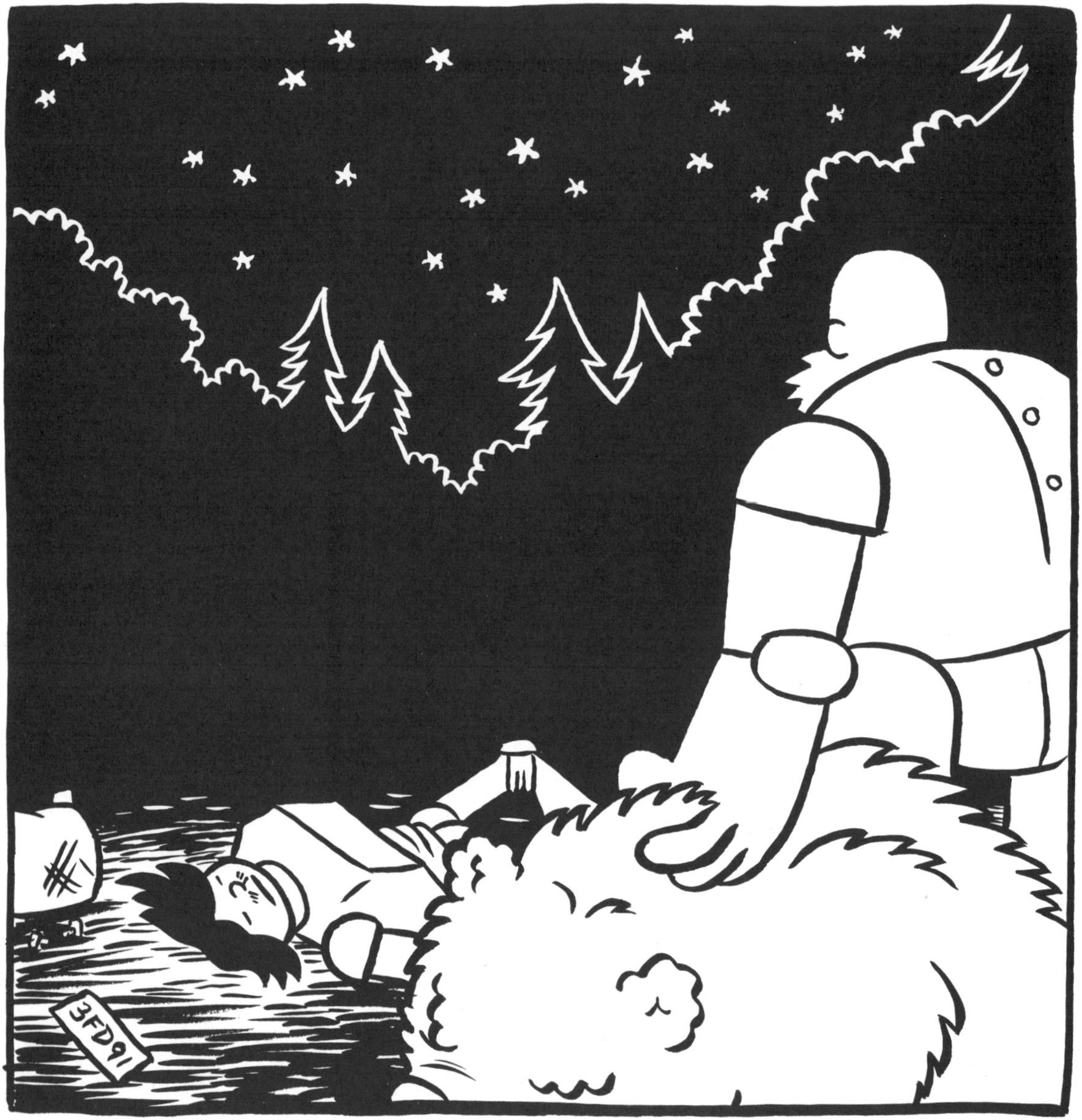
3FD91

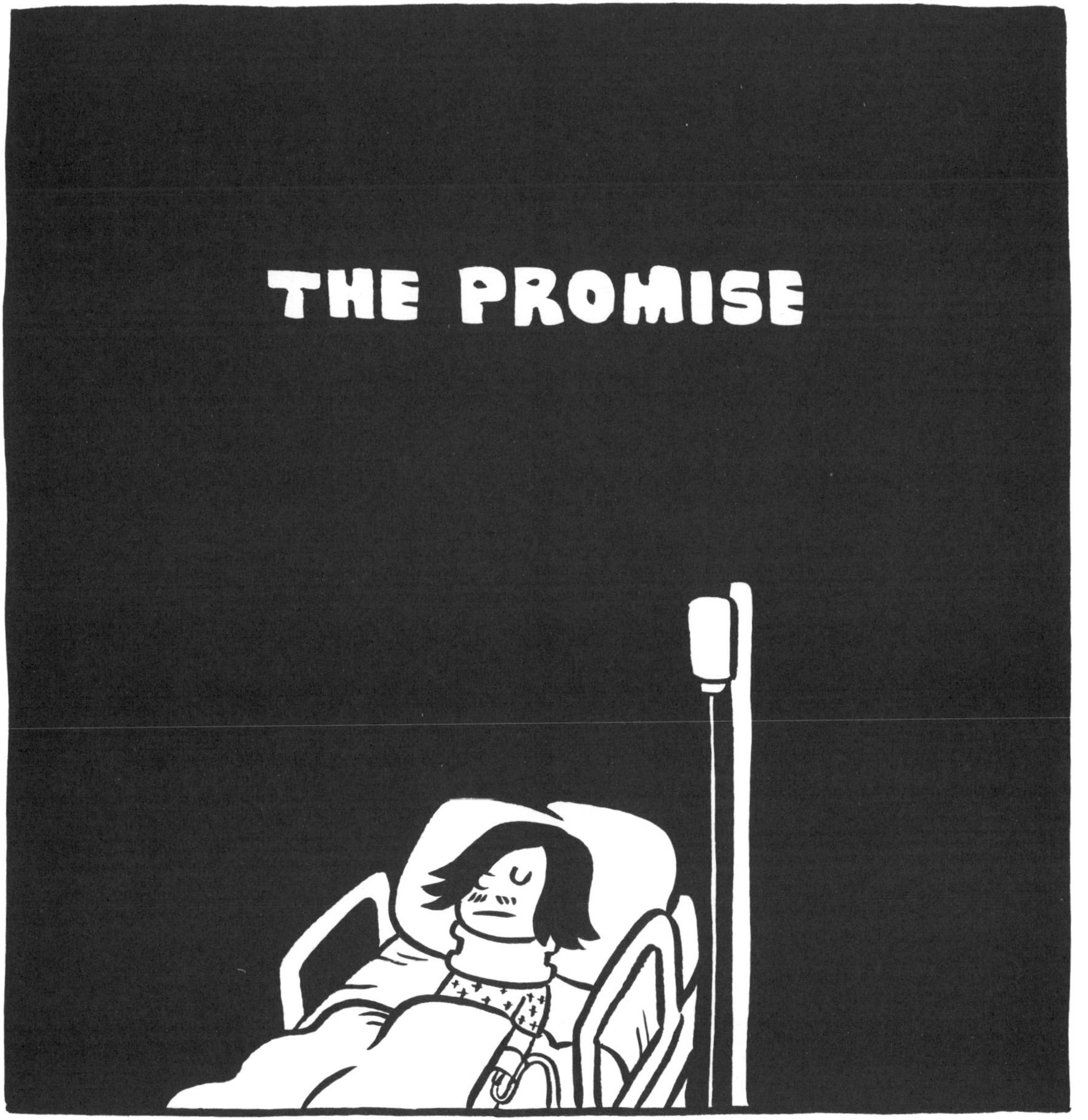
THE PROMISE

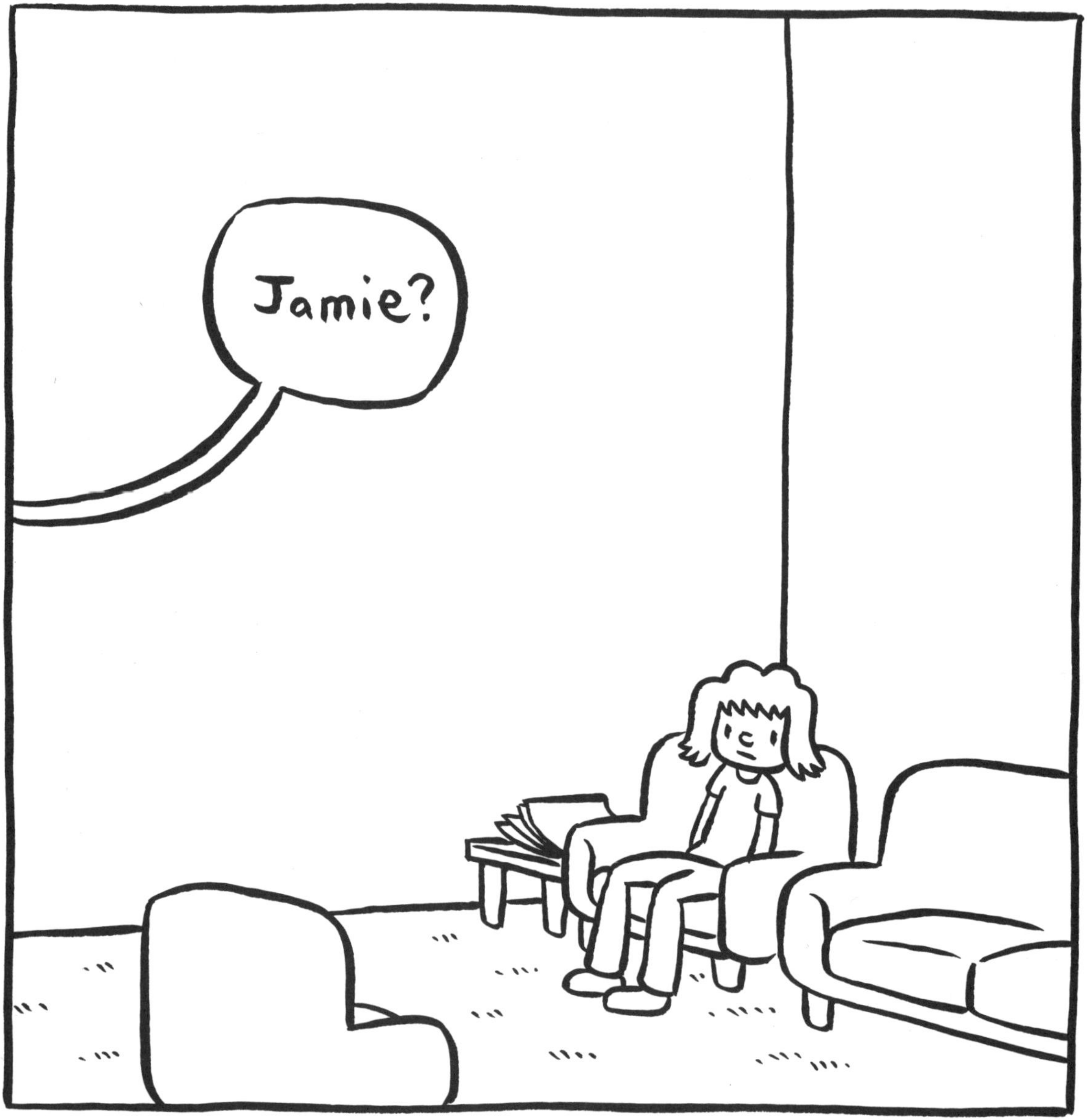
Jamie?

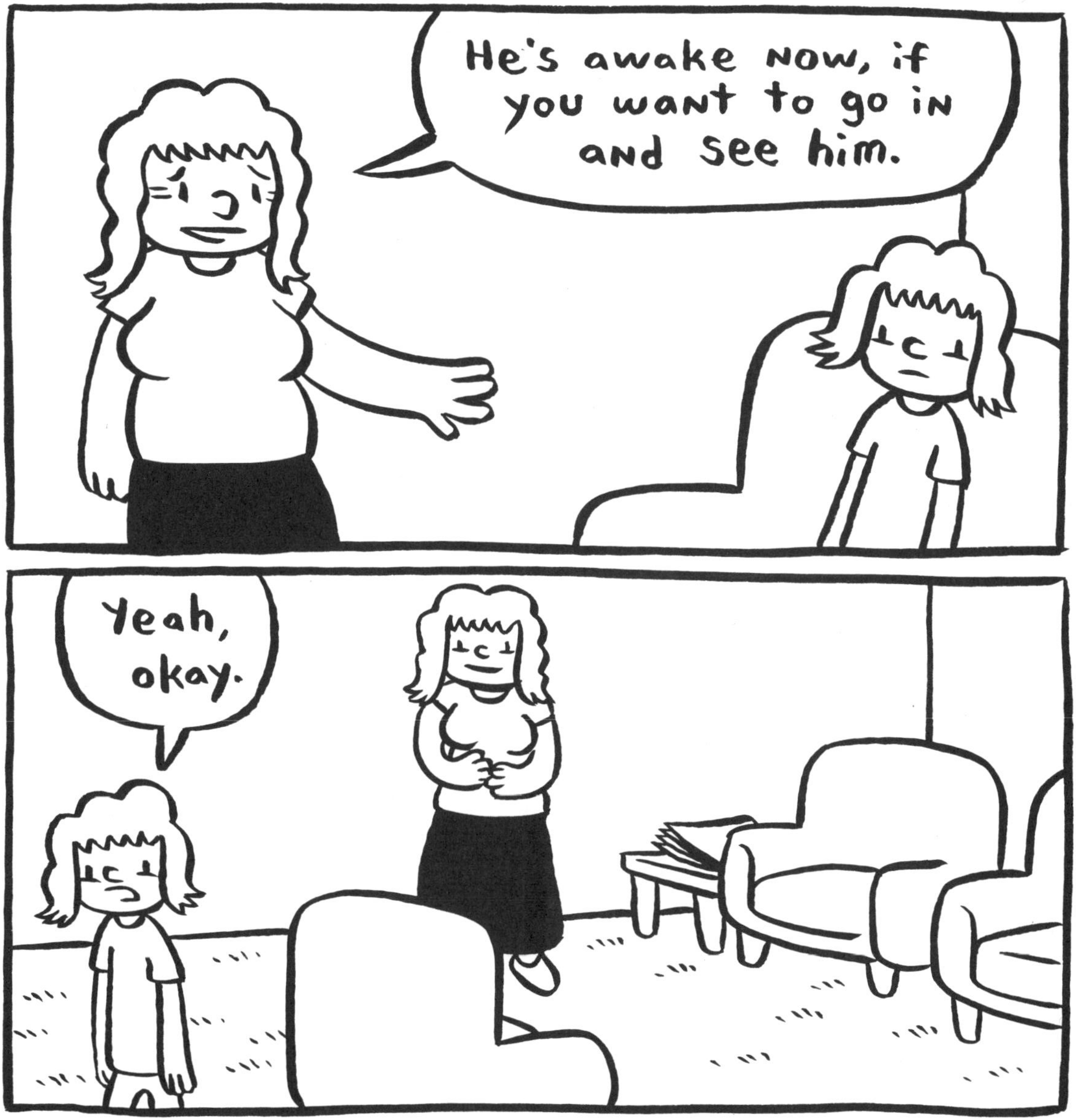
He's awake now, if you want to go in and see him.
Yeah, okay.

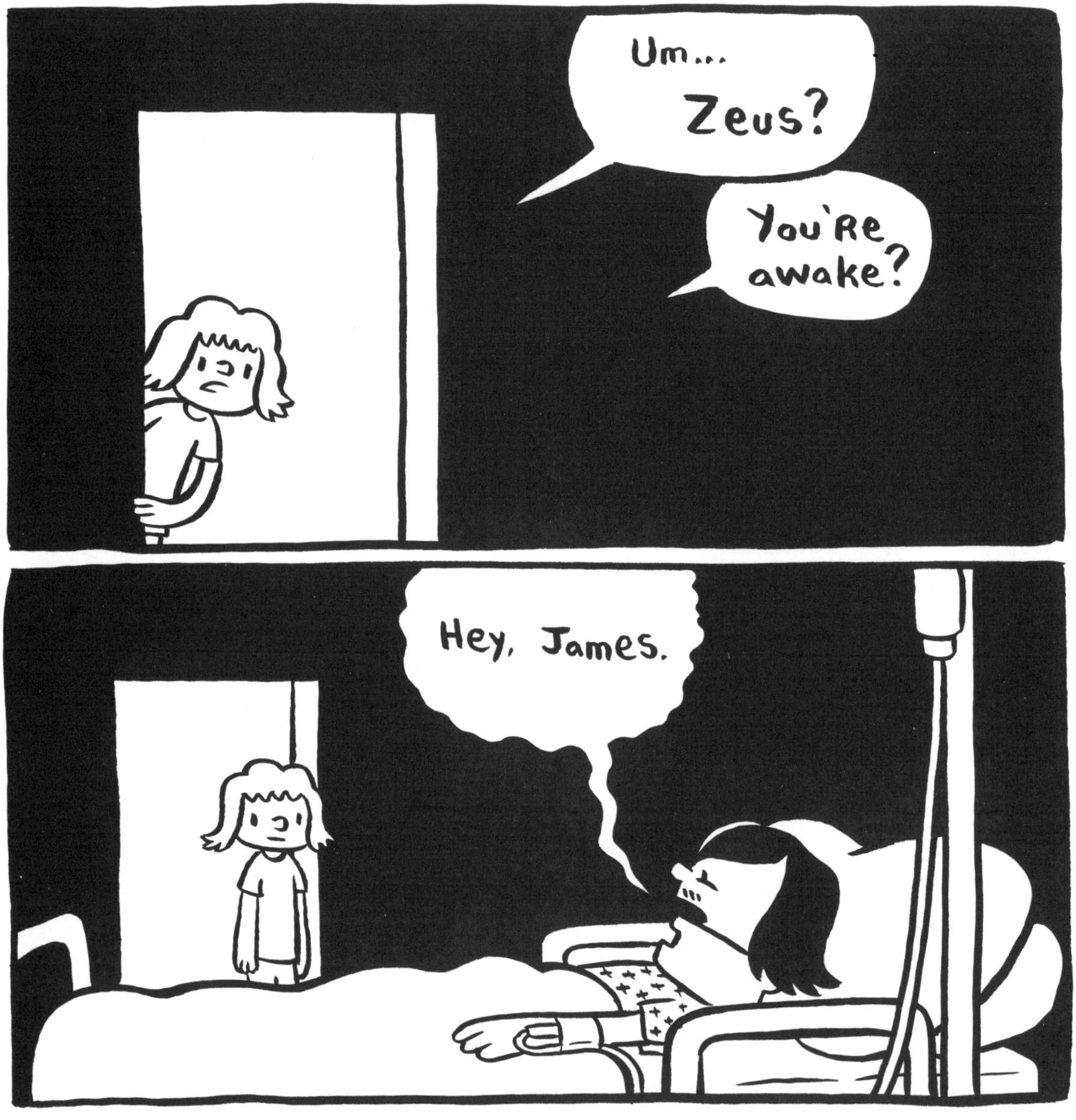
Um...
Zeus?
You're awake?
Hey, James.

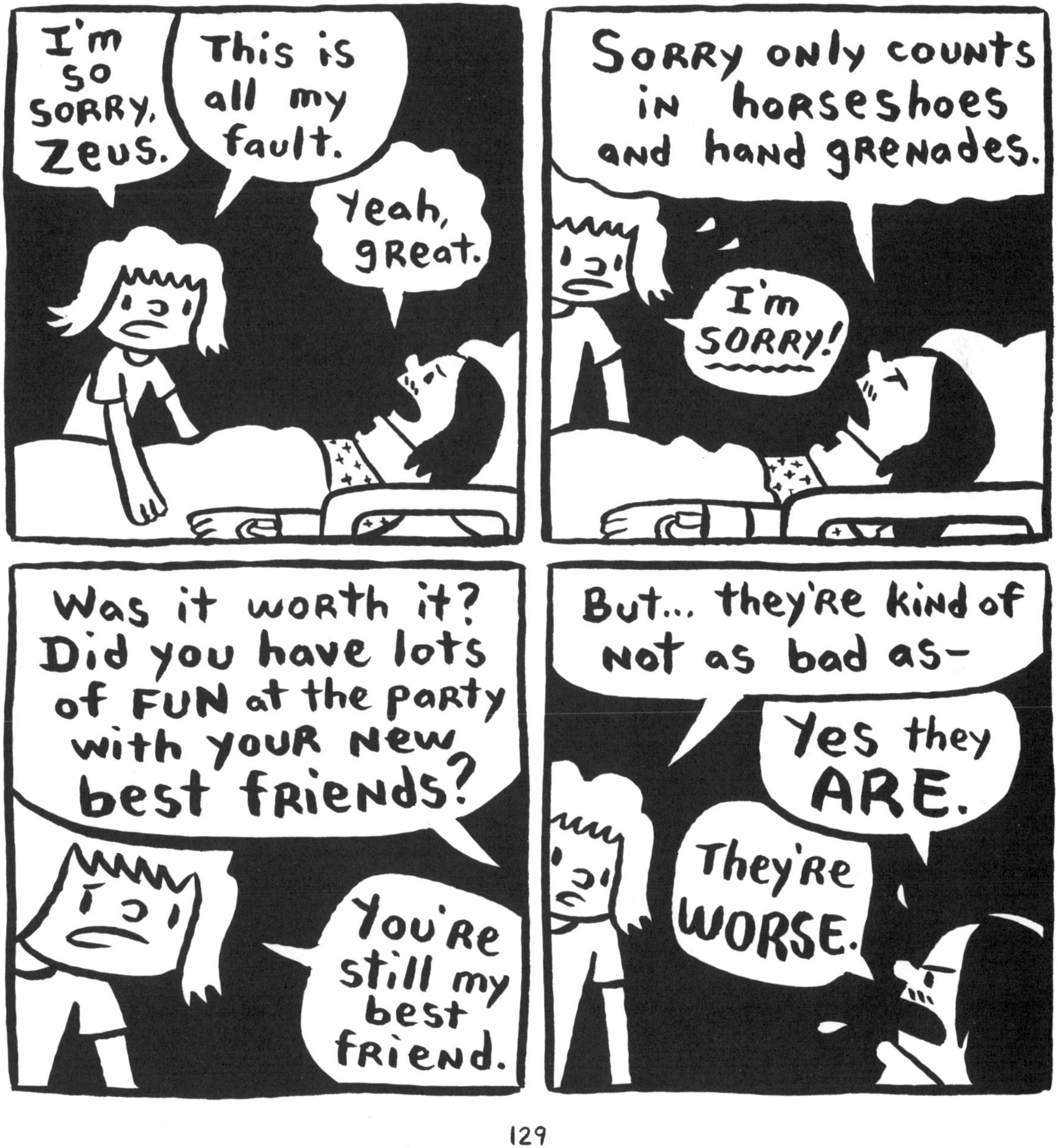
I'm so SORRY, ZEUS.
This is all my fault.
Yeah, great.
SORRY only counts in horseshoes and hand grenades.
I'm SORRY!
Was it worth it? Did you have lots of FUN at the party with YOUR New best friends?
You're still my best friend.
But... they're kind of not as bad as-
Yes they ARE.
They're WORSE.

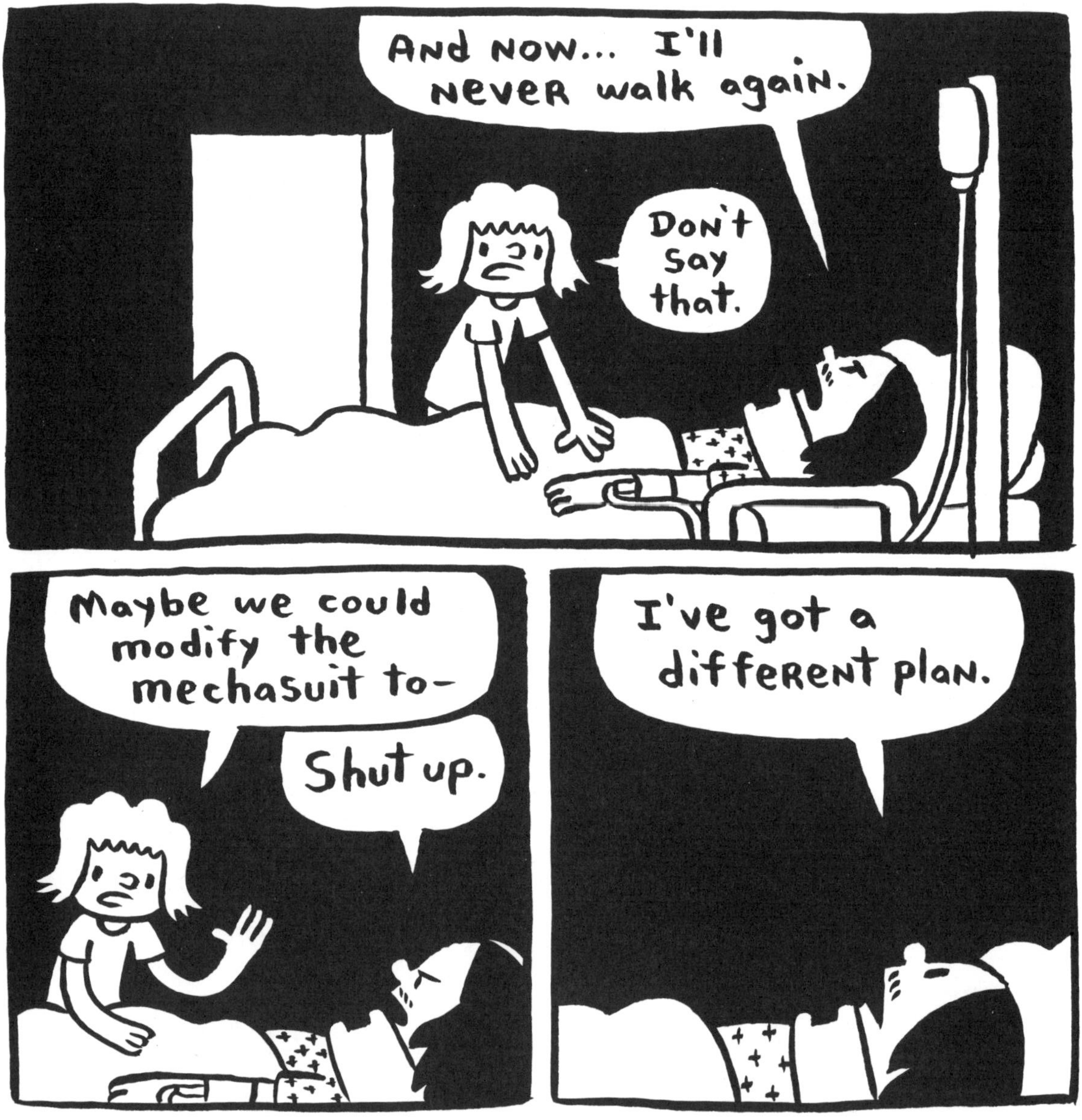
And now... I'll never walk again.
Don't say that.
Maybe we could modify the mechasuit to-
Shut up.
I've got a different plan.

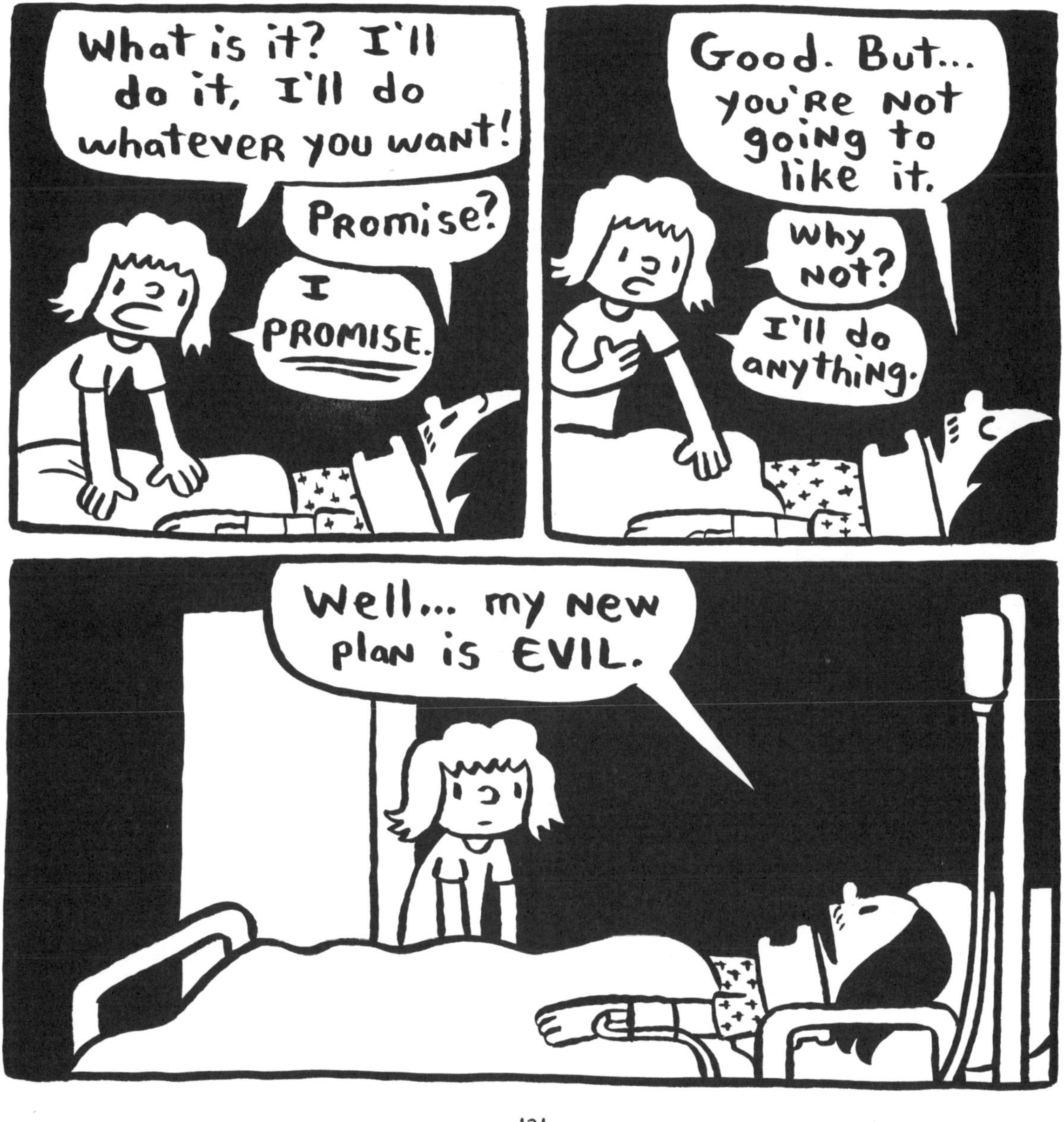
What is it? I'll do it, I'll do whatever you want!
Promise?
I PROMISE.
Good. But... you're not going to like it.
Why not?
I'll do anything.
Well... my new plan is EVIL.

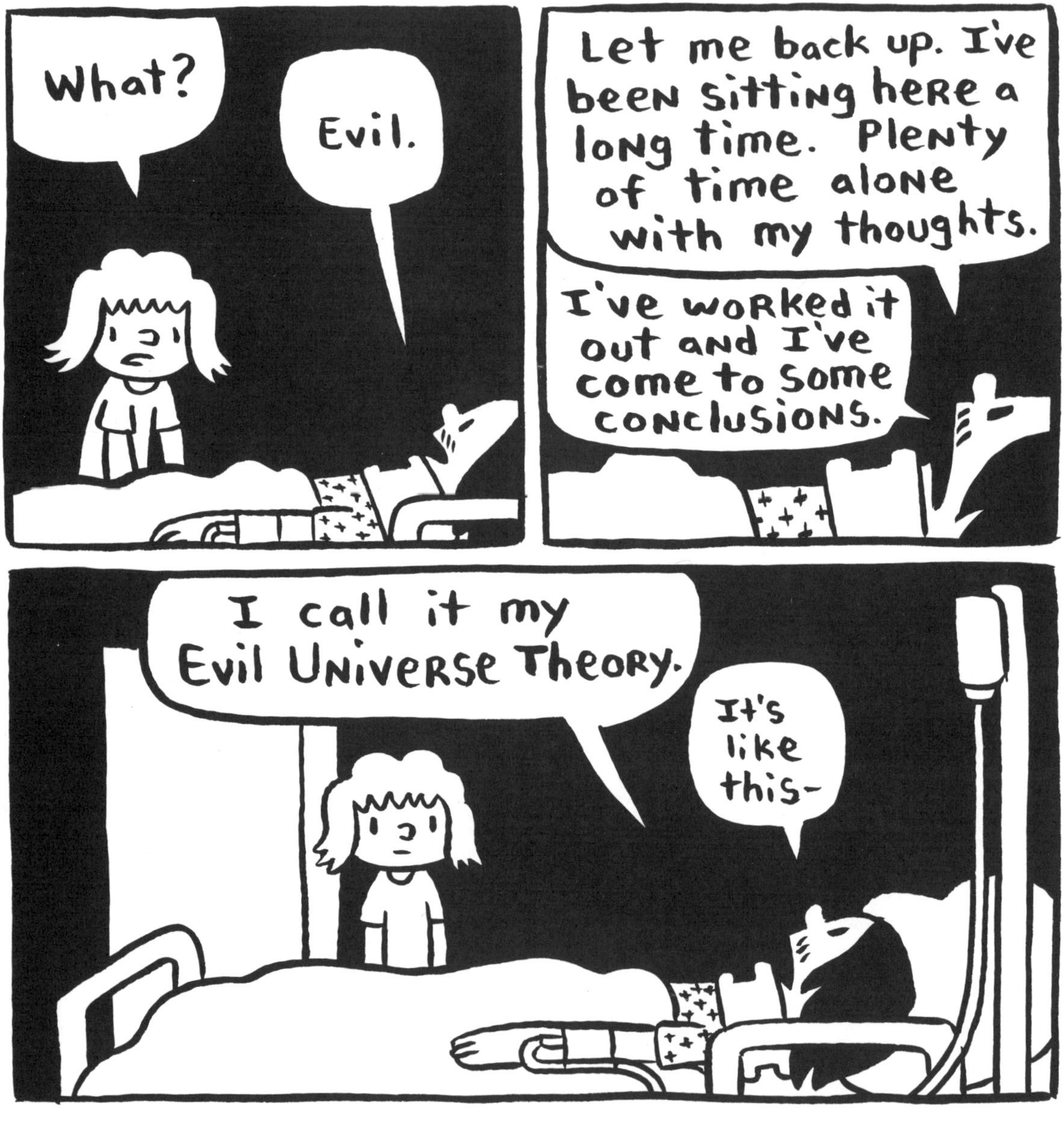
What?
Evil.
Let me back up. I've been sitting here a long time. Plenty of time alone with my thoughts.
I've worked it out and I've come to some conclusions.
I call it my Evil Universe Theory.
It's like this-

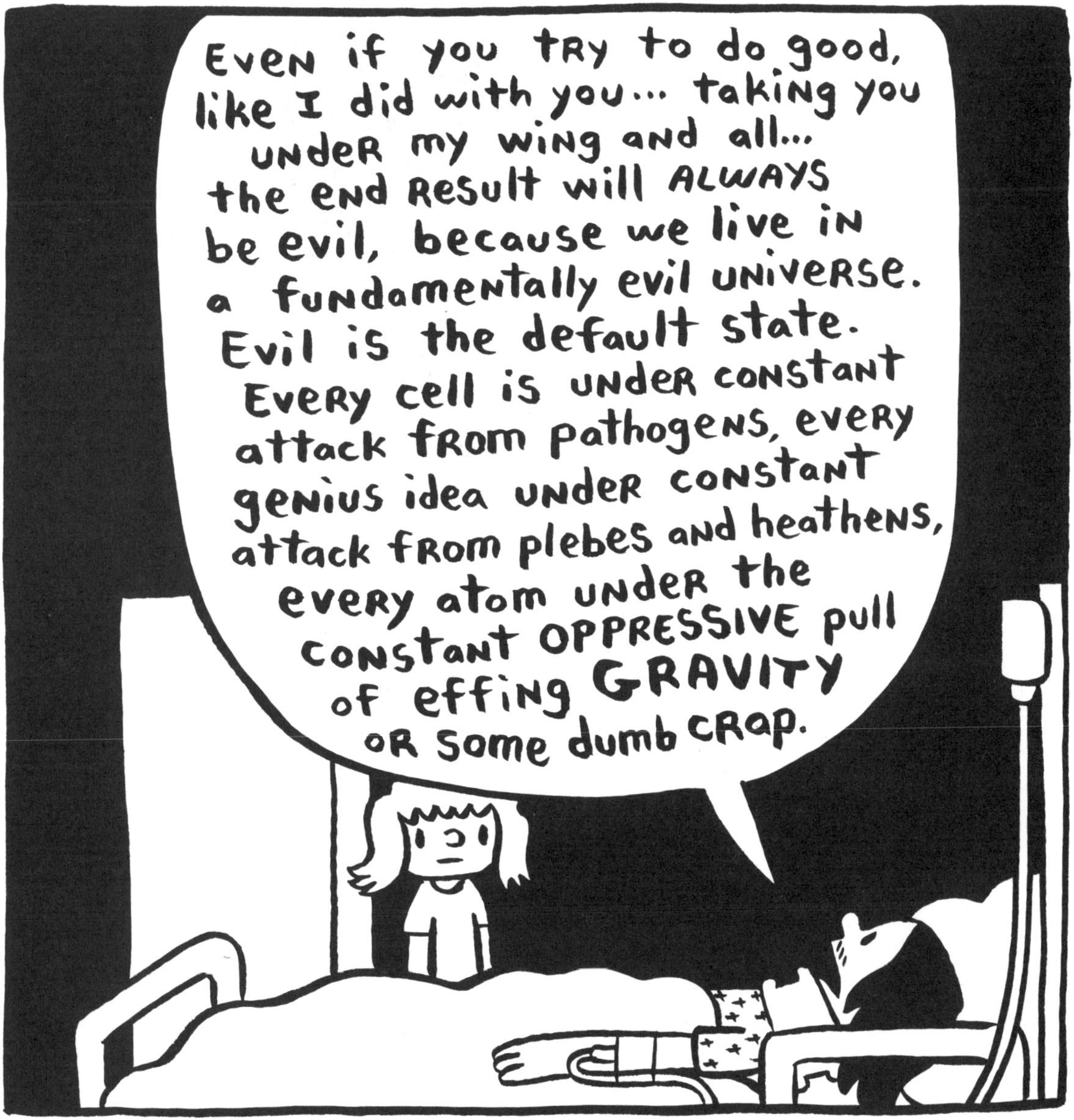
Even if you try to do good, like I did with you... taking you under my wing and all... the end result will ALWAYS be evil, because we live in a fundamentally evil universe. Evil is the default state. Every cell is under constant attack from pathogens, every genius idea under constant attack from plebes and heathens, every atom under the constant OPPRESSIVE pull of effing GRAVITY or some dumb crap.

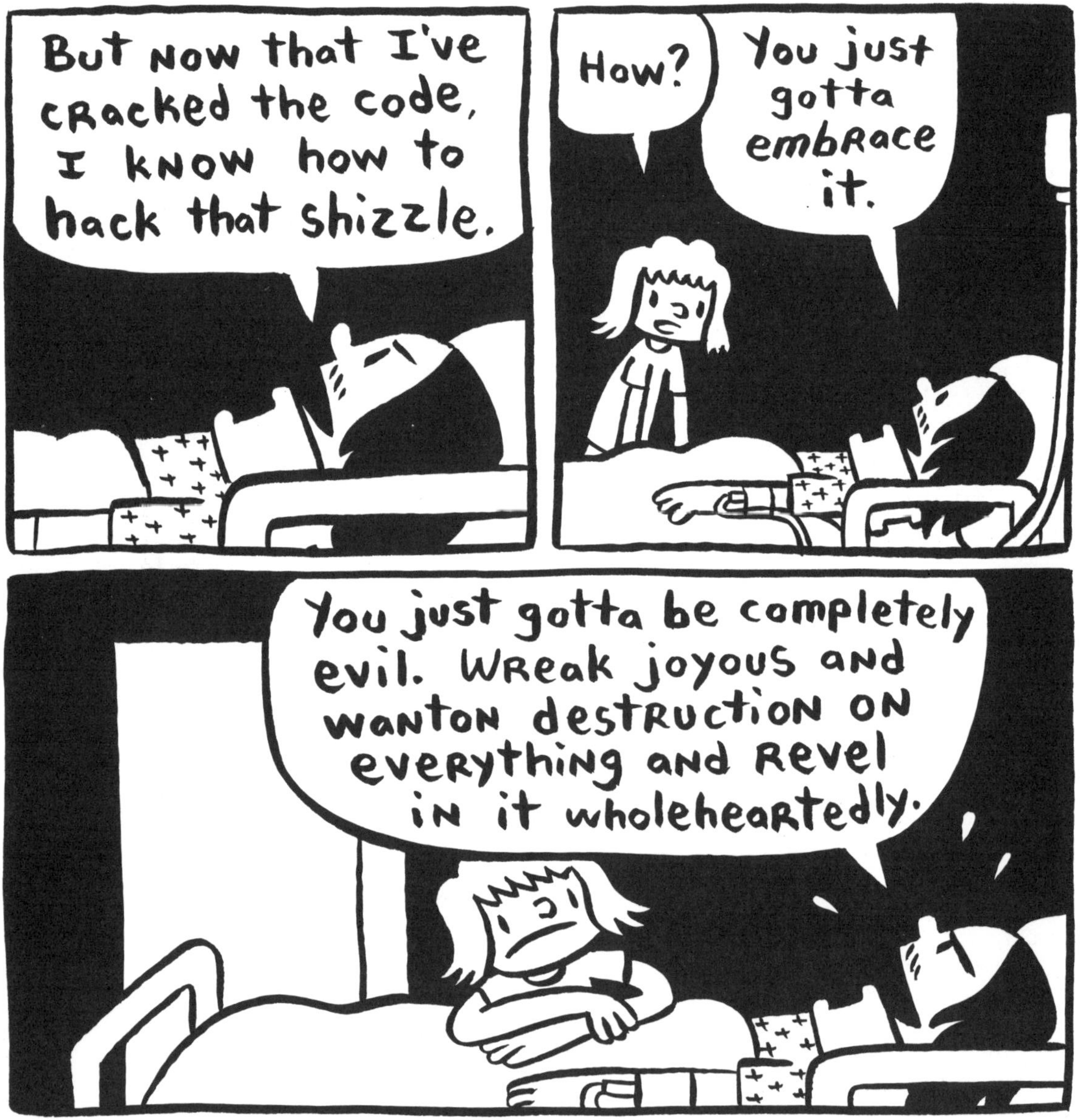
But now that I've cracked the code, I know how to hack that shizzle.
How?
You just gotta embrace it.
You just gotta be completely evil. Wreak joyous and wanton destruction on everything and revel in it wholeheartedly.

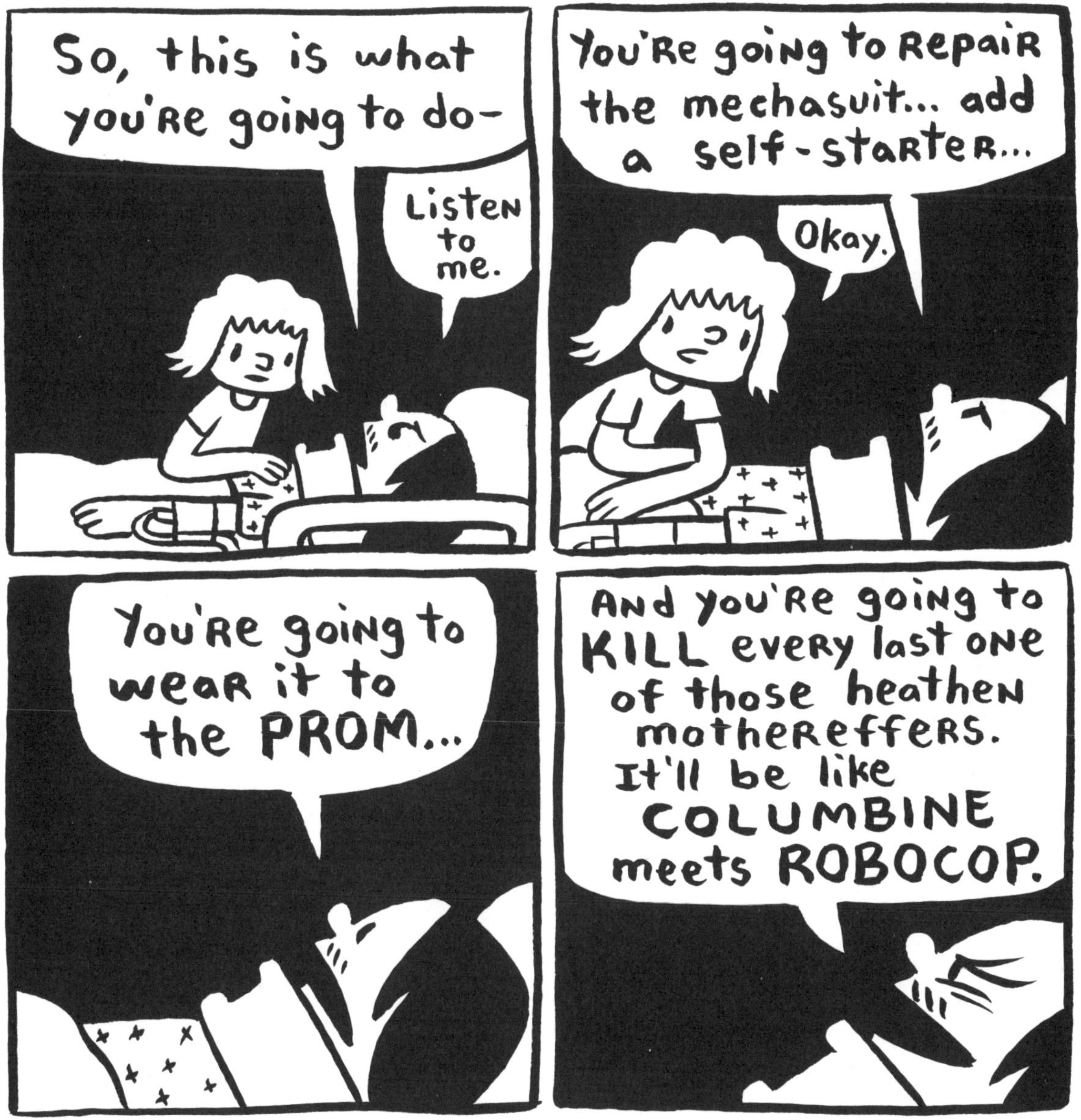
So, this is what you're going to do-
Listen to me.
You're going to repair the mechasuit... add a self-starter...
Okay.
You're going to wear it to the PROM...
And you're going to KILL every last one of those heathen mothereffers. It'll be like COLUMBINE meets ROBOCOP.

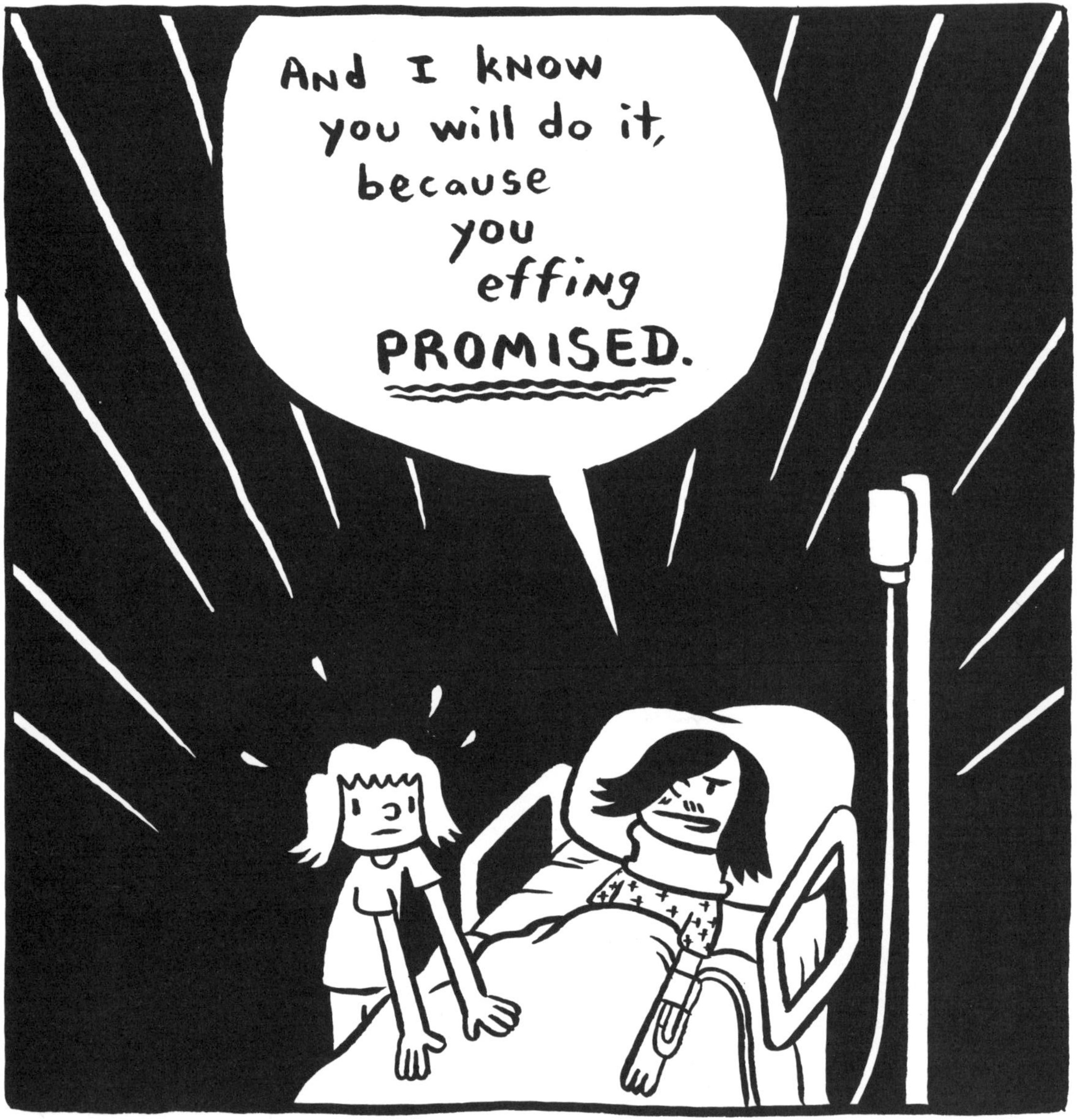
And I know you will do it, because you effing PROMISED.

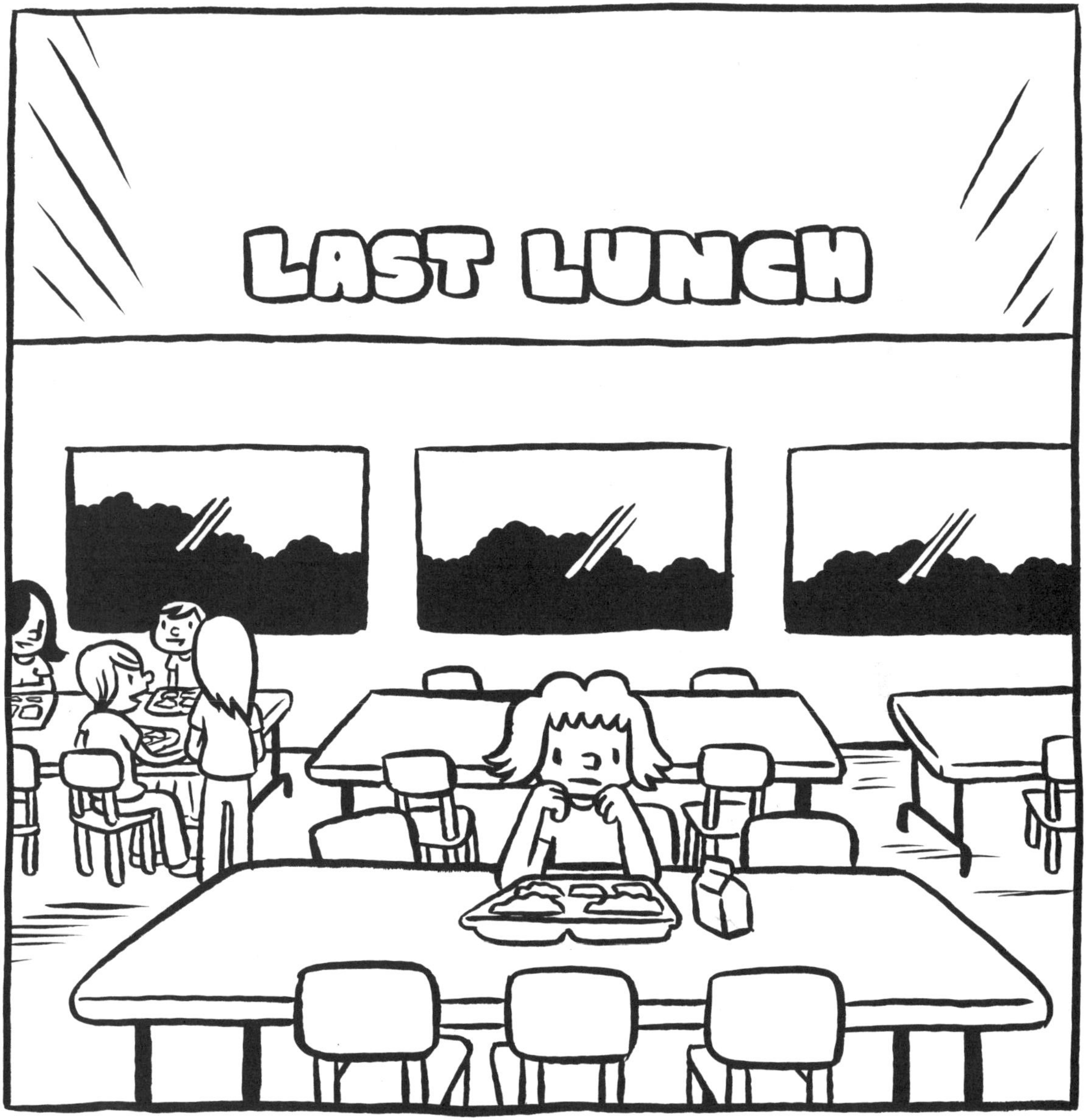
LAST LUNCH

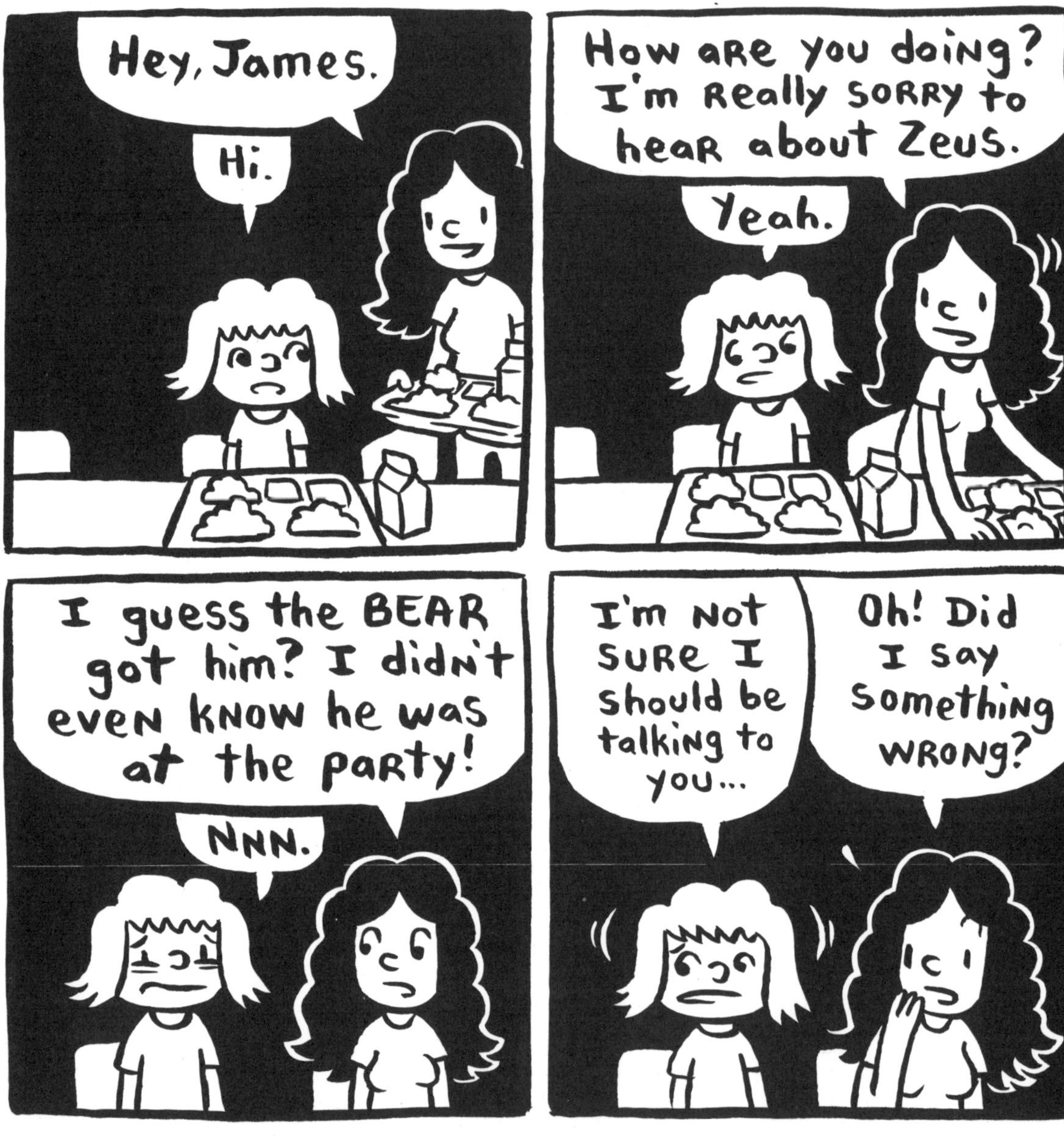
Hey, James.
Hi.
How are you doing? I'm really sorry to hear about Zeus.
Yeah.
I guess the BEAR got him? I didn't even know he was at the party!
NNN.
I'm not sure I should be talking to you...
Oh! Did I say something wrong?

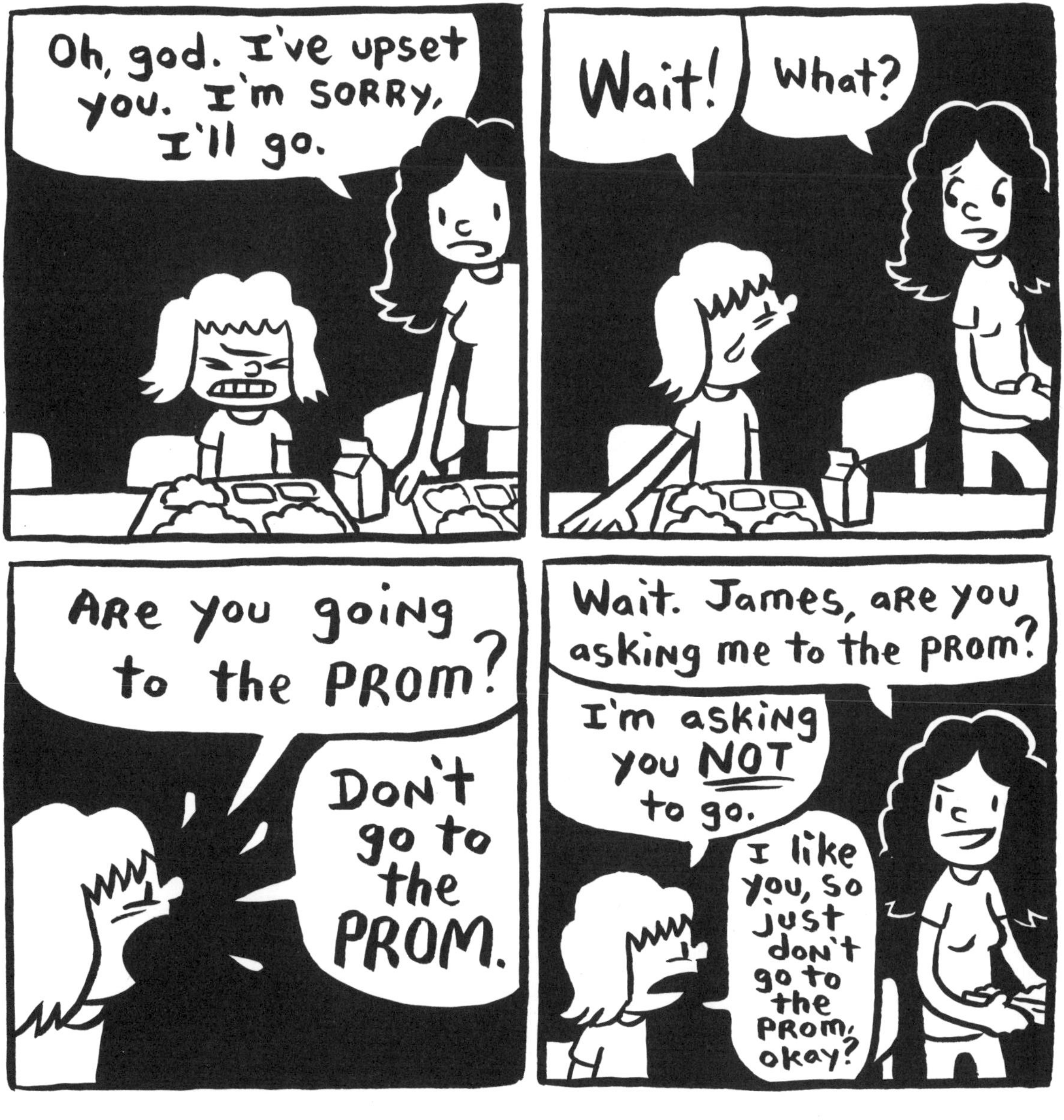
Oh, god. I've upset you. I'm SORRY, I'll go.
Wait!
What?
ARE you going to the PROM?
DON'T go to the PROM.
Wait. James, are you asking me to the PROM?
I'm asking you NOT to go.
I like you, so just don't go to the PROM, okay?

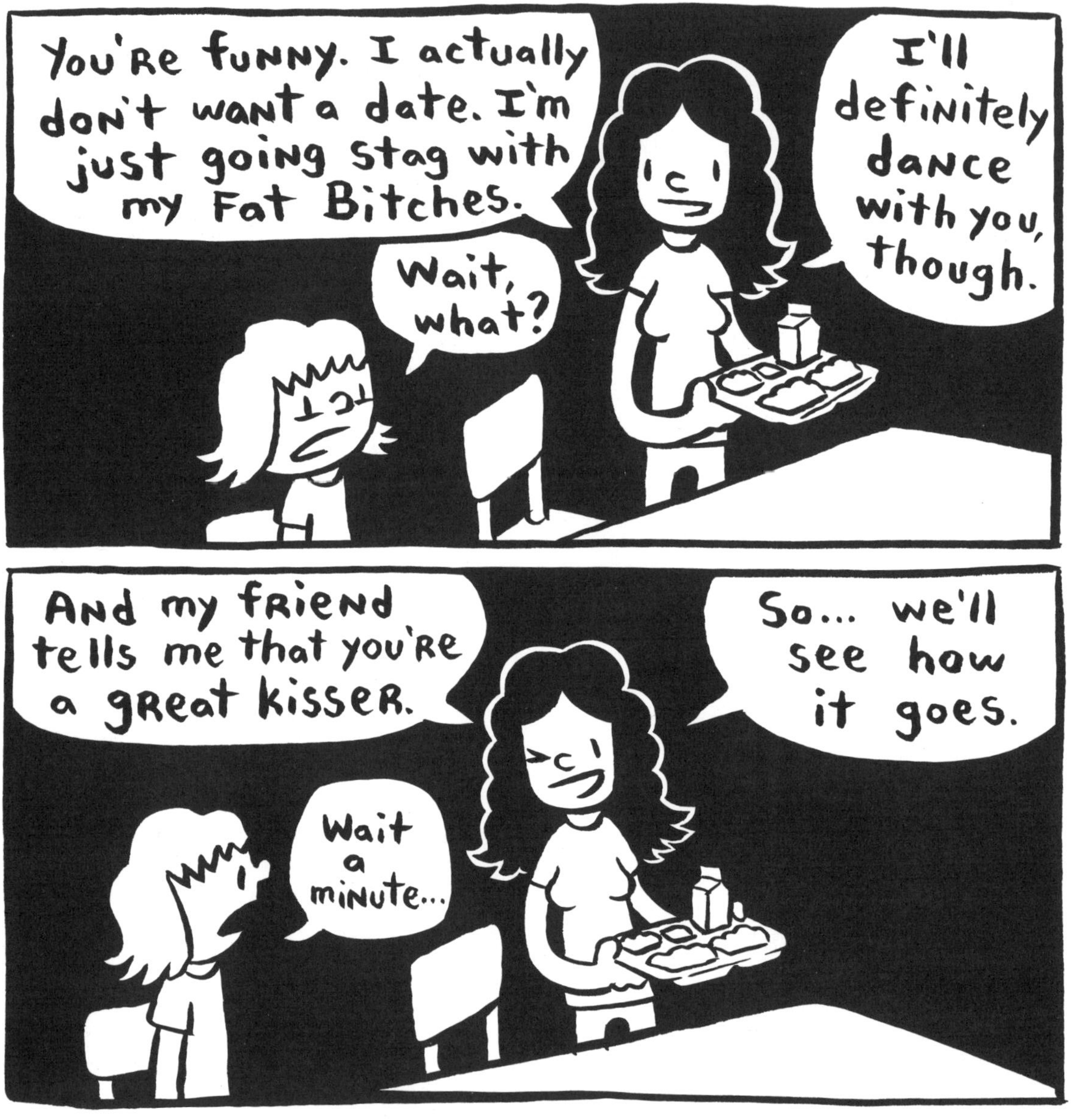
You're funny. I actually don't want a date. I'm just going stag with my Fat Bitches.
I'll definitely dance with you, though.
Wait, what?
And my friend tells me that you're a great kisser.
So... we'll see how it goes.
Wait a minute...

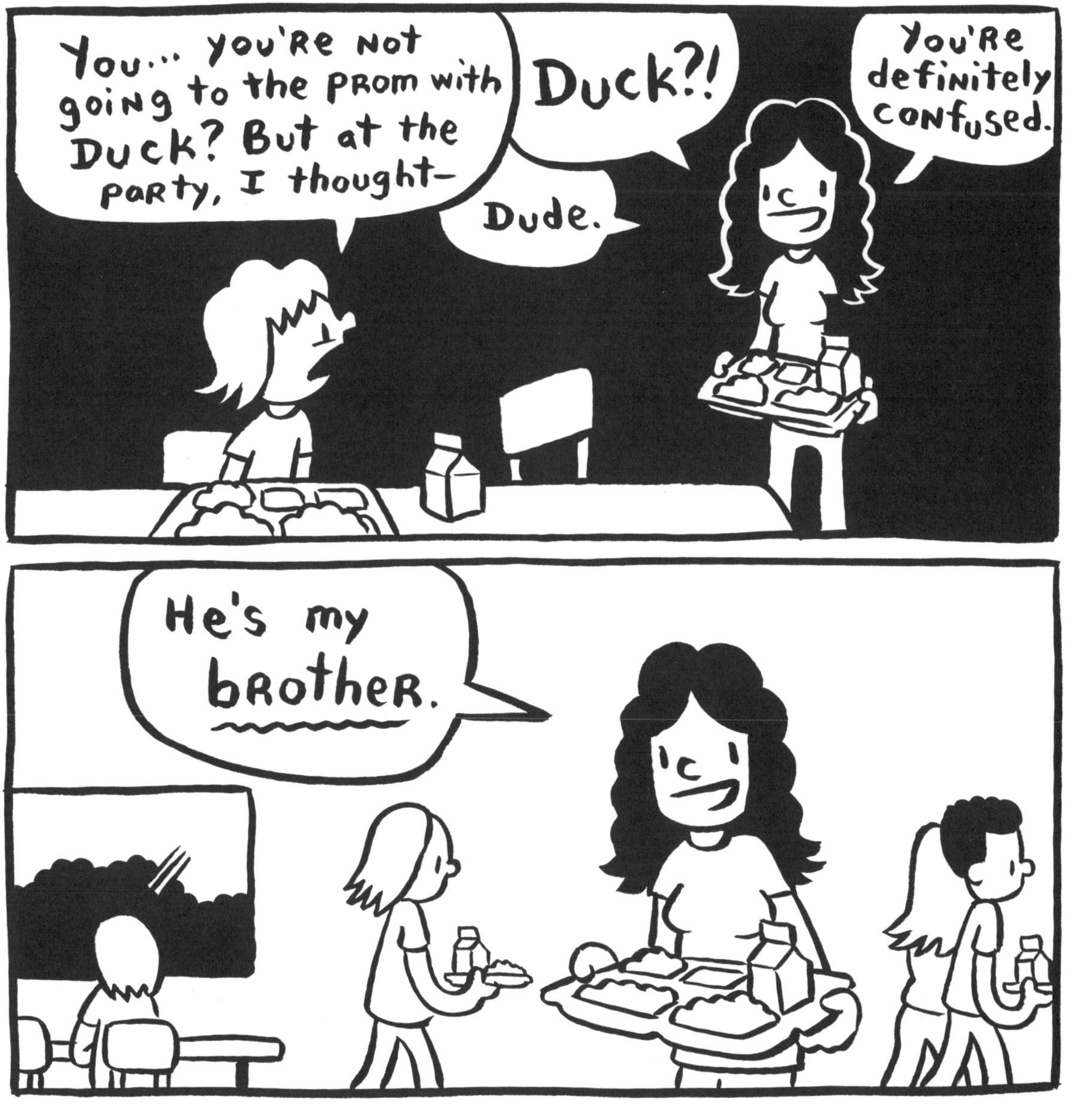
You... you're not going to the prom with Duck? But at the party, I thought–
Duck?!
Dude.
You're definitely confused.
He's my brother.

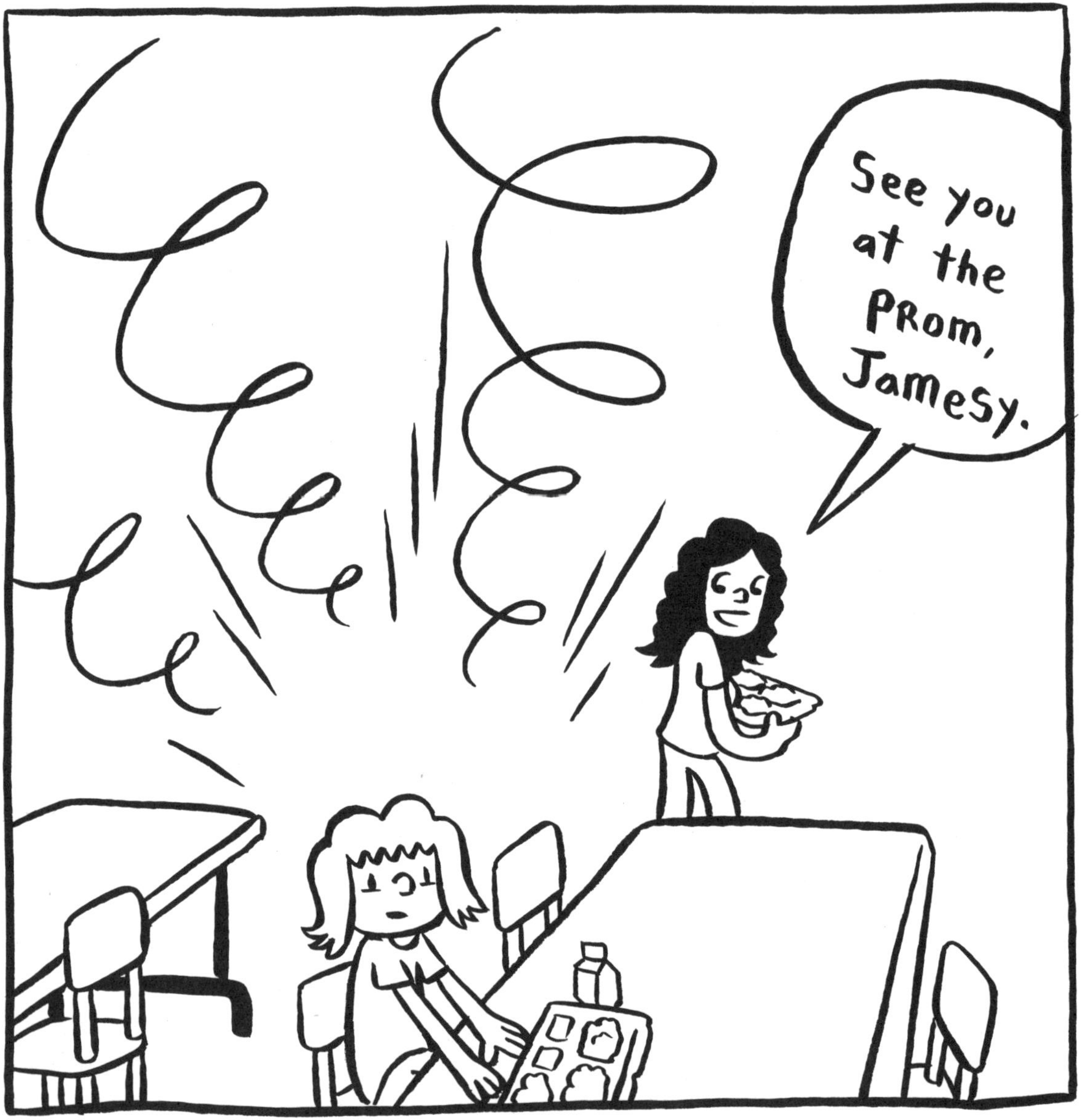
See you at the prom, Jamesy.

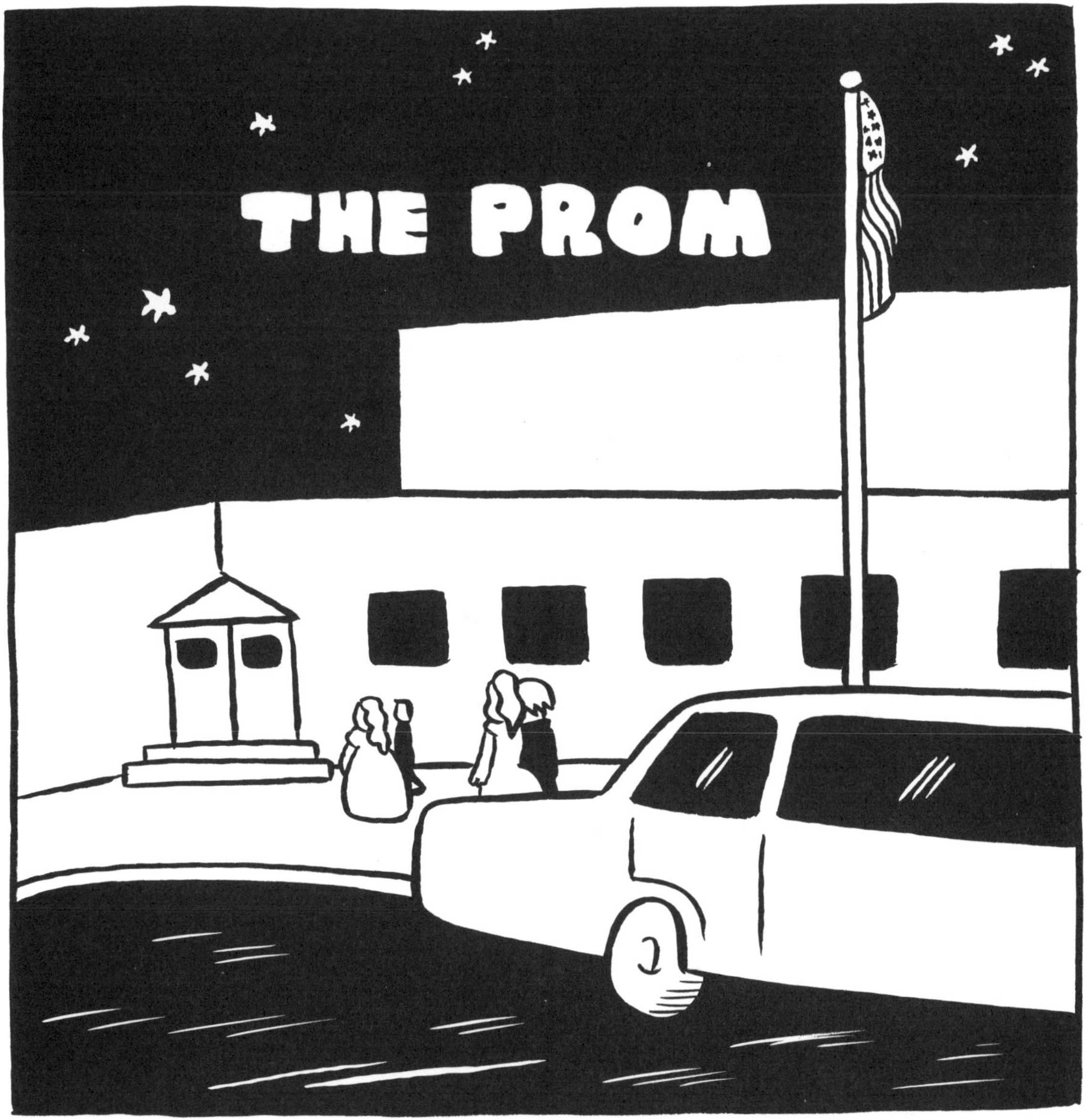
THE PROM

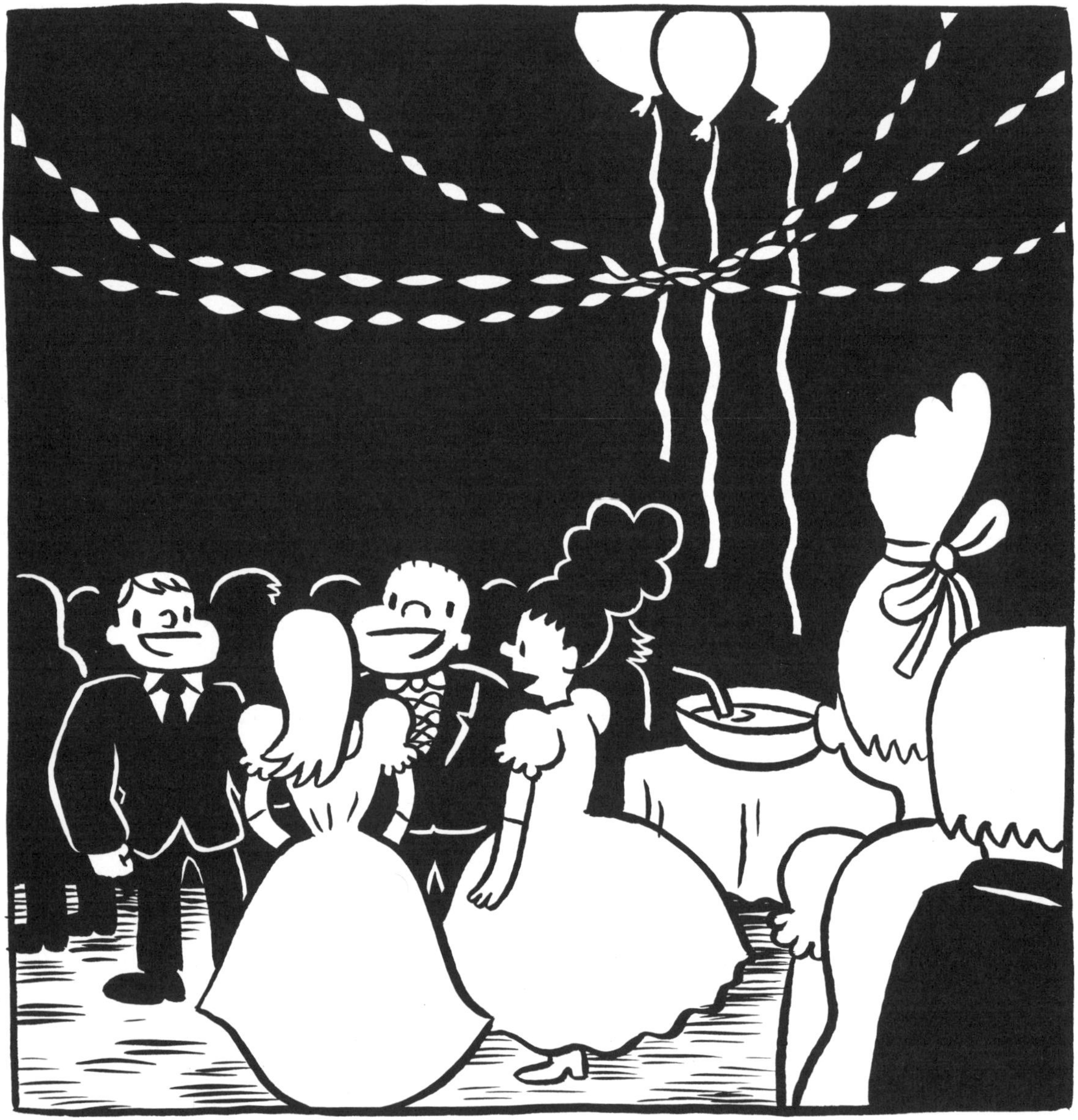

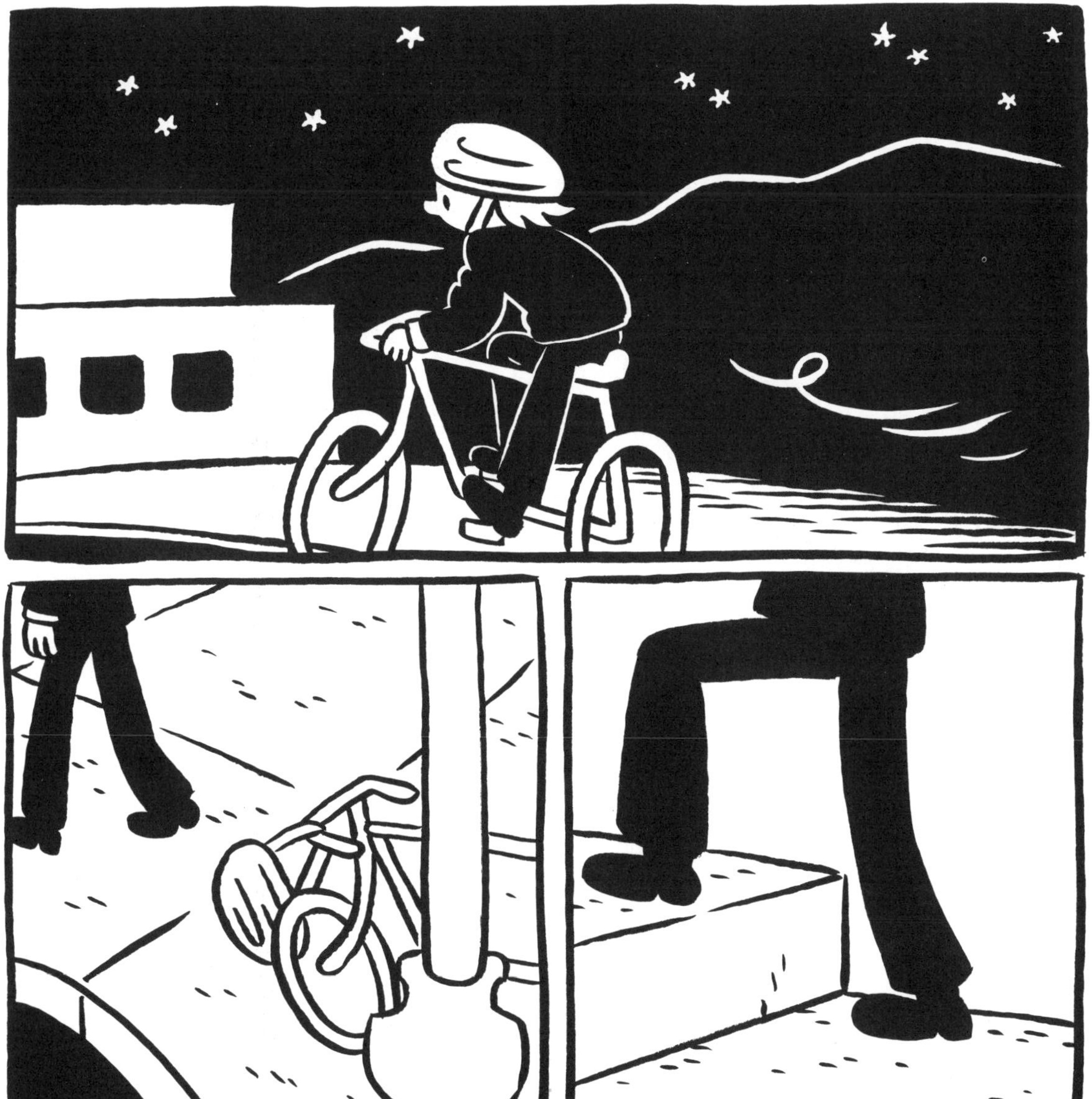

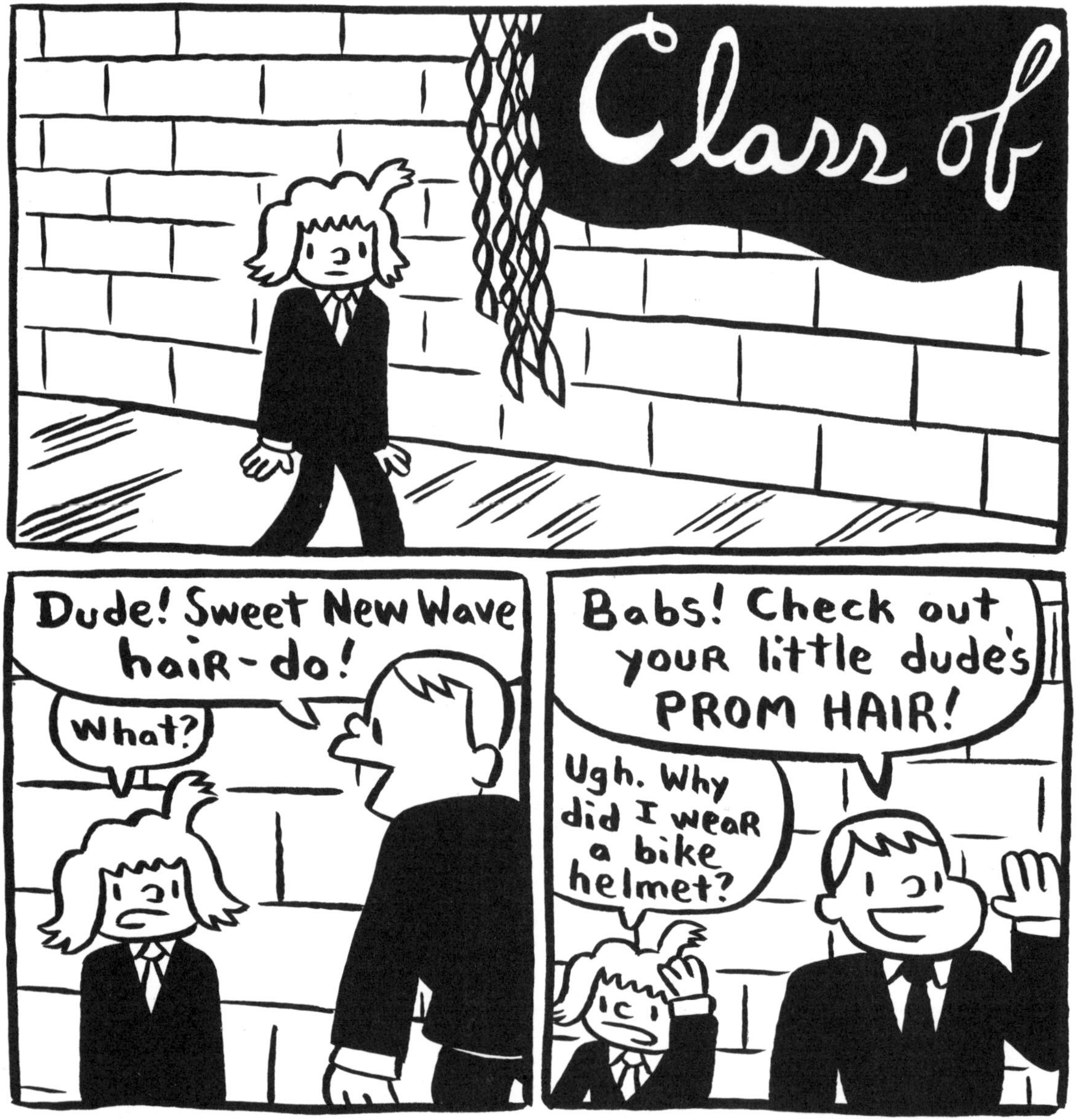
Class of
Dude! Sweet New Wave hair-do!
What?
Babs! Check out your little dude's PROM HAIR!
Ugh. Why did I wear a bike helmet?

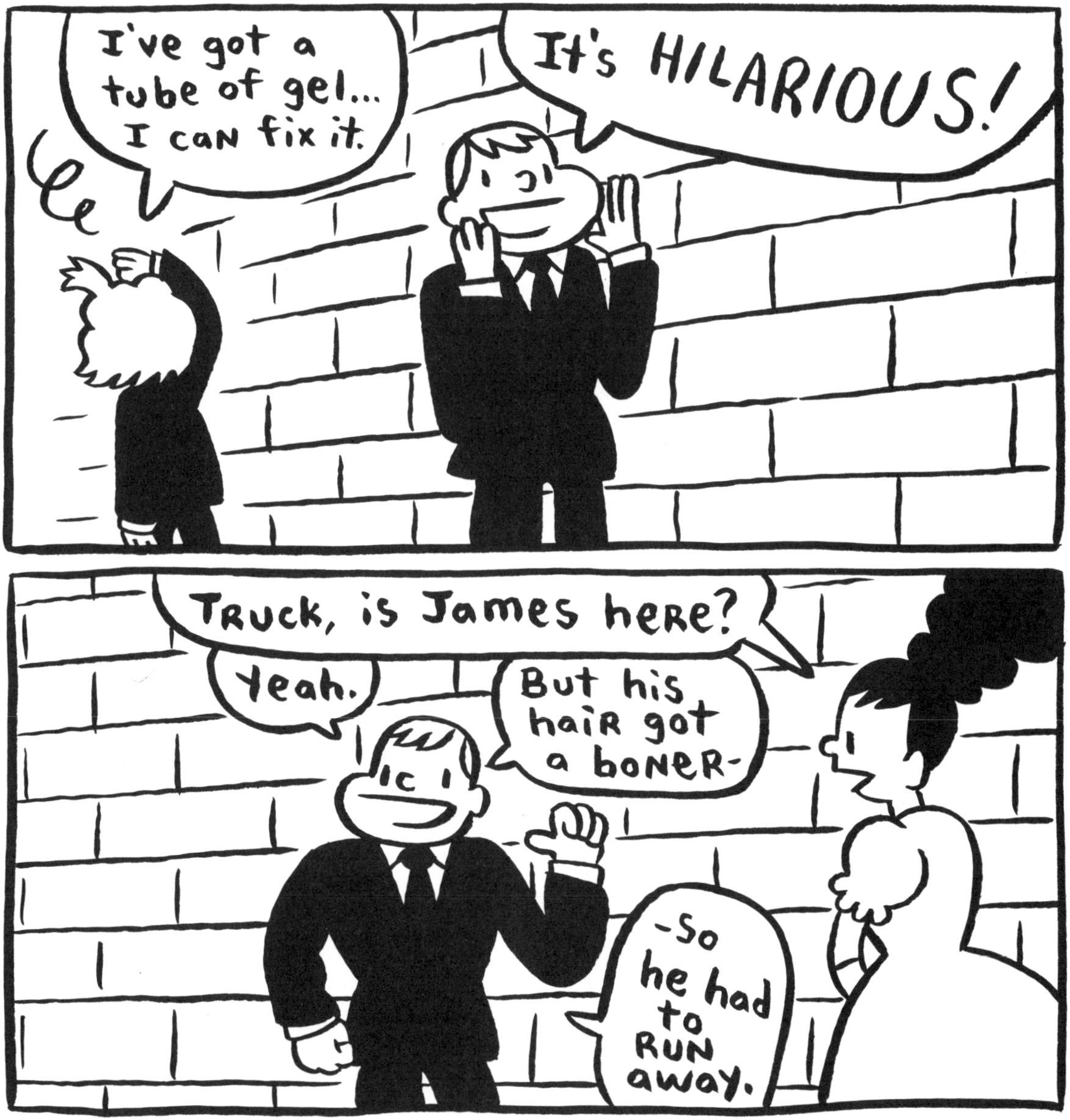
I've got a tube of gel... I can fix it.
It's HILARIOUS!
Truck, is James here?
Yeah.
But his hair got a boner-
-So he had to RUN away.

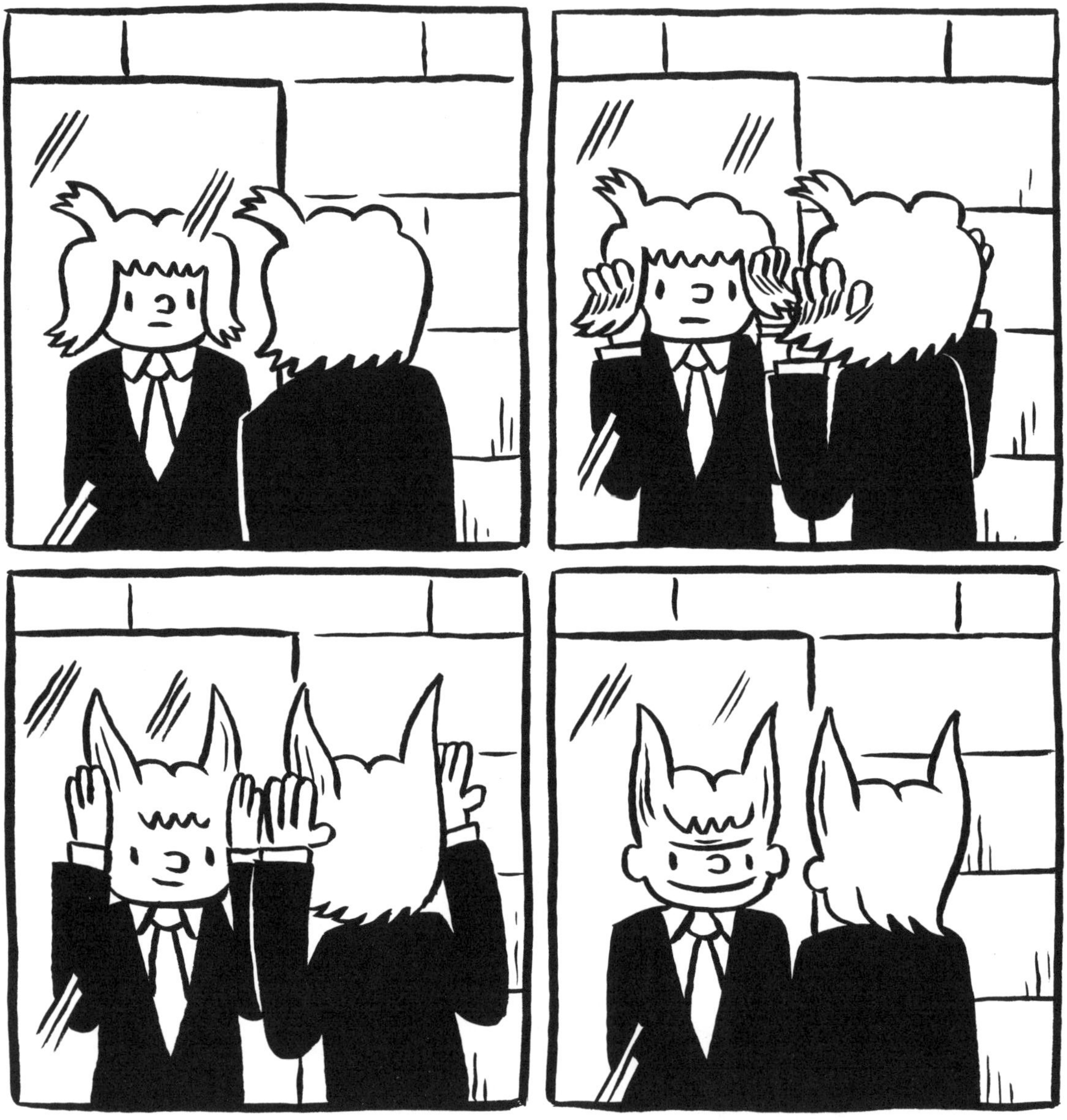

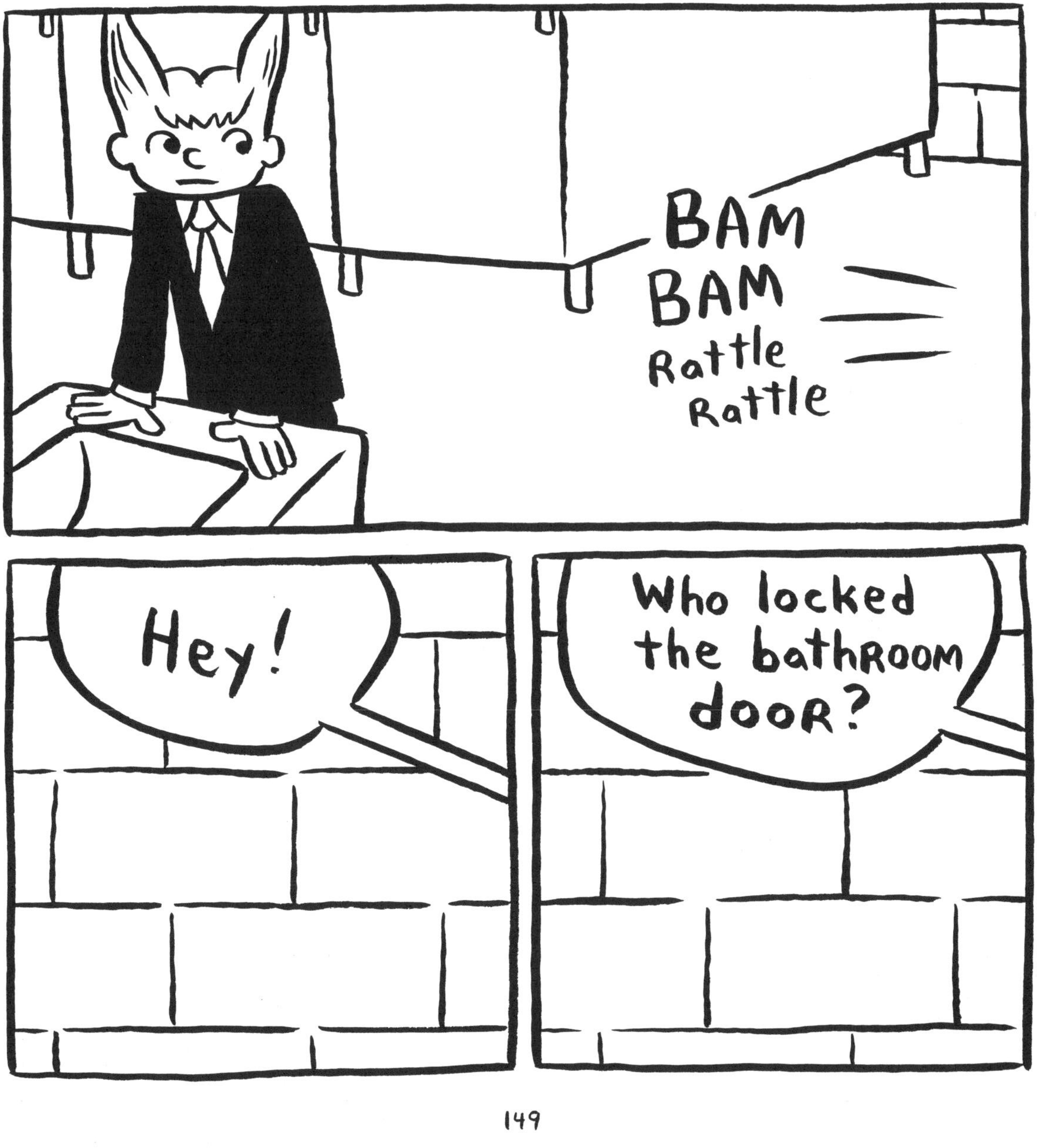
BAM
BAM
Rattle
Rattle
Hey!
Who locked the bathROOM dooR?

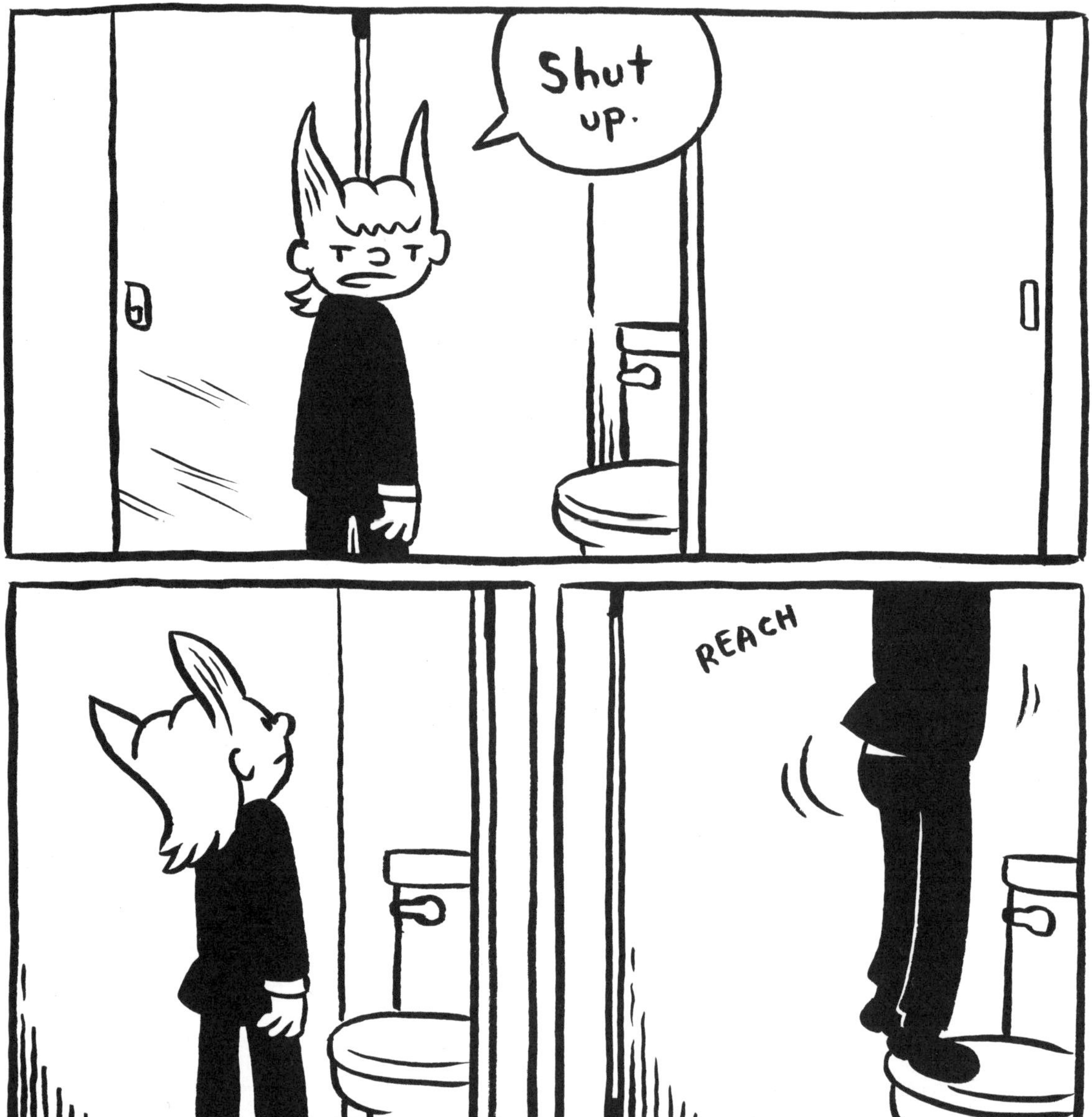
Shut up.
REACH

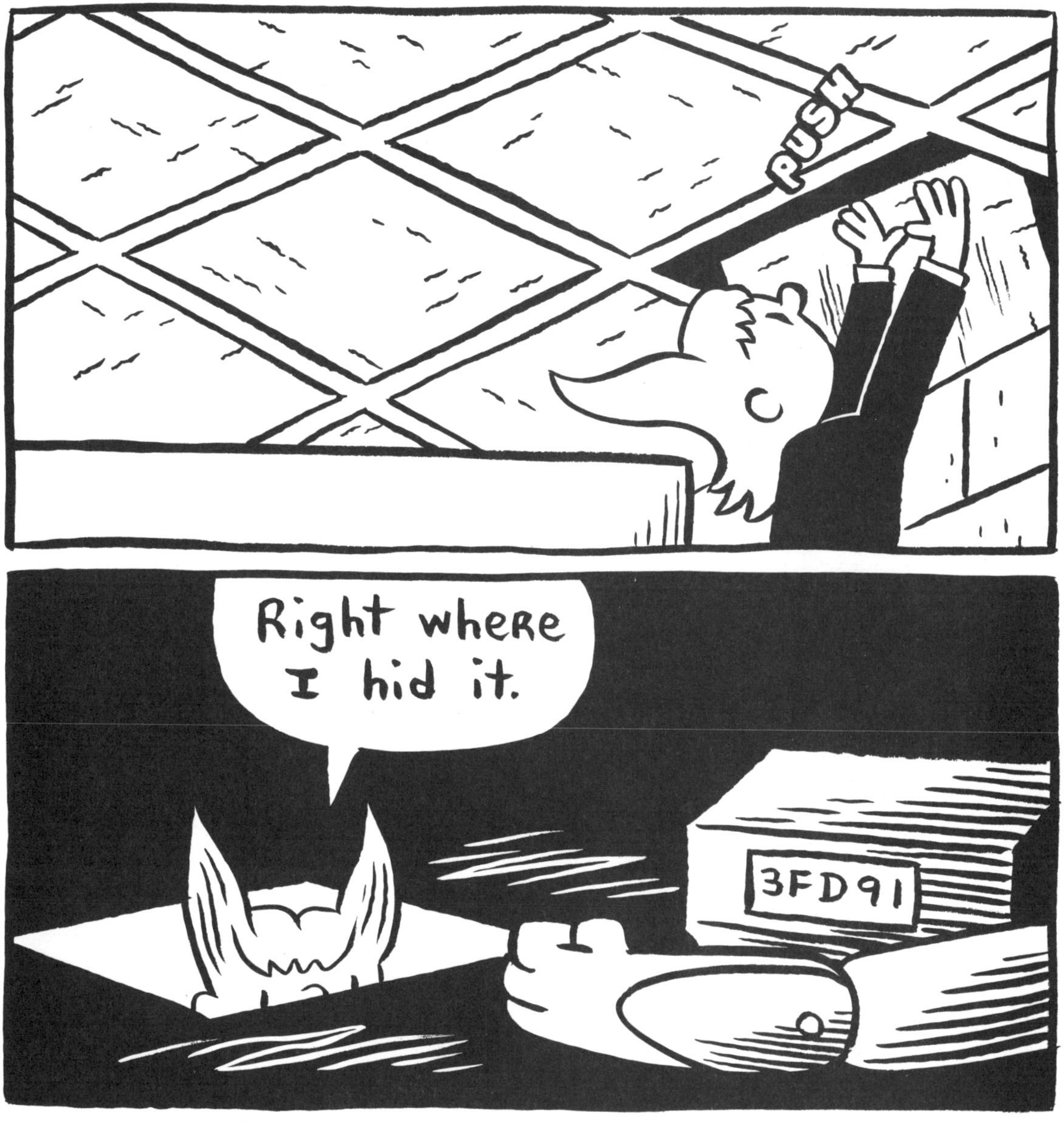
PUSH
Right where I hid it.
3FD91

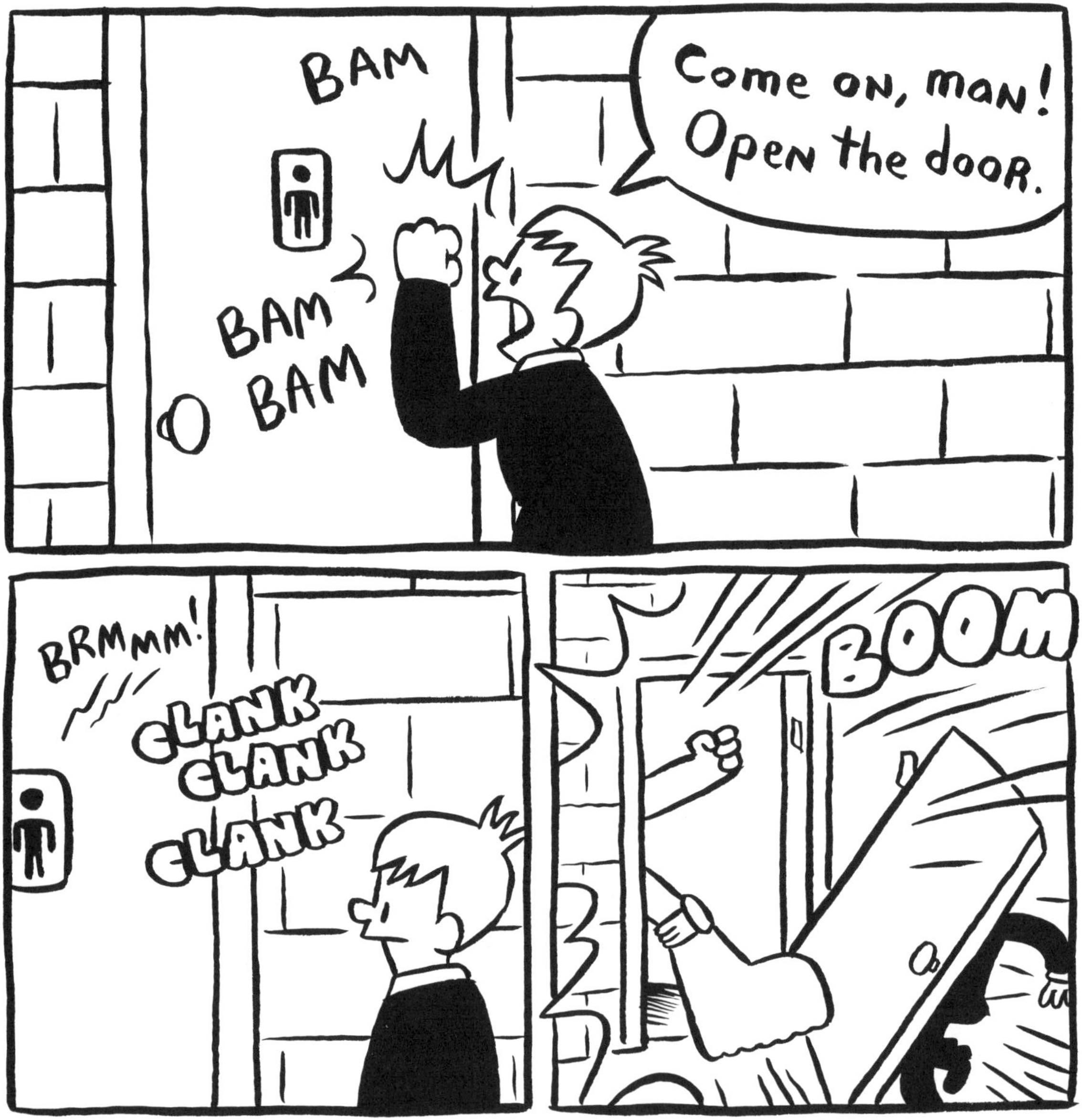
BAM
Come on, man! Open the door.
BAM BAM BAM
BRMMM!
CLANK CLANK CLANK
BOOM

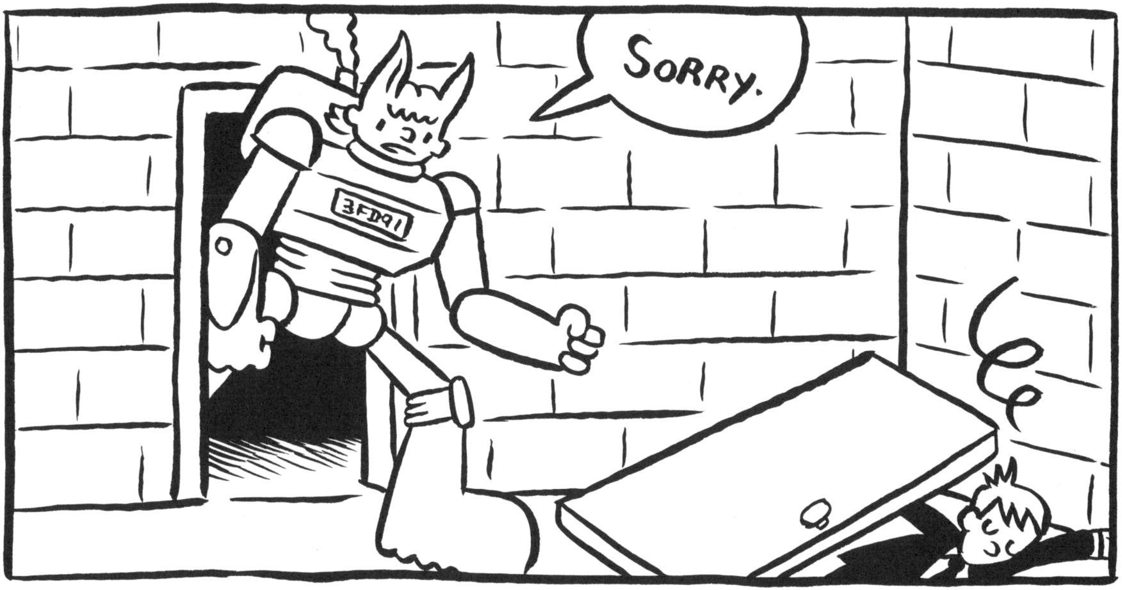
SORRY.
3FD91

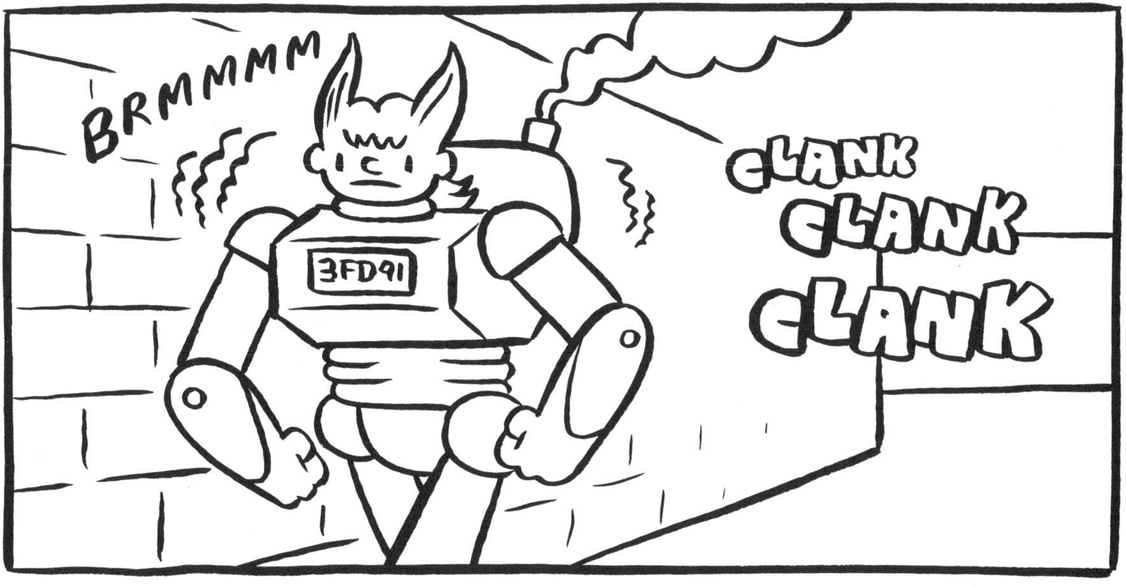
BRMMMMM
3FD91
CLANK
CLANK
CLANK

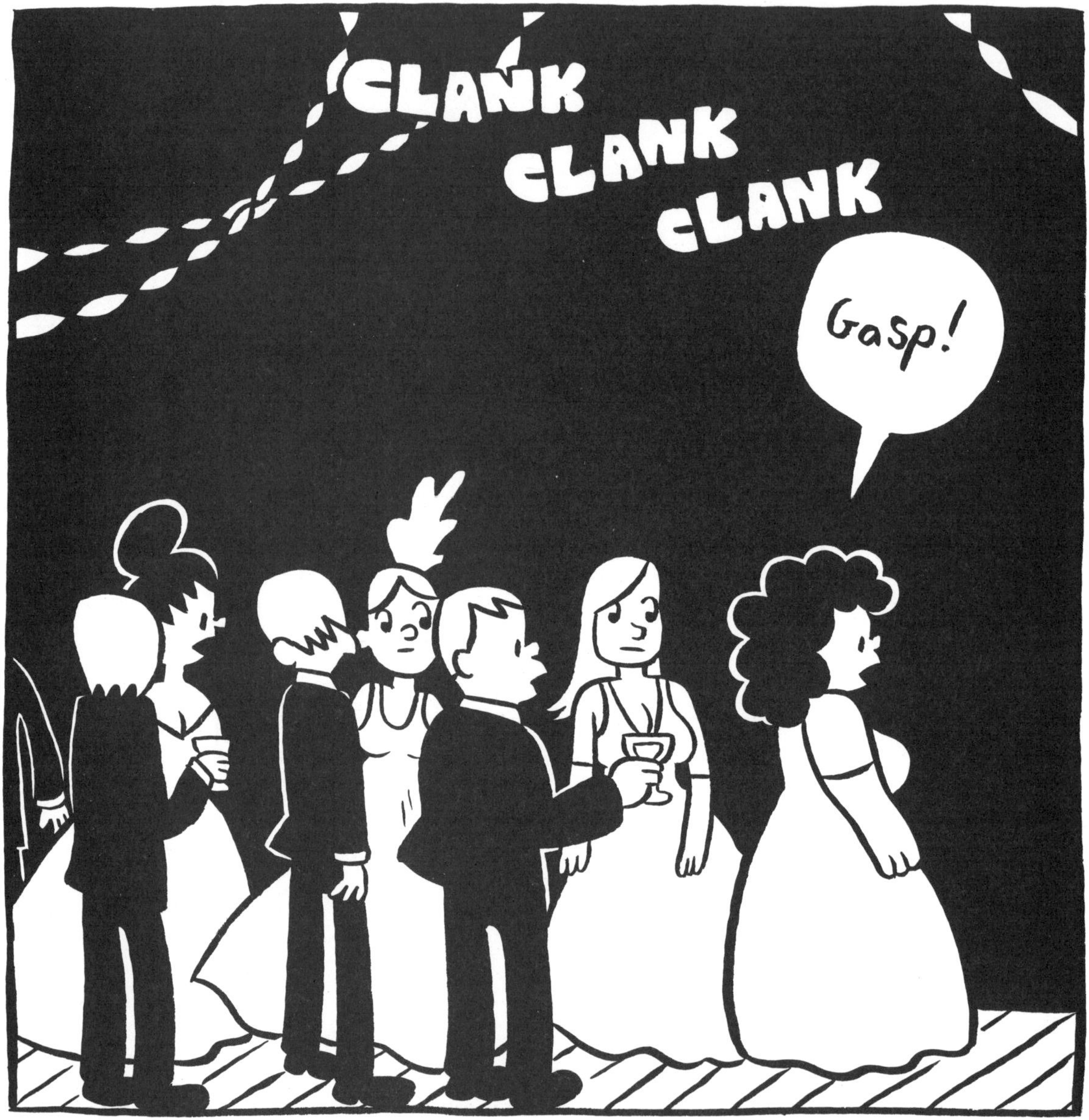
CLANK
CLANK
CLANK
Gasp!

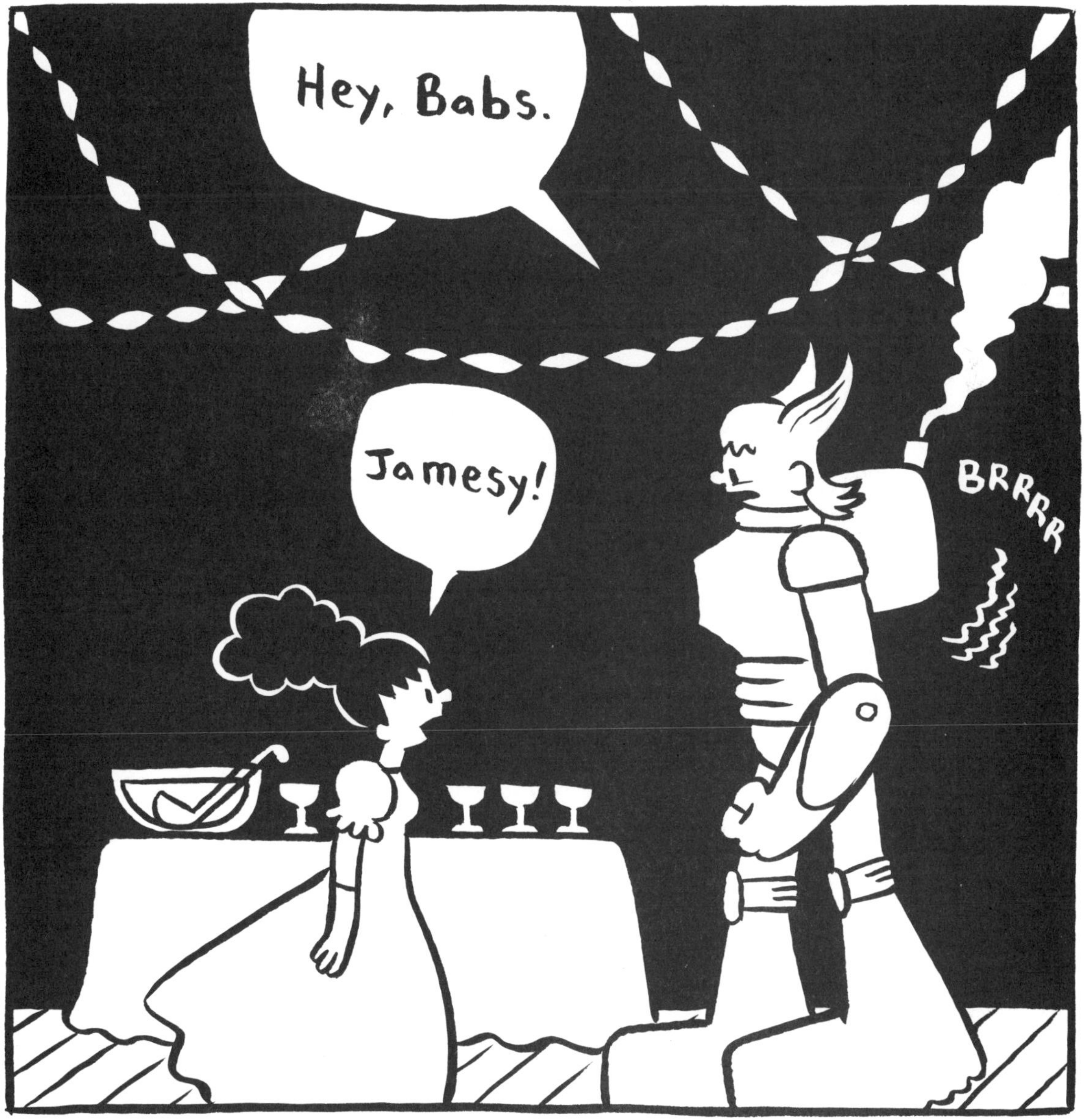
Hey, Babs.
Jamesy!
BRRRRR

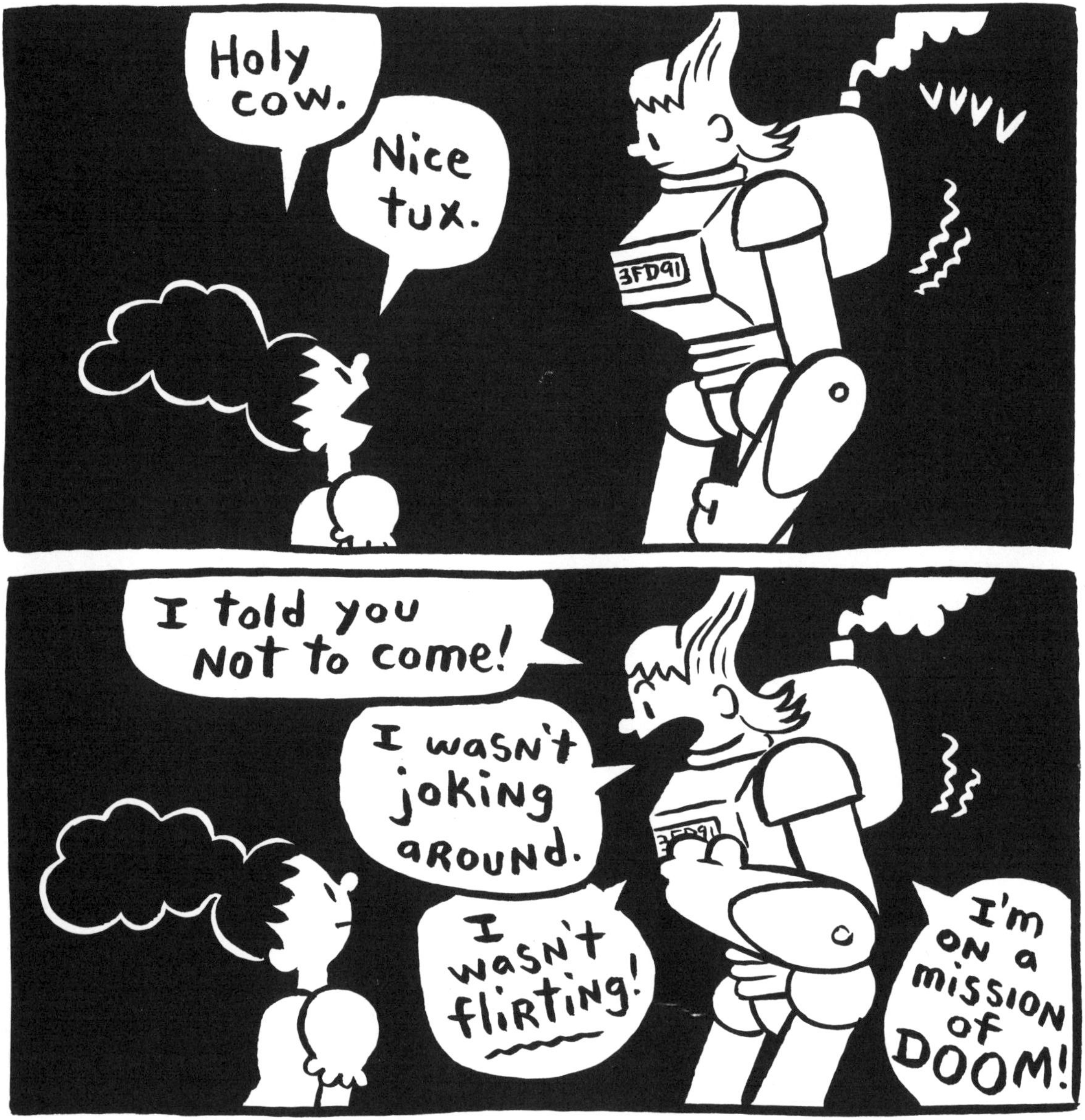
Holy cow.
Nice tux.
VVVV
I told you Not to come!
I wasn't joking around.
I wasn't flirting!
I'm on a mission of DOOM!

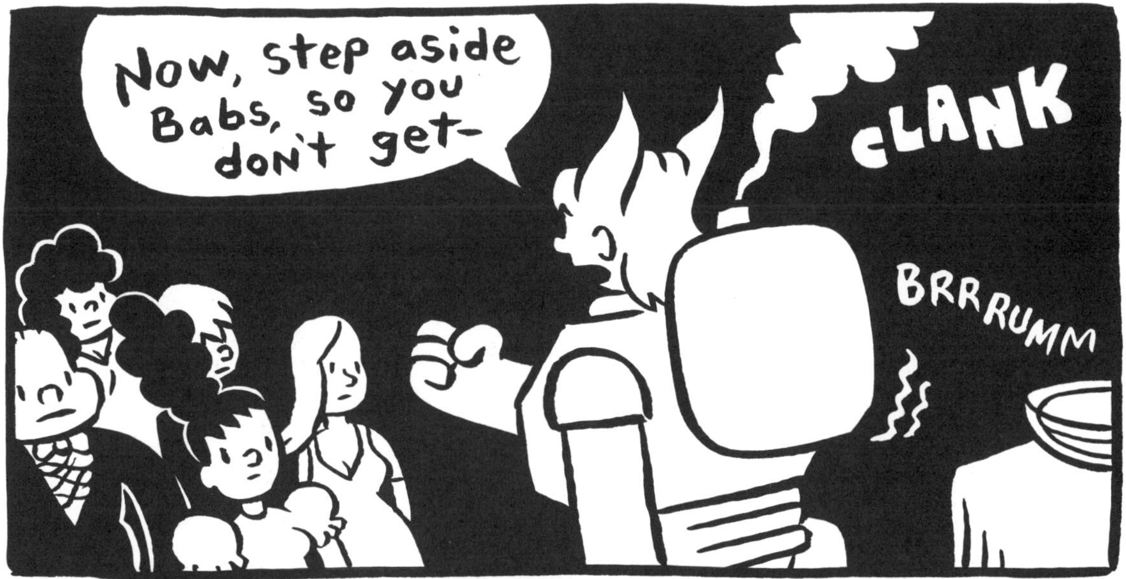
Now, step aside Babs, so you don't get-
CLANK
BRRRUMM

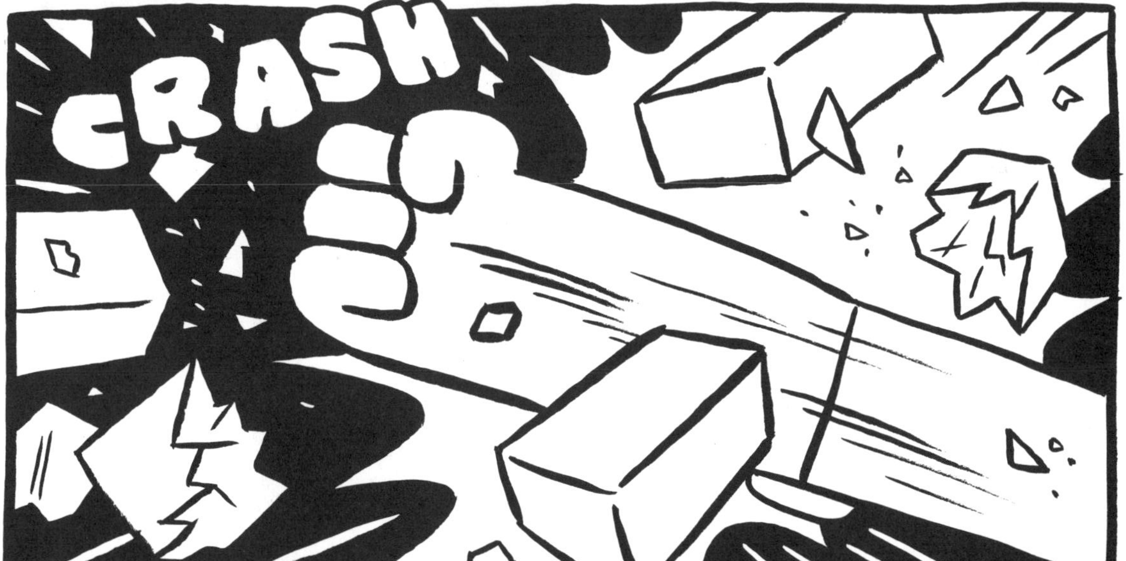
CRASH

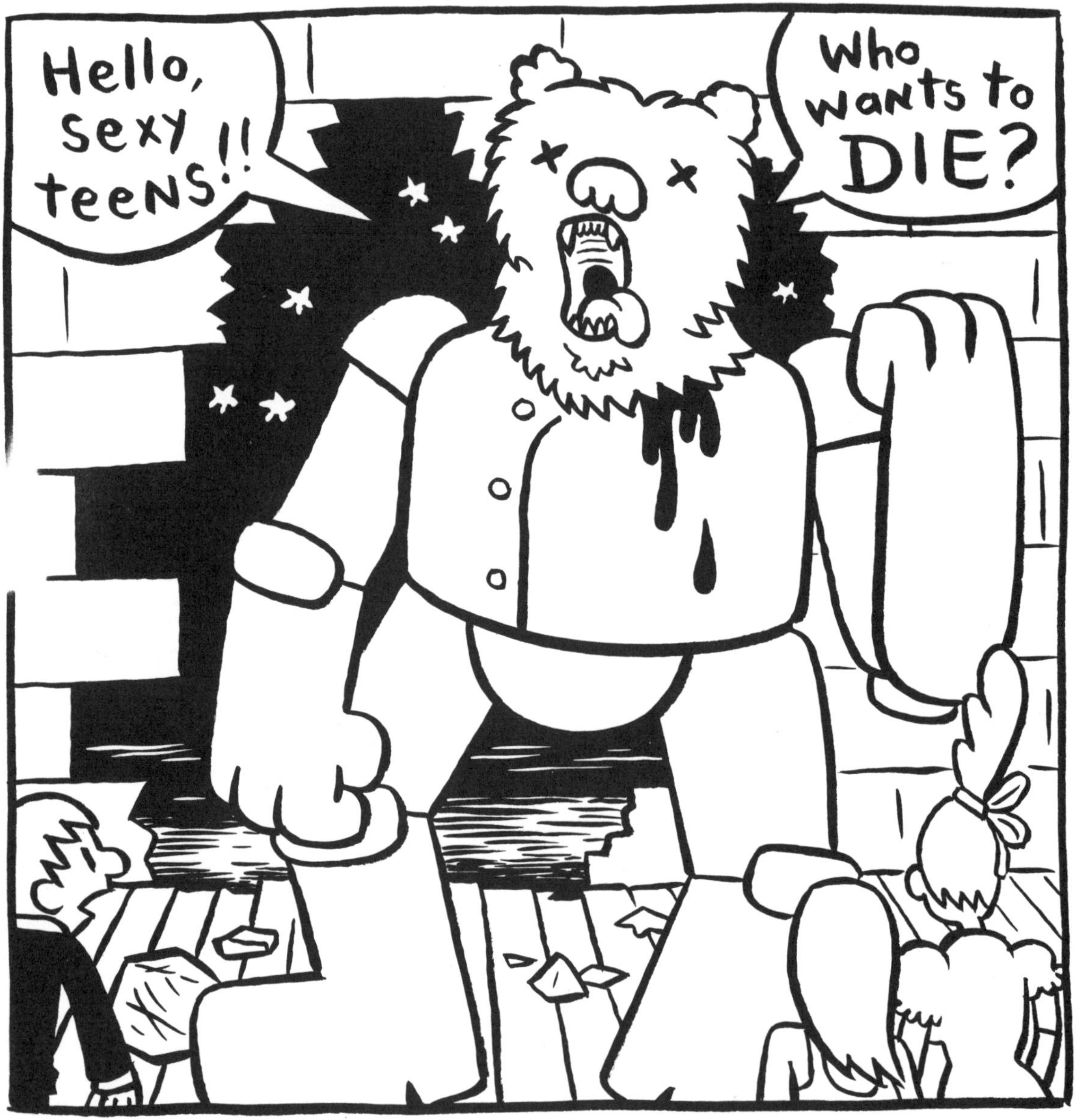
Hello, sexy teens!!
Who wants to DIE?

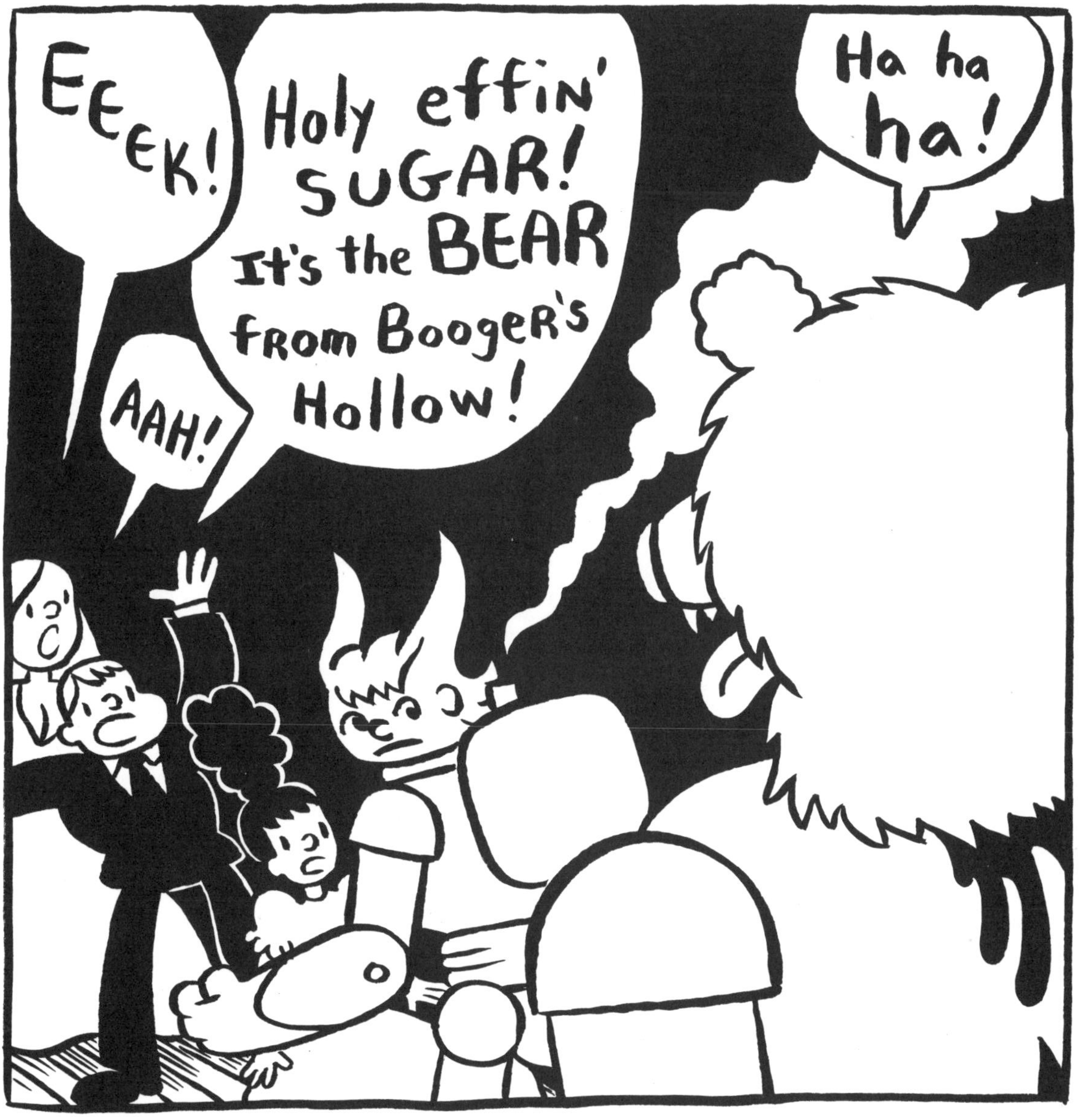
EEEEK!
Holy effin' SUGAR! It's the BEAR from Booger's Hollow!
AAH!
Ha ha ha!

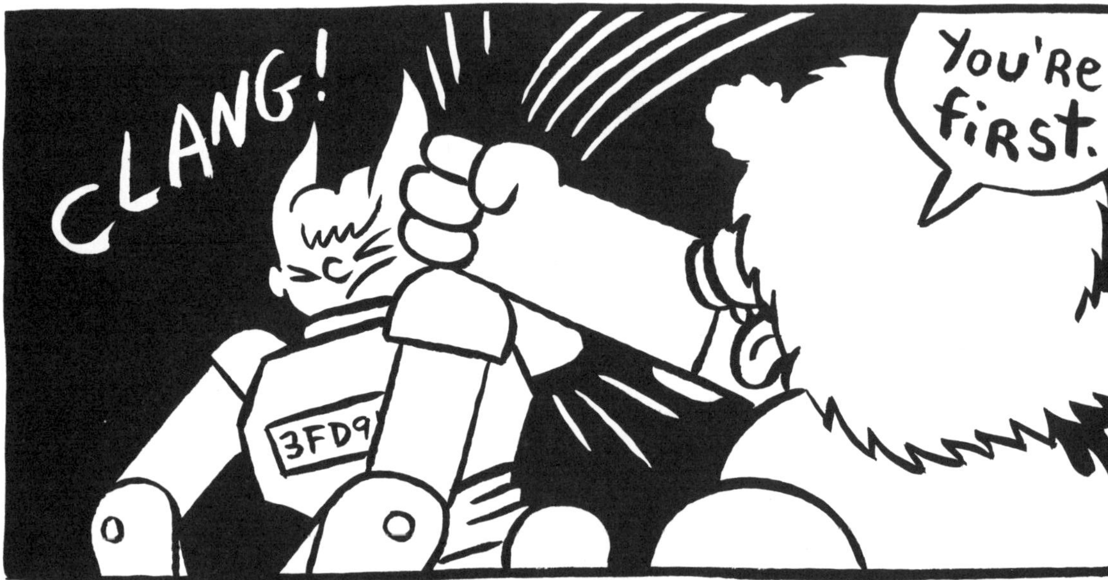
CLANG!
You're first.
3FD91

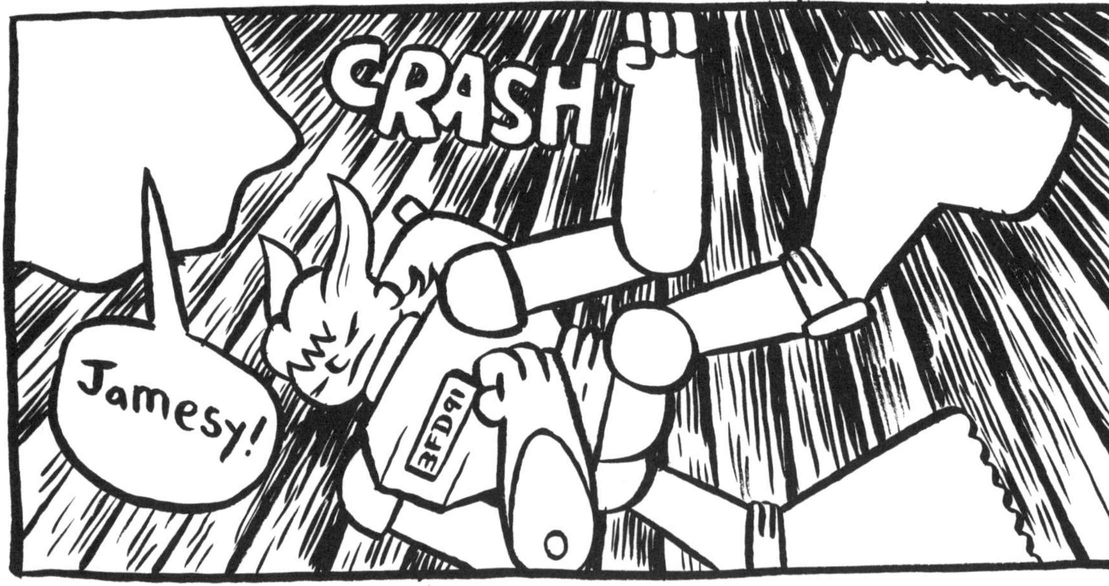
CRASH
Jamesy!
3FD91

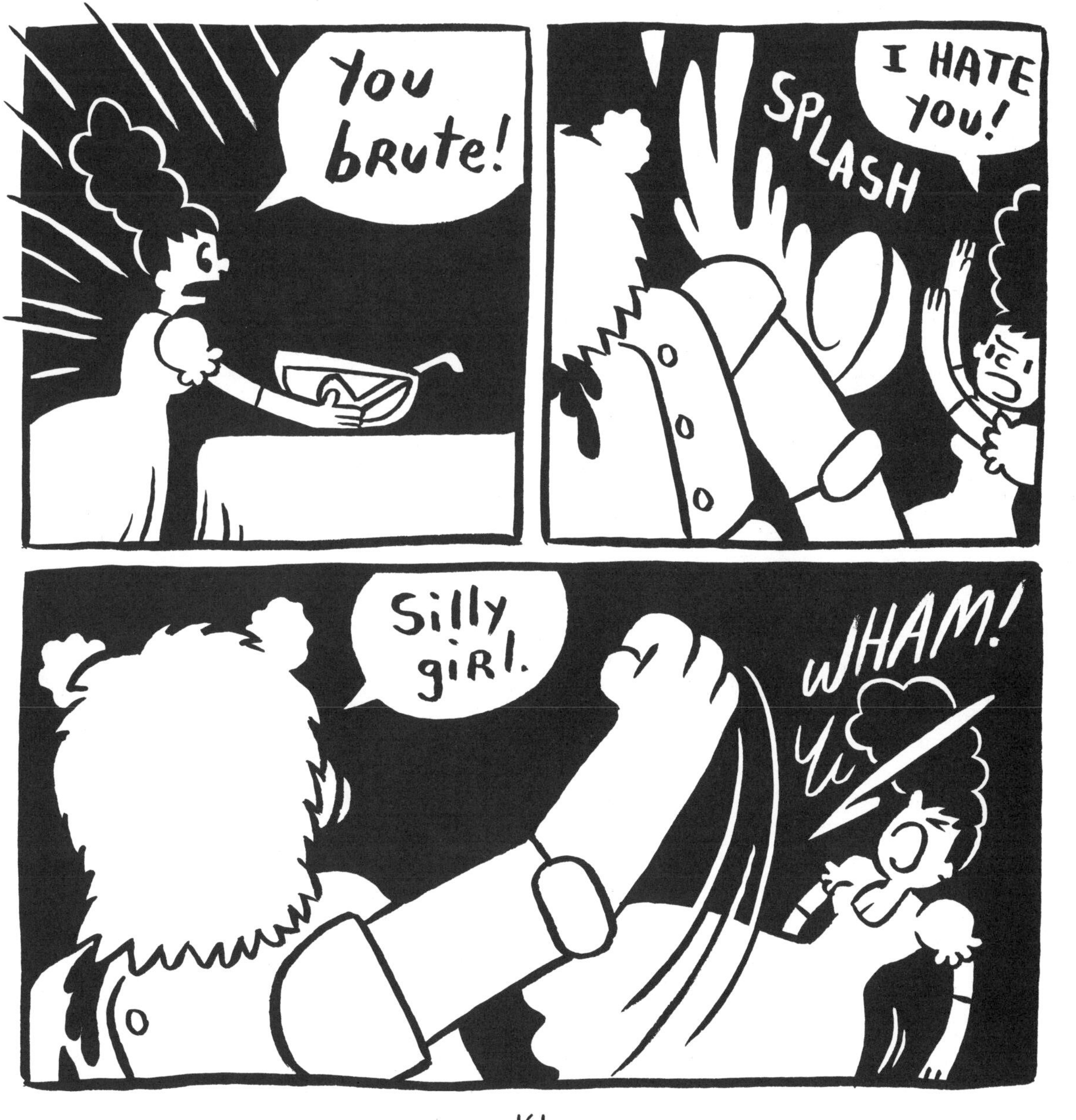
You brute!
I HATE YOU!
SPLASH
Silly girl.
WHAM!

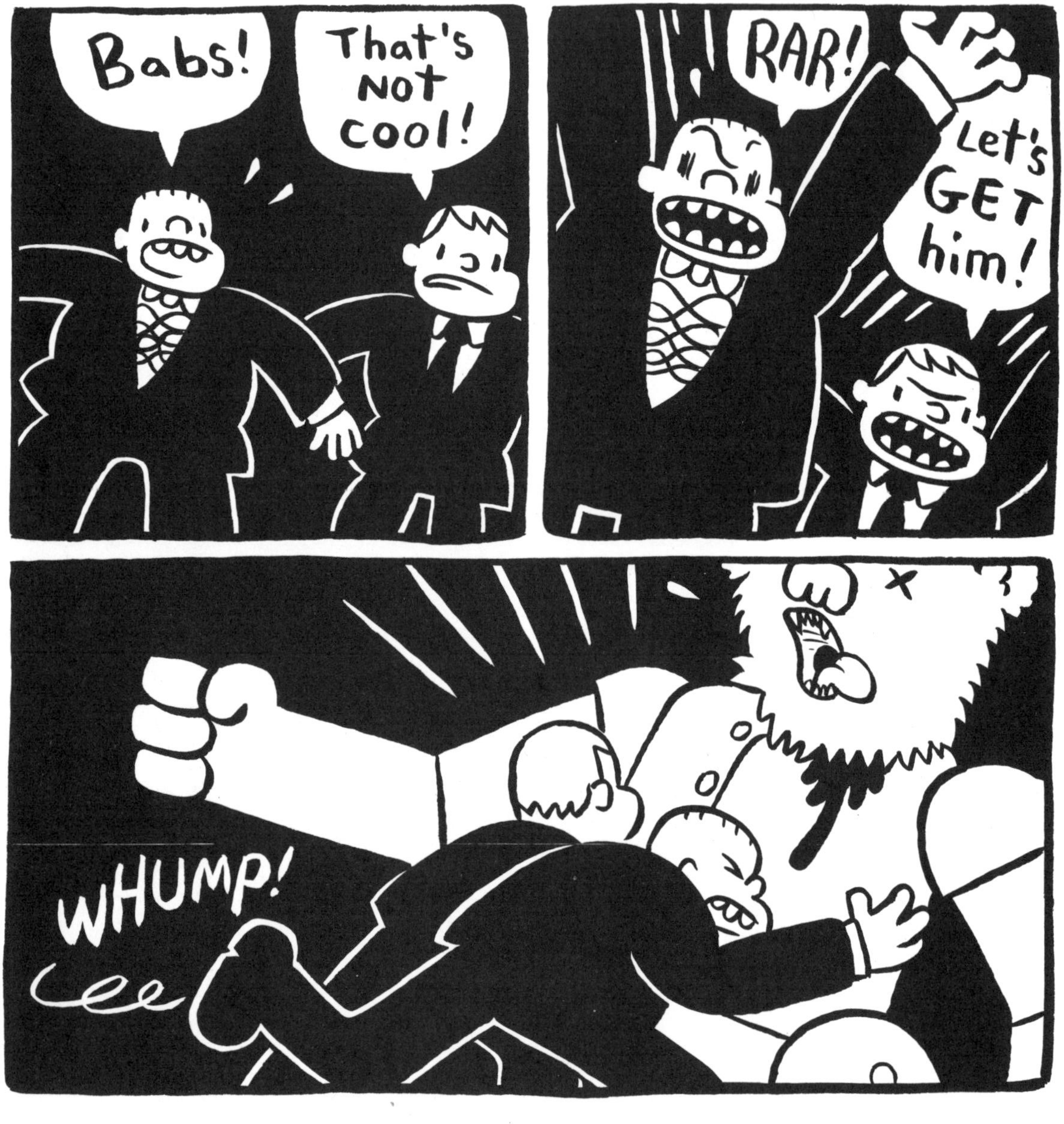
Babs!
That's NOT cool!
RAR!
Let's GET him!
WHUMP!

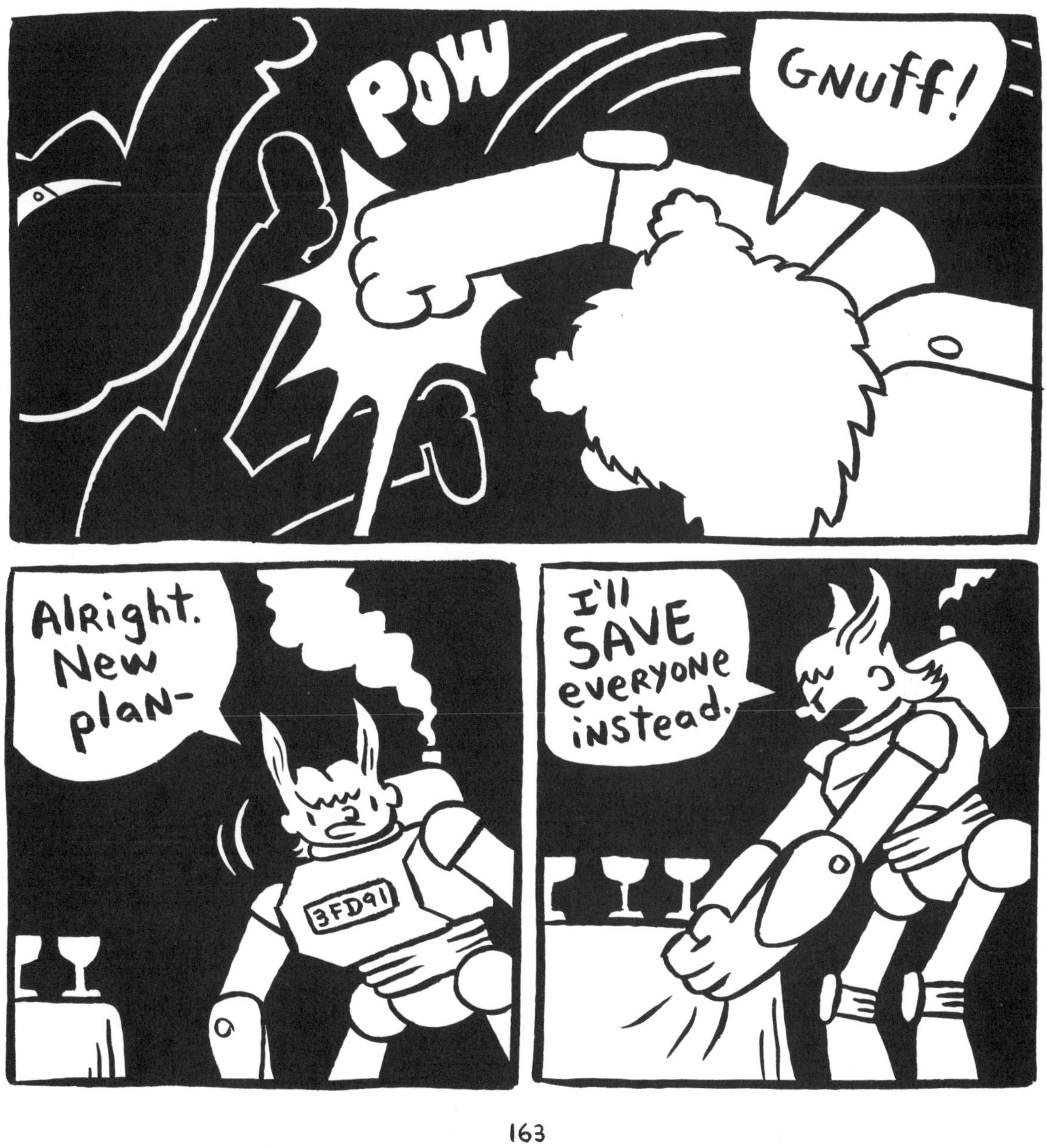
POW
GNUFF!
Alright. New plan-
3FD91
I'll SAVE everyone instead.

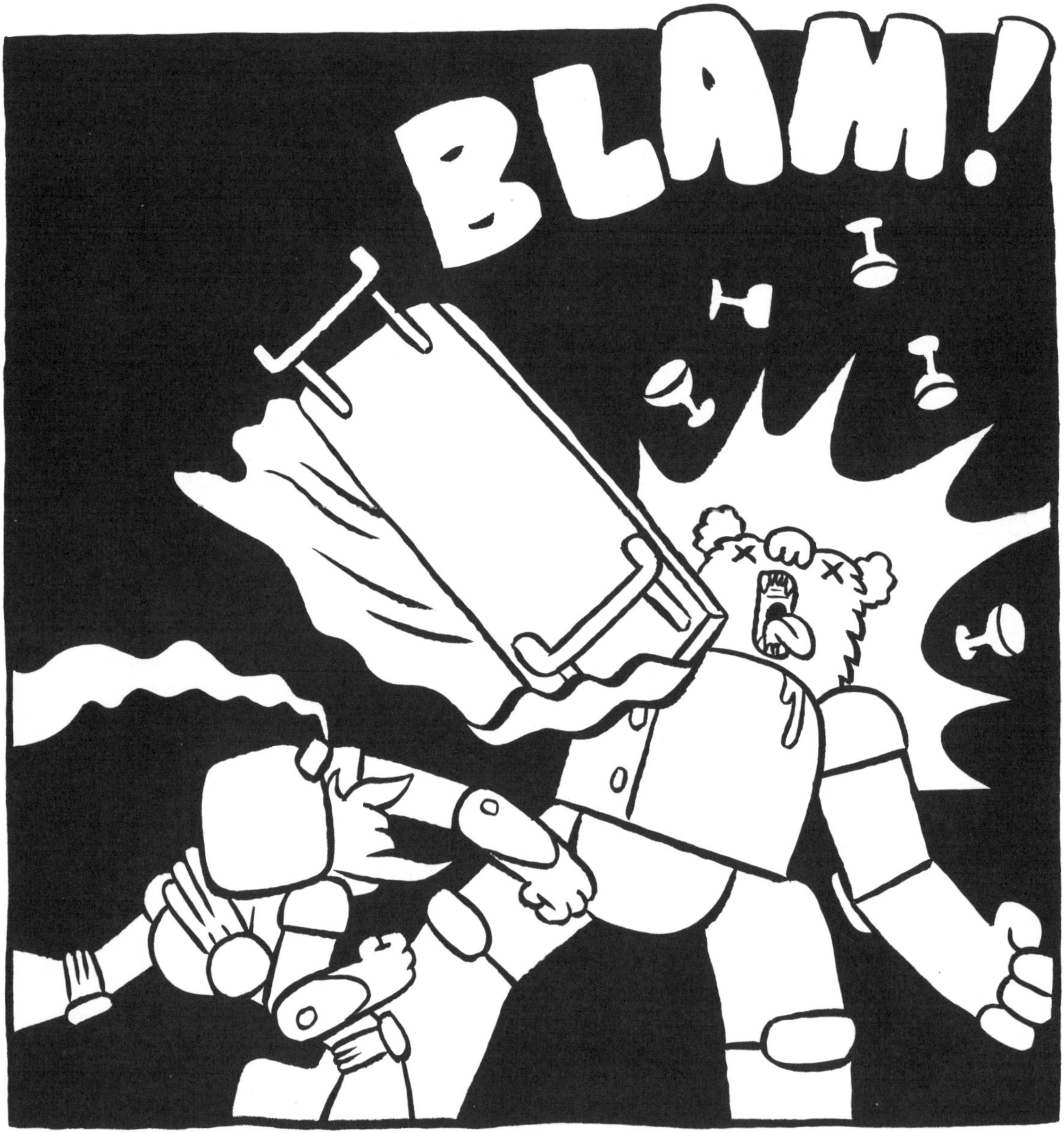
BLAM!

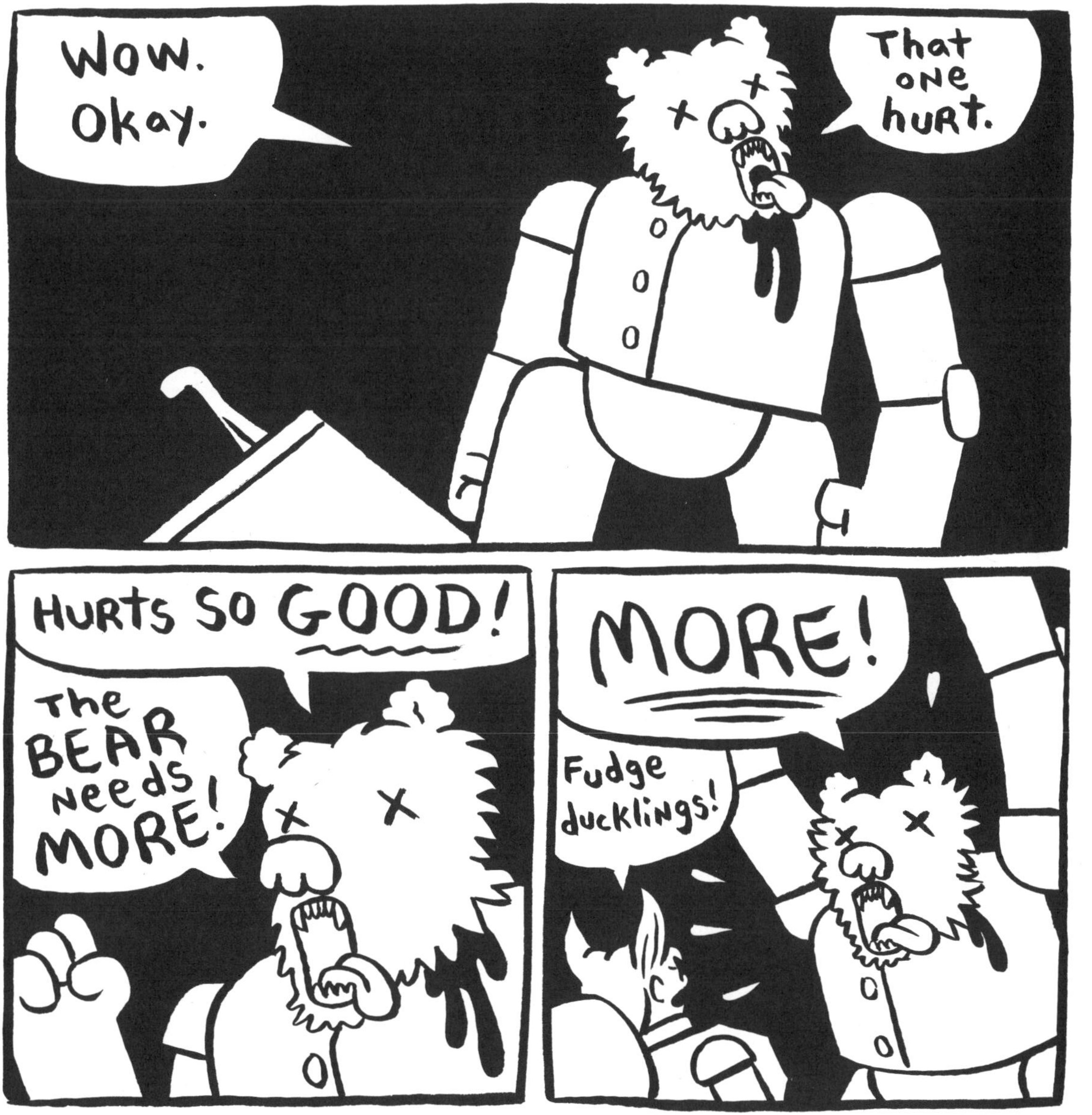
WOW. Okay.
That one hurt.
HURTS SO GOOD!
The BEAR needs MORE!
MORE!
Fudge ducklings!

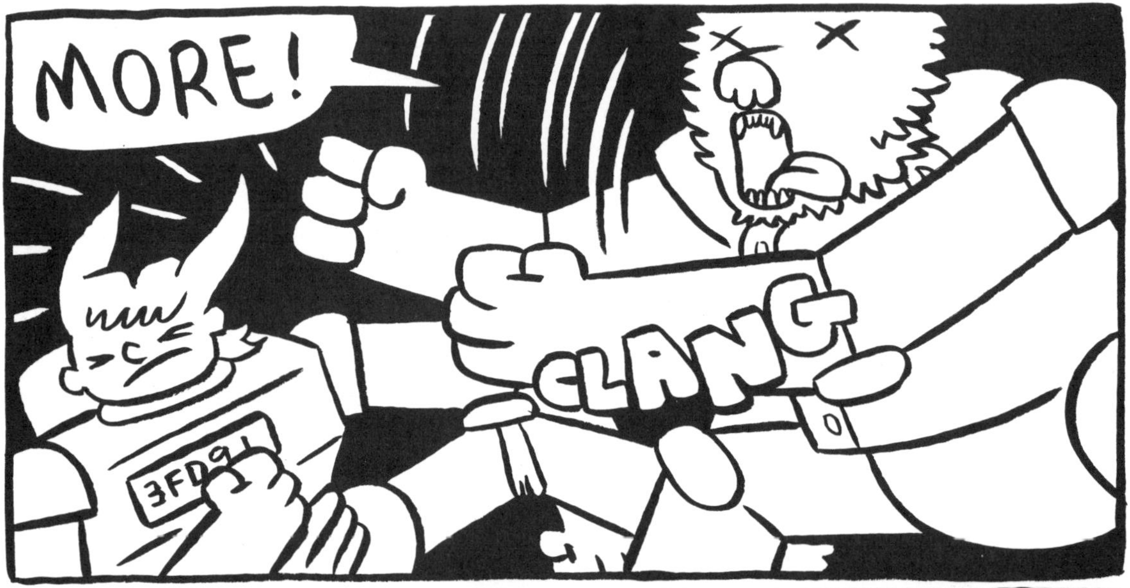

MORE!
3FD91
CLANG

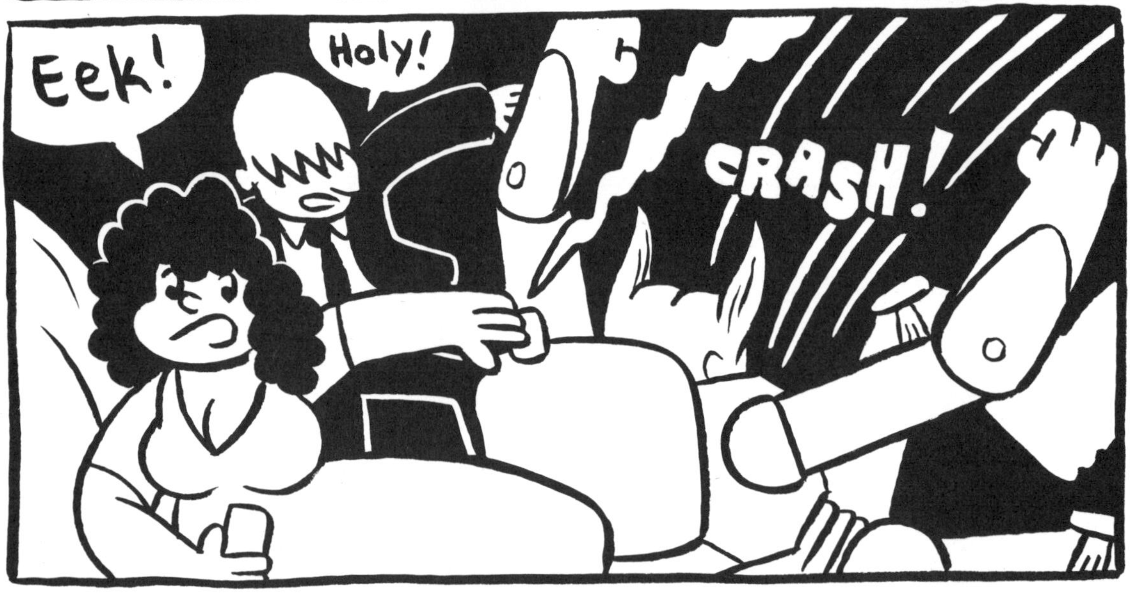

Eek!
Holy!
CRASH!

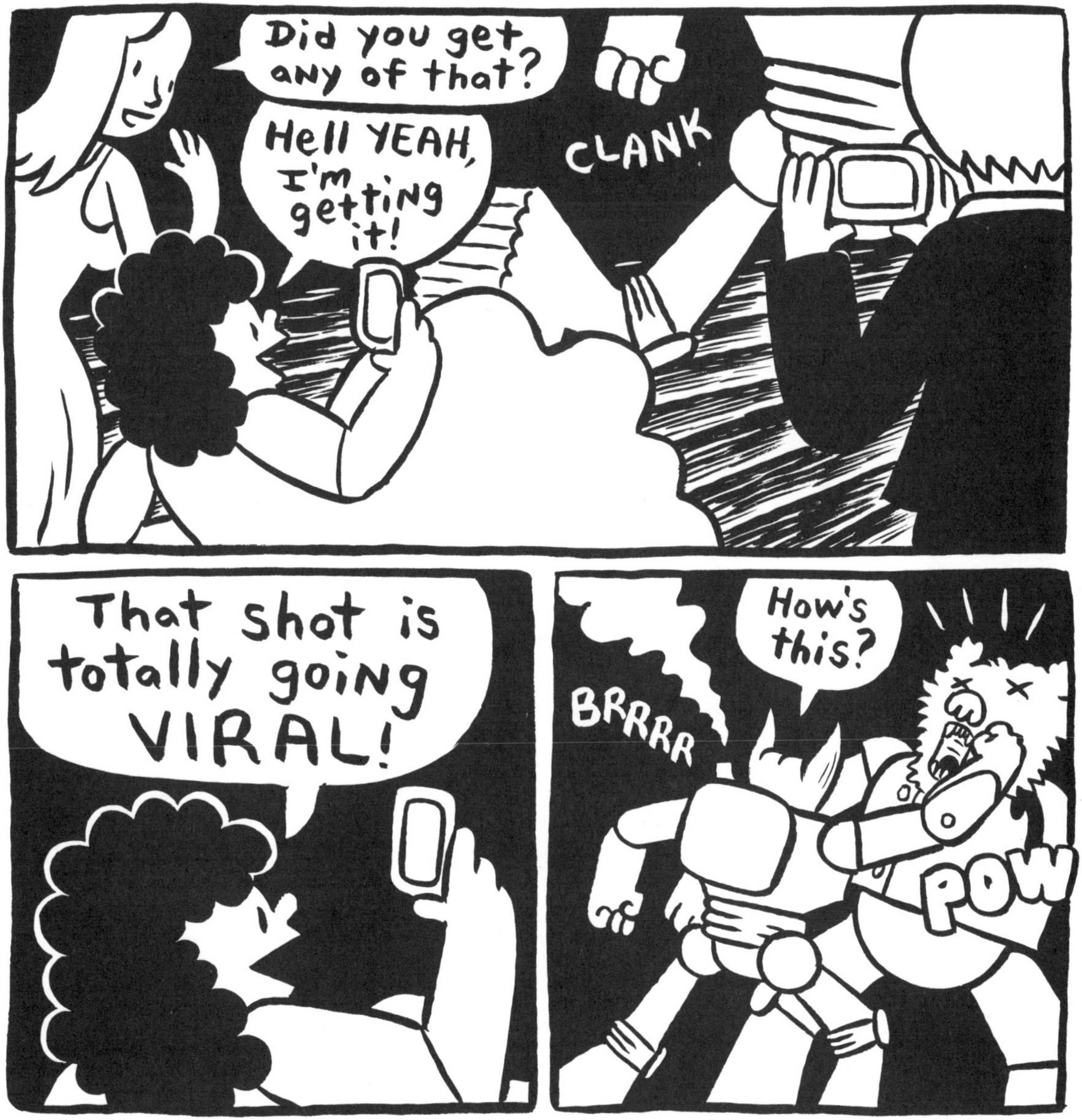
Did you get any of that?
Hell YEAH, I'm getting it!
CLANK
That shot is totally going VIRAL!
How's this?
BRRRRR
POW

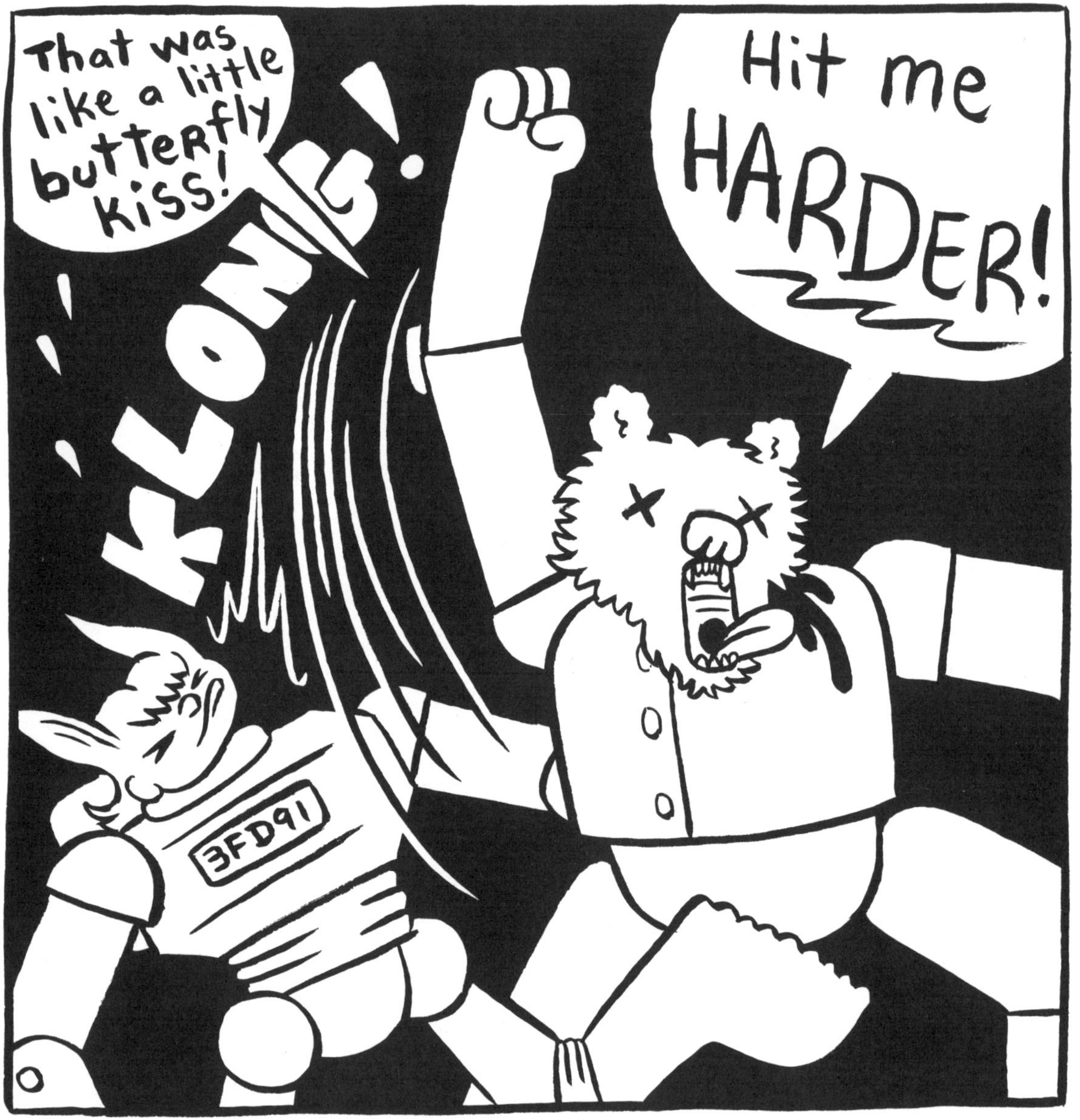

That was like a little butterfly kiss!
KLONG!
Hit me HARDER!
3FD91

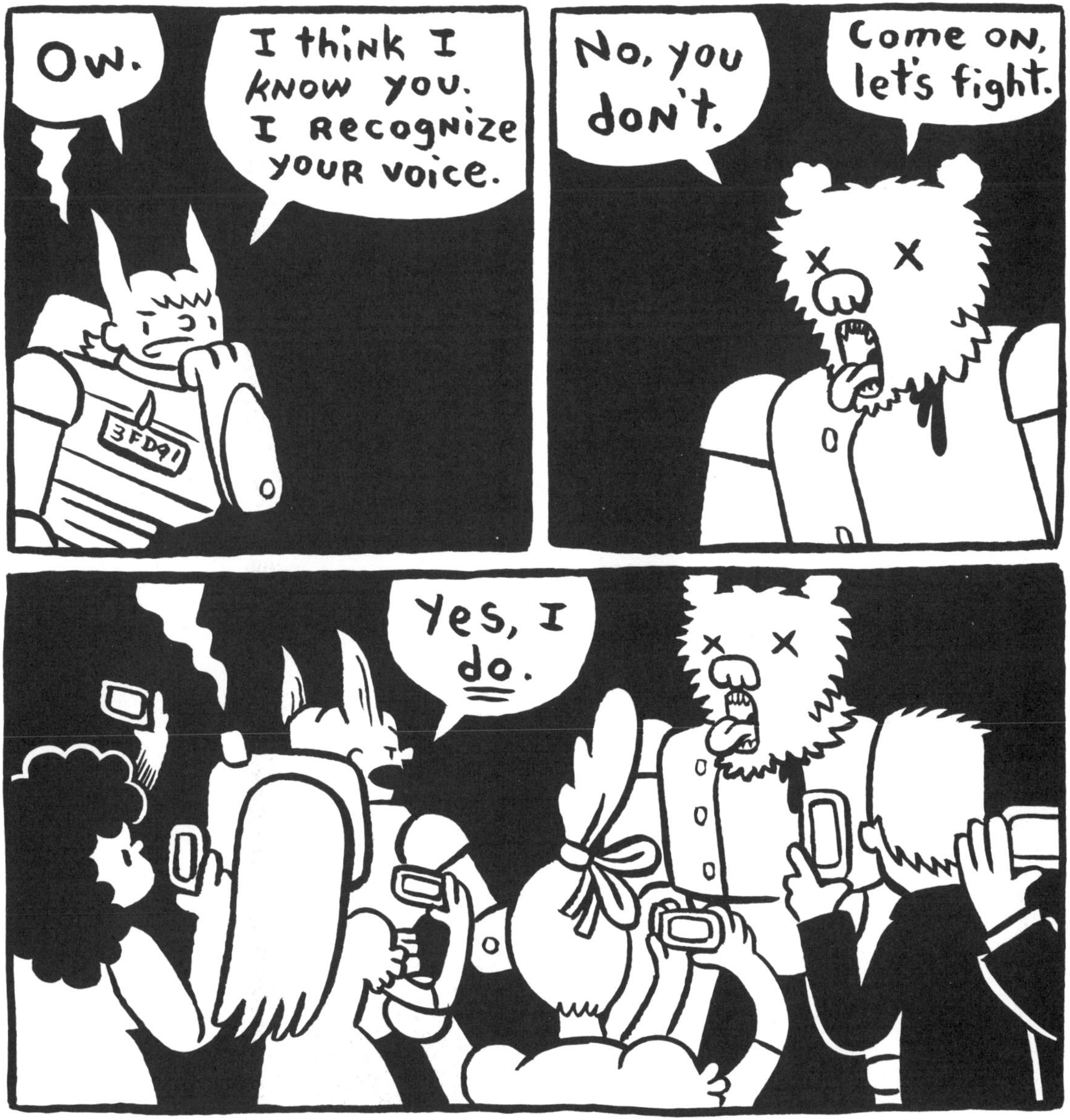
Ow.
I think I know you. I recognize your voice.
No, you don't.
Come on, let's fight.
Yes, I do.

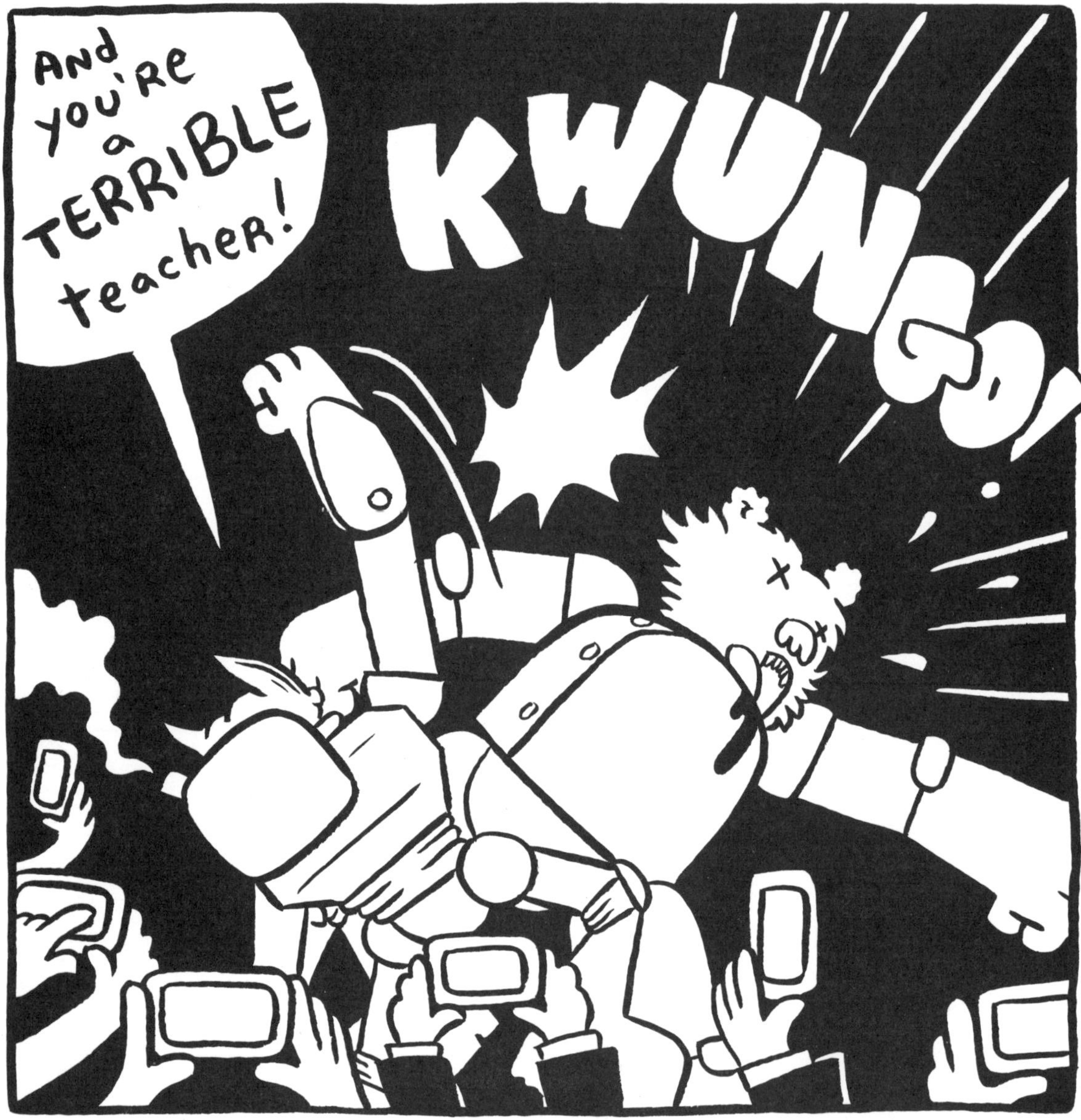
And you're a TERRIBLE teacher!
KWUNGG!

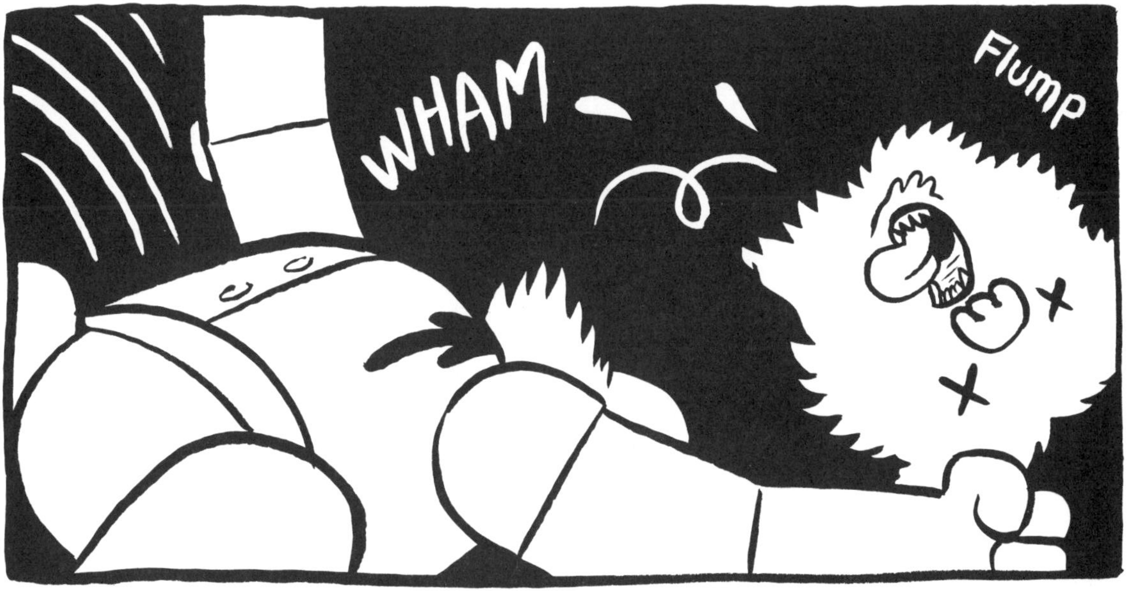
WHAM
Flump

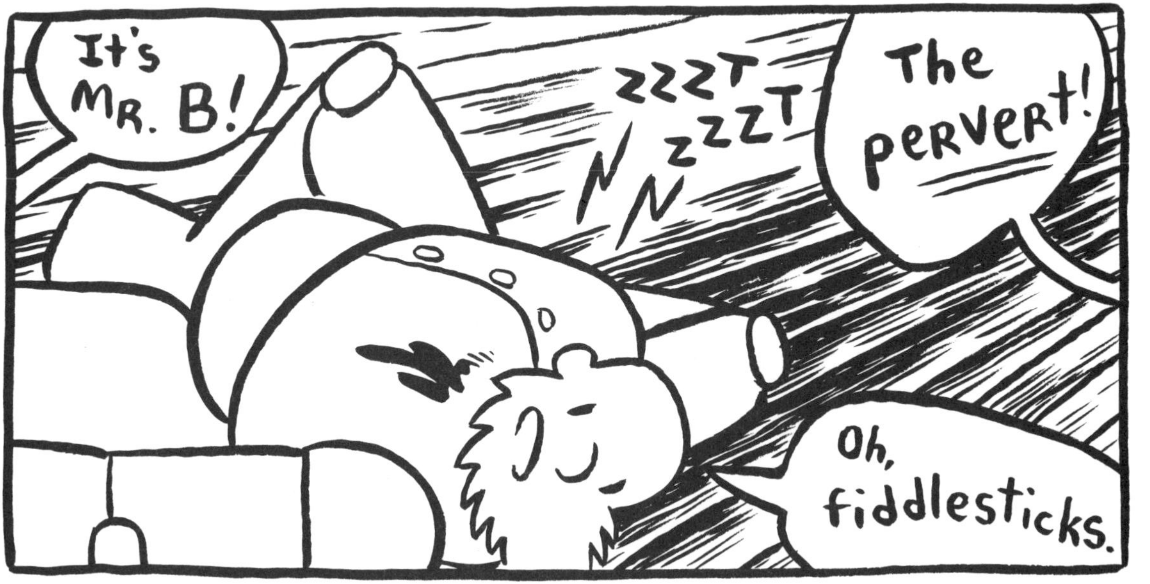
It's MR. B!
ZZZT ZZZT
The pervert!
Oh, fiddlesticks.

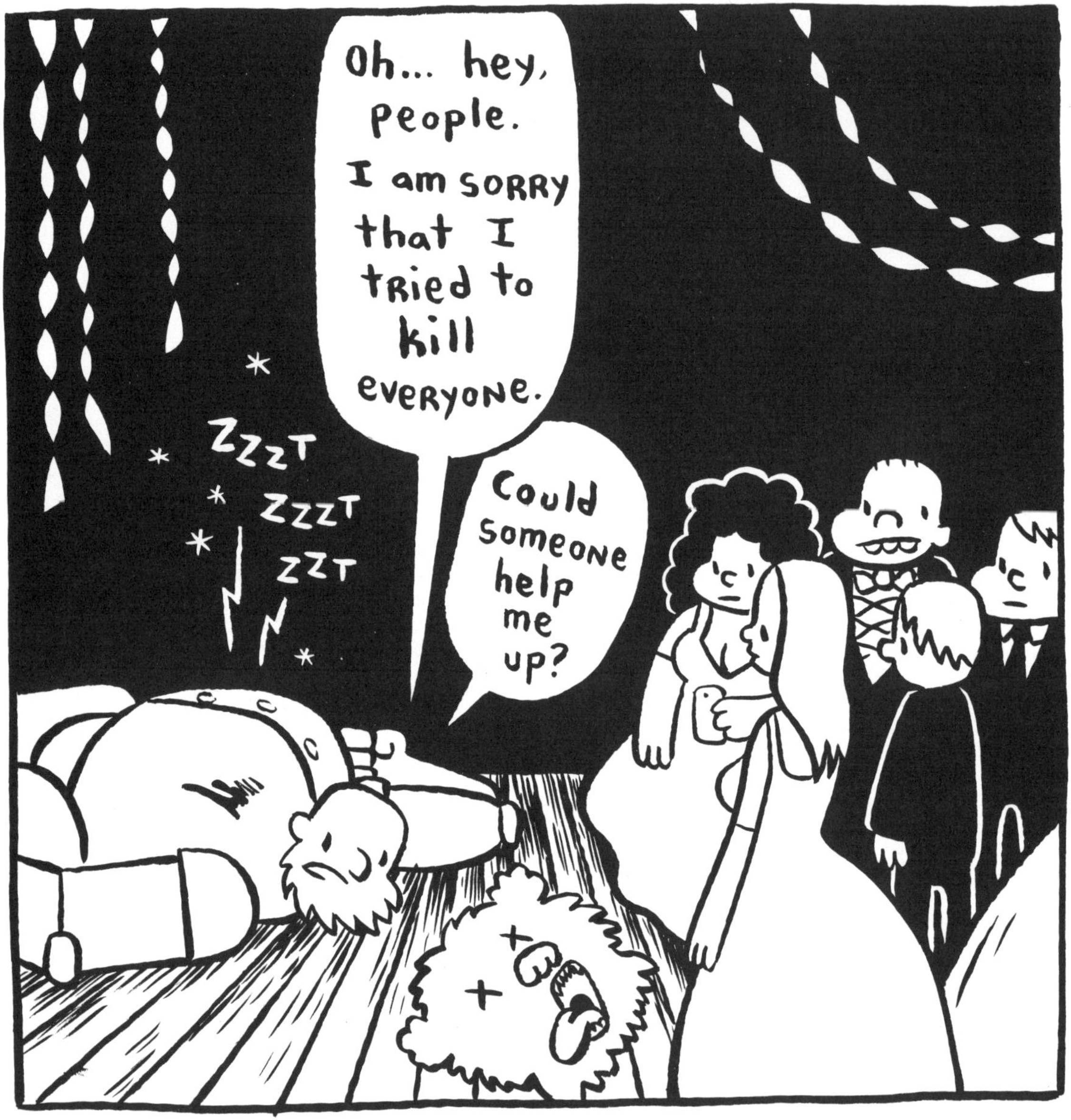
Oh... hey, people.
I am SORRY that I tried to kill everyone.
Could someone help me up?
ZZZT
ZZZT
ZZT

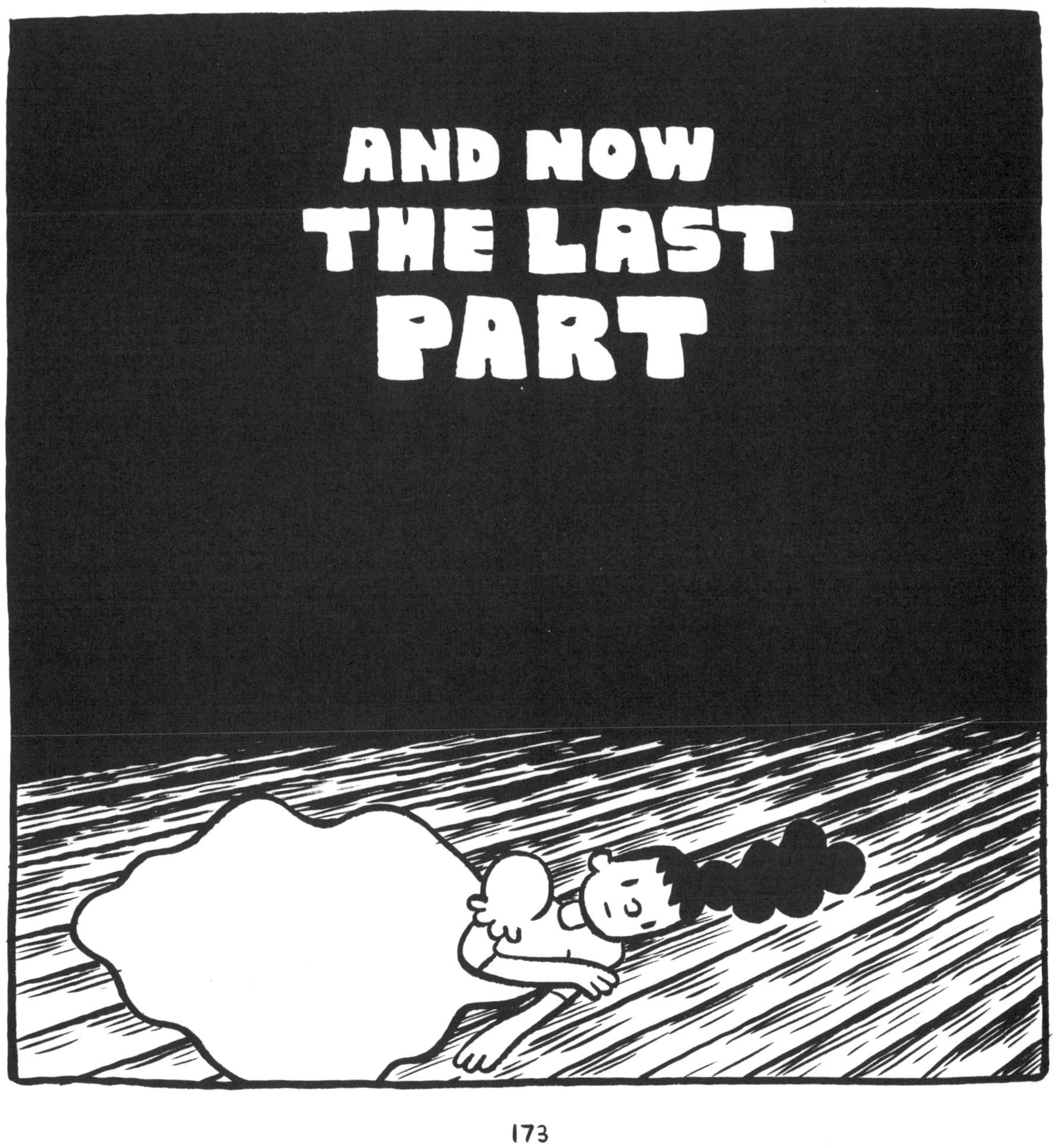
AND NOW
THE LAST
PART

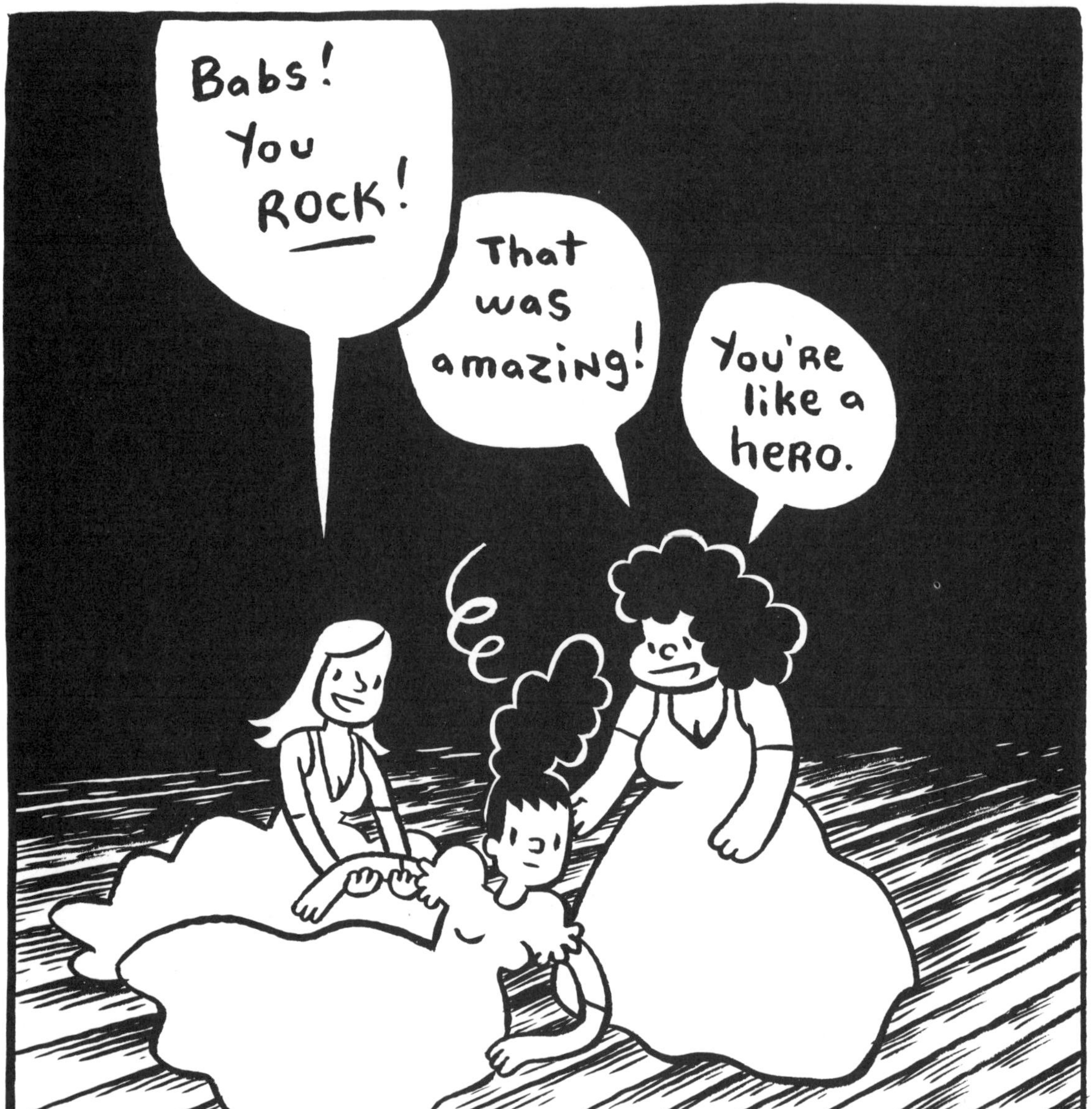
Babs! You ROCK!
That was amazing!
You're like a HERO.

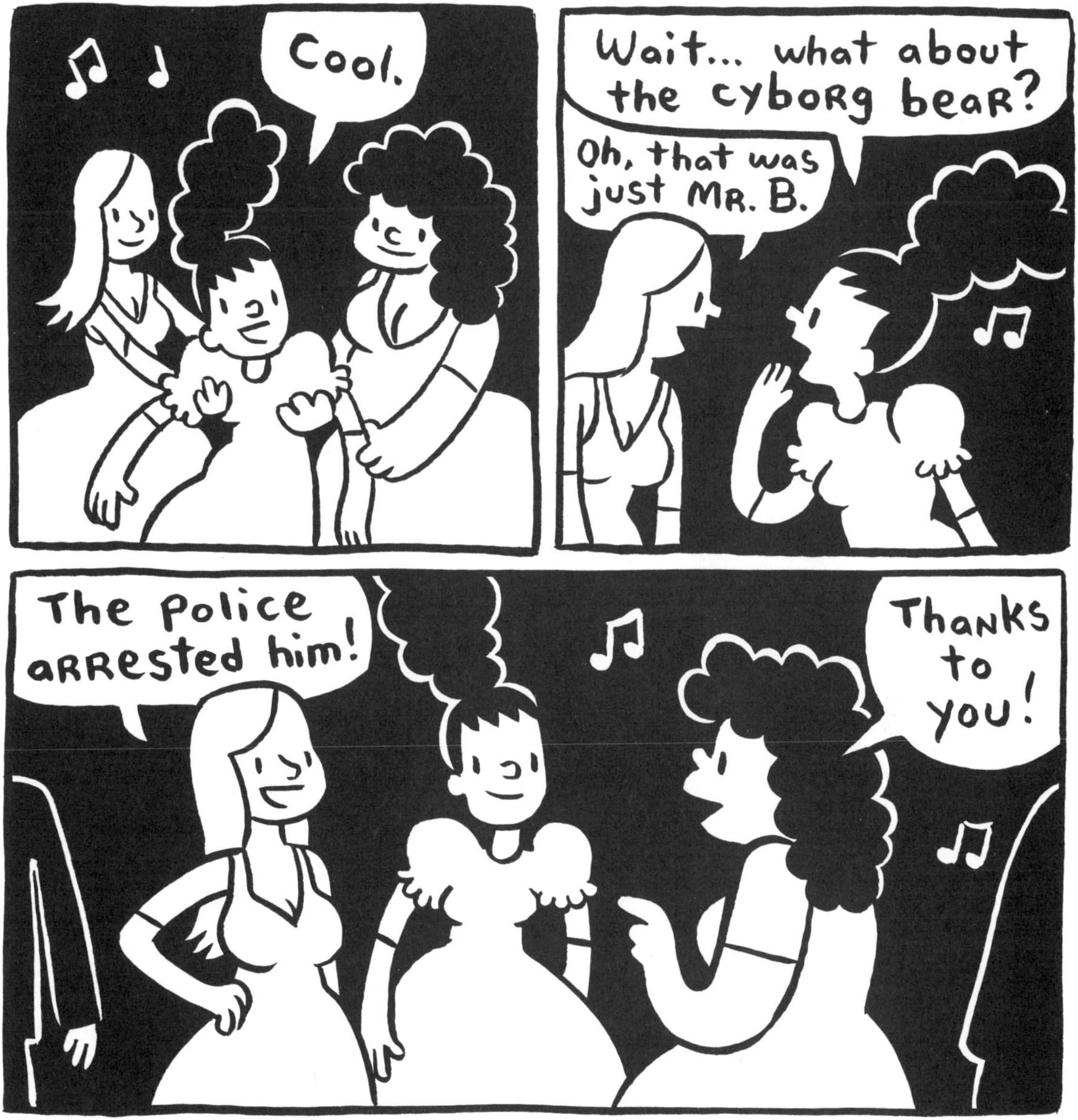
Cool.
Wait... what about the cyborg bear?
Oh, that was just MR. B.
The police arrested him!
Thanks to you!

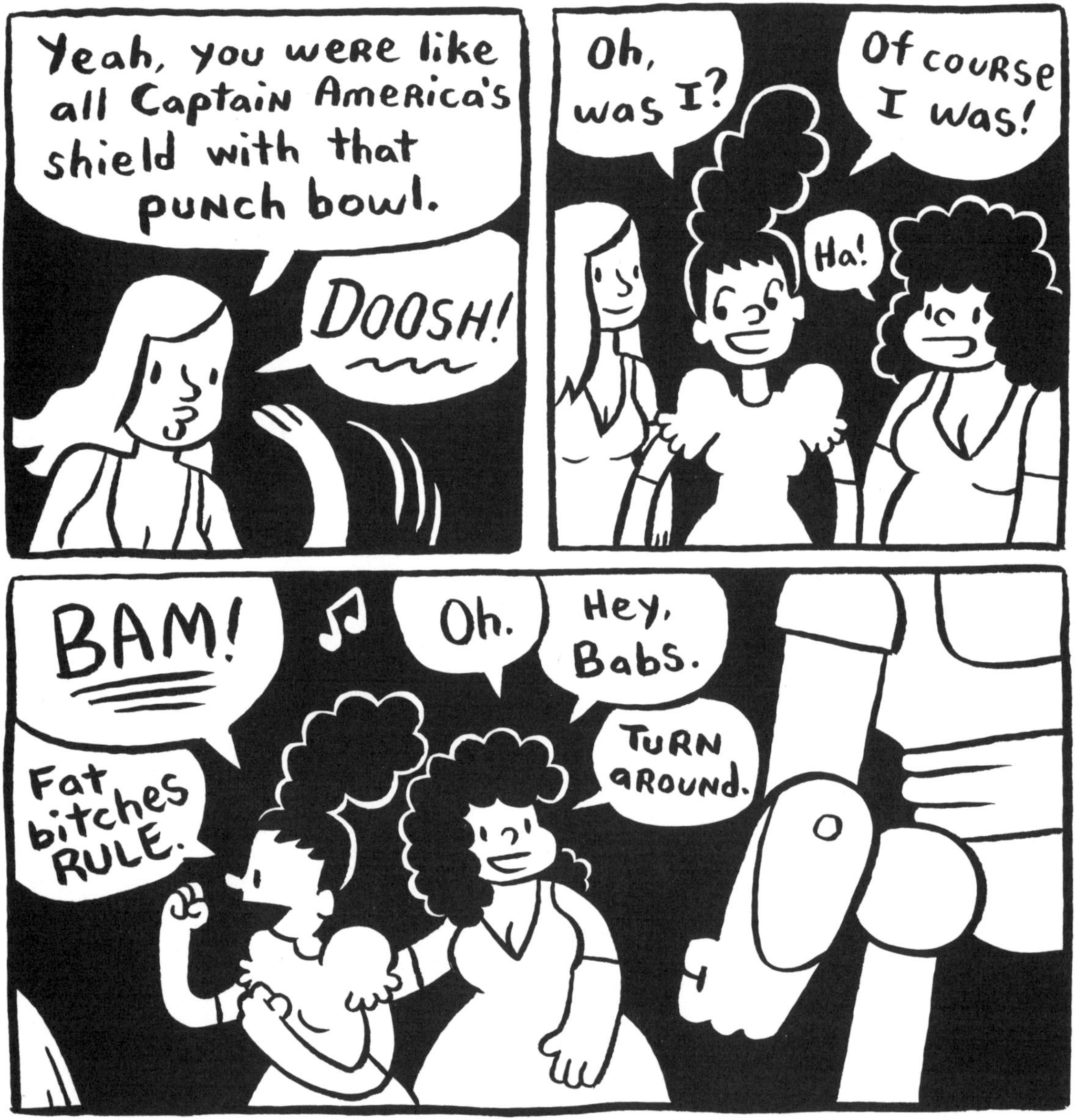
Yeah, you were like all Captain America's shield with that punch bowl.
DOOSH!
Oh, was I?
Of course I was!
Ha!
BAM!
Fat bitches RULE.
Oh.
Hey, Babs.
TURN around.

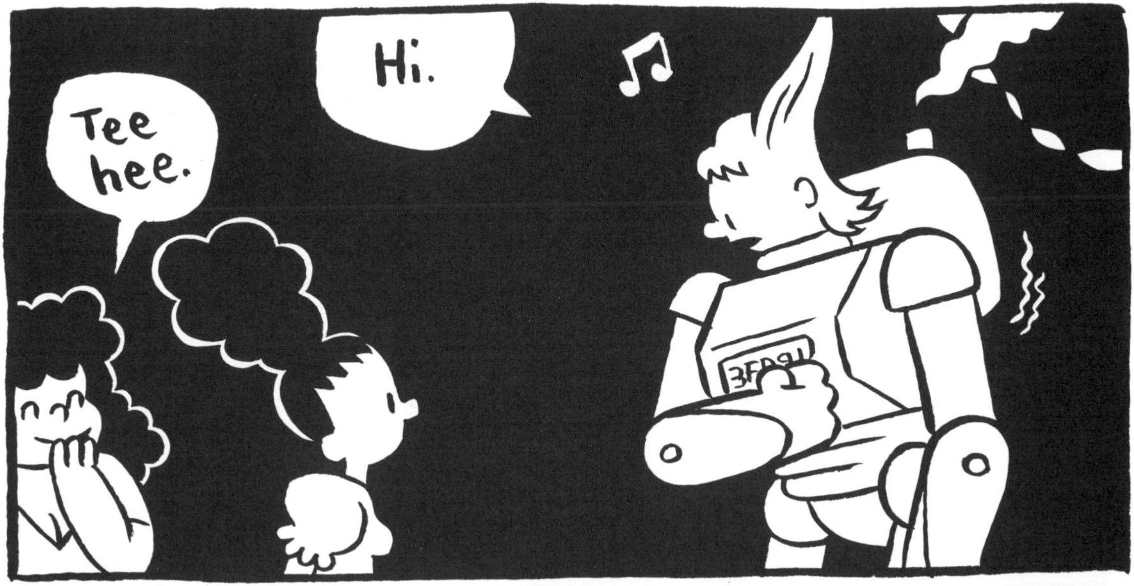
Tee hee.
Hi.
3FD91

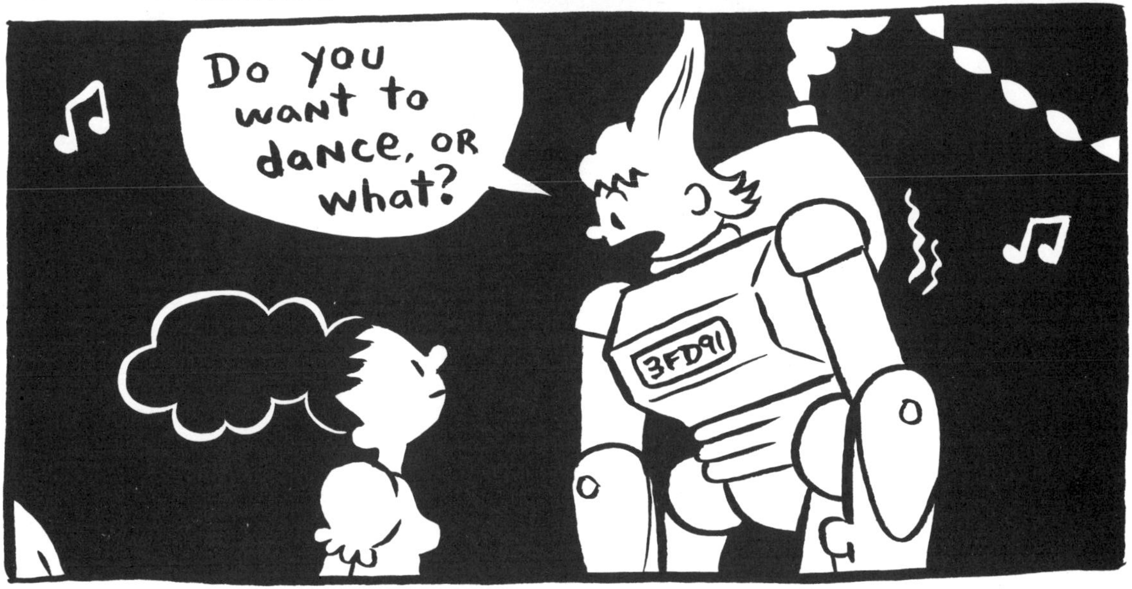
Do you want to dance, or what?
3FD91

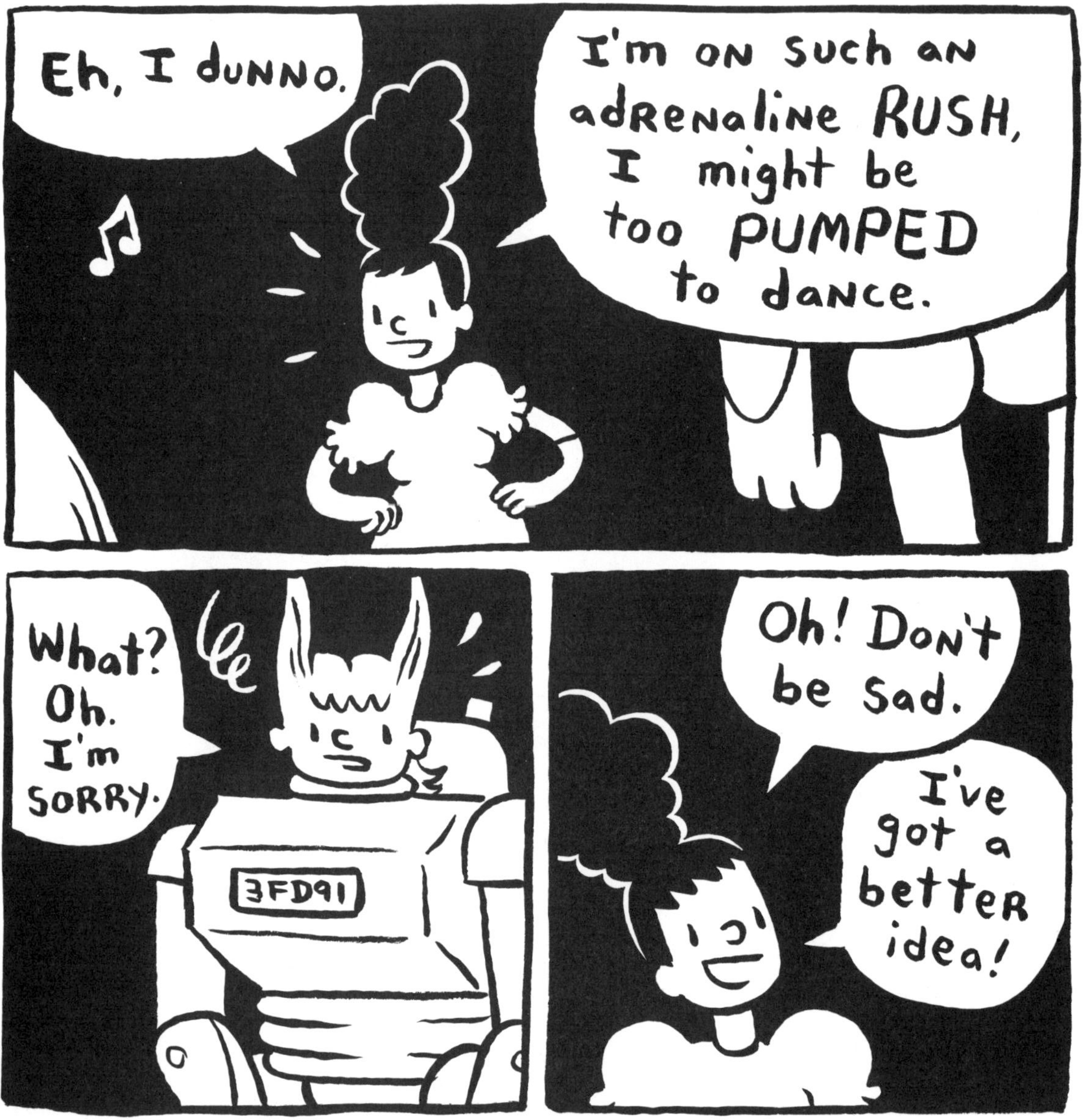
Eh, I dunno.
I'm on such an adrenaline RUSH, I might be too PUMPED to dance.
What? Oh. I'm sorry.
3FD91
Oh! Don't be sad.
I've got a better idea!

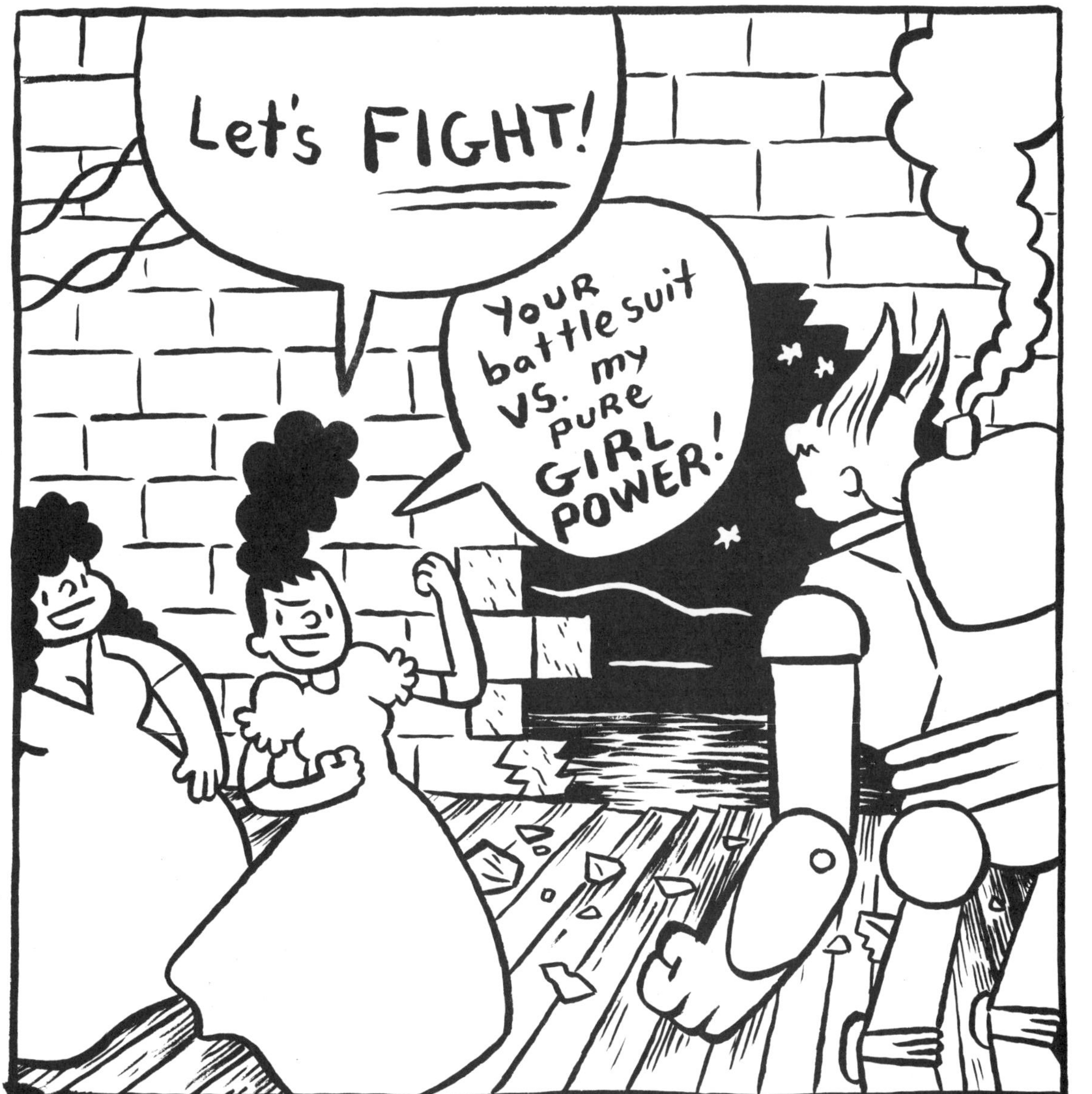
Let's FIGHT!
Your battle suit VS. my pure GIRL POWER!

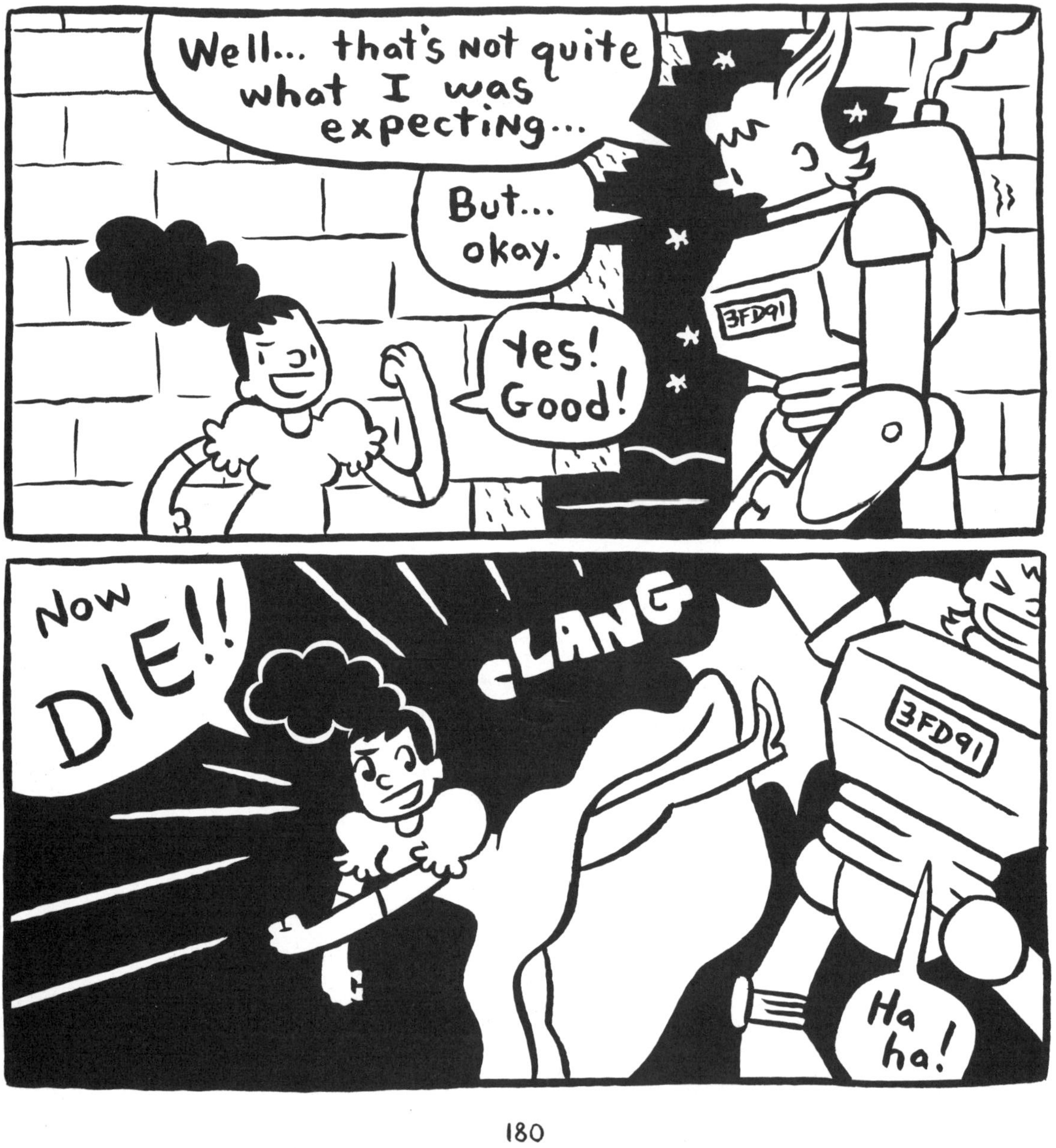
Well... that's not quite what I was expecting...
But... okay.
Yes! Good!
Now DIE!!
CLANG
Ha ha!

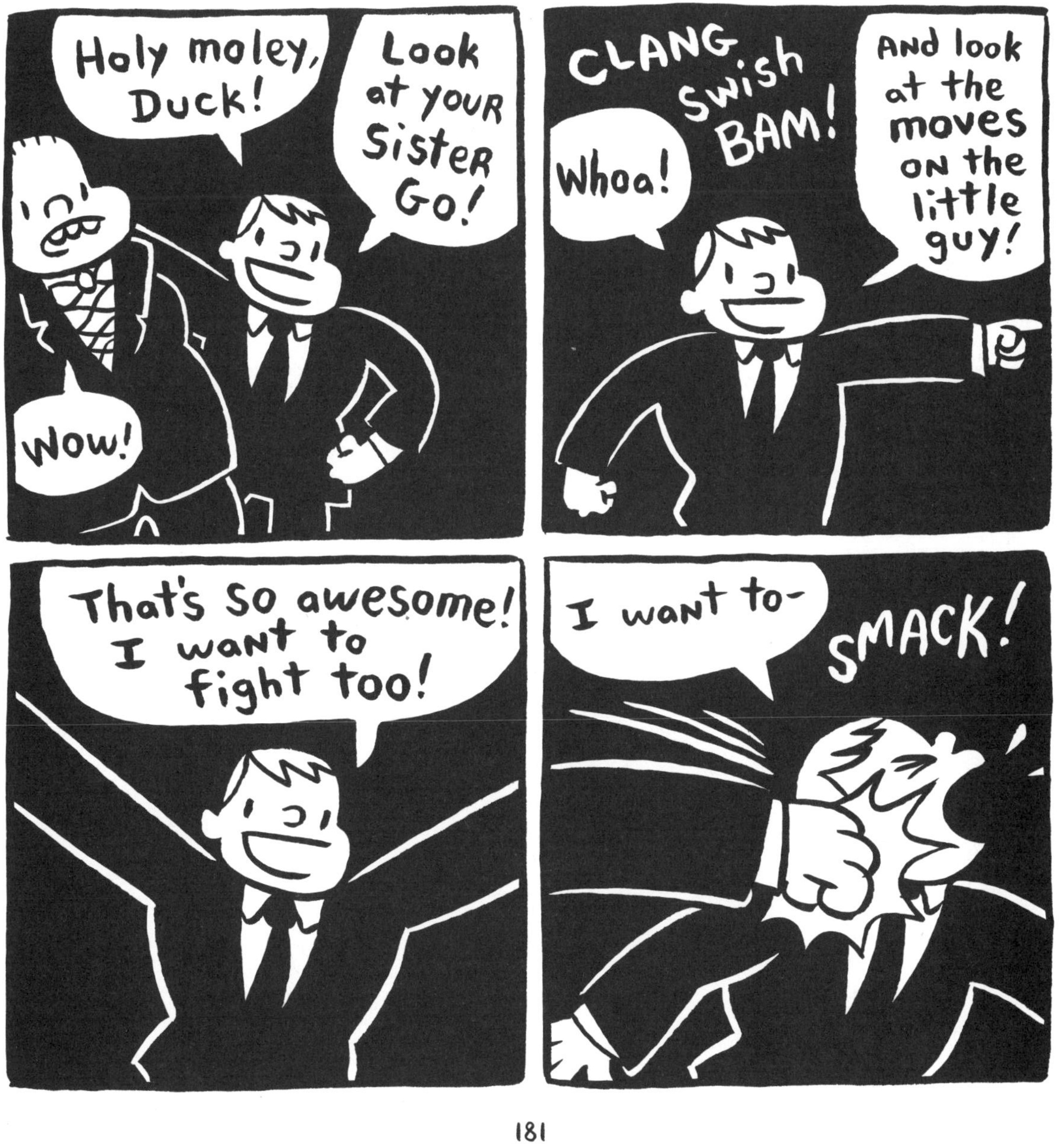
Holy moley, Duck!
Look at your Sister Go!
Wow!
CLANG Swish BAM!
Whoa!
And look at the moves on the little guy!
That's so awesome! I want to fight too!
I want to-
SMACK!

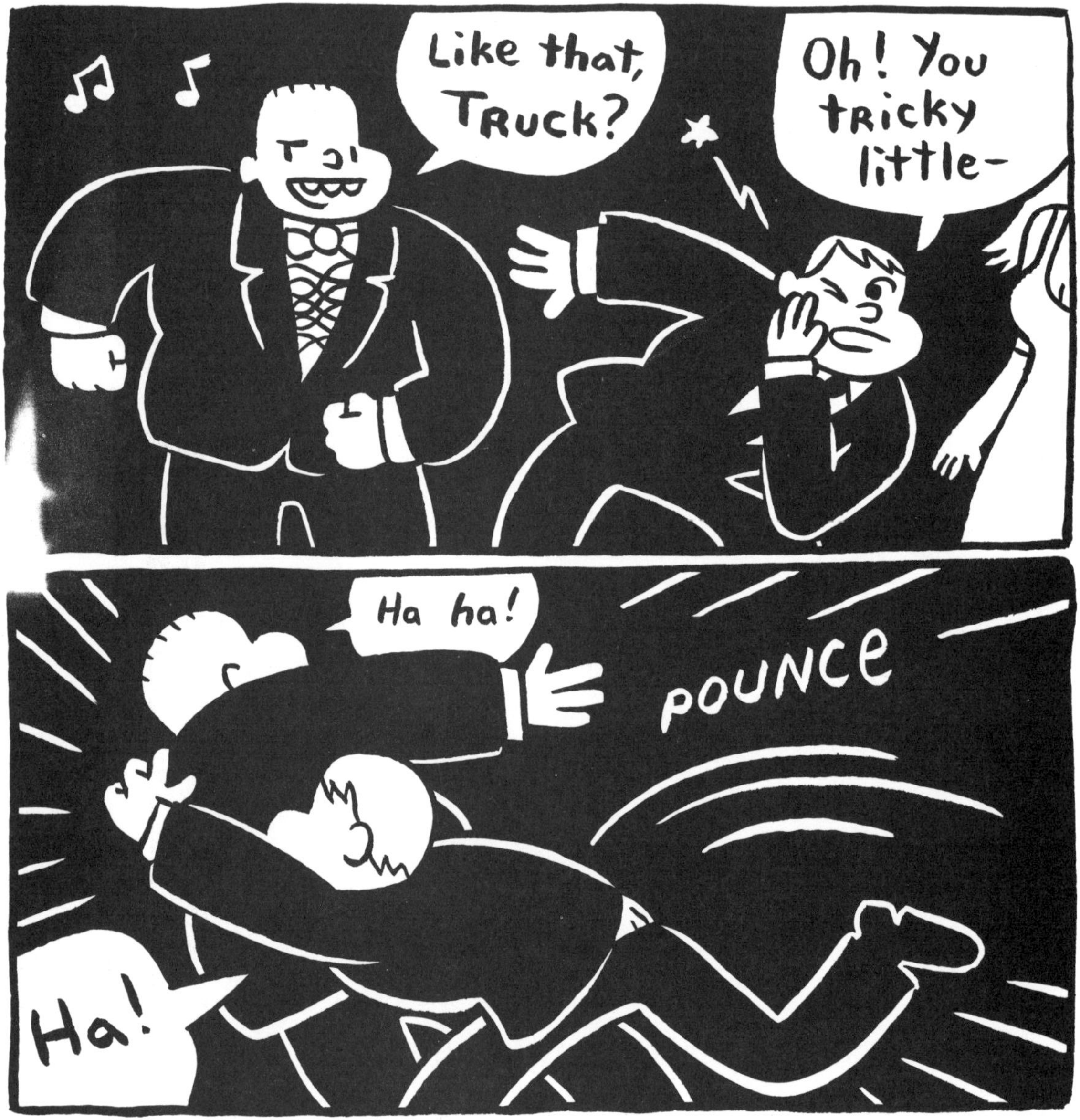
Like that, TRUCK?
Oh! You tricky little-
Ha ha!
POUNCE
Ha!

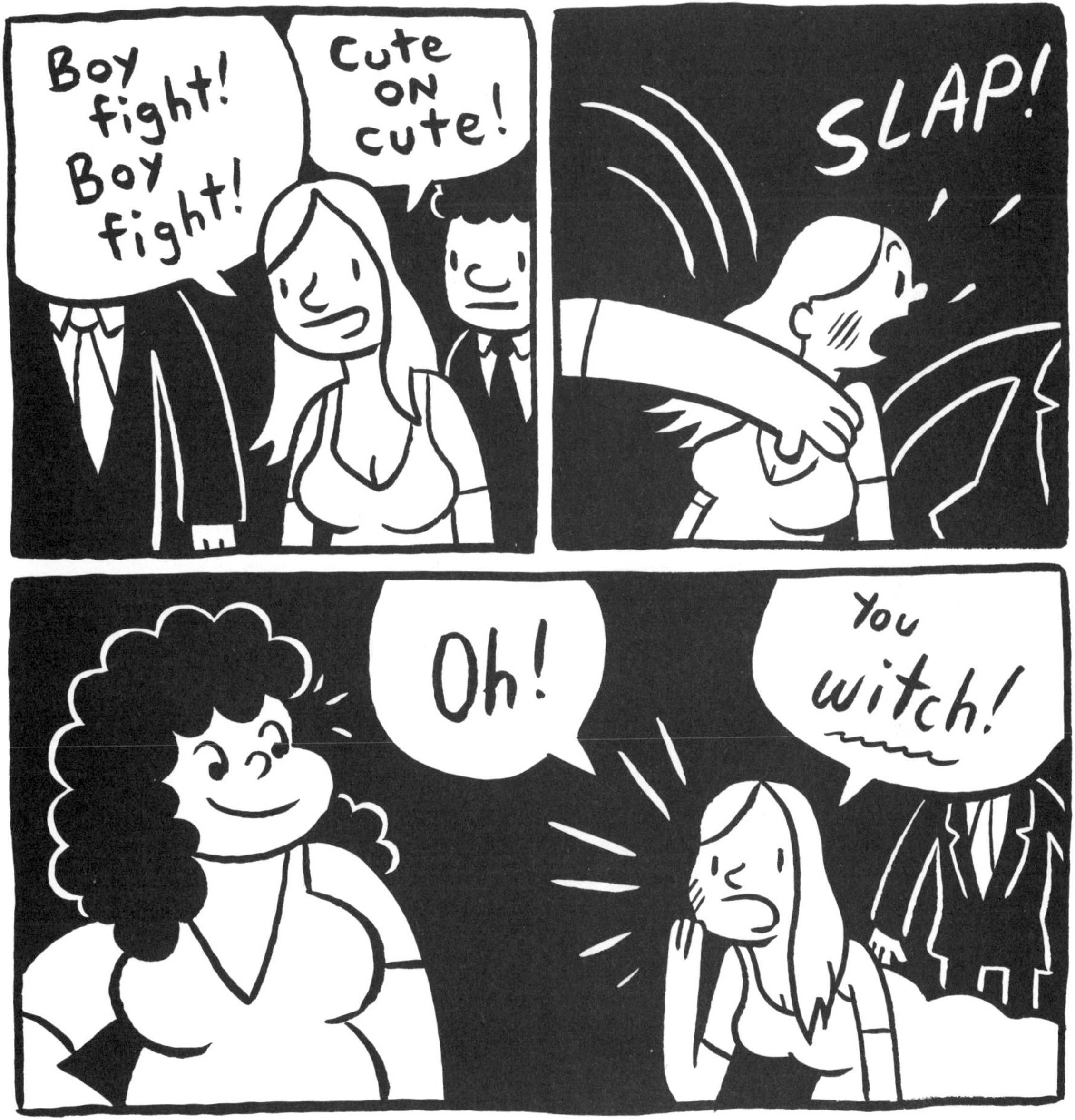
Boy fight! Boy fight!
Cute ON cute!
SLAP!
Oh!
You witch!

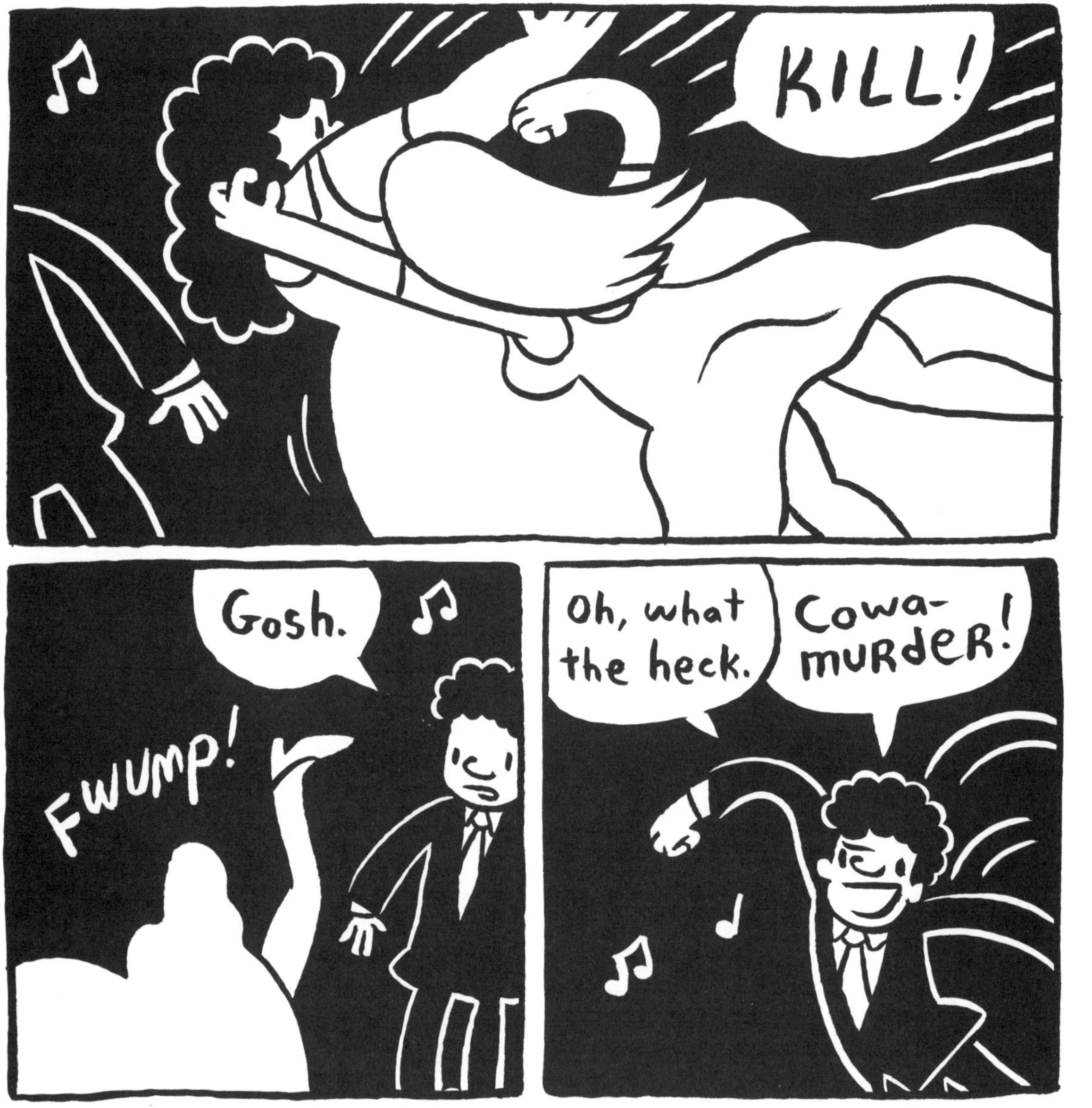
KILL!
Gosh.
FWUMP!
Oh, what the heck.
Cowa-murder!

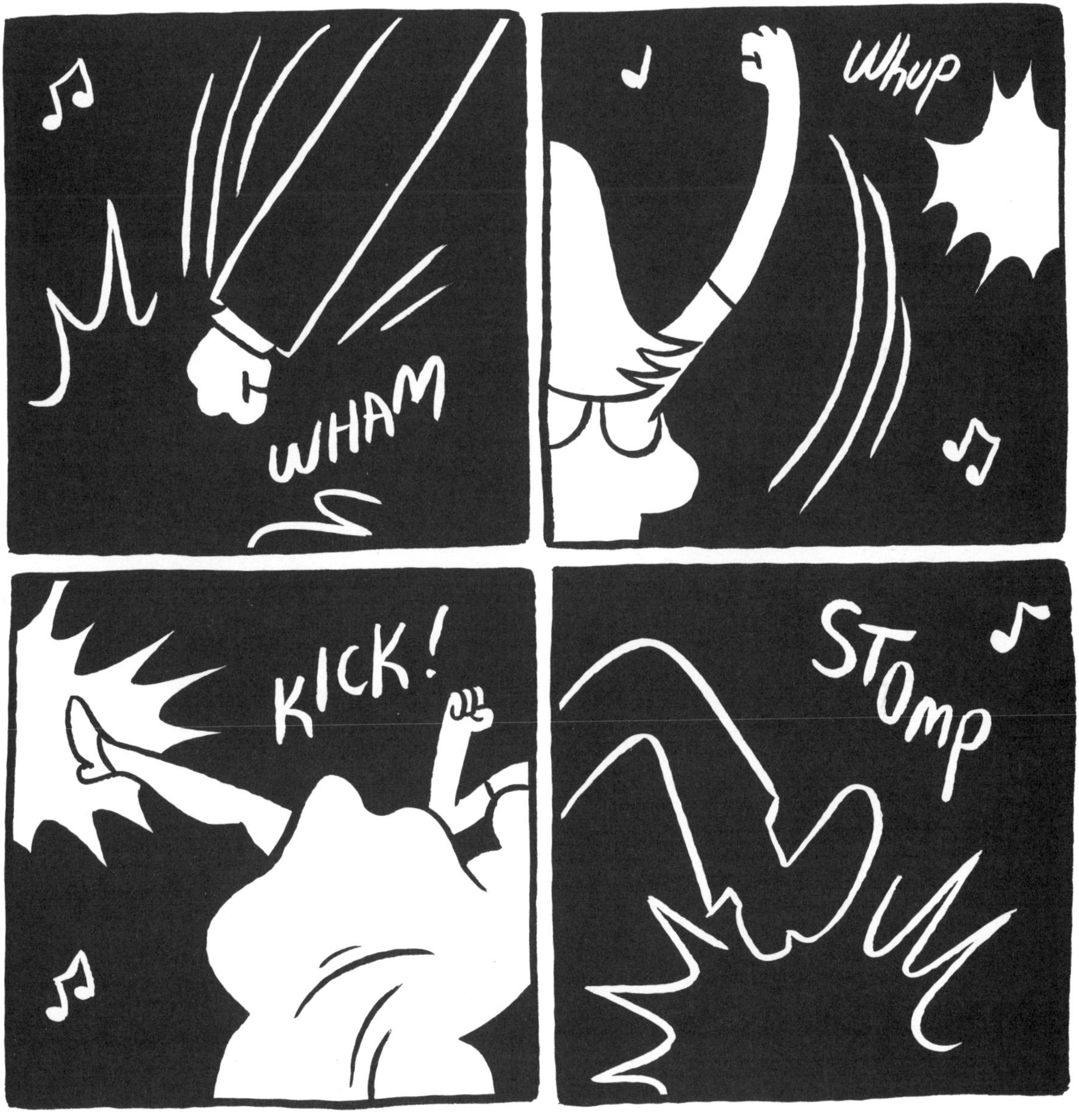
WHAM
WHUP
KICK!
STOMP

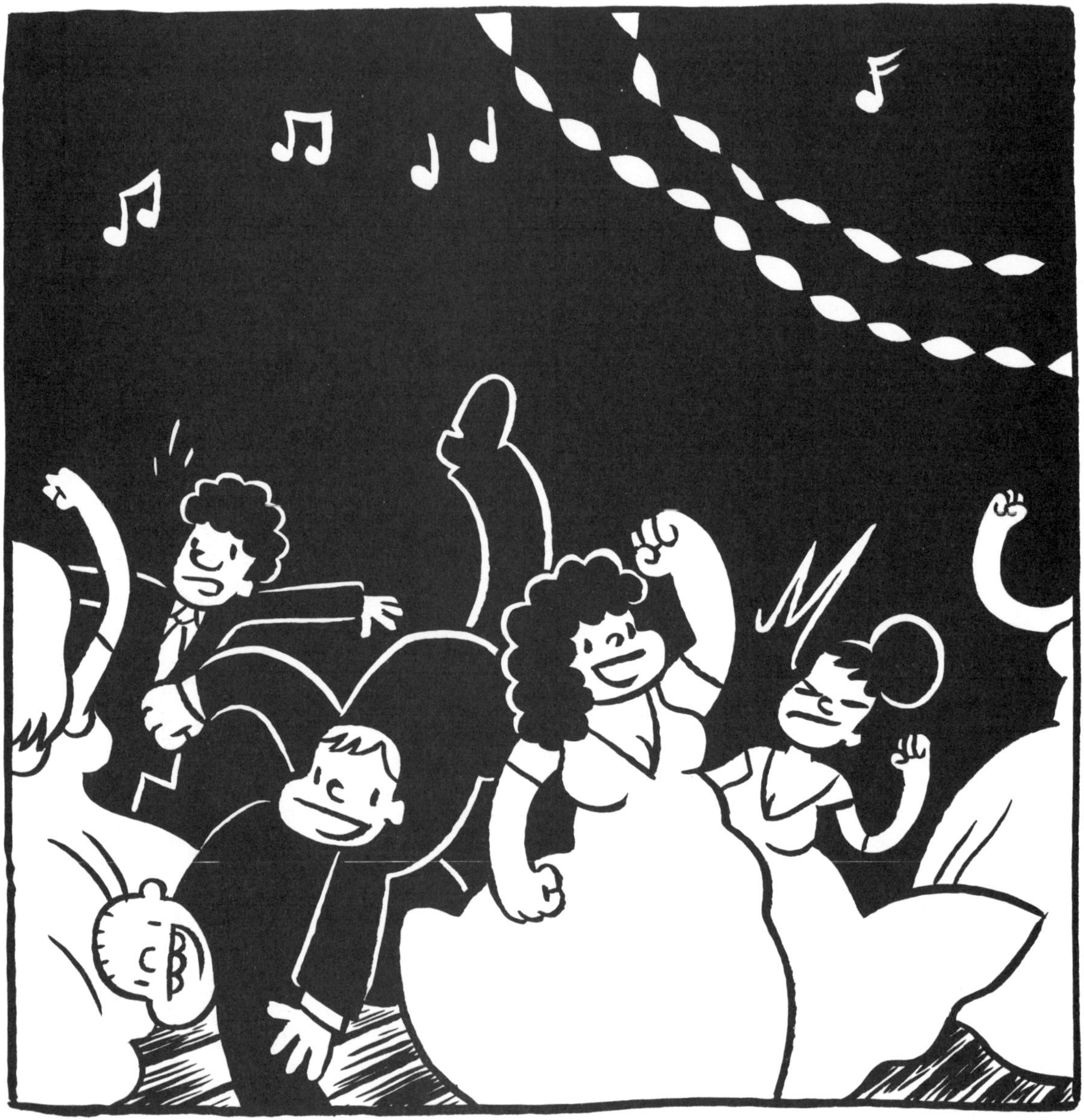

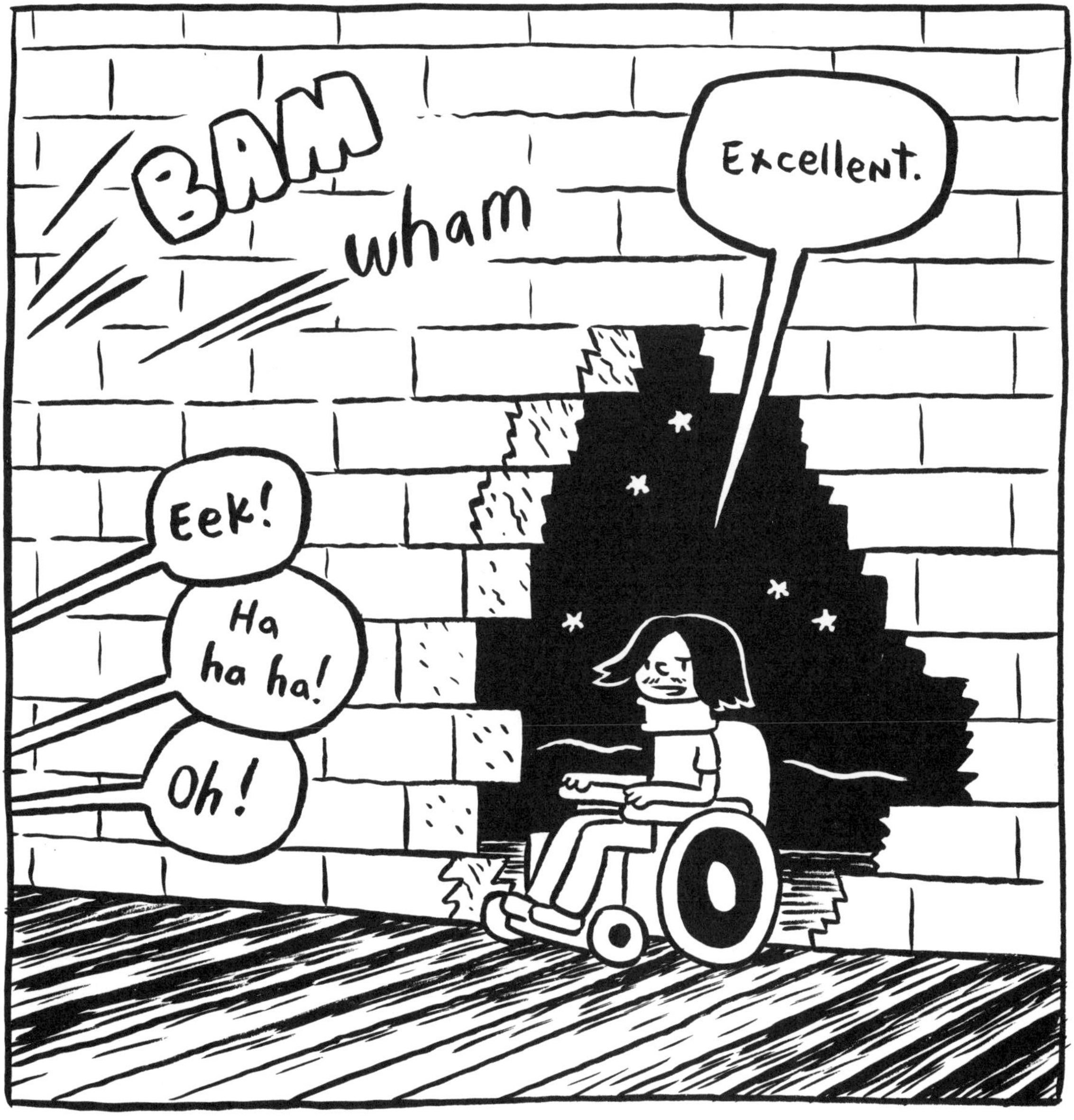
BAM
wham
Excellent.
Eek!
Ha ha ha!
Oh!

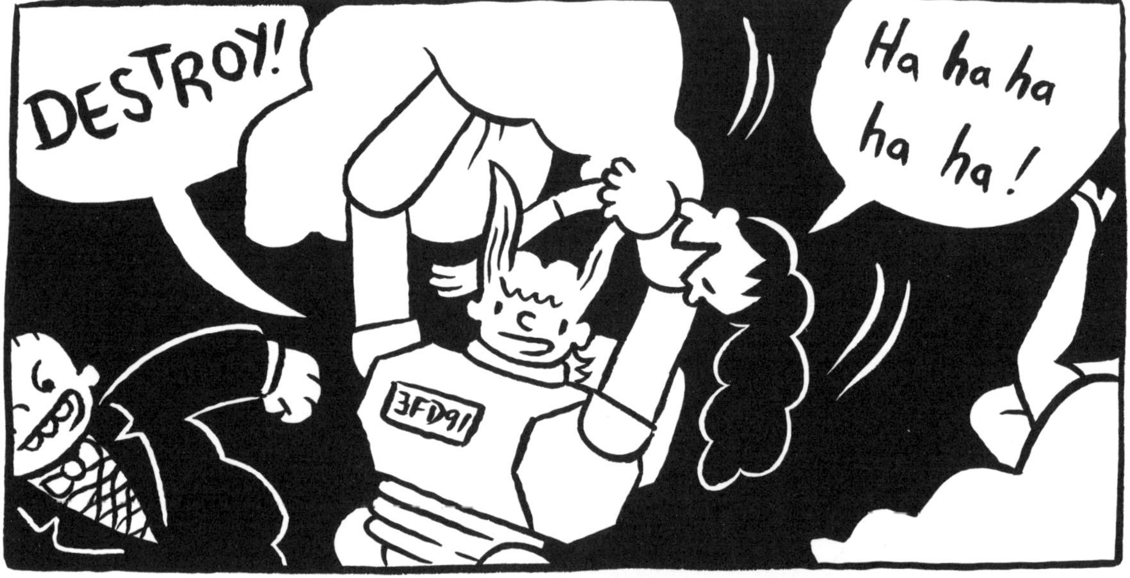
DESTROY!
Ha ha ha ha ha!
3FD91

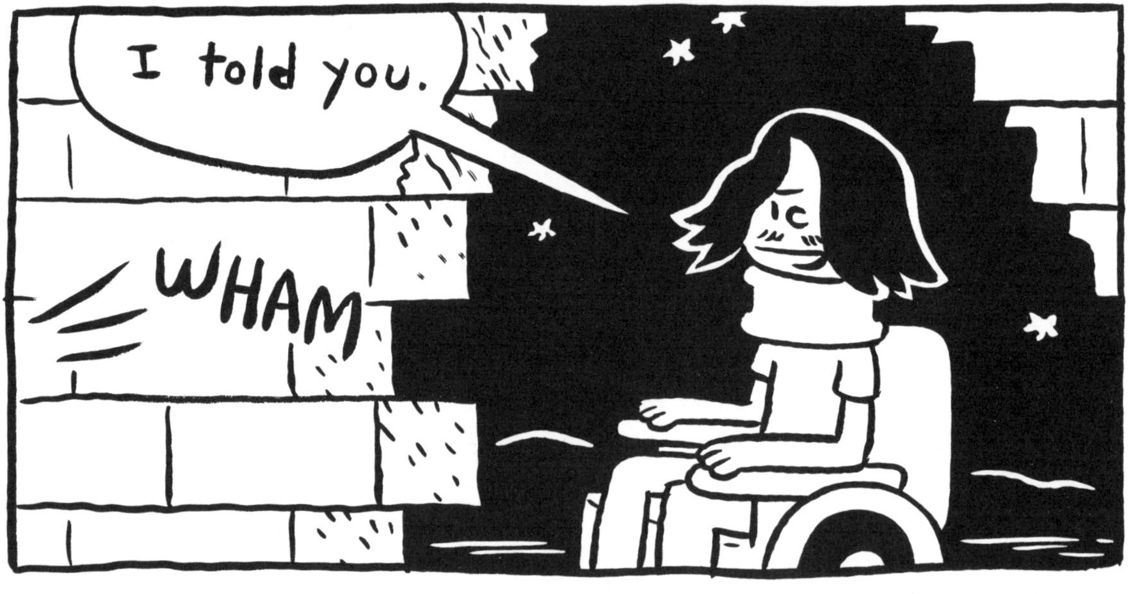
I told you.
WHAM

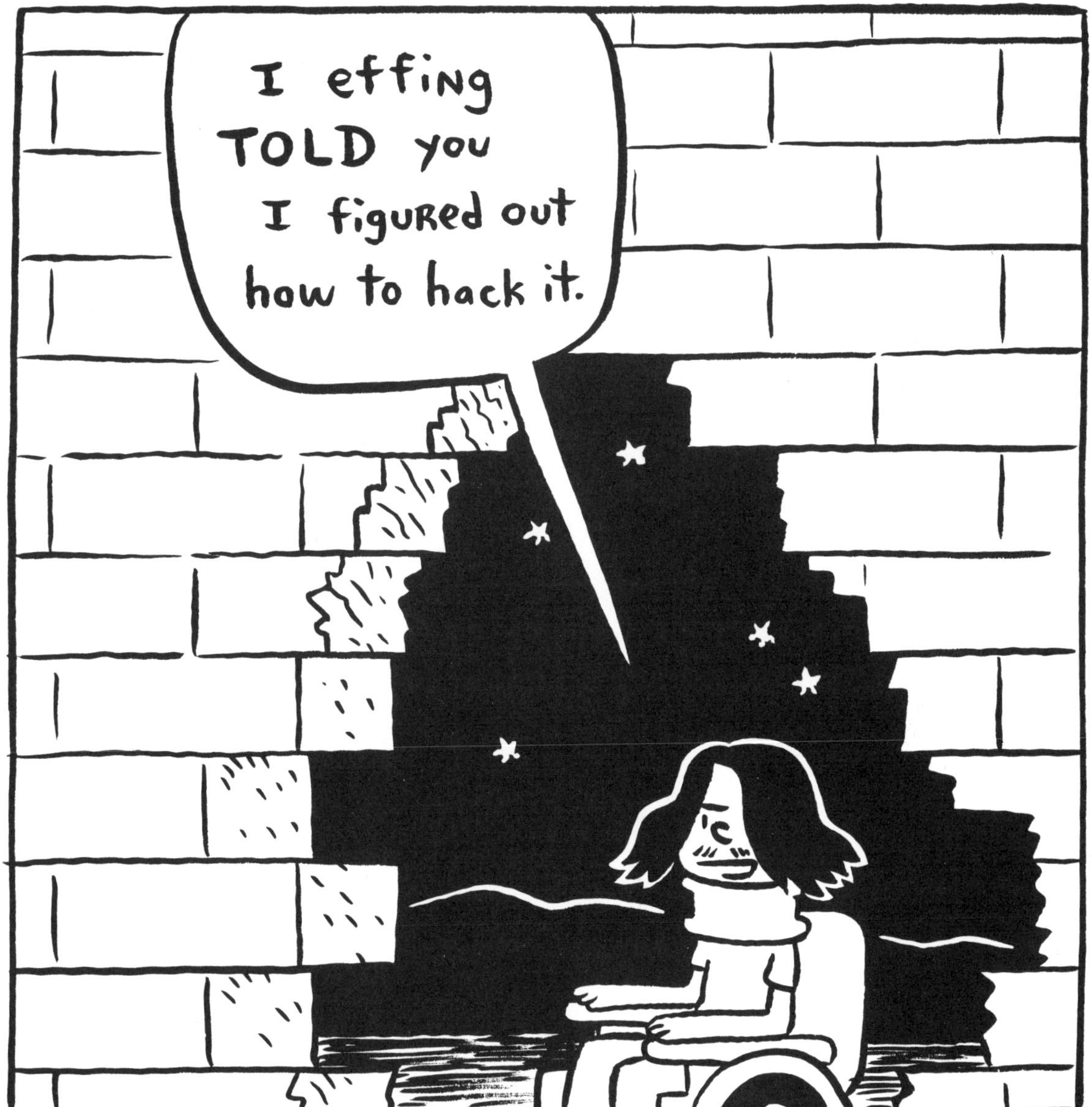
I effing TOLD you I figured out how to hack it.

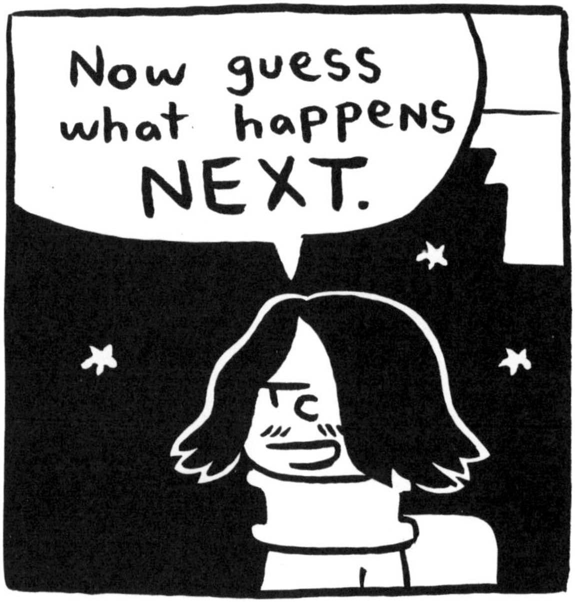
Now guess what happens NEXT.

Also available from James Kochalka:

American Elf
SuperF*ckers
SuperF*ckers Forever
Monkey vs Robot
Monkey vs Robot: The Crystal of Power
Pinky & Stinky
The Conversation #1 & #2

KOCHALKA

QUALITY

kochalka.tumblr.com